# Torah Tasting

## Journey Through GOD's Goodness With Jesus

**ELENA GLASSMAN**

DOVE
PUBLISHING HOUSE

Torah Tasting: Journey through GOD's Goodness with Jesus
Copyright © 2023 Elena Glassman
Dove Publishing House, LLC

All rights are reserved, including the right to reproduce this book
Or portions therefore in any form without express permission from
the author.

NKJV

Unless noted, scripture is from the New King James Version®.
Copyright © 1982 by Thomas Nelson. Used by permission.
All rights reserved.

Paperback ISBN 978-1-7365583-8-6
Hardback ISBN 978-1-7365583-9-3

Library of Congress
Printed in the United States of America

"I sought the Lord, and he answered me
and delivered me from all my fears.
Those who look to him are radiant,
and their faces shall never be ashamed.
This poor man cried, and the Lord heard him
and saved him out of all his troubles.
The angel of the Lord encamps
around those who fear him, and delivers them.
**Oh, taste and see that the Lord is good!**
Blessed is the man who takes refuge in him!
Oh, fear the LORD, you his saints,
for those who fear him have no lack!"

*~ Psalm 34:4-9*

# Introduction

I have always enjoyed writing. I handwrite my personal blessings and prayers on store-bought cards for my friends' birthdays to express my love and appreciation. Friends and family anticipate my annual Glassman Family Newsletter tucked inside the Hanukkah cards every December. My husband recognized the writing gift in me and bought me my first laptop 20 years ago, with the hopes that I'd write a book. After going through a few more laptops, my first book would not start and be written until the time was right.

Being married to a Jewish man who grew up in a New York Orthodox community, I am drawn to the Hebrew heritage of our Christian faith. Learning the Hebrew language and understanding the Jewish culture gives me a complete picture of our Messiah, and then pass on that heritage to our 2 Chinese Jewish children. It also has led me to develop a deep love for reading the Old Testament Bible in its original language. Years ago, when I first began my journey of learning about the Torah and researching, I found a book written on Torah Portions. I was disappointed that each weekly portion was brief and without much depth. I was hungry for more, but I did not find a book that I felt satisfied with that filled my hunger. I remember asking Father GOD for first-hand revelation, not getting fed off someone else.' My friend Jennifer once even gave me an encouraging word about seeing me like a child sitting on Papa GOD's lap as He taught me the knowledge of HIM, whispering into my ear His Living Word. This picture really confirmed how exactly the LORD teaches me, One on one. You could say I have been taught by the Master, the Best. Over the years, He has shown me so much that I want to share with others. So that they too, would experience His love and goodness.

There are countless commentaries, Christian and Jewish alike, scholarly and layman, written on the Torah and the Bible in general. I do not attempt to write yet another commentary, nor do I feel qualified to do so. However, in this book titled Torah Tasting, you will get a taste of a focus or a theme being highlighted in each week's Torah Portion. It possibly sheds some light on certain less discussed portions through inter-contextual closer-looks while I share some of my personal stories pertinent to the particular Parasha (Torah Portion in Hebrew) as a Jewish-Messiah-believing Gentile.

When our two children were going through their B'nei Mitzvah program (meaning Children of the Law, a two-year training program in biblical Hebrew, Torah-canting and Jewish studies) to prepare for their Bar/Bat Mitzvah (Son/Daughter of the Law, a coming-of-age ritual of 13-year-old Jewish children). Part of their B'nei Mitzvah program was reading the Torah Portions weekly. Each week's portion is divided into 7 aliyot (small portions) for daily readings. Each Parasha (Torah portion in Hebrew) also has a Haftorah portion (A selection of readings from the Books of Prophets to be read on Shabbats). In addition, believers in the Mashiach Yeshua (Jesus) have added a New Testament reading portion for the Messianic perspective to each portion.

The word Torah תרה, is often translated as the Law. However, it also means instruction or teaching. It comes from the root verb Yarah (ירה), to flow, to point out or to direct. GOD's Word directs us toward the target, the best plans GOD intends for us to live. His "Best" may look different from our perspective; nonetheless, it is the Best plans for us. GOD's Word is to direct us to LIFE, an abundant life. His teachings and instructions are universal. Rabbi Hillel, a revered 1st Century B.C. Jewish scholar and sage was once asked by a young man to explain the Torah standing on one foot. He took up the challenge and began to say these words while standing on one foot, "Do not do unto others that which you hate done unto yourself — that is the entire Torah. The rest is commentary, go and study it." Yeshua Jesus quoted Rabbi Hillel, flipping to a positive tone, saying "Do to them" instead of "Do not do unto others," which later was known as the Golden Rule — "And just as you want men to do to you, you also do to them likewise." —Luke 6:31

Each Torah Portion is packed with the richness of GOD's wisdom displaying His might and mercy. I believe each week's portion can be a stand-alone starting trigger point for in-depth self-study and research. Rabbis have been teaching these parashiot (Torah Portions in Hebrew) for generations. GOD's Word never becomes outdated or irrelevant. Each year at the festival of Simchat Torah (The Joy of Torah), Jews at every synagogue celebrate the conclusion of the public Torah reading annual cycle. At the following Shabbat service, the Torah scroll would be rewound to the beginning, and the first parasha (Torah Portion) Bereshit (Genesis 1-2) would be read. Thus, the reading cycle continues. Although we revisit the same portions each year, somehow, we manage to find new insights and revelations. The Word of GOD truly is living and powerful (Hebrews 4:12).

Reading the Torah Portion each week, I feel the LORD highlights something for me to see and learn. His Word is living and powerful indeed. It comes alive as we submerge in His Word and allow Him to reveal the hidden treasures from deep places. The phrase "Taste and See that the LORD is good" uses the sense of taste as an analogy. When we put something in our mouth, close our eyes and taste, attempting to shut off other senses, intensifying our taste buds to get the full experience of the flavor of the object being examined on the tongue. With our eyes closed, we are able to see beyond what our physical eyes see. I believe this is a poignant picture of what we are to do with GOD's Word. When we study the Torah, and meditate on His Word, breaking down each little bite, phrase by phrase, word by word, form by form, grammatically and structurally, the essence hidden behind the Word is then allowed to surface. The "Ah-Ha" moment comes with the revelation in the season of our life that is perfectly timed by the Sovereign LORD, to be received as a gift or to share with others as GOD manifests Himself in His Love and Hope. There are so many priceless gems discovered and explored when we seek the Face of GOD in His Word. I share my theories, some personal stories and what I feel the LORD has led me to see in these passages.

Coming from the hospitality industry myself and being married to a chef, I can relate to food and wine tasting. Before a big event like a wedding, the bride, her mother and the wedding planner typically are invited to a tasting to get a sample of what would be served at the wedding reception and dinner. An array of well-thought-out selections of delectable and bite-sized delicacies is presented to be enjoyed. There is a sense of anticipation and excitement at the tasting.

With certain Jewish traditions and contextual observation shared in this book, my hope is that you will get to taste and see the goodness of GOD, your appetite whetted, not yet satisfied and now you are ready to be set off on a life-changing journey with anticipation to find these hidden treasures for yourself and your family.

> "The <u>secret things</u> belong to the LORD our GOD,
> but the things that are revealed
> belong to us and to our children forever,
> that we may do all the words of this law."
> **- Deuteronomy 29:29**

Thank you for joining me on this Torah Tasting Tour! Whether you are a Christian (brand new or seasoned), a Jew, or someone who has never read the Bible before, I pray that you will be inspired and begin your own Torah-tasting journey and discover the deeper things the LORD has in store for you and your family.

# acknowledgements

This book would not have seen the light of day without the encouragement of my husband, Paul. The LORD knew what He was doing when He brought this girl out of the New York City of the Orient (Hong Kong) and joined her with a New Yorker Jewish boy from the Bronx. Thank you, Paul, for always believing in me. You saw a book in me before anyone else did, including myself.

There are a few more most influential people in my life that I'd like to acknowledge.

Firstly, it is my mother. Thanks, Mom, for all your sacrifice in raising me as a single mom, giving your family your all, and thinking of your children and your grandchildren in everything you've done and do. Your solid faith in the LORD inspires me, my sister, and your grandchildren. Thank you for showing us to never give up through your genuine and raw faith in Jesus Christ.

Matthew and Mollie, our two Chinese-Jewish children, you are the constant reminders of why we need to live for the LORD, so you, our children, can see GOD's faith in us and let our ceiling be the starting point of your faith walk upward. May your faith in Yeshua the Mashiach grow farther and deeper than your dad and I have grown and ever will go. May you grow to appreciate and learn of the amazing purposes of GOD, the Maker of Heaven and Earth created you for, as He has created you encompassing two of the oldest and greatest civilizations in World history. With that, you'll fulfill all that the LORD has made you to be to the fullest potential.

I'd like to thank Rabbi Marty for encouraging me many years ago to study Hebrew and inspiring me in more ways than he may even realize. There were many Hebrew teachers that I'd like to acknowledge over the years, like Terri Harper, Jonathan James, Jonathan Taylor, and Mark Esper.

Last, but not least, ALL GLORY TO GOD! This book truly would not have been possible without the constant love, encouragement, and inspiration from the ONE TRUE GOD of the Universe. My Heavenly Father, Thank You for entrusting me to write this book to somehow convey Your heart and Your love to Your children. I knew from the beginning of my writing journey that if not one page gets read, the time spent with You in the process would be my greatest gift that I'd cherish and be thankful for forever. I pray, in agreement with You, that the words written in this book will touch each reader's heart, that they will feel Your steadfast love and be filled with the desire to know You more.

# preface

The Torah, the first five books of Moses (Genesis, Exodus, Leviticus, Numbers and Deuteronomy), is divided into roughly 61 portions. Each week, according to the Jewish lunar/solar calendar, is assigned a portion. That same parasha (Torah Portion), chronologically, is designated to be read on Shabbat by Jews around the world in every synagogue, except for the Feasts of the LORD and certain High Holy Days; scriptures pertaining and assigned to those occasions are to be read instead. Sometimes two portions are paired up to make a double portion to be read on a Shabbat in order that all portions are included in the annual reading. That explains the 61 portions being read in the 52-week annual cycle.

The Parasha System, according to legend, was established by Ezra the Scribe after the Babylonian captivity and the destruction of the first Temple in the $6^{th}$ century BC. Without the central place of worship, the Temple, the Torah reading system was designed and unified for Jews to worship and read the Torah no matter where they were. Ezra the Scribe was instrumental in establishing the Temple service system, which later continued to be followed even after the Second Temple was constructed.

In this book, Yeshua HaMashiach and Jesus Christ, as well as Torah Portion and Parasha, are used interchangeably. GOD is spelled, instead of G-D, as in Judaism.

The regular Jewish year (i.e., not a leap year) is generally 354 days long. 354 divided by 7 is 50 weeks, with a remainder of 4 weeks, totaling 54 weeks in a Gregorian year. In other words, there are 50 or 51 Shabbats during a normal Jewish year.

There are also certain times when the normal weekly portion is not read on Shabbat. Such instances are during Passover and Sukkot when at least one day of the holiday happens on Shabbat, and other holidays which sometimes fall on Shabbat. Thus, there are at least two times during the year when the normal weekly portion is not read on Shabbat.

So now we're down to approximately 48 Shabbats each year when the weekly portion is read. (Actually, we only read 52 of the 54 portions on Shabbat: The first portion of the Torah, Bereshit, is always read on the Shabbat immediately following Simchat Torah. The last portion is always read on Simchat Torah, even though that holiday can never fall on Shabbat.)

**The way these problems get reconciled is that certain portions can be combined:**

- Vayakhel (Exodus 35:1-38:20) and Pekudei (Exodus 38:21-40:38)
- Tazria (Leviticus 12:1-13:59) and Metzora (Leviticus 14:1-15:33)
- Acharei (Leviticus 16:18:30) and Kedoshim (Leviticus 19:1-20:27)
- Behar Leviticus (25:1-26:2) Bechukotai (Leviticus 26:3-27:34)
- Chukat (Numbers 19:1-22:1) and Balak (Numbers 22:2-25:9)
- Matot (Numbers 30:2-32:42) and Masei (Numbers 33:1-36:13)
- Nitzavim Deuteronomy (29:9-30:20) and Vayelech (Deuteronomy 31:1-31:30)

*(Credit: Torahportions.ffoz.org)*

Some of these seven pairs of portions are combined each year to reconcile the number of Shabbat readings with the need to complete the annual Torah cycle.

# PREFACE

The 49 chapters of Torah Portions, including some double portions in this book, excluding Holy Days' scripture reading for the special Shabbats, are based on the Jewish Calendar Year 5781 (2021-2022) Torah reading schedule. 49 is 7 times 7, 7 is the number of perfection and completion. It seems to be a good number for the chapters in this book, with all 5 Books of Moses and their reading portions covered.

You may notice numbers are written out as numerals, rather than spelled out in English words as they are typically done in books. I feel that numbers are important to be shown as numerals in order to show patterns and symbolisms as well as a better flow of thought process. For example, "7 years ago" is written in this book instead of "seven years ago."

There may be variations in the English transliteration. Nonetheless, they mean the same in Hebrew. For example:

חנוכה = Hanukkah = Chanukah = Dedication

בראשית = Bereshit = Beresheet = B'rishit = Genesis = "In the beginning"

In addition, Every Hebrew alphabet derives from a pictographic script. Therefore, when combining to make a word, the essence of the word can be explored by dissecting the word into each Hebrew letter. A chart is provided for each Hebrew alphabet, its associated number, its symbolism and meaning for your reference. (Credits: Hebrew Word Pictures, Page 10, by Dr. Frank T. Seekins)

# Parashiot
## (Torah Portions)

| | |
|---|---|
| Introduction | vii |
| Acknowledgements | xi |
| Preface | xiii |
| Hebrew Alphabets | 23 |
| 1: Bereshit / In the Beginning | 25 |
| 2: Noach / Noa | 43 |
| 3: Lech Lecha / Go Forth | 53 |
| 4: Vayera / And He Appeared | 67 |
| 5: Chayei Sarah / Life of Sarah | 79 |
| 6: Toledot / Generations | 91 |
| 7: Vayetze / And He Went Out | 103 |

| | |
|---|---:|
| 8: Vayishlach / And He Sent | 115 |
| 9: Vayeshev / And He Dwelt | 129 |
| 10: Miketz / From the End | 143 |
| 11: Vayigash / And He Came Near | 153 |
| 12: Vayechi / And He Lived | 163 |
| 13: Shemot / Names | 177 |
| 14: Va'era / And I Appeared | 191 |
| 15: Bo / Come | 203 |
| 16: Beshalach / When He Sent | 213 |
| 17: Yitro / Jethro | 223 |
| 18: Mishpatim / Judgments | 231 |
| 19: Terumah / Heave Offering | 239 |
| 20: Tetzaveh / He Shall Command | 247 |
| 21: Ki Tisa / When You Take | 257 |
| 22: Vayakhel/Pekudei // And He Gathered / Countings | 269 |
| 23: Vayikra / And He Called | 277 |
| 24: Tzav / Command | 285 |
| 25: Shemini / Eighth | 293 |

26: Tazria/Metzora // She Will Conceive / Leper    303

27: Acharei Mot/Kedoshim // After the Death / Holy    319

28: Emor / Say    331

29: Behar/Bechukotai // On the Mountain / In My Statutes    341

30: Bemidbar / In the Wilderness    355

31: Naso /Take Up    363

32: Beha'alotecha / When You Came to Ascend    375

33: Shelach / Send    385

34: Korach / Korah    395

35: Chukat / Statute    407

36: Balak / Balak    415

37: Pinchas / Pinhas    427

38: Mattot/Massei // Tribes / Journeys    443

39: Devarim / Words    453

40: Va'etchanan / And I Pleaded    465

41: Eikev / Because    481

42: Re'eh / See    493

43: Shoftim / Judges    505

| | |
|---|---:|
| 44: Ki Tetze / When You Go Out | 519 |
| 45: Ki Tavo / When You Come In | 531 |
| 46: Nitzvaim / Stand | 545 |
| 47: Vayelech / And He Went | 559 |
| 48: Ha Azinu / Give Ear | 571 |
| 49: V'zot Habrachach / This Is the Blessing | 583 |
| Glossary | 595 |
| Torah Reading Calendar 2021-2023 | 597 |

# Hebrew Alphabets
## Associated Numbers / Pictures / Symbolic Meanings

1 א — Alef (picture as Ox, Bull) — Strength, leader, first

2 ב — Bet (Tent, house) — Household, in, into, family

3 ג — Gimmel (Camel) — To lift up, pride, benefit

4 ד — Dalet (Door) — Pathway, to enter

5 ה — Hey (Behold) — "The," to reveal

6 ו — Vav (Nail, Peg) — "And," to add, to secure

7 ז — Zayin (Weapon) — Cut, to cut off

8 ח — Chet (Fence, Inner Room) — Private, to separate

9 ט — Tet (Snake, Surround) — To surround

10 י — Yod (Hand) — Work, a deed, to make

20 כ — Kaf (Palm) — To cover, to open, allow

30 ל — Lamed (Cattle Goad) — Control, authority, the tongue

40 מ — Mem (Water) — Liquid, massive, chaos

50 נ —Nun (Fish) — Activity, life

60 ס — Samech (Prop) — Support, twist slowly, turn

70 ע — Ayin (Eye) — To see, know, experience

80 פ — Pey (Mouth) — To speak, a word, to open

90 צ — Tsade (Fishhook) — Catch, desire, need

100 ק — Qoof/Koph (Back of the Head) — Behind, the last, the least

200 ר — Resh (Head of a man) — A person, the head, the highest

300 ש — Shin (Teeth) — To consume, to destroy

400 ת — Tav (Sign) — To seal, to covenant

*Ch — pronounced as a H with a strong guttural sound
Tsa — pronounced as za in "pizza"
A — pronounced as a in "ma"
E — pronounced as e in "let"
I — pronounced as i in "inn"
O — pronounced as aw

**The transliteration of Hebrew words can vary. However, meaning and pronunciation stay the same, i.e., Alef is the same as Aleph — both refer to the first letter of the Hebrew alphabets.

(Credits: Hebrew Word Pictures, Page 10, by Dr. Frank T. Seekins)

# 1 א
# BERESHIT
## (In the Beginning)
בראשית

Genesis 1:1-6:8

Isaiah 42:5-43:10

John 1:1-17

Bereshit is the first portion of the Torah. בראשית Bereshit is the first word of the Torah, and of this portion, it means "In the beginning." The title of the first book of the Torah is Genesis, a Greek word meaning "origins." It tells the origins of the universe, of mankind and of the nation of Israel. This portion contains over 5 chapters with many well-known bible stories, such as the 6 days of creation and the LORD's day of rest, Adam and Eve, Cain and Abel, the first family's genealogy, and also the introduction of Noah and his family, who were surrounded by evil on earth.

There is significance in the first letter and the first word appearing in the Torah. The first time a word appears in the Torah often gives context and provides information on the essence and intent of the word. Obviously, being the first Torah Portion, Bereshit is filled with countless firsts. There is a whole world of fun mysteries to explore for sure.

The first verse of the entire Torah is —

> *In the beginning GOD created the heavens and the earth.*
> בראשית ברא אלהים את השמים ואת הארץ
> **Genesis 1:1**

This is the thesis statement of the bible. It is one of the most quoted bible verses. The whole premise of GOD's word hinges upon this statement.

In the first word בראשית Bereshit/In the beginning, a few words of clues seem to be snugly tucked inside, begging to be solved.

- בית — בראשית Beit House/Family
- בר — בראשית Bar Son
- ברית — בראשית Br'it Covenant
- ראש — בראשית Rosh Head/Top/Beginning.
- אש — בראשית Esh Fire

The first letter of the entire Torah is ב Bet, which is the second Hebrew alphabet of the 22 alphabets. Some sages say that the first Hebrew alphabet, א Aleph, is a silent letter representing the LORD. GOD is invisible yet very much present. ב Bet represents a house. The LORD begins the Torah with His intent of building a house, a home. GOD is the Head of the House/Home/Family, a house unseen and not yet built, a family not yet formed. Only the LORD can create and make a home out of emptiness and nothing. בראשית Bereshit/In the beginning is the Home/Family Head, who was there before the "beginning" and will be there after the "end." The One who is greater than anything and, above all, who desires to express love and to have His love reciprocated.

The word בראשית Bereshit consists of the word אש Esh Fire. GOD made a covenant with Abram with fire; GOD Himself appeared as fire —

# 1. BERESHIT / IN THE BEGINNING

*And it came to pass, when the sun went down and it was dark, that behold, there appeared a smoking oven and a burning (אש Esh Fire) torch that passed between those pieces.*
**Genesis 15:17**

His plan is to make a covenant as fire with His children, establishing a family/home. Fire provides light and warmth.

The word בר Bar Son is found within the word בְּרֵאשִׁית Bereshit "In the Beginning." This displays the Father's desire to build a home for His first son Adam, to build a nation through His son Abram, and to establish His covenant with and through His "only begotten Son"/ the Son of GOD and "the second Adam," Yeshua Jesus.

*[38] the son of Enosh, the son of Seth, the son of Adam, the son (בר Bar) of God.*
**Luke 3:38**

Yeshua Jesus was referred to as the Son (בר Bar) of GOD —

*And the Word became flesh and dwelt among us, and we beheld His glory, the glory as of the only <u>begotten of the Father</u>, full of grace and truth.*
**John 1:14**

*[20] Immediately he preached the Christ in the synagogues, that He is <u>the Son of God</u>.*
**Acts 9:20**

There is so much goodness of GOD that we can mediate on just in the first word of the Torah.

Isn't that amazing?

The LORD has a plan, and it can be seen from the beginning.

*In the beginning God created the heavens and the earth.* *² The earth was without form, and void; and darkness was on the face of the deep. And the Spirit of God was hovering over the face of the waters.*
**Genesis 1:1-2**

Genesis 1:1 transports us to the opening scene of a play.
Lights out… curtains up… complete darkness…
Nothing to see… Mysterious…
The Supreme Being, Ruler of all, is about to do something spectacular.
A dramatic voice of the narrator declares these words.
Powerful words.
These words make the entire uncreated world shake.

*"Let there be light"*
**Genesis 1:3**

This sets off the creation project by the Master of the Universe.

**Here are the first 3 Hebrew words in the Torah —**

ברשאית ברא אלהים Bereshit Bara Elohim

- בראשית Bereshit Beginning is also translated as choicest, the best in terms of firstfruits, the first part.
- ברא Bara Create/Shape/Fashion is almost exclusively used in regards to the LORD creating. He alone is able to create something out of nothing.
- אלהים Elohim God is in Hebrew plural form, and it is a general term for god or gods. However, here, it is referring to The One GOD. The plural form in God also suggests the plentitude of powers He possesses. Yet, the verb ברא Bara Create/Shape/Fashion is used in masculine singular form instead of in plural form. אלהים Elohim GOD, Creator of all, is establishing the framework of the ultimate masterpiece of all masterpieces. We will see later GOD created the heavens and the earth with his beloved mankind in

mind. אלהים Elohim GOD is the very first name of GOD that appears in the Torah.
- אלהים Elohim GOD is our Creator GOD.

Then in Genesis 1:26-27,

God (אלהים Elohim) said, "<u>Let Us</u> make man in <u>Our</u> image, according to <u>Our</u> likeness; let them have dominion over the fish of the sea, over the birds of the air, and over the cattle, over all the earth and over every creeping thing that creeps on the earth."

So God (אלהים Elohim) <u>created</u> (singular form) man in <u>His</u> (singular form) own image; in the image of God <u>He</u> (singular form) created him; male and female <u>He</u> (singular form) created them.

GOD is ONE, in plurality, the Father, the Son, the Holy Spirit. I believe Genesis 1:26-27 demonstrates this very well. Though the word "God (אלהים Elohim)" itself is a masculine plural form grammatically, it is paired with verbs that are in singular form. In English, it would be equivalent to saying, "They goes home," which is not in verb-subject agreement. Interestingly, it conveys a message that the LORD is ONE, yet a plurality in the ONE GOD. In synchrony, He created **him** (singular form), **male and female**, more than one in the man created. We (plural form again) are created after GOD's (One GOD) own image.

We can only attempt to comprehend an infinite God and his mysteries with our finite minds.

The LORD created man in his own image. He shows us that as His children, we are designed to do what our Father does. That is in our spiritual DNA!

He spoke words; things came into being.

Some rabbis believe when GOD spoke, each Hebrew letter with its essence was manifested into physical existence.

בראשית ברא אלהים

The first 3 Hebrew words mean "In the beginning GOD created," then the 4th word את Et is a direct object pointer (an untranslatable word) indicating what GOD created as follows. Because the 2 letters of the word את Et, א Aleph and ת Tav are the first and the last letters in the Hebrew alphabets. Some sages believe the first things GOD created were the Hebrew alphabets. Subsequently, He spoke words, which were made up of Hebrew letters; thus, creation came to be. That just gives a whole new revelation to see the first verse of the New Testament in the book of John.

> *In the beginning was the Word,*
> *and the Word was with God,*
> *and the Word was God.*
> **John 1:1**

The Hebrew language is a fascinating one. Much like Chinese, Hebrew was originally written in pictographic script. In its ancient form, each letter looks like a picture of something.

For example, the first Hebrew alphabet א Aleph looks like an ox head in its pictographic form. It means authority and strength. It is often referred to as a GOD letter, being the first, the head, the strength and authority, as well as it being silent like GOD being unseen yet omnipresent.

A rabbi once gives an example of the closest thing to the Hebrew language — Chemical compounds. The Hebrew alphabets liken the symbols in the Periodic Table. Each chemical symbol is a stand-alone element, like carbon and oxygen, with unique properties, atoms and molecules. When the elements are combined, different compounds are formed. Chemical reactions occur as a result and form beautiful or destructive things like diamonds and explosive materials. When 1 carbon (C) and 2 oxygens (O2) are combined, we get carbon dioxide $CO_2$. The chemical formula of $CO_2$ tells us what the compound and quantity it is made of.

Every Hebrew alphabet is associated with a picture, a concept. Each Hebrew alphabet is associated with a number. Almost every Hebrew word has a 3-letter Hebrew root that indicates the core concept of the word.

**Fascinating! For example, בית Beit House/Family is formed with the 3 Hebrew letters:**

- ב Bet — Inside / House
- י Yod — Hand / possessive term (of)
- ת Tav — Covenant

בית Beit is essentially Inside a House of Covenant. A house is not merely a built structure, but it is built with its habitants or occupants in mind. The patriarch, the matriarch, their children, and servants that would reside inside. House of Israel and House of Jacob refer to the family rather than an actual house.

The Hebrew words in the Torah are filled with examples like this to demonstrate the LORD's original intent for the word.

No wonder some rabbis came up with the "Bible Code" several years ago. It is believed that the LORD encoded many messages in the Torah. They are not merely words randomly chosen to be written in the Torah.

I do believe there are nuggets of wisdom and truth hidden in the Torah to be discovered. Clues are left like breadcrumbs, so we can trace them to find GOD's heart. The Word of GOD is also referred to as the Living Word. We can read the same passage 100 times and still get something new that is timely and personable. Only the Almighty GOD can do that.

*²Now the earth was formless and empty, darkness was over the surface of the deep, and the Spirit of God was hovering over the waters. And God said, "Let there be light," and there was light.*
*⁴God saw that the light was good, and he separated the light from the darkness. 5 God called the light "day," and the darkness he called "night." And there was evening, and there was morning — the first day.*
**Genesis 1:2-4**

The very first thing GOD created was light. He spoke light, and light came to be. The Hebrew word for light is אור Or. Perhaps that is where they got the English word, aura?

- א Aleph — represents the LORD
- ו Vav — add/combine/nail or peg
- ר Resh — head/person

Light is when the LORD fills our head. He is the light. We have light when we fill our head and our whole being with GOD.

*This is the message which we have heard from Him and declare to you, that <u>God is light</u> and in Him is no darkness at all.*
**1 John 1:5**

*In the beginning was the Word, and the Word was with God, and the Word was God. ² He was with God in the beginning. ³ Through him all things were made; without him nothing was made that has been made. ⁴ <u>In him was life, and that life was the light of all mankind.</u> ⁵ The light shines in the darkness, and the darkness has not overcome it.*
**John 1:1-5 4**

"Life was the light of all mankind" explains Genesis 1's Day One creation of light very well.

When Jesus spoke again to the people,

# 1. BERESHIT / IN THE BEGINNING

> *He said, "<u>I am the light of the world</u>.*
> *Whoever follows me will never walk in darkness, but will have the*
> *light of life."*
> **John 8:12**

If GOD is light, when He created light, He essentially imparted part of Himself into the world that we would have a piece of Him. The Ruler of the Universe was giving and duplicating Himself in order to be known and seen.

That is powerful!

The LORD has commanded us to be light to the world as He is the light.

> *For it is the God who commanded light to shine out of darkness, who*
> *has shone in our hearts to give the light of the knowledge of the glory*
> *of God in the face of Jesus Christ.*
> **2 Ephesians 4:6**

We have a Jack Russell/Yorkie Poo-mix dog named Jack. We adopted him during one Passover when he was still a puppy. Thus, he is our sweet Passover puppy. He has all-white hair that even makes him look like a Passover lamb. One of the things about Jack is that he is a light-chaser. On any sunny afternoon when light shines through the window into our kitchen, you'll find Jack going crazy chasing after the light reflected on our kitchen cabinets. At first, we had no idea why he would be so fixated on the cabinet door, then try to pounce his cushioned paws on it like he wanted to catch it… then we saw the light. It is pure entertainment to watch Jack chasing the different light spots in our kitchen. For that reason, Jack was nicknamed our light-chaser. I believe while the light of the world resides in us, when we know the LORD as our Mashiach, we need to be like Jack and see where the LORD is shining His light, the dark corners being lit up, the shadowy cabinet doors with light shone on it, and we are to go after them. I do believe that we need to be sensitive to the Holy Spirit and pay attention to where He is at work, where He is shining the light, so that we can bring the "Light of the knowledge of the glory of the LORD" to the world. Let the LORD be magnified.

> *For so the Lord has commanded us: 'I have set you as a light to the Gentiles, That you should be for salvation to the ends of the earth…"*
> **Acts 13:47**

Have you ever been around or know someone that, after a few moments spent with them, you feel exhausted and mentally drained? They always see the glass half-empty. They speak the language of Hopelessness fluently. They choose to see the possibility of things getting worse rather than getting better, seeing every bit of the woes instead of blessings. I call them light-zappers. Even the little bit of light and hope you have, they will zap that right out of you, leaving you emotionally drained after a brief encounter.

On the other hand, have you ever met someone when they walk into the room, they light up the whole atmosphere; they carry the Hope of Glory inside them? Oftentimes without a word said?

I actually grew up with someone like that, my Mother.

Mom possesses the confidence and wisdom from some tough life experiences. However, the faith in the all-things-possible GOD, the beauty and the glory of Yeshua Jesus, shines brightly on and from within her. Not only does she dress elegantly, she always has on red lipstick and red nail polish impeccably. By the way, red represents the Blood of Yeshua Jesus. She has a "trademark" image, hazelnut-colored Margaret-Thatcher-hairstyle and Chanel-perfume-scented, that makes an impression that is not easily forgotten. Her presence commands attention. Being a Hong Kong businesswoman in a men's world in Mainland China for many years and the only female at a boardroom table more times than she cares to count, Mom has learned to speak and conduct herself confidently no matter what and where she is. I have watched her turn a bully into an admirer, respecting and honoring the person that she is. Without trying,

Mom's faith in the LORD and her self-assurance lights up any place she goes. Those around her cannot help but elevate higher into the place GOD has created them to be with the gifts created in them. They feel like they can do anything.

One of the first businesses she started in China when the communist country had just begun to open to "foreign" investors like herself from Hong Kong (still a British colony until 1997) in the early 80s was a little dessert shop. They served traditional Chinese desserts like red-bean soup. Since those humble times, a few of her employees have become successful business owners themselves after working for Mom. One of them is Little Li. Little Li became a successful entrepreneur and opened a café in one of the most popular tourist cities in China. 'Til this day, when Mom visits Guilin and meets Li, Li would not let her pay for anything at her businesses. She still speaks of how Mom inspired and helped launch her to accomplish the success she has today.

The light of GOD really illuminates from within us, even if we do not see with our physical eyes. Our spirits recognize it.

> *For with You is the fountain of life;*
> *In Your light we see light.*
> **Psalm 36:9**

> *"You are the light of the world. A city that is set on a hill cannot be hidden.* $^{15}$ *Nor do they light a lamp and put it under a basket, but on a lampstand, and it gives light to all who are in the house.*
> $^{16}$ <u>*Let your light*</u> *so shine before men, that* <u>*they may see your good works and glorify your Father in heaven.*</u>
> **Matthew 5:14-16**

The light and glory we carry of the Father ought to be able to open eyes so that people see the vision GOD has for them. They are encouraged by the Father's light and love through us, our kindness and words of grace that they feel refreshed from the weariness the world has burdened them with. We shine light into dark places and resurrect hope. They feel alive and lighter, able to enter GOD's rest. Mashiach Yeshua Jesus says:

> *Come to Me, all you who labor and are heavy laden, and I will give you rest.* [29] *Take My yoke upon you and learn from Me, for I am gentle and lowly in heart, and you will find rest for your souls.* [30] *For My yoke is easy and My burden is light.*
> **Matthew 11:28-30**

The LORD is referred to as Father of lights.

> [17] *Every good gift and every perfect gift is from above, and comes down from the Father of lights, with whom there is no variation or shadow of turning.*
> **James 1:17**

> *For you were once darkness, but now <u>you are light in the Lord</u>. Live as <u>children of light</u>* [9] *(for the fruit of the light consists in all goodness, righteousness and truth)* [10] *and find out what pleases the Lord.* [11] *Have nothing to do with the fruitless deeds of darkness, but rather expose them.*
> **Ephesians 5:8-11**

> [4] <u>*In him was life, and that life was the light of all mankind.*</u> [5] *The light shines in the darkness, and the darkness has not overcome it.*
> **John 1:4-5**

Science is slowly catching up with GOD's Word. His Word is truth. A few years ago, news sources reported that a bright flash of light at conception (an egg meeting a sperm) had been captured on video. That seems like a re-enactment of Genesis 1. In the middle of nothingness and darkness, light came to be and brought life. Life begins at conception indeed.

GOD is light, and His light brings life.

## 1. BERESHIT / IN THE BEGINNING

Wow! We are the children of light, literally.

We are made with His light inside of us.

Light dispersion in physics demonstrates to us that when lights pass through a triangular prism, it separates into visible lights of different colors like green, yellow, blue and violet. We are created to shine the light of GOD in our own unique ways, different and beautiful, glorifying the Source Light, our Father.

The first thing that GOD called good is the light He brought into the world. Somehow the Genesis 1 light being good reminds me of David's words of praise to GOD that He is good. The LORD is light; the LORD is good. His goodness lives inside of us, just as His light within us.

האור <u>כי טוב</u>

*HaOr <u>Ki Tov</u>*

*The light is good.*

**Genesis 1:3**

הודו ליהוה <u>כי טוב</u>

*Hodu L'Adonai <u>Ki Tov</u>*

*Give thanks to the LORD for He is good.*

**Psalm 106:1**

Our Father is the Father of lights that spoke creation into existence, including the light, we, as His children, are children of lights and we have been given full authority and power over the enemies by our Mashiach Yeshua Jesus to call things as they shall be.

*[19] Out of the ground the Lord God formed every beast of the field and every bird of the air, and brought them to Adam to see what he would call (קרא Qara Call) them. And whatever Adam called (קרא Qara Call) each living creature, that was its name.*

**Genesis 2:19**

This is what the authority the LORD originally has given to mankind. Whatever we call, it shall be, just like our Father did…

> *⁵ God called (קרא Qara Call) the light Day, and the darkness He called Night.*
> **Genesis 1:5**

Our words hold the power of death and life! Wow!

> *Your word is a lamp to my feet*
> *And a light to my path.*
> **Psalm 119:105**

> *Death and life are in the power of the tongue,*
> *And those who love it will eat its fruit.*
> **Proverbs 18:21**

Can you imagine speaking GOD's word to light up darkness? In the midst of confusion, we can speak the Word of GOD to break up deception and bring clarity. We can speak GOD's Word to bring light to any situation and light up the path where we are directed to go!

Like our Father, our spoken words hold creative powers.

> *And <u>God said</u>, "Let there be light," and <u>there was light</u>.*
> *⁴ <u>God saw that the light</u> was good, and he separated the light from the darkness. ⁵ <u>God called</u> the light "day,"…*
> **Genesis 1:3-5**

**Here are the 4 things observed in the above verses:**

1. GOD said
2. There was light
3. GOD saw light
4. GOD called/proclaimed.

# 1. BERESHIT / IN THE BEGINNING

Notice that the Light was there before GOD "saw" it.

Just because we do not see physically, it does not mean it is not there. Walking by faith is knowing the truth, despite the lack of physical evidence. We just know.

I have heard a saying, "There is a fine line between faith and insanity."

When Noah built the ark, no one had ever seen rain before. He may have looked insane to others. He had complete faith in GOD when building the ark for an upcoming catastrophic storm. He believed in GOD's Word, and his whole family was saved.

I believe the LORD is calling us to a new level of faith. Speaking our words in alignment with His will in bold faith, even when we do not see the "why" and the "how." Our audacious proclamation of GOD's Word and His will leads to blessings in future generations, our House. GOD created the world with provision for His Family, you and me, in mind. He chose to build the heavens as His throne and the earth His foot stool (Isaiah 66:1) so that the Creator of the Universe could be with us. "In the beginning GOD created…" is the framework, a foundation built and established a home of covenant with the love of the LORD for His children. From the beginning, He has loved us. Every alphabet in His every word is enveloped with His longing to be near us and that we would grow to know His love and His goodness for eternity.

Let's pray:

### Our Father in Heaven אבינו שבשמימ,

Thank You for being the Light and for creating the light in the world that we can see. You are the Father of lights and we are your children. As we begin our journey of this new year reading the Torah, Your love letters to us, we ask that You will deepen our understanding of what it means to be the light of the world, that You will give us a greater revelation of how to shine brighter Your glory through our words and deeds that the world will see and glorify You, Our Father in heaven.

B'Shem Yeshua HaMashiach בשם ישוע המשיח.

In Jesus' Name we pray. Amen.

# 1. TORAH TASTING
## *REFLECTION*

1. What is the word, picture or theme the LORD is highlighting to you in this chapter and Torah Portion?

2. What comes to mind when you hear the LORD had plans in creation of building a house "with you in mind"?

3. Was there a time you felt you were completely in the dark in a situation? What were your emotions? Was there eventually light shining in there that led you to see in clarity? How did it change your perspective after seeing the situation in the light?

# 2 ב
# noach
## (Noah)
## נח

Genesis 6:9-11:32

Isaiah 54:1-55:5

Luke 17:10-27

Last week's Torah Portion, Bereshit, ended with the opening of Genesis 6, filled with turmoil and sinfulness of mankind. GOD announced that He would destroy His creation, both man and beast, as well as creeping and flying creatures. The last verse in Torah Portion Bereshit is, "But, Noah found grace in the eyes of the LORD." A glimpse of hope in a righteous man named Noah is the cliff-hanger.

This week's Parashat Noach begins with the protagonist Noah, as in its title. It includes some of the popular Bible stories like Noah building the ark, the worldwide flood, GOD's covenant with Noah (the rainbow as a sign of the covenant), the Tower of Babel, descendants of Shem and Terah.

This parasha has been made into movies many times, from animation to Hollywood epic productions. The context of the story is filled with violence, depravity, and immorality. One can only imagine the world Noah and his family were living in. Unfortunately, it somewhat resembles the one we are in, evil and wickedness is being justified and promoted. The housing and feeding of hundreds and hundreds of animals is anything but cute and fluffy, as some children's books portray.

*⁸ But Noah found <u>grace</u> (חן Chen Favor) in the eyes of the Lord. This is the genealogy of Noah. Noah was a <u>just</u> (צדיק Tzadik Righteous) man, <u>perfect</u> (תמים Tamim Blameless) in his generations. Noah walked with God. ¹⁰ And Noah begot three sons: Shem, Ham, and Japheth. The earth also was corrupt before God, and the earth was filled with violence. ¹² So God looked upon the earth, and indeed it was corrupt; for all flesh had corrupted their way on the earth.*
**Genesis 6:8,9-12**

*Thus Noah did; according to all that God commanded him, so he did.*
**Genesis 6:22**

The 3 words used to describe Noah are:

- חן Chen — Favor/Grace
- צדיק Tzadik — Righteous/Just
- תמים Tamim — Blameless/Perfect/Complete/Unblemished/Without Defect

This is the first time these 3 words appear in the Torah. Later, they are associated with some well-known heroes as well.

Here are just a few examples.

- חן Chen Favor/Grace — Abraham, Moses, Joseph and Esther
- צדיק Tzadik Righteous/Just — the LORD and David

- תמים Tamim Blameless/Perfect/Complete/Unblemished/Without Defect — sacrificial offerings for the LORD

Noah is the first man that found favor with the LORD, the first righteous and blameless man recorded. He did all that GOD commanded him. We can only imagine the mockery he faced following GOD in those days. His obedience amidst the ungodly world displayed his extraordinary courage.

> [20] *Now the sons of Noah who went out of the ark were Shem, Ham, and Japheth. And <u>Ham was the father of Canaan.</u>* [19] *These three were the sons of Noah, and from these the whole earth was populated. And Noah began to be a farmer, and he planted a vineyard.* [21] *Then he drank of the wine and was drunk, and became uncovered in his tent.* [22] *And <u>Ham, the father of Canaan,</u> saw the nakedness of his father, and told his two brothers outside.* [23] *But Shem and Japheth took a garment, laid it on both their shoulders, and went backward and covered the nakedness of their father. Their faces were[b] turned away, and they did not see their father's nakedness. So Noah awoke from his wine, and knew what his younger son had done to him.* [25]
> *Then he said, "Cursed be Canaan;*
> *A servant of servants*
> *He shall be to his brethren."*
> **Genesis 9:18-25**

There are many theories as to what happened in this account of the uncovering of Noah's nakedness. Nonetheless, we know Canaan was cursed and Ham was his father and Noah his grandfather. Ham did the dirty deed, yet Canaan was cursed, suffering the consequence. There must be more to the story. However, what we want to focus on is that the cursed one, Canaan, would go on to father some interesting characters and became a name to a land of huge significance to GOD's people.

Abram was called to go to Canaan. His descendants were later enslaved in Egypt. Fast forward 400 years, the LORD would deliver the Hebrews from slavery and guide them back to Canaan, the "Promise Land." Turning the cursed land, Canaan, into the Promised Land? Only our awesome GOD can do such a thing, reversing the curse.

Canaan כנען appears 8 times in this Torah Portion, Parashat Noach. The number 8 is symbolic of grace and a new beginning. The Hebrew root of Canaan is כנע Kana, meaning "to be humbled."

*And being found in appearance as a man, He humbled Himself and became obedient to the point of death, even the death of the cross.*
**Philippians 2:8**

Another clue to GOD's redemption plan is through the humble Mashiach.

*Now the whole earth had one language and one speech. ² And it came to pass, as they journeyed from the east, that they found a plain in the land of Shinar, and they dwelt there… And they said, "Come, let us build ourselves a city, and a tower whose top is in the heavens; let us make a name for ourselves, lest we be scattered abroad over the face of the whole earth." And the Lord said, "Indeed the people are one and they all have one language, and this is what they begin to do; now nothing that they propose to do will be withheld from them. ⁷ Come, let Us go down and there confuse their language, that they may not understand one another's speech." ⁸ So the Lord scattered them abroad from there over the face of all the earth, and they ceased building the city. ⁹ Therefore its name is called [c]Babel, because there the Lord confused the language of all the earth; and from there the Lord scattered them abroad over the face of all the earth.*
**Genesis 11:1-2,4,6-9**

Genesis 11 gives the account that the world all had one language at one point. Then, GOD confused their language, and they scattered all over the earth. Some believe that this fable tale-like parasha did not actually happen, even within the Jewish and Christian circles. However, I have heard archeologists discover evidence of the Great Flood, as well as the

Tower of Babel. That confirms what the Torah has told us, as well as the traditions and stories in many different cultures that have been passed on orally from generation to generation.

Our ancestors were all there and knew of Noah, the Ark and the flood. They told their children the stories they had heard from their fathers. Many cultures around the world have their own version of the worldwide flood story.

Several years ago, I came across a book titled "The Discovery of Genesis: How the Truths of Genesis Were Found Hidden in the Chinese Language" by C.H. Kang and Ethel R. Nelson. The topic is fascinating and one that I had never heard of. Learning to read and write Chinese beginning at age 3 as my native language, yet I had never realized the information I am about to share with you here.

The Chinese language has no alphabet. It is composed with characters. Many characters are pictographs in their ancient form. For example, anything that is related to water has the water 水 radical, which looks like 3 rain drops as in 河 River, 海 Sea, 湖 Lake. Kang's book makes the case that many accounts in the Book of Genesis are hidden in the Chinese language. The spoken Chinese language has many dialects, sort of like regional languages, American English versus Irish English, except the Shanghai-ese dialect is completely incomprehensible to a Beijing-ese native, though both are regional Chinese dialects. Thankfully, most Chinese speak Mandarin and Cantonese, Mandarin being the official dialect in Mainland China and Cantonese being the second most spoken dialect among Chinese around the world. Nonetheless, there is only one written traditional form of the Chinese language. There is a simplified version being used in Communist Mainland China, but that is another topic for another time. The Chinese language is one of the most ancient languages in the world. When I discovered some of these words that tell of the Genesis stories, I knew they were not mere coincidence. For example, the word for boat is 船 , it is made up of 3 parts: 舟 Boat, 八 Eight, and 口 Mouth. The original boat/vessel had 8 mouths/people on it. What are the chances that this word matches up with Noah's ark with 8 people on it? How about the word for flood 洪? It is the 3 Rain Drops + 共 Total (with the words "altogether" and there were 八, "8"). Again, there were 8 people on Noah's Ark during the flood. There are hundreds of words supporting the theory that the Chinese ancestors hid the Creation and Torah stories in their language. Here is my favorite. The word for Righteousness is 義, made up of 2 words: Lamb 羊 +/over Me 我. Righteousness is when the Lamb of GOD covers me or when I kneel humbly at the feet of the Lamb of GOD.

*Knowing that you were not redeemed with corruptible things, like silver or gold, from your aimless conduct received by tradition from your fathers, [19] but with the precious blood of Christ, as of a lamb without blemish and without spot.*
**1 Peter 1:18-19**

*But by His doing you are in Christ Jesus, who became to us wisdom from God, and righteousness and sanctification, and redemption.*
**1 Corinthians 11:3**

*"Behold, the days are coming," says the Lord,*
*"That I will raise to David a <u>Branch of righteousness</u>;...*
*A King shall reign and prosper,*
*And execute judgment and <u>righteousness</u> in the [c]earth.*
*[6] In His days Judah will be saved,*
*And Israel will dwell safely;*
*Now this is His name by which He will be called:*
*The LORD Our <u>Righteousness</u>.*
**Jeremiah 23:5-6**

Another book titled "Finding GOD in Ancient China" by Chan Kei Thong and Charlene L. Fu discusses the GOD whom the Chinese had worshipped thousands of years ago, with evidence recorded in historic ancient literatures long before Buddhism or Taoism, 2 most popular religions, among the Chinese being introduced in 500-600 B.C.. This book presents the fact that the One True GOD, King of the Universe, is not merely some old White man with flowy white hair and a deity imported from the West to corrupt the Chinese. One time when I was sharing about the LORD with a relative, he cynically responded, "The Christian thing is not for me. I am Chinese." But when I brought up the Chinese words with the Genesis stories in them, he was surprised and intrigued. He became open to what I had to say about the LORD. I believe we are living in the Harvest Time; the LORD is giving us harvesting tools. Just like shears and knives, we are being shown tools like hidden messages in the languages to reach those who are seeking GOD.

There are also tremendous similarities between the 2 ancient languages, Chinese and Hebrew. Of course, it just blesses me that I hold these 2 languages dear to my heart. When I see the messages that GOD had tucked inside them to be found, at discovery, my whole being just leaps in joy.

*And we know that <u>all things work together for good to those who love God</u>, to those who are the called according to His purpose.*
**Romans 8:28**

*For it pleased the Father that in Him all the fullness should dwell, ²⁰<u>and by Him to reconcile all things to Himself</u>, by Him, whether things on earth or things in heaven, having made peace through the blood of His cross.*
**Colossians 1:19-20**

Noah's name נח Noach means comfort and rest.

*Lamech lived one hundred and eighty-two years, and had a son. ²⁹ And he called his name Noah, saying, "This one will comfort us concerning our work and the toil of our hands, because of the ground which the Lord has cursed."*
**Genesis 5:28-29**

**Noah's name נח Noach has two Hebrew letters:**

- נ Nun — Life (number 50)
- ח Chet — Enclosed (number 8)

The 2 numbers add up to 58, the same number as וגה HaGan The Garden.

Is it a coincidence Noah, as rest and comfort, also shows us a picture of life and rest within an enclosure? The number 58 shows us life and rest in The Garden. This depicts the original Garden that the LORD has provided for mankind. GOD had Noah populate the earth after the flood, just as He had commanded Adam to do.

GOD had a restoration plan through Noah to reverse the curse. The Torah does not tell stories isolated from other cultures. This parasha reminds us that all were created by the One True GOD. We have the same root. We were once scattered, but GOD has provided a redemption plan to gather us all together as a reunion through the Righteous One, the Lamb of the world.

Let's pray:

> **Our Father in Heaven** אבינו שבשמימ,
>
> Thank You for Your mercy. You saved the world when there was only one righteous man, Noah. When none was righteous, You provided righteousness to cover us through our Mashiach Yeshua Jesus. In the days of the Harvest, as we are in now, help us to see the tools You are giving us to reach Your people. Their hearts are ready, ripe to receive and see Your love. Show us one by one that they will be gathered back to Your heart.

Isaiah 54:1-3 —

*"Enlarge the place of your tent,*
*And let them stretch out the curtains of your dwellings;*
*Do not spare;*
*Lengthen your cords,*
*And strengthen your stakes.*
*³ For you shall expand to the right and to the left,*
*And your descendants will inherit the nations,*
*And make the desolate cities inhabited."*
*Yes, LORD! We are ready! Let Your Word be done!*
*B'Shem Yeshua HaMashiach* בשם ישוע המשיח.

*In Jesus' Name we pray. Amen.*

# 2. TORAH TASTING
## *REFLECTION*

1. What is the word, picture or theme the LORD is highlighting to you in this chapter and Torah Portion?

2. Is there a culture or heritage that fascinates you? Even in its non-religious traditions, does it somehow point to the LORD's handiwork?

3. GOD is purposeful in His creation. Looking back on your own upbringing or background (where you grew up, cultural or social elements, ...), or perhaps someone you know, does it connect to the LORD's big-picture purposes?

# 3 ג
# Lech Lecha
## (Go Forth)
## לך לך

Genesis 12:1-17:27

Isaiah 40:27-41:16

John 8:51-58

*The title of this week's Torah Portion is לך לך Lech Lecha Go Forth. The Lord had said to Abram, "Go from your country (land), your people (relatives) and your father's household (people closest to him) to the land I will show you.*
**Genesis 12:1**

This Parasha covers GOD calling Abram to go to the land that would be given to him and his descendants, Abram going to Egypt with Sarai, the battle between the kings (5 kings versus 4 kings) in the Valley of Siddim, Abram helping the King of Sodom to win the battle while rescuing Lot (Abram's nephew), GOD establishing a covenant with Abram, the birth of Ishmael and finally, circumcision being commanded as a sign of the covenant between GOD and Abram.

The fifth and the sixth Hebrew words of this portion is לך לך Lech Lecha. The word לך Lech is Go Forth. It comes from the Hebrew root הלך Halach Go. לך Lech is a command form of "Go." Then, לך Lecha is a preposition To/For, along with the object pronoun of you. Literally, these 2 words can mean "Go, for you". I sense that GOD called Abraham to go for his own sake.

לך Lecha is not translated in this verse. We only see "Go … from your country.…"

I feel that it is significant and not to be ignored.

This Parasha opens with the LORD speaking to Abram, לך Lecha "for you," commanding him to go away from the land in which he had grown up. I believe GOD called Abram to go in order to bless him for the sake of Abram. Yes, I know the LORD does things to reveal Himself and to accomplish His purposes, but so much He does have us in mind as well. GOD did not just give a command, "Go…," but לך Lecha "for you" somehow has an intimate and personal tone to that. Abram is not just a pawn, but the LORD delighted in him and his righteousness (Genesis 15:6) that Abram would later become father of many nations.

לך לך Lech Lecha are 2 identical Hebrew words with only 2 consonants each but with different vowels. The first word is a verb and the second one is a preposition with a pronoun. Since there are no vowels indicated on the Torah scrolls, is it possible that both לך לך means Go, Go … as an emphasis? Possibly so, but either way, the use of both לך לך is interesting as the first words spoken to Abram from the LORD.

In the word picture, the first letter ל Lamed is a shepherd's rod and the second letter כ/ך Kaf is an open hand as to reveal something. It looks like GOD holds a shepherd's rod in one hand and waving his other hand with His palm open to guide Abram in the direction He is showing him to go. He would go from the land that he was able to see and knew well to a place full of unknowns and uncertainty. The Hebrew root word for "show" in the phrase "GOD would show him" is ראה Ra'ah See.

However, it seems the journey to Canaan had already begun long before this point...

> <u>Terah became the father of Abram, Nahor and Haran.</u> *And Haran became the father of Lot.* <sup>28</sup> *While his father Terah was still alive, Haran died in Ur of the Chaldeans, in the land of his birth.* <sup>29</sup> *Abram and Nahor both married. The name of Abram's wife was Sarai, and the name of Nahor's wife was Milkah; she was the daughter of Haran, the father of both Milkah and Iskah.*
> <sup>31</sup> *Terah took his son Abram, his grandson Lot son of Haran, and his daughter-in-law Sarai, the wife of his son Abram, and together they set out from Ur of the Chaldeans to go to Canaan. But when they came to Harran, they settled there.*
> **Genesis 11:27-29**

Basically, Terah had 3 sons, Abram, Nahor and Haran. Haran died and his brother married his niece, Milkah (Haran's daughter). I know, that sounds strange to us modern Western-minded people. Nonetheless, Haran had another daughter, Iskah. What's interesting is that Terah set out to leave the land of Ur, where they had lived, into Canaan and settled in Harran. This is the backdrop of this Torah Portion, Parashat Lech Lecha.

It seems the journey to Canaan had already been set in motion somehow before the LORD even called Abram. By the way, Terah had not taken along his other son Nahor and wife Milkah on their journey. Interesting! But for whatever reason, Terah brought his son Abram, daughter-in-law Sarai and grandson Lot with him to leave Ur, Abram's heart was prepared to go to Canaan.

By divine providence, it did not come as a surprise to Abram about Canaan being the end goal, with detours along the way.

At this time, Abram was called out of everything familiar to him at age 75, leaving behind everything he grew up knowing in Harran:

His land/country — his customs, traditions

His relatives — those who had influence over him, his peers, and people that looked like him

His father's house — those who had the same bloodline

Abram was completely uprooted from his past into his future in order to receive the eternal blessings the LORD had for him. From here on, it is the LORD and Abram, along with his wife and nephew.

Coincidentally, my husband (Paul) and I can relate to Abram's leaving Harran so well.

Paul was born and raised in the Bronx, New York City, while I came from Hong Kong, the opposite side of the globe. Both cities are alike, crowded metropolitans, filled with noise and pollution, known for exciting city life with people everywhere. By the time we met in Washington, D.C., working in the U.S. Capital city, Paul had already been away from New York (his birthplace), living in Maryland (just right outside of Washington, D.C.); whereas I had already been living in the South in the U.S. for high school and college, away from Hong Kong (my native land). Paul's family lived on the East Coast; they were a close family. After we met, an opportunity came for Paul to move to Ohio, job promotions and raises happened in 3 moves within 30 months. During that time, we got married and moved away from all that was familiar.

Nope, GOD did not appear to us and spoke the words, "Go!," like He did with Abram. We did feel prompted to go to the Midwest, then later settled in Texas.

Paul grew up in the Orthodox Jewish community, and reading the Torah was a weekly tradition they had on Shabbats. Christianity was something they were told to stay away from. Then… he met me. Obviously, I tried to "convert" him to know and accept Jesus as LORD and Savior, dragging him all over the place to different churches hoping the light bulb would come on and he would become a "Christian." Well, it did not happen that way. GOD had other plans and they were far better than mine. There was a series of events in our faith-seeking journey, en route to Texas that eventually led him to know his Jewish Messiah. Being away from the East Coast, Paul was completely out of his comfort zone. His strong New York accent highlights him in a crowd like a neon sign when he opens his mouth in a fun way. We were both taken out of the land, the relatives and family familiar to us, and placed in new communities, making new friends. We had no family close by to influence or guide our faith journey. It was just the two of us and GOD in our center, with the people and circumstances He placed in our path.

And it is in Texas that we got to meet the GOD we had never known. Paul began to understand many of the traditions he grew up with, following those traditions in the way GOD intended, in a Messianic perspective. Our GOD is not a foreign GOD, not Greek, not Caucasian, not Blonde with blue eyes. His love and character transcend all things that would hinder us from getting to know Him.

When Paul came to accept Yeshua Jesus as His Deliverer and LORD, he did not convert. Instead, he became a "Complete Jew," knowing his Jewish Mashiach. To this day, Paul attributes his finding GOD or seeing who He is to being removed from home, taken out of his element.

Have you ever been taken out of your element before? Not necessarily geographically, maybe circumstantially? Maybe you are feeling led to a place unfamiliar to you? Perhaps the LORD is about to show you new things, and in order for that to happen, He needs you to put down any and all pre-conceived notions?

GOD can make even enemies' land a place of refuge. Throughout history, Egypt is not friendly territory to GOD's people. We see that from Moses, most notably when the Hebrews were enslaved in Egypt for 400 years.

> *<u>Now there was a famine in the land, and Abram went down to Egypt to live</u> there for a while because the famine was severe.*
> **Genesis 12:10**

> *When a man's ways please the Lord,*
> *He makes even his enemies to be at peace with him.*
> **Proverbs 16:7**

Abram went and lived in Egypt for a while to ensure a sufficient food supply. How ironic that a place that provided a safe haven for his family temporarily would someday be a place of bondage for his descendants?

It seems like before something big happens, the LORD would lead His people out of their comfort zone to deliver them from famine and harm so that His glory would be on full display!

Here are a few examples —

Naomi's family fled to Moab for food due to famine:

> *Now it came to pass, in the days when the judges ⁽ᵃ⁾ruled, that there was a famine in the land. And a certain man of Bethlehem, Judah, went to ⁽ᵇ⁾dwell in the country of Moab (unfriendly land), he and his wife and his two sons.*
> **Ruth 1:1**

And it was in Moab that Naomi gained the daughter-in-law and that through her GOD would bring redemption and deliverance to her and her nation!

Jacob's sons went to Egypt for food due to famine:

*The famine was over all the face of the earth, and Joseph opened all the storehouses and sold to the Egyptians. And the famine became severe in the land of Egypt. 57 So all countries came to Joseph in Egypt to buy grain, because the famine was severe in all lands. When Jacob saw that there was grain in Egypt, Jacob said to his sons, "Why do you look at one another?" 2 And he said, "Indeed I have heard that there is grain in Egypt; go down to that place and buy for us there, that we may live and not die."*
**Genesis 41:56-42:1-2**

Joseph and Mary went to Egypt for safety from Herod:

*Now when they had departed, behold, an angel of the Lord appeared to Joseph in a dream, saying, "Arise, take the young Child and His mother, flee to Egypt, and stay there until I bring you word; for Herod will seek the young Child to destroy Him."*
**Matthew 2:13**

GOD's Word shows us so many times that His redemption is just waiting right around the corner even when we resist and avoid the "Egypt's," the seemingly dreadful place and circumstance. Abram's promises from GOD would come after his descendants' 400 years of slavery in Egypt, but GOD never forsook His Word and He never will.

We can always count on GOD's Word.

*As the sun was setting, Abram fell into a deep sleep, and a thick and dreadful darkness came over him. 13 Then the Lord said to him, "<u>Know for certain that for four hundred years your descendants will be strangers in a country not their own and that they will be enslaved and mistreated there.</u> 14 But I will punish the nation they serve as slaves, and afterward they will come out with great possessions. 15 You, however, will go to your ancestors in peace and be buried at a good old age. 16 In the fourth generation your descendants will come back here, for the sin of the Amorites has not yet reached its full measure."*
**Genesis 15:12-16**

The LORD had to tell this tough and hard-to-swallow truth to Abram during his sleep.

Speaking of bringing promises in our sleep. Another "Lech Lecha" moment in my life really speaks to that. So often, GOD calls us, not in a way He did Abram, Samuel, or Moses, but in subtle ways.

14 years ago, I was a mother of two young children, ages 4 and 2.

A few new friends of mine were homeschooling their children. While the idea was intriguing or even exotic, I could not envision myself wearing long dresses with head scarves, schooling our children while raising chickens and gardening.

Lots of homeschooling-mom stereotypes, as you can see.

After interacting more with these "cool" homeschool moms who were nothing I'd expected, I realized their children were normal, and not weird, nor socially awkward. I slowly warmed up to the idea.

Still, I was stuck at the "I don't have a teaching degree and can never teach our children" mode. I wrestled with GOD and gave him all kinds of reasons why it would not be a good idea. Of course, The LORD spoke to me ever so gently. Starting our 4-year-old firstborn child for the 2-hour session once a week at a Chinese school was a "no-brainer," an easy start. Before having children, we knew our children would learn the Chinese language and specifically speak Cantonese (a dialect of HongKongese), which they did learn from birth.

I felt the nudging growing stronger from the LORD to homeschool our kids. Like Gideon, one of my favorite prophets that asked, "LORD, if it is you speaking, please show me…," I needed confirmations too. Then, GOD gave me a dream. He spoke words to me in my sleep, like He did Abram. In this dream, I saw our bedroom with a tiny closet (it was our actual bedroom upstairs). I opened the small closet. To my surprise, it led into a huge room…

Kind of like my Narnia wardrobe moment.

The room looked like a classroom, equipped and furnished with everything needed for children to learn, white boards, markers, stickers, pens, crayons, posters, etc. You name it, all the things you can imagine in a classroom were in this room. I woke up from this dream, and instantly, I knew the LORD was saying, "You have been fully equipped to teach your children." Not 1, not 2, but 3 times, GOD gave me this same dream to confirm to me He led me to this point and will continue to lead me on this journey. I am not alone, as if He was saying, "Go! For you and your family…"

Dipping my toes in the water, so to speak, I bought workbooks to begin teaching our children ABCs and 123s, saying to myself, "At least I can't mess them up with the basic alphabets and numbers, right?" A wise homeschool mom once encouraged me, "All moms are teachers to their children. After all, we teach them how to brush their teeth and tie their shoes. Moms are natural teachers, with or without a college teaching degree." Before I knew it, I was surrounded by new and veteran homeschool parents. The LORD told me to look at this as an annual contract, a year-by-year decision. So, every summer, we sought the LORD and asked if we should continue. As our children grew older, we involved them in the conversation and decision-making. Our son graduated high school 14 years later with an associate degree, as an Eagle Scout, then onto a 4-year university with scholarships. From the beginning, homeschooling was a faith journey, going into something completely unfamiliar and trusting in what GOD would do for our family, taking fear out of the equation. The blessings on this journey of going from the familiar into the unknown are tremendous and beyond what we can see, impacting our children for many years to come. We would not trade our experience for anything.

What's your לֶךְ לְךָ Lech Lecha moment?

A new job opportunity? A new friend that sparks your interest in a new interest for hobby or career idea or business that you'd never known nor considered?

An acquaintance or a "random" stranger you have just met that their kindness leads you to a new way of thinking or seeing people or circumstances around you, possibly seeing GOD's hand and work in your midst?

The course of world history would be entirely altered if Abram did not say yes, or would it? Would someone else be raised up for the call?

Just like Esther, the unseen hand, through her uncle Mordecai, guided her to enter the Kingdom beauty pageant, and eventually, she became Queen of the mighty Persian Empire. That ultimately gave her the power to call for a massive, fast and prayer movement, which led to the strategies she executed beautifully, saving the Jews, her own people. However, if not Esther, someone else would have been raised up for a time such as this, according to her uncle Mordecai.

If not you, then who?

When the LORD said, "Whom shall I send, and who will go for Us?" Are you willing to be the one that answers, "Here I am. Send me," as Isaiah said to GOD in Isaiah 6:8?

I am here. All that I am.

Here I am. Send me. Not perfection, just all that I have been created and all that I am now.

Is GOD nudging you and saying to you,

"Go. Go forth. Go for you and your family's sake."

"Go and I will go with you and show you things you have not seen before."
"Go, in order that I can bless you with eternal blessings and My Glory will be there for all to see."?

This Parasha takes us on the adventures GOD led Abram, leaving his homeland to a foreign place where he would be caught up in an intense battle as a victorious warrior, meeting the mysterious king/priest Melchizedek, with GOD's covenant and promises reassured multiple times, seeing into a future that would sustain him through many setbacks. GOD would seal the covenant with Abram and his descendants with circumcision, a mark of GOD's people that, 4000 years later, it still stands. Even Moses called for circumcision of the heart so that we would not be stubborn but be tender-hearted toward the LORD (Deuteronomy 10:19).

*Circumcise yourselves to the LORD, and remove the foreskins of your heart, men of Judah and inhabitants of Jerusalem.*
**Jeremiah 4:4**

The mark of the LORD is our spiritual circumcision, the circumcision of the heart. Our tender heart and affection toward the LORD and doing His will is a sign the world sees that we belong to the One True GOD.

**Let's pray:**

**Our Father in Heaven** אבינו שבשמימ,

Thank You for Your words, Lech Lecha, to Abram. Those words still ring true today when You call us out from what we can see and know well to a place full of promises and blessings. We ask You to mark us with circumcised hearts that we follow and obey Your Word promptly so that we won't miss anything You've prepared for us. And let our circumcised hearts be a sign, like the circumcised Hebrews, set apart for the world to know that our lives belong to You. We are ready for the adventures that await us when we go forth as You guide us. We say to You today, "LORD, here I am, send me."

B'Shem Yeshua HaMashiach.

In Jesus' Name we pray. Amen.

## 3. TORAH TASTING
### *REFLECTION*

1. What is the word, picture or theme the LORD is highlighting to you in this chapter and Torah Portion?

2. Is there a time the LORD nudged you to go, leaving behind what is familiar to you? What did you learn from that experience?

3. Do you feel a call into the next season that GOD is calling you to that will require tremendous faith?

# 4 ד
# Vayera
## (And He Appeared)
## וירא

Genesis 18:1-22:24

2 Kings 4:1-37

Luke 17:28-37

Vayera is the title of this week's Torah Portion, taken from its very first Hebrew word וירא Vayera. This portion is filled with many familiar Bible stories, from the promise and fulfillment of a son to Abraham and Sarah, Abraham's son by his Egyptian servant along the way, sins and destruction of Sodom and Gomorrah, Abraham's pleading and failure to save Sodom and Gomorrah, the testing of Abraham's faith in GOD through the command of the sacrifice of Isaac, and subsequently the reaffirmation of GOD's promises to Abraham.

The Hebrew word וירא Vayera means "And he appeared." It derives from the Hebrew root Ra'ah See.

*Then the Lord <u>appeared</u> to him by the terebinth trees of Mamre, as he was sitting in the tent door in the heat of the day. ² So he <u>lifted his eyes</u> and <u>looked</u>, and <u>behold</u>, three men were standing by him; and when he <u>saw</u> them, he ran from the tent door to meet them, and bowed himself to the ground, ³ and said, "My Lord, if I have now <u>found favor in Your sight/eyes</u>, do not pass on by Your servant.*

**Genesis 18:1-3**

This parasha opens with "the LORD appeared," the word "appeared" is essentially "allowed or caused to be <u>seen</u>" by Abraham. The backdrop of this Torah Portion is Abraham being in a resting position at the entrance of his tent (his resting place) on a warm summer day, and then the LORD showed up. The LORD's name here is a tetragrammaton YHWH יהוה. Some refer it to "Yahweh," adding vowels to the four consonants, YHVH. This unpronounceable name is solely referred to The One True GOD of the universe, who came to meet Abraham in 3 persons.

This Torah Portion opens with a day that seems like any ordinary day, yet extraordinary things are about to happen. After every male had been circumcised in Abraham's household, on this day, he was sitting at the door of his tent. Three men manifested before his eyes. Three specific ways described how Abraham saw these three men:

1. He lifted his eyes וישא עיניו Vayisa Einav
2. and saw/looked וירא Vayara
3. and behold (or O, here, see) והנה Hineh

Is it possible that those are the 3 ways he saw the men individually and respectively?

I speculate so. Perhaps Abraham saw 3 distinct characters in them? Or the 3 phrases/words were used to show the progression of how Abraham noticed them. I believe there is possibly another mystery to be further discovered.

More fun adventures for another time.

Grammatically, I see that Abraham was speaking to those 3 men in terms of a singular person. The LORD was showing up to meet Abraham in 3 people. Some rabbis state that Abraham likely was addressing the chief of the 3 people. While that's a possibility, I'd like to suggest to you that mysteriously Abraham was speaking to one person knowing somehow it was a supernatural encounter with the Holy One. This is the only Torah reference that the LORD appeared to someone in "three men." Let's explore the significance in the other "three-men" mentioned in the Torah that we can glean from.

*<u>Preparation of claiming GOD's promise of inheritance</u> —*
*(When spies were sent to scout out the Promise Land)*
*Pick out from among you **three men** for each tribe, and I will send them; they shall rise and go through the land, survey it according to their inheritance, and come back to me*
**Joshua 18:4**

*<u>GOD's anointing of a king, beginning of the Kingdom age</u> —*
*(When Samuel was sent to anoint Saul to be the first king of Israel)*
*Then you shall go on forward from there and come to the terebinth tree of Tabor. There **three men** going up to God at Bethel will meet you, one carrying three young goats, another carrying three loaves of bread, and another carrying a skin of wine.*
**1 Samuel 10:3**

<u>Righteousness</u> —

*Even if these **three men**, Noah, Daniel, and Job, were in it, they would deliver only themselves by their <u>righteousness</u>," says the Lord God*
**Ezekiel 14:14**

GOD's words to be heard —

> [19] While Peter thought about the vision, the Spirit said to him, "Behold, **three men** are seeking you. [20] Arise therefore, go down and go with them, doubting nothing; for I have sent them." Then Peter went down to the men [h]who had been sent to him from Cornelius, and said, "Yes, I am he whom you seek. For what reason have you come? And they said, "Cornelius the centurion, a just man, one who fears God and has a good reputation among all the nation of the Jews, was divinely instructed by a holy angel to summon you to his house, and to hear words from you." [23] Then he invited them in and lodged them.
>
> ## Acts 10:19-23

For some reason, Abraham's three-men visit reminds me of something many Chinese are familiar with, the 3 gods (stars or symbols), 福 Fu Fortune/Prosperity/Wealth/Blessings, 祿 Lu Status/Good Career, 壽 Shou Longevity/Long Life. They represent the 3 ultimate earthly happiness anyone would desire. They are embodied in 3 smiley men with a long beard dressed in exquisite robes. The 壽 (long life) deity is an old man. I do not remember worshipping them as a child. They are like good-luck symbols commonly seen in Chinese society. They are depicted in paintings, statutes, and movies and deeply engrained in Chinese culture. You may even have seen them in Chinese restaurants. These three men are synonymous to Good Luck and Happiness anywhere they are seen. They are always seen together, never apart. They come as a "package deal." They are 3 individual characters, yet seen as a unified entity.

Speaking of 3, I once witnessed angels in our home when our children were toddlers. One night, I heard some rattling noise and thought it was our daughter that had crawled out of her crib in the middle of the night playing. I got out of bed and saw nothing in our game room. Kids were sound asleep. I got back into bed and looked out. I saw 3 angels outside our bedroom, 2 looking up and 1 looking at me as if they were signaling GOD's blessings were upon us. They disappeared soon after. I said to myself, "I am not dreaming. I am not dreaming. I am not dreaming," so

I would remember the incident did indeed happen, not merely a dream. I woke up in the morning recalling the incident. I told my husband about it. He said I must have been dreaming. I responded with the emphatic "No!" I have heard that when GOD's divine visit and glory is so strong, sometimes, electrical things are interfered. That morning, I put our kids in our minivan and proceeded to start the engine but found the battery dead. Fortunately, Paul was still home to help me. He went to his car with the intent to pull around to the garage, where I was to give my battery a jump. A few minutes later, he returned and said, "I believe you were not dreaming." I said, "Why do you say that?" He said, "You are not going to believe it. My car battery is dead too." In addition, the battery of one of our electrical devices was dead as well. Three dead batteries! Later in the week, Paul shared with me that our son Matthew had a dream on that fateful night which gave clues to the messages of the three angels' visitation. His dream had 3 specific items; they led me to a verse in Proverbs 24.

> *Through <u>wisdom</u> a house is built,*
> *And by <u>understanding</u> it is established;*
> *⁴ By <u>knowledge</u> the rooms are filled*
> *With all precious and pleasant riches*
> **Proverbs 24:3-4**

As if the 3 angels represent wisdom, understanding and knowledge, during that year's Christmas season, I received 3 different angel figurines as gifts from 3 different friends. I had never received angel figurines as a gift before, let alone 3.

Since then, the LORD continued to unfold the revelation of what He wanted to say to us in blessing us through this unforgettable event beyond the message of "wisdom, understanding and knowledge."

It is an encounter I will never forget.

> *There is a saying: Good things come in 3's. One of my favorite scriptures is the words spoken to the Prophet Jeremiah by the LORD in Jeremiah 33:3 — Call to Me, and I will answer you, and show you great and mighty things, which you do not know.*
> **Jeremiah 33:3**

Indeed, there are wonderful things associated with the number 3: Humans are made of Body, soul and spirit. The patriarchs of Abraham, Isaac and Jacob. The LORD Yeshua Jesus the Mashiach was resurrected on the 3rd day. Of course, the Holy Trinity of the ONE GOD is in GOD the Father, the Son and the Holy Spirit. The 3rd Hebrew Alphabet is Gimel, in the shape of a camel, representing to give or benefit. I sense that the LORD appearing to Abraham in the 3 men has significance beyond our finite mind. It set off a series of events that have an eternal impact.

> *And the Lord said to Abraham, "Why did Sarah laugh, saying, 'Shall I surely bear a child, since I am old?' 14 Is anything too hard (wonderful, extraordinary) for the Lord? <u>At the appointed time I will return to you, according to the time of life</u>, and Sarah shall have a son."*
> **Genesis 18:13-14**

Throughout the Torah, the appointed time Moed מועד is used to refer to the Feasts of the LORD. The appointed season according to the time of life, gives the sentiment of mystery. Despite the unspecified time, the LORD reassured the provision of Sarah having a son. Also, "the LORD" and the "3 men" in this portion are used interchangeably, there is no question that the LORD manifested Himself in these 3 men and Abraham knew it. Even so, Sarah laughed at the absurd idea of her giving birth in her old age. When caught, she denied it. Nonetheless, GOD's will stands despite her lack of faith. That's remarkable! GOD can fulfill His promises by doing His part will, even if we don't believe. When we declare GOD's will be done, it will be done at the appointed time, according to the time of life. GOD's promises are yes and amen, not a minute late or early.

## 4. VAYERA / AND HE APPEARED

Between the 3-men visit to Abraham and Sarah prophesying the birth of their child and Sarah giving birth to their son is the destruction of Sodom and Gomorrah for their depravity after Abraham's failed attempt to save it. Abraham then journeyed to the South and met Abimelech. Abraham misled Abimelech about Sarah being his sister, and thus Abimelech's household was struck with the plague of infertility.

> *So Abraham prayed to God; and God healed Abimelech, his wife, and his female servants. Then they bore children;[18] for <u>the Lord had closed up all the wombs of the house of Abimelech because of Sarah</u>, Abraham's wife. <u>And the Lord visited Sarah</u> as He had said, and the Lord did for Sarah as He had spoken. [2]<u>For Sarah conceived and bore Abraham a son</u> in his old age, at the set time of which God had spoken to him.*
> **Genesis 17-21:1-2**

The fulfillment of GOD's Word of Sarah conceiving and bearing a son came interestingly after Abraham had prayed and GOD's healing of Abimelech's household from barrenness. I cannot help but wonder about this very first time someone's prayer bringing forth a miraculous healing is a way of showing us that we can pray for someone else for the very prayer for which we ourselves are still waiting for the answer to the same prayer request. Would you be willing to pray for someone and celebrate their answered prayer with joy genuinely while you are still waiting for your own? The LORD chose even an imperfect man like Abraham to perform the first healing miracle with and through. Praise GOD... There is hope for us.

The Hebrew root word צחק Tsachaq Laugh appears in the Bible 13 times, out of the 13 times, 7 of them are in this Parasha.

But before Sarah laughed, Abraham already laughed once himself at the very idea of them having a son when GOD gave him the word.

*Then Abraham fell on his face and laughed, and said in his heart, "Shall a child be born to a man who is one hundred years old? And shall Sarah, who is ninety years old, bear a child?" ¹⁸ And Abraham said to God, "Oh, that Ishmael might live before You*
**Genesis 17:17**

Later, Abraham named their son Isaac.

*And Abraham called the name of his son who was born to him — whom Sarah bore to him — Isaac.*
**Genesis 21:3**

The name Isaac comes from the Hebrew root צחק Tsachaq Laugh. Laugh symbolizes the disbelief of Abraham and Sarah. It is with this symbol that they named their child. GOD does the miraculous and the impossible things, and Isaac is the walking testament to that. The LORD turned laughter of doubts into laughter of joy.

For eternity, GOD's faithfulness to His Word is commemorated in the 2nd Patriarch's name, Isaac. His name is a constant reminder of the LORD's might and power. When doubts seep in, we can laugh and know that the LORD can and will turn that into laughter of joy.

**GOD is referred to the GOD of Abraham, Isaac and Jacob. The literal meaning of the Patriarch's names is:**

- Abraham — Father of many
- Isaac — Will laugh
- Jacob — Heels, grasp

Yaacov Jacob comes from the Hebrew roots of עקב Aqev Heel. Here is the first mention of עקב Aqev Heel in the Torah when GOD cursed the serpent.

## 4. VAYERA / AND HE APPEARED

*And I will put enmity*
*between you and the woman,*
*and between your offspring⁽ᵃ⁾ and hers;*
*he will crush⁽ᵇ⁾ your head,*
*and you will strike his heel* עָקֵב *Aqev.*
**Genesis 3:15**

The names "Abraham, Isaac and Jacob" form an eternal prophetic word:

The Father of many (our LORD) will laugh at the Heel-grasper (the serpent).

Laughter is a powerful weapon!

*Do not grieve, for the joy of the Lord is your strength.*
**Nehemiah 8:10**

Laughing in the enemy's face, as well as resting in the LORD's faithfulness and love can scatter demons. Did you know that?

Our emotions are powerful. They send vibrations to the people around us. Anxiety and fear can be sensed and smelled by animals, and so can joy and confidence. Being anxious gives the enemy power. On the other hand, being restfully confident to the point that we rejoice and laugh in a seemingly impossible and desperate circumstance empowers us and sends the signal to those around us that fear and hopelessness are not tolerated.

Do you need a holy visitation today to reaffirm GOD's promises to you? Do you need a miracle in your life that you laugh at the absurdity of that coming to pass? Do you know that praying for the same miracle for someone else, like Abraham did, may bring about the delivery of your own miracle? The LORD sees the end from the beginning. He laughs at the enemy's (the serpent) heel being struck at the end from the beginning when Adam sinned. Despite our human frailty, GOD's strength is made perfect through our weakness.

Hallelujah!!! Let's burst a victory laugh with the LORD!

Let's pray:

**Our Father in Heaven** אבינו שבשמימ,

Thank You for causing us to see You manifested in our midst. Abraham saw You in the 3 men. In our everyday life, we can see You in Your Word, in the kindness and love in people sent on our path. You have the appointed times Moed מועד for everything. We trust in Your perfect timing. Thank You for being the GOD that turns laughter of doubts to laughter of victory.

B'Shem Yeshua HaMashiach בשם ישוע המשיח.

In Jesus' Name we pray. Amen.

# 4. TORAH TASTING
## *REFLECTION*

1. What is the word, picture or theme the LORD is highlighting to you in this chapter and Torah Portion?

2. Do you have a prayer request that you are waiting for GOD to move and answer? Would you be willing to seek out others who have the same need and pray for them while you are still waiting for your own miracle?

3. Is there a situation that you could cry about, but instead, you will choose to laugh in the face of the enemy and watch GOD deliver you?

# 5 ה
# Chayei Sarah
## (Life of Sarah)
חיי שרה

Genesis 23:1-25:18

Kings 1:1-31

John 4:3-14

This Torah Portion is titled Chayei Sarah חיי שרה, the life of Sarah. It narrates the death and burial of Sarah, Abraham purchasing the cave of Machpelah to bury Sarah, a wife being found for Isaac and his marriage to Rebekah, Abraham marrying Keturah, his death and the list of Ishmael's descendants. A funeral and a wedding are backdrop stories that guarantee some serious drama, for sure.

This week I have been pondering on the emphasis of this Parasha about Sarah's life, not her death. It is no coincidence that today I just attended a memorial service, a celebration of the life of a friend, Avie R. With her husband's permission, Jerry R., prior to his passing, I am sharing her story. Avie lived life fully for the LORD. She was a devoted wife and mother who served her community with purpose and passion. One of the stories told of her was when she and her husband, Jerry, were dining in a restaurant many years ago. She found out their young waitress was going to drop out of school. She pulled her aside and encouraged her to stay in school. In sharing the love of GOD, she promised to give her $500 upon graduation to start her next chapter in life. She kept in touch with her throughout the rest of her academic year. The young lady did finish school, and Avie kept her word and gave her $500 as promised. Avie is an inspiration who lived her life for Yeshua Jesus.

This Torah Portion opens with GOD celebrating Sarah's life.

> ויהיו חיי שרה מאה שנה ועשרים שנה ושבע שנים שני חיי שרה
> Sarah שרה lived one hundred (שנה years) and twenty (שנה) years) —
> seven (שנה) years; these were the years of (שני) the life of Sarahשרה .
> **Genesis 23:1**

The literal translation of the verse is "Sarah lived one hundred years, twenty years seven years; these were the years of the life of Sarah," as if we are to ponder on her life and to read this first verse very, very, very slowly. Instead of Sarah's death, GOD highlights her life, the years and days lived for the glory of GOD as the first matriarch of Israel, GOD's chosen people. She is the mother of the nations, married to Abraham, the father of nations.

> *And I will bless her (Sarah) and also give you a son by her; then I will bless her, and <u>she (Sarah) shall be a mother of nations</u>; kings of peoples shall be from her."*
> **Genesis 17:16**

What's more?

The LORD changed her name from שרי Sarai to שרה Sarah.

שרי Sarai means princess, derives from שר Sar as in שר שלום Sar Shalom Prince of Peace.

# 5. CHAYEI SARAH / LIFE OF SARAH

GOD substituted the letter י Yod (work/deed) with the letter ה Hey (reveal/behold).

שרַי Sarai => שרָה Sarah

This insinuates that GOD is showing Sarah that living for him is not about "work and striving" but instead "behold in faith" and seeing His goodness come to pass for her. Despite her human flaws, this name change was to prepare her for things to come that would require her faith in the LORD instead of depending on her own ability.

The letters ה Hey and י Yod together make the Name of GOD יה YAH.

Even in the Hebrew word for "Years," שנה Shanah that is repeated 3 times, and then the Hebrew word for "Years Of" שני Shanei, they have the ה Hey and י Yod endings. It may sound crazy to you, but I sense that the 3 ה Heys and 1 י Yod signifies the life she lived for the glory of GOD, fulfilled GOD's purpose for her, she did transform from work and living by sight to being led by faith relying on GOD's spirit's guiding. The ה Heys and י Yod endings in this verse are too much to ignore. The LORD is intentional with His Word. GOD gave the Founding Father of Israel a beautiful bride, with His own Name Yah יה adorned on her in the name change.

The word Years שנה Shanah derives from the root for two or repeat again. I believe this Torah Portion's first verse is to declare to us that Sarah's legacy is to be repeated for generations to come in the daughters of GOD. Although Sarah only had one son, she did become a mother of nations, as the LORD had promised. That is the kind of miraculous exponential multiplication GOD can do, from one son to too many to count.

Sarah went with Abram when they made their journey to Canaan, even before GOD blessed them. She honored her husband and went along with him when he was not completely truthful to Abimelech about their relationship out of self-defense. Later on, in order to have children, she pushed her servant on her husband, to bear a child after 10 years of struggling with infertility herself. Childbearing was the primary job of a wife. Sarah didn't allow her inability to get in the way of perpetuating their family bloodline. She was a faithful wife and loving mother. We can see how much she was remembered and loved in the way Isaac, her son, mourned for his mother. Through many battles, infertility struggles, and other adversities, Sarah was a supportive wife, the wind beneath Abraham's wings.

A traditional Shabbat blessing over our daughters goes like this:

"May God make you like Sarah, Rebekah, Rachel, and Leah."

Every time we say this blessing over our daughters, we are speaking the perpetuation of the virtues, beauty and faith of our matriarchs into them, according to the will of GOD.

Sarah, Rebekah and Rachel were all beautiful inside and out.

Sarai/Sarah

> *¹¹ And it came to pass, when he was close to entering Egypt, that he said to **Sarai** his wife, "Indeed I know that you are a woman of beautiful countenance (יפת מראה Yefat Mareh) (beautiful to look at).*
> **Genesis 12:11**

Rebekah — She was given a choice to go or not to be Isaac's bride when Abraham's servant came and found her to be his future daughter-in-law.

Her heart of kindness made her stand out beyond her physical beauty.

## 5. CHAYEI SARAH / LIFE OF SARAH

*15 Before he had finished praying, Rebekah came out with her jar on her shoulder. She was the daughter of Bethuel son of Milkah, who was the wife of Abraham's brother Nahor. 16 **The woman was very beautiful** (טבת מראה Tovat Mareh, **Good/Pleasant to look at**), a virgin; no man had ever slept with her. She went down to the spring, filled her jar and came up again.*
**Genesis 28:15-16**

*67 Then Isaac brought her into his mother Sarah's tent; and he took Rebekah and she became his wife, and he loved her. So **Isaac was comforted after his mother's death**.*
**Genesis 24:67**

Rachel — She waited patiently for another 7 years to marry the love of her life after her father tricked Jacob into marrying her older sister Leah first. She possessed inner and outer beauty that captured Jacob's heart for life.

*Leah's eyes were delicate, but **Rachel was beautiful of form and appearance** (יפת תאר ויפת מראה Yefat Toar V'Yefat Mareh)*
**Genesis 29:17-18**

I believe Sarah, Rebekah and Rachel were chosen and destined to be the Patriarchs' brides for their beauty and virtues, even the word beautiful מראה Moreh was used to describe all 3 of their beauty.

Sarah שרה Sarah — means Princess
Lived for 127 years. 127 is associated to the word עזים Ezim Female Goat.
Rivkah רבקה Rebekah — means Calf/stall
Rachel רחל Rachel — means Sheep

It seems unflattering to call a woman a sheep or goat. However, these women are somehow associated with sacrificial animals. Yes, we are to live a life as living sacrifices, just as these godly women did for the LORD and for their future generations.

> *I beseech you therefore, brethren, by the mercies of God, that you present your bodies a living sacrifice, holy, acceptable to God, which is your reasonable service.*
> **Romans 12:1**

Let's look at the first marriage in history —

> And the Lord God said, "It is not good that man should be alone; I will make him a helper comparable to him."… ²⁰ So Adam gave names to all cattle, to the birds of the air, and to every beast of the field. But for Adam there was not found a helper comparable to him…
>
> *And Adam said, "This is now bone of my bones*
> *And flesh of my flesh;*
> *She shall be called Woman* אשה *(Ishah) ,*
> *Because she was taken out of Man* איש *(Ish)."*
> ²⁴ *Therefore a man shall leave his father and mother and be joined to his wife, and they shall become one flesh.*
> **Genesis 2:18,20,23-24**

> ²⁰ And Adam called **his wife's name Eve** חוה *(Chavah) because she was the mother of all living.*
> **Genesis 3:20**

**Eve** חוה Chavah means Life-giver or To Tell/Declare.

The LORD created Eve, the first woman, the first wife, the mother of all living. Interesting how Sarah was called to be mother of nations. She somehow was blessed with Eve's mantle.

Eve's name alludes to the fact that she was to be a mother with the gift and power to tell and declare! What a revelation!

Could it possibly be the call of women? To declare the Word of GOD!

# 5. CHAYEI SARAH / LIFE OF SARAH

*The Lord gave the word; Great was the company (Female/women) of those who proclaimed it.*
**Psalm 68:11**

To paraphrase: Mighty and Powerful are the Women-Proclaimers of GOD's word!!!

The serpent deceived Eve with words. Eve persuaded Adam with words that led to their fall.

But GOD has provided the redemption plan. We can declare His Word and bring life into our families.

We give life through our speech and declaration.

- אִישׁ Man — Ish
- אשה Woman — Ishah

The unfathomable mystery of the Hebrew language again shows us something with the letters י Yod and ה Hey here, like in Sarah's name mentioned earlier.

The word איש Ish Man and אשה Ishah Woman both have the Hebrew letters אש the א Aleph and ש Shin. Meanwhile, איש Ish Man has the י Yod and אשה Ishah Woman has the ה Hey.

First of all, it is noteworthy that Man has the י Yod symbolic of work, and Woman has the ה Hey symbolic of Behold to Reveal and the Spirit/Breath of GOD. The י Yod and the ה Hey together make יה YAH, the Name of GOD.

The original design of the union in a man and a woman is with GOD inside, which makes the marriage perfect and complete. However, if GOD is taken out of the marriage or absent to begin with, with the י Yod and the ה Hey removed from them, אש Esh remains, that is Fire and Destruction.

Behind every successful man, there is a strong woman. Women need to use their superpower of words of declaration wisely, like the epitome of a good wife illustrated in Proverbs 31.

> *She opens her mouth with wisdom,*
> *And on her tongue is the law of kindness.*
> **Proverbs 31:26**

Wow!!!

The minute a bride says, "I do," there is a mantle and anointing on her tongue. Her words of blessings rule her household and elevate her husband!!!

No wonder GOD says this about finding a wife.

> *He who finds a wife finds a good thing,*
> *And obtains favor from the Lord.*
> **Genesis 18:22**

In history, many First Ladies are the strength behind our heroic U.S. Presidents, from Martha Washington, Dolley Madison to Jacqueline Kennedy. Also, many wives of missionaries courageously and quietly supported their husband's calling. Nate Saint was a U.S. missionary pilot in the 1950's. He felt called to evangelize in the South American jungle areas in Ecuador. Eventually, he and his 4 teammates were speared to death. Nonetheless, the mission was continued by his wife, Marjorie, and family. Marjorie, who had served alongside her husband prior to his death, kept on sharing the Good News of the love of GOD, despite many challenges and disappointments. Their selfless servants' hearts to the point of death advancing GOD's Kingdom are beyond admirable.

> *Greater love has no one than this, than to lay down one's life for his friends.*
> **John 15:13**

Marjorie did not grow bitter after her husband's murder. She, along with 4 other widows, stayed in Ecuador, carrying on the mission with their children. Many came to know and accept the LORD Yeshua.

Their story was featured in Life Magazine, books and even a feature film named, "End of The Spear." The testimony of their self-sacrificing love for GOD's people touched many around the world.

By no means, does all this talk of wives supporting their husbands diminishes their own individual calling and purposes. Quite the contrary, many women see their purposes completed while serving with their husbands.

I believe our Matriarch Sarah fulfilled her calling in mighty ways serving the LORD, and GOD honored her. There are only a handful of Parashiot (Torah Portions) with someone's name in the titles. Sarah is one of them. She was no ordinary woman!

Although marriage is not for everyone, GOD instituted marriage to display His glory. A good marriage reflects GOD's goodness to everyone around the couple when they choose to serve one another selflessly above their own interest.

When our first son was born, my husband and I decided that I would leave my career to stay home and raise our children. It is a partnership. Paul honors me in recognizing my gift of writing and encouraged me to write and teach in pursuing the call GOD placed on my life. I am Paul's support, and he is mine. I want to see him be all that GOD has created him to be, and he feels the same way for me. Most importantly, we desire to have GOD יה YAH in the center of our marriage. GOD completes us. He guides us in all we do, individually and in partnership.

*Now the Lord is the Spirit; and where the Spirit of the Lord is, there is liberty.* <u>*¹⁸ But we all, with unveiled face, beholding as in a mirror the glory of the Lord, are being transformed into the same image from glory to glory, just as by the Spirit of the Lord.*</u>

2 Corinthians 17-18

By the Living Spirit of GOD יה YAH, we are transformed into the image of GOD, which we behold and in our work we go from glory to glory.

**Let's pray:**

**Our Father in Heaven אבינו שבשמימ,**

We thank You for ordaining the first earthly relationship in marriage and making it sacred. We pray for those who have experienced pain in marriages, that You bring about healing and redemption in ways only You can and will do. We declare according to Your will and Your Word for our sons to find a wife that is a complement to him, that he will see and behold his destiny fulfilled in faith while he works to provide. And, for our daughters, they'd be a good helper to her husband; in turn, her husband is the provider and protector gifted by You that together they reflect Your glory, just like Sarah, Rebekah and Rachel.

B'Shem Yeshua HaMashiach בשם ישוע המשיח.

In Jesus' Name we pray. Amen.

# 5. TORAH TASTING
## *REFLECTION*

1. What is the word, picture or theme the LORD is highlighting to you in this chapter and Torah Portion?

2. Is there a woman's life and legacy you are reminded of to celebrate today? What impact did she have on you or on those around her?

3. What is an example being centered in her life that points to GOD's presence?

# 6 ו
# toldot
## (Generations)
## תולדות

Genesis 25:19-28:9

Malachi 1:1-2:7

Matthew 10:21-38

This Torah Portion is titled תולדות Toldot Generations/Descendants/Geneology. It tells the birth of Issacs's twin sons, Esau and Isaac, Esau selling his birthright, Isaac and Abimelech, Isaac blessing Jacob instead of Esau, Jacob fleeing from Esau and Esau marrying Ishmael's daughter.

The first verse of this Parasha says:

This is the genealogy of Isaac, Abraham's son. Abraham begot Isaac.

Genealogy is important to the LORD. Throughout the Torah, we see family trees meticulously recorded. GOD commanded Adam to be fruitful and multiply פרו ורבו P'ru Urvu (Genesis 1:22, 28). After the Great Flood destroyed every man except for Noah's family, GOD commanded

Noah to be fruitful and multiply פרו ורבו P'ru Urvu (Genesis 8:17, 9:1, 9:7). GOD commanded Ishmael to be fruitful and multiply פרו ורבו P'ru Urvu (Genesis 17:20). GOD called Jacob to be fruitful and multiply פרו ורבו P'ru Urvu (Genesis 28:3, 35:11). As we read in the Torah that being fruitful and multiply is not something we have complete control, infertility would keep a woman from being fruitful. However, what GOD commands His people to do, He promises to do His part to accomplish the commandment.

GOD's promise to Abraham —

> *Blessing I will bless you, and multiplying I will multiply your descendants as the stars of the heaven and as the sand which is on the seashore; and your descendants shall possess the gate of their enemies.*
> **Genesis 22:17**

GOD's promise to Isaac —

> *And <u>I will</u> make your descendants multiply as the stars of heaven; I will give to your descendants all these lands.*
> **Genesis 26:4**

GOD's promise to Jacob —

> *¹³ And behold, the Lord stood above it and said: "I am the Lord God of Abraham your father and the God of Isaac; the land on which you lie I will give to you and your descendants. ¹⁴ Also <u>your descendants shall be</u> as the dust of the earth; you shall spread abroad to the west and the east, to the north and the south; and in you and in your seed all the families of the earth shall be blessed. ¹⁵ Behold, I am with you and will keep[c] you wherever you go, and will bring you back to this land; for I will not leave you until I have done what I have spoken to you."*
> **Genesis 28:13-15**

## 6. TOLEDOT / GENERATIONS

*And blessed be His glorious name forever! And let the whole earth be filled with His glory. Amen and Amen.*
**Psalm 72:19**

*"Holy, holy, holy is the Lord of hosts;
The whole earth is full of His glory!"*
**Isaiah 6:3**

So, the LORD commanded His people to be fruitful and multiply, follow Him wholeheartedly, then the whole earth would be filled with GOD's glory, as GOD's people unreservedly love Him spreading His glory everywhere they go to fill the whole earth.

My mother spent a good deal of time in Mainland China for many years for business. Since our children were babies, I began to bring them to visit her every year during the Chinese New Year. On one of those trips, Mom organized a 10-day visit to China for us. We would go to 11 cities in 10 days. I arrived in Hong Kong with a mild cold, which eventually turned into a severe cold/flu. There might even have been a sinus infection on top of that. My energy was completely zapped out of me. We stayed at different hotels almost nightly. It was a hectic trip for a sick person caring for 2 little children. I had lost my appetite, with a runny nose and a sore throat, as well as fighting severe fatigue. I did not feel like getting out of the hotel room bed, let alone getting myself up to get my 2 little ones dressed and packed our luggage all over again for another overnight trip each day. Riding in a car for hours on bumpy country roads did not help the situation. Everything was a blur when all I wanted to do was to sleep this illness off. I did not have a good attitude about the trip at all, but I knew Mom wanted to show off her grandchildren from halfway around the world to her friends.

I complied, not without complaint though, maybe silently. I was grumpy at times.

I remember hearing the LORD's voice saying, "What if I told you that you have a mission on this trip?"

"What?" I said the idea of a mission was so foreign to me.

Then, I felt Him nudge me to shift my perspective about this trip.

"What if there is a bigger purpose here than visiting family and friends?"

"What if I am to take territory for the Kingdom of GOD every step that I tread in all the places we go? as GOD told His people in Deuteronomy 11:24-25-

'Every place on which the sole of your foot treads shall be yours… No man shall be able to stand against you; the Lord, your God, will put the dread of you and the fear of you upon all the land where you tread, just as He has said to you.'"

Suddenly, I got excited. Yes, indeed, I was carrying GOD's presence and His glory with me everywhere we went, whether I realized it or not. GOD has placed me on a mission trip?!

I began praying for the people placed in our path. I declared that every step treaded was being claimed back for the Kingdom of GOD. After returning home, I was so exhausted from the journey with jetlag I slept for 3 whole days. My sweet husband did wake me up to feed me once a day. I'd never slept for 3 days straight before and have not done so since. But it was an experience I will never forget. It is such a privilege that the LORD has chosen me for this mission.

Have you been on a mission before? You never know when GOD calls you on one. Be ready!

> [18] *And Jesus came and spoke to them, saying, "All authority has been given to Me in heaven and on earth.* [19] *Go therefore and make disciples of all the nations, baptizing them in the name of the Father and of the Son and of the Holy Spirit,* [20] *teaching them to observe all things that I have commanded you; and lo, I am with you always, even to the end of the age." Amen.*
> **Matthew 28:18-20**

> *Every place on which the sole of your foot treads shall be yours...*
> **Deuteronomy 11:24**

The LORD told His people that every place their foot treaded would be theirs. I believe there is tremendous spiritual significance in these words. Territory is important according to GOD's Word. We need to stake the claim and show the enemy the truth that GOD is bigger than him, and we know it. Yeshua Jesus said He has given us all authority to go to all the nations and spread His Name and fame. Perhaps that is spiritual fruitfulness and multiplication, referring back to GOD's commandment to His children.

> *Every good gift and every perfect gift is from above, and comes down from the **Father of lights**, with whom there is no variation or shadow of turning.*
> **James 1:17**

We are birthed from the Father of lights. We are the little lights that originated from the Father. And we have His light inside us. When we turn toward Him and connect to His heart, His light shines through us, and it is the source of the light that touches people in our paths. Our smiles, acts of kindness, words of encouragement and attitude of hope can make a world's difference in someone's life at the appropriate times. The one store cashier or restaurant waitress we encourage can be like our light sparks something inside them, reviving hope. They can then turn around and touch 10 other people with a renewed outlook on life. That looks like spiritual fruitfulness and multiplication in simple terms.

If each one of us knows the Father as our source of light and goes out to do what we were created to do, igniting others with His light, the whole earth will be filled with His glory. Amen. Let it be so, In Yeshua's Name.

Parashat Toldot starts with the genealogy of Isaac. Isaac couldn't ride on his daddy's faith coattail anymore. Isaac had to hold his own. He too, would be the father of many, just like his father, Abraham. He was taking over the baton from Abraham to follow GOD. He inherited His father's blessings from the LORD, but he had to establish his own faith walk with GOD. He even had a personal holy visitation.

> *Then the Lord appeared to him and said: "Do not go down to Egypt; live in the land of which I shall tell you. ³ Dwell in this land, and I will be with you and bless you; for to you and your descendants I give all these lands, and I will perform the oath which I swore to Abraham your father.*
> **Genesis 26:2-3**

Abraham had an encounter with Abimelech, king of Gerar, and Isaac had one with Abimelech, king of the Philistines. What are the chances both kings had the same name, and at both times, the kings desired to take the patriarchs' wives? Nonetheless, both Abraham and Isaac later left being tremendously blessed. But unlike his father Abraham, that went down to Egypt during a famine, Isaac was told not to go to Egypt during another famine. Instead, he went to Abimelech, the king of the Philistines in Gerar. He had to find his own path.

The Torah lists the genealogy of the lineage of Abraham, Isaac and Jacob. GOD cares about genealogy. We too, care about where we come from and why we are the way we are. That's why many adopted children want to find their biological parents, no matter how much their adoptive parents love them. They want to find out where they came from, things about their biological parents who gave life to them and the circumstances surrounding the adoption. They perhaps could help explain certain struggles in life. People spend lots of money to research their ancestry. Knowing our past and being aware of what made us who we are helps us to live to the fullest in the present and move forward into the future.

My maternal grandfather's youngest brother, as the last living sibling, was on a mission to create their family tree in the 1980's. He uncovered history dating back 200 years, revealing the glorious days of his ancestors' accomplishments during the Chinese imperial era, as well as Sino-Japanese Wars and the Revolutionary Wars between the Nationalists and the Communists. A small mountain in my grandfather's hometown Guilin (in GuangXi Province), had been purchased and established as a family burial site where most of our family members were buried until it was confiscated by the Communists when they took over. Then, Mom overcame many bureaucratic obstacles and repurchased it so that my maternal grandparents could be brought back there from Hong Kong to be buried, to fulfill their lifelong yearning. This reminds me so much of Machpelah, where Abraham had purchased to bury Sarah. Since then, it has become the official burial site for Israel's patriarchs and matriarchs.

There is a deep desire inside each of us that wants to know…

"Who created me?"

"What purpose am I created for?"

Knowing our heavenly father is the first step in discovering many life mysteries.

This Parasha's title is Toldot, the generations after Isaac, yet it begins with the fact that his wife Rebekah was barren.

> *This is the genealogy (תולדות Toldot) of Isaac, Abraham's son. Abraham begot Isaac.²⁰ Isaac was forty years old when he took Rebekah as wife, the daughter of Bethuel the Syrian of Padan Aram, the sister of Laban the Syrian. ²¹ Now Isaac pleaded with the Lord for his wife, because **she was barren** (עקר Akar); and the Lord granted his plea, and Rebekah, his wife, conceived.*
> **Genesis 25:20-21**

Similarly, we were introduced to the genealogy of Abram's father with the same exact words.

> *This is the genealogy (תולדות Toldot) of Terah: Terah begot Abram, Nahor, and Haran. Haran begot Lot. ²⁸ And Haran died before his father Terah in his native land, in Ur of the Chaldeans. ²⁹ Then Abram and Nahor took wives: the name of Abram's wife was Sarai, and the name of Nahor's wife, Milcah, the daughter of Haran the father of Milcah and the father of Iscah. ³⁰ But **Sarai was barren** (עקר Akar); she had no child.*
> **Genesis 11:27-30**

Both of the above verses begin by telling us about the generations following Abram and Isaac, but ironically, the first fact given was the barrenness of Sarai and Rebekah.

> *³¹ When the Lord saw that Leah was unloved, He opened her womb; but **Rachel was** barren (עקר Akar)… ²² Then God remembered Rachel, and God listened to her and opened her womb.*
> **Genesis 29:31, 30:22**

And then, later in Genesis 29, we are told Rachel dealt with the same issue.

Why would the wives of Abraham, Isaac and Jacob all struggle with barrenness while they were called to be fruitful and multiply?

What irony!

## 6. TOLEDOT / GENERATIONS

The main role of a wife in those days was childbearing. Speaking of the pressure to reproduce. While GOD promised their husbands that their descendants would be too many to count, they carried the responsibility of birthing the first offsprings. Every passing day not being pregnant was a disappointment.

However, we know the anxiety of the temporarily-infertile matriarchs would simply dissipate if only they realized the truth... The truth is...

None of us is responsible for bringing GOD's Word and promises to pass; ONLY GOD IS!

> [45] *Not one of all the Lord's good promises to Israel failed; every one was fulfilled.*
> **Joshua 21:45**

> [12] *The Lord said to me, "You have seen correctly, for I am watching[b] to see that my word is fulfilled."*
> **Jeremiah 1:12**

> [28] *"Therefore say to them, 'This is what the Sovereign Lord says: None of my words will be delayed any longer; whatever I say will be fulfilled, declares the Sovereign Lord.'"*
> **Ezekiel 12:28**

> *God is not human, that he should lie,*
> *not a human being, that he should change his mind.*
> *Does he speak and then not act?*
> *Does he promise and not fulfill?*
> **Numbers 23:19**

The LORD is faithful to His WORD.

- The Hebrew word for barren is עָקָר Akar.
- ע Ayin — means See/Experience
- ק Qoof — means Following
- ר Resh — means the Highest

Essentially, עָקָר Akar Barrenness is to experience something following the highest. Its root is עָקָר Eker which means off shoot or descendants. Deep down in barrenness is the promise of birthing descendants, an experience of seeing what GOD intends for us when we follow after Him.

While we are unsure why those women were barren, we do know for certain that Sarah and Rebekah's barrenness ended when their husbands prayed. Rachel became pregnant because GOD heard her prayers. It was GOD's will for these women to have children. Despite the circumstances, when they prayed, whatever stood in the way of fulfilling GOD's promises lifted. Through barrenness, the opposite of what is destined, praying according to GOD's will and His call on the women, they were able to experience what it is like to follow the GOD Most High. Spiritual barrenness is like being stuck in the waiting room for GOD's promises to come. It is a time of frustration and helplessness when one focuses on the physical circumstances and human solution to the problem. Spiritual barrenness is knowing our calling and what we are destined to do, and yet circumstantial evidence points to impossibilities. It is reports like, "You will never…" and "Things will always be…."

I believe that the solution to spiritual barrenness is spiritual fruitfulness and multiplication… Knowing we come from the Father of lights, with whom there is no variation or shadow of turning. He does not change, and His Word is constant. We are to fixate on GOD's Word that is eternal and unchanging, much like His character. We are to focus on Him being the light and allow His light to shine through us. Even during the temporary barren season, we know GOD is true to His Word. He, not we, are responsible for bringing His Word to pass. During this season, we are to experience and gain invaluable blessings by following the LORD at all costs. The result is just like what our Matriarchs, Sarah, Rebekah and Rachel experienced; we will see His promises come to pass that will marvel us beyond our wildest dreams.

"This is the genealogy… She is barren" —

Her temporary barrenness is miniscule compared to the generations she will birth forth!

**Let's pray:**

**Our Father in Heaven אבינו שבשמימ,**

Thank You for the promises amidst the challenges in life. You have commissioned us to go and show the world Your goodness. Remind us daily to see You as our Father of lights and we are the light of the world. Show us how to reach and touch each person You place in our path. Let Your children of lights around the world light up one person at a time, be fruits and multiply Your love and hope that fills the whole world with Your glory. LORD, please help us see temporary spiritual barrenness in Your eternal perspective.

B'Shem Yeshua HaMashiach בשם ישוע המשיח.

In Jesus' Name we pray. Amen.

## 6. TORAH TASTING
### *REFLECTION*

1. What is the word, picture or theme the LORD is highlighting to you in this chapter and Torah Portion?

2. Regarding spiritual fruitfulness and multiplication, when was there a time you brought forth GOD's light and blessed someone, or you being the receiver of such a blessing that someone else brought GOD's light into your life?

3. Abraham prayed and blessed someone while he himself was struggling with the same issues. How do you think he did that? Where did he get that mental strength?

4. Torah Portion Toldot is about from generation to generation. What are some of the life lessons, spiritual or physical blessings you've inherited from your parents, grandparents, or great-grandparents?

5. Like Isaac had to get to know the LORD for himself, rather than taking his father's faith for granted, is there any example that your spiritual journey looks different from the last generation in your family? You had to carve your own path, so to speak?

# 7 ז
# vayetze
## (And He Went Out)
## ויצא

Genesis 28:10-32:3

Hosea 12:12-14:10

John 1:41-51

Parashat Vayetze is another episode packed with drama, worthy for a movie — a supernatural dream of an open heaven meeting GOD, wholeheartedly devoted romance and love of a lifetime, Jacob's fleeing from his brother and later fleeing from his father-in-law.

This Torah Portion opens with this —

*Now Jacob went out (יצא **Yatza Go/Bring Forth**) from Beersheba (Well of Seven) and went toward Haran (Crossroads).* <sup>11</sup> *So he came to a certain place (מקום **Makom**) and stayed there all night, because the sun had set. And he took one of the stones of that place (מקום **Makom Place**) and put it at his head, and he lay down in that place (מקום **Makom Place**) to sleep.*
### Genesis 28:10-11

At this time, Jacob was on the run from his brother Esau after stealing his blessings. He went out from Beersheba (Well of Seven) toward Haran (Crossroads). Ironically, the names of the places he ran from and toward seem to mirror his current situation. Beersheba, meaning Well of Seven, is symbolic of prosperity and hopeful promises. Haran means crossroads. Jacob had a comfortable life with his parents. However, his actions led to the consequences of running toward a crossroads of the uncertain future. He "happened" to come to a "certain place" (מקום Makom Place).

The first time מקום **Makom Place** appears in the Torah is in Genesis 1-

> *⁹ Then God said, "Let the waters under the heavens be gathered together into* one place (מקום *Makom), and let the dry land appear;"* and it was so.
> **Genesis 1:9**

It is no coincidence that the first time יצא **Yatza Go/Bring Forth** shows up in the Torah is in the same chapter as well.

> *¹² And the earth brought forth (*יצא *Yatza Go/Bring Forth) grass, the herb that yields seed according to its kind, and the tree that yields fruit, whose seed is in itself according to its kind. And God saw that it was good. ¹³ So the evening and the morning were the third day.*
> **Genesis 1:12**

On the third day of Creation, the LORD spoke and the waters were gathered into one Place and dry land was formed. Then, the LORD brought forth vegetation and fruits.

It seems that the place (מקום **Makom**) was intentionally established so that fruits and plants could sprout and grow. The "seemingly ordinary" place is symbolic of circumstances set up, ready for something extraordinary to happen. That "something" is an earth-shaking and life-altering event. When Jacob came to this "certain place," did he expect amazing things to happen?

Probably not. It was getting dark, and he just needed a place to crash for the night.

He found a stone to use as a pillow and fell asleep. GOD gave him a dream to show him magnificent things and reaffirm promises made to his father and grandfather. GOD infused hope into him during his sleep when he was running away hopelessly from Esau, his brother. It was a fateful day that would forever change his life.

Jacob's "certain place" (מקום Makom) reminds me of my own מקום Makom. I attended an all-girls' Catholic school from kindergarten at age 3 all the way to high school graduation at 17. During the 1980s Hong Kong, everyone was anxious at the news of Hong Kong returning to Communist China from being a British colony for over 100 years since China's defeat in the First Opium War with Great Britain. Many HongKongese were feeling uncertain about the future. Would democracy and free speech be a thing of the past? What control would the new government impose on the once free-market metropolitan city? No one had a clue. Those with resources scrambled to immigrate to English-speaking countries to obtain citizenship and hope to someday return once the post-1997-turnover Hong Kong proved to be stable. With Mom being our sole provider, the only way out for our family was me going to school overseas, which would provide some sort of insurance for our future. Many of my classmates had plans to go to the U.K., Australia or Canada upon graduation. I, on the other hand, aspired to study hotel management and found an ideal school in Switzerland. It was like GOD had already prepared me for this because, by this time, I'd been in the French immersion program at L'Alliance Française Hong Kong. I would be comfortable going to Switzerland to study, as French is the main spoken language in the Swiss region I planned to go.

Around our school were posters displayed providing post-secondary-school and vocational career opportunities information. I still remember as if it was yesterday, the moment I was standing in front of a certain poster on the bulletin board in the school yard about a scholarship program for foreign exchange students in the U.S.. Ironically, the United States was not on my radar when exploring school options. The United States?

No way. I had seen enough movies showing drug and crime-infested streets in New York and Los Angeles. The stereotype of American pop culture did not appeal to me at all, to say the least. But GOD had a different plan… This opportunity offered a year of amazing cultural exchange experience. The scholarship was very enticing since my mother would not have to pay much if I was selected for the program. It would only be one year; then, I would be Europe-bound.

Little did I know that moment in time, standing and studying the poster would lead me on a path that the LORD would bless me beyond my wildest imagination.

*A man's heart plans his way,*
*But the Lord directs his steps.*
**Proverbs 16:9**

*The steps of a good man are ordered by the Lord,*
*And He delights in his way.*
**Psalms 37:23**

*For my thoughts are not your thoughts,*
*neither are your ways my ways, declares the Lord.*
**Isaiah 55:8**

[16] *Then Jacob awoke from his sleep and said, "Surely the Lord is in this place, and I did not know it."*
**Genesis 28:17**

GOD's plans are always better than ours. I do see that moment standing before that poster being in the "certain place" (מקום Makom) as a crossroads moment for me.

## 7. VAYETZE /AND HE WENT OUT

Like Jacob, I had no idea how the LORD's hand was on me, simply drawing my attention to an ordinary poster. Did it catch anyone else's attention? Was it there just for me?

Divine providence is a wonderful thing!

It led me on a path that I could never have imagined. Jacob's being in that certain place (מקום Makom) resting for the night would lead to his supernatural encounter with the LORD. He built a memorial that he knew this place was marked for eternal greatness for his life.

Have you ever had a "certain place (מקום Makom)" kind of experience? At the time, it might have looked like an ordinary moment, but it turned out to be life-transforming and brought forth life and fruits.

Or perhaps, you are in that place right now, waiting, unknowingly stumbling upon a crossroads? When you choose to follow the LORD, know that He is trustworthy. He wants to meet with you as much as you want to have an encounter with Him. He has good plans for your life beyond your wildest dreams. I know that to be true, first-hand.

It is fascinating that the word "Place" מקום Makom appears 12 times in this Parasha. I cannot help but wonder that this possibly points to the 12 tribes that would be brought forth from Jacob, just like "the place מקום Makom" brought forth life and fruits in Genesis 1.

> *Then Jacob rose early in the morning, and took the stone that he had put at his head, set it up as a pillar, and poured oil on top of it. ¹⁹ And he called the name of that place Bethel; but the name of that city had been Luz (לז/Almond Tree or Wood) previously.*
> **Genesis 28:18**

As soon as Jacob got up, he anointed this place with oil. He did not want to forget this experience, and his stone pillow would remind him of the incredible promises GOD made to him.

The place Jacob experienced GOD's presence is called Luz; the word's origin has to do with an almond tree or wood. He then called it Bethel, House of GOD.

The Almond tree in Jeremiah gives us a clue as to what it might mean in Jacob's supernatural experience.

*Moreover the word of the Lord came to me, saying, "Jeremiah, what do you see? And I said, "I see a branch of an almond tree." Then the Lord said to me, "You have seen well, for I am ready to perform My word."*
**Jeremiah 1:11-12**

The LORD showed Jeremiah through the almond tree branch that He is about to fulfill His Word and make it happen.

*Now it came to pass on the next day that Moses went into the tabernacle of witness, and behold, the rod of Aaron, of the house of Levi, had sprouted and put forth buds, had produced blossoms and yielded ripe almonds. 9 Then Moses brought out all the rods from before the Lord to all the children of Israel; and they looked, and each man took his rod.*
**Numbers 17:8**

Aaron's rod was the only one of the 12 rods that sprouted and produced ripe almonds. It demonstrates GOD's miraculous power, and it was to be placed in the Tabernacle (the presence/house of GOD). Luz, Almond tree, and the House of GOD all tie back to commemorate the Holy visitation of GOD with Jacob. As the third patriarch, Jacob, has heard all about the LORD's promises to his father and grandfather, he too, like his father, had to know GOD firsthand and understand the tremendous blessings and responsibilities that come with being the father of GOD's people.

According to this Torah Portion, Jacob's first encounter with Rachel was around tending sheep. They were both experienced shepherds. Even when Laban and Jacob had a dispute over Jacob's wages, they used sheep and goats to settle the matter. There are a few other well-known shepherds that are noteworthy.

The first shepherd in history, Abel, was brutally murdered by his brother.

> ² *Then she bore again, this time his brother Abel. Now Abel was a keeper of sheep (root רעה Ra'ah Pasture), but Cain was a tiller of the ground…⁴ Abel also brought of the firstborn of his flock and of their fat. And the Lord respected Abel and his offering,⁵ but He did not respect Cain and his offering. And Cain was very angry, and his countenance fell… ⁸ Now Cain talked with Abel his brother; and it came to pass, when they were in the field, that Cain rose up against Abel his brother and killed him.*
> **Genesis 4:2,4,5,8**

The second and third times the word רעה Ra'ah To Pasture/Tend was used was referring to Jacob and Rachel.

> ⁷ *Then he (Jacob) said, "Look, it is still [a]high day; it is not time for the cattle to be gathered together. Water the sheep, and go and feed (רעה Ra'ah Pasture) them…Now while he was still speaking with them, Rachel came with her father's sheep, for she was a shepherdess (רעה Ra'ah Pasture).*
> **Genesis 29:7,9**

The fourth time the word רעה Ra'ah To Pasture/Tend is seen when introducing the future king of Israel, David.

> ¹¹ *And Samuel said to Jesse, "Are all the young men here?" Then he said, "There remains yet the youngest (David), and there he is, keeping the sheep (רעה Ra'ah Pasture).*
> **1 Samuel 16:11**

רעֹה Ro'eh Shepherd comes from the Hebrew root רעה Ra'ah To Pasture/Tend/Graze.

- ר Resh — represents head, person
- ע Ayin — represents eye, see
- ה Hey — represents, what comes from
- A shepherd is a person that watches over the sheep.
- The word רעה Ro'eh Shepherd can be divided into 2 parts:
- רע Ra — means evil
- ה Hey — represents reveal or open

A shepherd recognizes and sees evil, as well as protects the sheep from being open to evil and harm. Keeping the sheep safe is a shepherd's main task.

Although shepherding was a common profession in ancient Hebrew days, I believe certain Torah's protagonists were specifically mentioned as being shepherds for a reason. Abel pleased the LORD with his shepherding skills and the fruits of his labor while his brother Cain was a farmer. Jacob was a shepherd, whereas his brother Esau was a hunter. Later, Jacob brought his expertise to his uncle Laban that prospered their household. Jacob first met Rachel when she was tending the flock. Not many women are mentioned in the Torah as shepherds like Rachel. It was a demanding job requiring patience and loving care for the flock. Jacob and Rachel are the first and perhaps the only shepherd couple explicitly mentioned in the Torah.

Years of shepherding leadership training prepared David for the call of his life as a warrior and reigning king for the LORD and His people.

Possibly the most famous Psalm, written by the Shepherd King David, calls GOD our Shepherd.

> *The Lord is my shepherd;*
> *I shall not want*
> **Psalm 23:1**

The LORD is our Ultimate Shepherd, the One that protects us from harm and provides our every need. We have no want, no other desires, completely satisfied and whole in Our Good Shepherd.

Yeshua, Our Mashiach, refers to Himself as Our Shepherd that would lay down his own life for the sheep.

> "I am the good shepherd. The good shepherd gives His life for the sheep. [14] I am the good shepherd; and I know My sheep, and am known by My own.
> **John 10:11,14**

> Now it was **the Feast of Dedication** (Hanukkah, 25th day of Kislev) in Jerusalem, and it was winter. [23] And Yeshua Jesus walked in the temple, in Solomon's porch. [24] Then the Jews surrounded Him and said to Him, "How long do You keep us in doubt? If You are Christ (The Mashiach/Messiah), tell us plainly."
> Yeshua Jesus answered them, "I told you, and you do not believe. The works that I do in My Father's name, they bear witness of Me. [26] But you do not believe, because you are not of My sheep, as I said to you. [27] My sheep hear My voice, and I know them, and they follow Me. [28] And I give them eternal life, and they shall never perish; <u>neither shall anyone snatch them out of My hand.</u> [29] My Father, who has given them to Me, is greater than all; and <u>no one is able to snatch them out of My Father's hand.</u> [30] <u>I and My Father are one."</u>
> **John 10:22-30**

A fascinating observation: This Torah Portion for this year (2021) falls on the Shabbat (9th day of Kislev) 2 weeks from Hanukkah (25th day of Kislev). The Shepherd-theme is highlighted in Jacob and Rachel's story. Yeshua speaks of Himself as a Shepherd of His people in the Only One Time Hanukkah is mentioned in his recorded Word.

His statement, "I and My Father are one.," resonates with Himself as a Shepherd as well as the LORD as King David's Shepherd in Psalm 23.

In the Festival of Lights (Hanukkah), GOD being the Source of all lights, is a time to celebrate GOD as our Miracle-Maker. Hanukkah comes from a story ending with rededicating the Temple to the LORD. Hanukkah (meaning dedication) is a joyous season reminding us of the Temple dedication. During this time, we once again stand in awe of GOD's greatness. Yeshua Jesus chose this time to speak of GOD as Our Shepherd at the Temple. Like the Maccabees supernaturally defeated the enemies, the strongest military force at that time, against impossible odds, Our Mashiach reminds us that with GOD, we have nothing to fear! All things are possible.

From Jacob's fateful crossroad-moment encounter with GOD to the shepherding theme in Parashat Vayetze, we see that the Divine Providence sets up the stage of Jacob seeing GOD as The Shepherd of all shepherds. His uncertain future was completely secure in the LORD's hand. The LORD would be faithful to His Word to Jacob, his father and grandfather. Jacob's going-forth would prove to bring life and fruits as GOD had intended. Approaching the Hanukkah season, Parashat Vayetze reminds us that GOD is our Good Shepherd. Hearing His voice and following Him places us securely in the Father's Hand. No one can snatch us out of His Hand.

No One!

Do you believe that?

Let's pray:

**Our Father in Heaven** אבינו שבשמימ,

Thank You for being our Good Shepherd. You can lead us from the ordinary "Going-forth" moments to an extraordinary future that You have good plans prepared for us that would produce life and fruits. LORD, teach us to hear You clearly and follow You closely no matter what so that we will always feel secure and not anxious at the unforeseeable uncertainty. Yeshua Jesus, we trust that You are our Ultimate Shepherd, keeping us out of harm's way and we have all that we need in You.

B'Shem Yeshua HaMashiach בשם ישוע המשיח.

In Jesus' Name we pray. Amen.

# 7. TORAH TASTING
## *REFLECTION*

1. What is the word, picture or theme the LORD is highlighting to you in this chapter and Torah Portion?

2. Have you ever had a "certain place (מקום Makom)" kind of experience? At the time, it might have looked like an ordinary moment, but it turned out to be life-transforming that brought forth life and fruits?

3. Whether you live in the city, suburbs, or rural areas, at one point or another, you have seen pastures with sheep somewhere, perhaps even in movies or photos. What sentiments do you feel when you come across that scenery? What comes to mind when you hear about shepherds or "The LORD is my shepherd?" How does that encourage you about the LORD being your shepherd today?

# 8 ח
# vayishlach
## (And He Sent)
## וישלח

Genesis 32:3-36:43

Hosea 11:7-12:12, Obadiah 1:1-21

Matthew 2:13-23

The first word in its first verse gives the title of this Torah Portion Vayishlach.

> <u>Then Jacob sent</u> (שלח *Shalach*) messengers before him to Esau his brother in the land of Seir, the country of Edom.
> **Genesis 32:3**

This portion tells us about Jacob sending presents to his brother Esau as appeasement after stealing his birthright, his wrestling with GOD at Peniel, his reunion with Esau, his sojourning at Shechem and the rape of his daughter Dinah, his sons' revenge-seeking justice for the crime against their sister, Jacob's returning to Bethel, Rachel's death at Benjamin's birth, Jacob's father Isaac's death, Esau's descendants and clans and kings of Edom.

The recurring theme in this Parasha is "names being called."

Just in this portion, the Hebrew word שם Shem Name is used 20 times! —

Gen. 32:27, 28, 29, 29, 30, 33:17, 35:8, 10, 10, 10, 10, 15, 18, 36:10, 32, 35, 39, 39, 40, 40.

*¹⁰ Now a river went out of Eden to water the garden, and from there it parted and became four riverheads. ¹¹ The name (שם Shem) of the first is Pishon; it is the one which skirts the whole land of Havilah, where there is gold.*
**Genesis 2:10-11**

The first time the word שם Shem is used in the Torah refers to the river that watered the Garden of Eden and parted 4 ways, the first riverhead is Pishon, and it has gold.

The 2 Hebrew letters in the word Shem is ש Shin (Destroy/Consume) and מ Mem (Chaos/Water), representing "destroy chaos." The ultimate Name, the Name of all names, is the LORD's Name, יהוה, the 4-letter Name of GOD with no consonant, cannot be pronounced. Jewish people refer to GOD as השם HaShem, "The Name," for His Name is too holy to be uttered. GOD is The Chaos-Destroyer! When His created things fulfill their original divine purposes, He can indeed destroy chaos.

Jacob's name change would bring about destruction to the enemy in the Name of the LORD. That is Israel's destiny!

*So He said to him, "What is your name?"*
*He said, "Jacob."*
*And He said, "Your name shall no longer be called Jacob, but Israel; for you have struggled with God and with men, and have prevailed (יכל Yachol Able/Have power/Endure)."*
**Genesis 32:27-28**

The LORD has given Jacob power and authority to bring about victory through his bloodline, a king and kingdom that would have no end.

*And He (The Mashiach to be born) will reign over the house of Jacob forever, and of His kingdom there will be no end."*
**Luke 1:33**

*Of the increase of His government and peace*
*There will be no end,*
*Upon the throne of David and over His kingdom,*
*To order it and establish it with judgment and justice*
*From that time forward, even forever.*
*The zeal of the Lord of hosts will perform this.*
**Isaiah 9:7**

A name shapes a person or a thing's destiny. What you call someone or something matters!

Words matter. Definitions matter.

Let's look at another word closely used with שם Shem Name here.

Just in this portion, the Hebrew word קרא Qara Call is being used 10 times! —

Genesis 32:30, 33:17, 33:20, 35:7, 8, 10, 10, 15, 18, 18.

The first time this word was used is after GOD created light and called it day on the first day of creation.

*God <u>called (קרא Qara)</u> the light Day, and the darkness He called (קרא Qara) Night. So the evening and the morning were the first day.*
**Genesis 1:5**

קרא Qara also means to proclaim. Just as the LORD spoke creation into existence, proclamation comes in power. What the LORD proclaims and calls, He has authority over that. The moment GOD gave Jacob the name Israel, the LORD proclaimed ownership of Israel's destiny, not just his family, but the blessings and promises made to His people, the land and inheritance. Instead of taking hold of his brother's heel to take charge of his destiny, Jacob became Israel, surrendering control of his destiny to the LORD. The GOD-given name of Israel ישראל Yisrael. The Hebrew root of ישראל Yisrael, שרה Sarah, means to persevere and prevail as a prince/commander שר Sar. Israel would eventually bring forth the Kingdom of GOD through the Mashiach Messiah Yeshua Jesus, who is called שר שלום Sar Shalom (Prince of Peace, Isaiah 9:6).

**The word שלום Shalom Peace is made up of 4 Hebrew alphabets:**

- ש Shin- represents Destroy/Consume
- ל Lamech- represents Authority
- ו Vav-represents Establish
- מ Mem-Chaos

שלום Shalom Peace essentially is destroying the authority that establishes chaos (Seekins, p.193). Peace is not free of chaos, but instead, it is having the calmness and the stillness to know that the LORD is GOD. שר שלום Sar Shalom, Prince of Peace, is the Ruler of all things, even over chaos and destruction.

The word שם Shem Name is tucked inside the word שלום Shalom Peace. Without The Name above all names (the Name of the LORD), there can be No Peace. He is the Beginning and the End of our Peace!

In Genesis, the LORD gave Adam the task to name all living creatures and to rule over His creation.

# 8. VAYISHLACH / AND HE SENT

*<sup>19</sup> Out of the ground the Lord God formed every beast of the field and every bird of the air, and brought them to Adam to see what he would call (קרא Qara) them. And whatever Adam called (קרא Qara) each living creature, that was its name.*
**Genesis 2:19**

*What is man that You are mindful of him,*
*And the son of man that You visit him?*
*<sup>5</sup> For You have made him a little lower than the angels,*
*And You have crowned him with glory and honor.*
*<sup>6</sup> You have made him to have dominion over the works of Your hands;*
*You have put all things under his feet,*
*<sup>7</sup> All sheep and oxen —*
*Even the beasts of the field,*
*<sup>8</sup> The birds of the air,*
*And the fish of the sea*
**Psalm 8:4-8**

A ruler has dominion over his subjects. That is what GOD had given Adam the authority to do, reigning over all created things, "the works of His hands," until Adam's Fall and disobedience of GOD's Word. Some believe that Adam called forth the nature and destiny of each created thing that he named. For example, the Hebrew word for dog is כלב Kelev, which literally means as/like a heart. Dogs are known for their loyalty and faithfulness as "Man's best friend." They love people with their hearts. Given the name כלב Kelev, dogs' nature is called forth. By the way, כלב Kelev is Caleb in English. Caleb was a loyal and devoted leader in Israel. How about a cat חתול Chatul? It comes from the Hebrew root חתל Chatel, that makes the word חתל Chitul for diaper, which means to wrap around. A cat is flexible and wraps around your arm when he/she wants to show affection.

But the LORD provided a plan to restore that authority of proclamation back to us through Yeshua the Mashiach, Jesus Christ.

*And Jesus came and spoke to them, saying, "<u>All authority has been given to Me in heaven and on earth.</u> ¹⁹ Go therefore and make disciples of all the nations, baptizing them in the name of the Father and of the Son and of the Holy Spirit, ²⁰ teaching them to observe all things that I have commanded you; and lo, I am with you always, even to the end of the age." Amen.*
Matthew 28:18-20

*² Grace and peace be multiplied to you in the knowledge of God and of Jesus our Lord, ³ as <u>His divine power has given to us all things</u> that pertain to life and godliness, through the knowledge of Him who called us by glory and virtue, ⁴ by which have been given to us exceedingly great and precious promises, that through these you may be partakers of the divine nature, having escaped the corruption that is in the world through lust.*
2 Peter 1:2-4

*¹⁹ Behold, <u>I (Yeshua Jesus) give you the authority</u> <u>to trample on serpents and scorpions, and over all the power of the enemy</u>, and nothing shall by any means hurt you.*
Luke 10:19

Not only have we been given authority to rule and reign on earth and in heaven, in the Name of Yeshua Jesus, what we call and proclaim is subjected to our words of authority.

Here are a few names being called in this Torah Portion that are noteworthy.

## ISRAEL – GOD STRIVES / PENIEL – FACE OF GOD

*Then Jacob was left alone; and a Man wrestled with him until the breaking of day. ²⁵ Now when He saw that He did not prevail against him, He touched the socket of his hip; and the socket of Jacob's hip was out of joint as He wrestled with him. ²⁶ And He said, "Let Me go, for the day breaks." But he said, "I will not let You go unless You bless me!"*
*So He said to him, "<u>What is your name?</u>"*
*He said, "<u>Jacob.</u>"*
*And He said, "<u>Your name shall no longer be called Jacob, but Israel</u>; for you have struggled with God and with men, and have prevailed."*
*Then Jacob asked, saying, "Tell me Your name, I pray."*
*And He said, "Why is it that you ask about My name?" And He blessed him there.*
*So <u>Jacob called the name of the place Peniel</u>: "For I have seen God face to face, and my life is preserved."*
**Genesis 32:24-30**


## SUKKOT – TENTS

*But he said, "What need is there? Let me find favor in the sight of my lord." ¹⁶ So Esau returned that day on his way to Seir. ¹⁷ And Jacob journeyed to Succoth, built himself a house, and made booths for his livestock. Therefore <u>the name of the place is called Succoth</u>.*
**Genesis 33:16-17**

## EL-ELOHE-ISRAEL — GOD-GOD OF ISRAEL

*$^{18}$ Then Jacob came safely to the city of Shechem, which is in the land of Canaan, when he came from Padan Aram; and he pitched his tent before the city. $^{19}$ And he bought the parcel of land, where he had pitched his tent, from the children of Hamor, Shechem's father, for one hundred pieces of money. $^{20}$ Then he erected an altar there and <u>called it El Elohe Israel</u>.*
**Genesis 33:18-20**

## EL BETHEL — GOD HOUSE OF GOD

*Then God said to Jacob, "Arise, go up to Bethel and dwell there; and make an altar there to God, who appeared to you when you fled from the face of Esau your brother."… And they journeyed, and the terror of God was upon the cities that were all around them, and they did not pursue the sons of Jacob. $^6$ So Jacob came to Luz (that is, Bethel), which is in the land of Canaan, he and all the people who were with him. $^7$ And he built an altar there and <u>called the place</u> <u>El Bethel</u>, because there God appeared to him when he fled from the face of his brother.*
**Genesis 35:7**

## ALLON BACHUTH — OAK OF WEEPING

*Now Deborah, Rebekah's nurse, died, and she was buried below Bethel under the terebinth tree. <u>So the name of it was called Allon Bachuth</u>.*
**Genesis 35:8**

## BETHEL — HOUSE OF GOD

*And <u>Jacob called the name of the place</u> where God spoke with him, <u>Bethel</u>.*
*Genesis 35:8*

## BEN-ONI-SON OF MY SORROW / BENJAMIN-SON OF THE RIGHT HAND

*Now it came to pass, when she (Rachel) was in hard labor, that the midwife said to her, "Do not fear; you will have this son also." ¹⁸ And so it was, as her soul was departing (for she died), that <u>she called his name</u> Ben-Oni; but <u>his father called him Benjamin</u>.*
*Genesis 35:17-18*

Following are the names being called in the examples just listed in this Torah Portion-

- Israel — GOD strives
- Peniel — Face of GOD
- Sukkot — Tents
- El-Elohe-Israel — GOD-GOD of Israel
- El Bethel — GOD House Of GOD
- Allon Bachuth — Oak of Weeping
- Bethel — House of GOD
- Ben-Oni — Son of My Sorrow
- Benjamin-Son of the Right Hand

What I see in these names is that Jacob went from taking matters into his own hands and running away from the consequences of his action to maturity and taking responsibility of his life, trusting in GOD more than ever. His wrestling with GOD shows us his boldness and courage, determination to take up the mantle passed onto him from his father and grandfather. The tents, Bethel, the House of GOD kept reoccurring to remind him where he came from and where the LORD was taking him. He built altars and worshiped the One GOD, burying sorrows and turning that into Hope. The Right Hand symbolizes power and authority, as given to the Mashiach, the Messiah.

> *The Lord said to my Lord,*
> *"Sit at <u>My right hand</u>,*
> *Till I make Your enemies Your footstool."…*
> *The Lord is at <u>Your right hand</u>;*
> *He shall execute kings in the day of His wrath…*
> *He shall drink of the brook by the wayside;*
> *Therefore He shall lift up the head.*
> **Psalm 110:1, 5, 7**

> *If we truly believe every good gift comes from GOD, everything good happens because of GOD, and He only wants good things for us. Then, we can acknowledge and proclaim His Name when circumstances are good. But even when they are not good, we can call forth His goodness that He indeed can and will turn all things into good.*
> And we know that all things work together for good to those who love God, to those who are the called according to His purpose.
> **Romans 8:28**

About people's names, I have a dear friend named Kathy, who loves sharing the love of GOD with people. When she meets someone new while out and about, she likes to address them by name. With her spunky personality, Kathy would say, "Hey, Melissa, do you know what your name means?" Sometimes they respond yes, sometimes no. No matter what the answer, Kathy would get on her phone and look up the name's meaning. After all, everyone loves to hear their name being called. Kathy would then talk about the meaning of the name and ask if she could pray with them. There is such a purpose and destiny tied in with every name. Kathy does not pass up an opportunity to speak GOD's name into people, in the name of Yeshua Jesus, and watch His beloved children be amazed and touched by His grace.

Isn't that a brilliant idea?

The authority of naming and proclamation given to Adam was lost at the Fall, but Yeshua has reclaimed it back to GOD's children that we can speak and call forth destiny and purposes with power for GOD's glory.

When the enemy says, "Remember that hurt you have experienced? Remember the mistake you made that time? You should feel bad, ashamed and embarrassed…," our answer should be, "No, the name I call that time in my life is 'the Season of GOD's grace.'"

Responding with the Name of GOD eradicates the enemy's plan of making us depressed and ashamed, keeping us from being stuck in the past with things that cannot be undone or changed.

When the enemy says, "Remember the shameful things you have done? How could GOD ever love you for that?" Our answer should be, "Yes, wow! What a place the LORD has rescued me from. The name I call that incident is 'Covered in GOD's Mercy'!"

Agree with the enemy that I remember, but the name I call it is completely different from his.

I proclaim the goodness of GOD, despite of challenges we face in this season.

What we proclaim now shapes how certain situations will manifest in the future.

Are we naming them hope in faith or despair in fear?

Instead of calling oneself a victim, a survivor is more empowering. A victim has been violated and that label keeps that person in the state of victimhood helplessly and endlessly. A survivor is someone that has lived through an experience. Many survivors have even triumphed over their ordeal and choose to make something good of it somehow.

> *And it shall come to pass That whoever **calls** (קרא Qara) on the **name** (שם Shem) of the Lord Shall be saved.*
> **Joel 2:32**

Calling the Name of the LORD brings salvation.

Like Jacob, has the LORD given you a new name and a new destiny? Or do you simply need to proclaim His Name to demolish and defeat disorder and lawlessness in your life?

What name we call a person, a thing or a situation makes the world's difference.

We proclaim and call the Name of GOD over a situation or someone, the Name above all the names as in Yeshua the Mashiach, and the ultimate Name that destroys chaos and brings peace everywhere whenever The Name is spoken!

## 8. VAYISHLACH / AND HE SENT

Let's pray:

**Our Father in Heaven** אבינו שבשמימ,

Thank You for restoring the authority back to us through Yeshua to speak Your Goodness forth in anything or anyone that we proclaim Your Name. Teach us how to turn victims into survivors by infusing hope in faith. LORD, remind us that our words matter. What we label either gives it life or death. We receive Your Name over us that covers us with Your Perfect Peace, which surpasses all understanding and guards our hearts and minds through the Mashiach.

B'Shem Yeshua HaMashiach בשם ישוע המשיח.

In Jesus' Name we pray. Amen.

# 8. TORAH TASTING
## *REFLECTION*

1. What is the word, picture or theme the LORD is highlighting to you in this chapter and Torah Portion?

2. Is there a name of a person or a thing in your life that is significant to you? Perhaps a nickname that turns out to be prophetic? Can you dig deeper into that meaning and significance to explore what the LORD may be saying to you?

3. Naming or renaming someone or something can change the course of their destiny. Do you have a name you would like to speak over yourself that aligns with GOD's vision for your future and call?

# 9 ט
# Vayeshev
## (And He Dwelt)
### וישב

Genesis 37:1-40:23

Amos 2:6-3:8

Matthew 1:18-25

This Torah Portion's titled וישב Vayeshev, meaning "And He Dwelt" from the first verse.

> *Now Jacob dwelt in the land where his father was a stranger, in the land of Canaan. ² This is the history (generations) of Jacob.*
> **Genesis 37:1**

This Parasha tells about Joseph's dreams, which provoked his brother's jealousy and hatred toward him. Thus, they sold him into slavery. Then, it narrates the accounts of Judah and Tamar, his daughter-in-law, and concludes with Joseph being falsely accused by Potiphar's wife and thrown into jail, as well as the 2 dreams he interpreted while in prison.

The Hebrew Root of this Portion title is וישב Vayeshev. Its root ישב Yashav means Remain, Sit, Dwell. How ironic the title references sit and settle, but this week's portion is full of movements, anything but sitting still. Joseph went to Shechem to see his brothers, not finding them, then went to Dothan; later, he was sold into slavery in Egypt. Judah went away from his brothers to visit an Adullamite man named Hirah and married Shua's daughter. We see nothing settling and remaining still. However, I believe ישב Yashav is a subtle clue to what is in the background. It is the LORD's presence that remains and dwells. His steadfast love and mercy steadily guide His children.

Genesis 37 begins with the story of Joseph, Jacob's favorite son, by his beloved wife, Rachel. He told his 2 dreams to his brothers, showing off his tunic of many colors given by his father. Most are familiar with the rest. Genesis 38 seems to abruptly interrupt the flow of the storytelling and interject the story of Judah marrying a wife in Canaan and having 3 sons.

> *And <u>Judah</u> saw there a daughter of a certain Canaanite whose name was Shua, and he married her and went in to her. ³ So she conceived and bore a son, and he called his name <u>Er</u> (Er ער Awake). ⁴ She conceived again and bore a son, and she called his name <u>Onan</u> (On אין Vigor/Wealth). ⁵ And she conceived yet again and bore a son, and called his name <u>Shelah</u> (שלה Shalah Be quiet/At Ease). He was at Chezib (כזב Kazav To Lie/Liar) when she bore him.*
> **Genesis 38:2-5**

The story tells us that Judah found his son Er a wife named Tamar. Er was evil, and the LORD killed him. Then, Judah gave Tamar to his second son, Onan, as a wife to have children, according to the levirate law, for the sake of posterity. Onan purposely kept Tamar from conceiving, and the LORD killed Onan. Judah told Tamar to remain a widow until his third son got older, but he really had no intention of giving Shelah to Tamar as a husband. Tamar later planned to deceive Judah that he would have sexual relations with her, thinking she was a prostitute. Judah gave her a signet and cord as a pledge for payment. She became pregnant with Judah's child. 3 months later, she was brought forth being accused of harlotry.

There are several things that demand attention. Let's start with the name of Tamar.

The word תמר Tamar means palm tree. Throughout the Haftorah (The Prophets and the Law portion of the Old Testament), the Hebrew root תמר Tomer speaks about the palm tree of Prophetess and Judge, Deborah (Judges 4:5), and the palm tree being upright (Jeremiah 10:5). Deborah was a prophetess and mother of Israel (Judges 5:7). A name can tell the nature, character and often the destiny of a person. However, not much is known about where Tamar came from other than she lived in the land of Canaan, possibly a pagan. That never stopped GOD from partnering with the unlikely heroes/heroines doing great things.

**The name תמר Tamar consists of the 2 parts: the letter Tav ת and the word מר Mor.**

- ת Tav — meaning Covenant
- מר Mor — meaning Myrrh

Myrrh is an anointing oil, and it was used as an embalming perfume. One of the most known references of Myrrh is at the birth of the Messiah Yeshua Jesus. The wise men brought him 3 gifts, gold, frankincense and myrrh. Myrrh was a costly perfume symbolic of sanctification and suffering. Is it possible that even the name Tamar, the Covenant sealed with Myrrh (suffering and sanctification), was foretelling about the Mashiach, coming from the bloodline of Judah and Tamar?

> *So Judah said, "Bring her (Tamar) out and let her be burned!" When she (Tamar) was brought out, she sent to her father-in-law (Jacob), saying, "By the man to whom these belong, I am with child." And she said, "Please determine whose these are — the **signet and cord, and staff**." [26] So Judah acknowledged them and said, "She has been more <u>righteous</u> than I, because I did not give her to Shelah my son." And he never knew her again.*
>
> **Genesis 38:24b,25**

The first time the word צדק Tzadak Righteous is used in the entire Torah is here... on a woman named Tamar! She risked everything she had in order to do what was right.

Tamar's name means palm tree and uprightness. Her righteous act was rewarded with twin boys. Like the Prophetess Judge Deborah sitting under the palm tree, Tamar too is a mother of Israel, as the First Righteous Woman mentioned in the Torah. From her, came forth the greatest shepherd king of Israel, David, and later eventually, the Messiah!

The word צדק Tzadak Righteous has 3 letters:

- צ Tsade— Hook/Desire
- ד Dalet— Door/Entry
- ק Qoof — Last

Righteous is the desire to enter last. Doing what is right is to think less of oneself. Tamar did not care what others would think of her. She took matters into her own hand, and doing the right thing, earned her the "Righteous" title. She named her twin boys Perez and Zerah.

## 9. VAYESHEV / AND HE DWELT

*Now it came to pass, at the time for giving birth, that behold, <u>twins</u> were in her womb.* <sup>28</sup> *And so it was, when <u>she was giving birth</u>, that the one put out his hand; and the midwife took a scarlet thread and bound it on his hand, saying, "This one came out first."* <sup>29</sup> *Then it happened, as he drew back his hand, that his brother came out unexpectedly; and she said, "How did you break through? This breach be upon you!" Therefore his name was called Perez.* <sup>30</sup> *Afterward his brother came out who had the scarlet thread on his hand. And his name was called Zerah.*

**Genesis 38:27**

Just like Judah's father, Jacob and Esau, that were twins, the kingship line of Judah would come from twins, Perez and Zarach.

**Here are the names of Judah's 3 sons from his first wife and his 2 sons with Tamar:**

- יהודה Yehudah Judah — Praised
- ער Er — Awake
- אונן Onan — Vigor/Wealth
- שלה Shelah — Be quiet/At ease / PEACE
- פרץ Perez- To Break through
- זרח Zarach — To Rise / Come forth

These names together can mean — Praised is the Awake and Vigor and PEACE would break through, rise and come forth.

Signet ring (חתמת Chotemet), cord (פתיל Patil) and staff (מטה Mateh) were requested and given to Tamar by Jacob as a pledge for her service. Those 3 words also have never been seen in the Torah before prior to this story. They make a grand entrance announcing something significant.

The signet ring represents authority and kingship. One example is in Esther. The king's signet ring gave the decree in authority. The cord is seen in Aaron's priestly garment (Exodus 28:28). The staff also represents authority and guidance, and most notably, the shepherd's staff of Moses later in Exodus. These 3 pledge items seem to symbolize the Mashiach that would be prophesied by Jacob over Judah. Somehow these items connected to the conception of Tamar's children preluded the prophecy. These 3 pledge items tie in with the family line of Judah that would produce the King of the Kingdom that has NO End.

> *Your throne, O God, is forever and ever;*
> *A scepter of righteousness is the scepter of Your kingdom.*
> **Psalm 45:6**

> *Once I have sworn by My holiness;*
> *I will not lie to David:*
> *[36] His seed shall endure forever,*
> *And his throne as the sun before Me;*
> **Psalm 89:35-36**

> *Then the angel said to her, "Do not be afraid, Mary, for you have found favor with God. [31] And behold, you will conceive in your womb and bring forth a Son, and shall call His name Jesus. [32] He will be great, and will be called the Son of the Highest; and the Lord God will give Him the throne of His father David. [33] And He will reign over the house of Jacob forever, and of His kingdom there will be no end."*
> **Luke 1:30-33**

Many acknowledge the following verses, the last words from Jacob to his son Judah, as Messianic prophecy.

## 9. VAYESHEV / AND HE DWELT

> "Judah, you are he whom your brothers shall praise;
> Your hand shall be on the neck of your enemies;
> Your father's children <u>shall bow down</u> before you.
> ⁹ Judah is a lion's whelp; From the prey, my son, you have gone up.
> He ⁽ᶜ⁾bows down, he lies down as a lion;
> And as a lion, who shall rouse him?
> ¹⁰ <u>The scepter shall not depart from Judah,</u>
> Nor a lawgiver from between his feet,
> Until **Shiloh** (שילה) comes;
> And to Him shall be the obedience of the people.
> ¹¹ Binding his donkey to the vine,
> And his donkey's colt to the choice vine,
> He washed his garments in wine,
> And his clothes in the blood of grapes.
> ¹² His eyes are darker than wine,
> And his teeth whiter than milk.
> **Genesis 49:8-12**

Shiloh (שילה) is a title of the Mashiach, Messiah. This is the only spelling of שילה Shiloh as such and is the only time Shiloh as a person is used in the Torah. Other ones are used as a name of location.

Parashat Vayeshev consists of 4 prophetic dreams, 2 in Genesis 37 and 2 in Genesis 39-40. The first 2 foretold Joseph's brothers bowing to him when he would ultimately save his family from famine after his time in slavery. The last 2 dreams of the cup-bearer and the baker of Pharoah, interpreted by Joseph, would lead to his eventual liberation and promotion. What a turnaround!

> Now Joseph had a dream, and he told it to his brothers; and they hated him even more. ⁶ So he said to them, "Please hear this dream which I have dreamed: ⁷ There we were, binding sheaves in the field. Then behold, my sheaf arose and also stood upright; and indeed your sheaves stood all around and <u>bowed down to my sheaf</u>."
> **Genesis 37:5-7**

The bowing-down part in Joseph's dreams would later coincide with Judah's prophecy regarding the Mashiach. His brothers would bow down and praise the coming Messiah.

Some Jewish sages said the Joseph and Judah-Tamar stories in Genesis 38-40 did not happen chronologically. The Judah-Tamar narrative (Genesis 38) is inserted in the middle of the Joseph's story, between him provoking his brothers to hatred, being sold into Potiphar's house (Genesis 37) and his false accusation that landed him in prison (Genesis 39). Some say it is placed there to contrast Judah's harlotry misconduct to Joseph's godly character in Potiphar's house. I'd like to say that it is to highlight 2 heroic people. Both Tamar and Joseph's stories started out tragic. Tamar was widowed and childless, and Joseph was sold into slavery with no hope of escaping his fate. Both could've ended badly without GOD's supernatural intervention —

-Tamar's perfect timing of her pre-meditated encounter with Jacob, her father-in-law, and conception of child.

-Joseph's precise interpretation of the cup-bearer and the baker's dreams, then 2 years later, the cup-bearer suddenly remembers Joseph when Pharoah had his dreams.

Though GOD was not mentioned in the text, like in the book of Esther, He was very much working behind the scenes.

Not all dreams are from GOD, but those that are most certainly bring redemption, and peace and can transform lives. I've had a few powerful prophetic dream testimonies. One of them is about my friend, Ginny (not her real name):

Ginny had just gotten married and had recently gone on her honeymoon.

<u>In my very short dream</u>…

I asked Ginny, "Are you pregnant?"

Ginny said, "I don't know."

I further probed, "Are you sure?"

She said, "Maybe, but I am not sure."

The End… That was it.

I woke up thinking that probably has nothing to do with babies. Dreams are often symbolic, as in spiritual pregnancy and childbirth. Besides, she'd just gotten married; they probably did not want children right away. My spiritual mother, Gaye, has taught me when you have a dream, ask GOD if it is from Him and ask for revelation; also, to put the dream under the Blood of Jesus. That is what I did. Sometimes, the LORD would lead me to intercede and pray for the person(s) without sharing the dream with them.

Over the course of the next several weeks, the dream was brought to my mind to pray for Ginny. One day I woke up and felt it was time to tell Ginny about the dream.

I needed reassurance and asked GOD, "Are you sure You want me to call her?"

I felt Him answer, "Yes!"

So, I called Ginny on the phone and told her about the dream, and added,

"You know, dreams are usually symbolic of something. I am sure it is not about you actually being pregnant."

She responded, "Interesting that you said that. I felt something different but was not sure what. Now you mention it; maybe I am pregnant."

I asked Ginny, "Are you pregnant?"

Ginny said, "I don't know."

I further probed, "Are you sure?"

She said, "Maybe, but I am not sure."

The dialog happened just like it did in my dream.

At this point, she seriously suspected that she may be pregnant and said she would be tested for it. I told her I needed her to tell me as soon as she found out.

A few days later, she texted me, "Positive. I am pregnant."

I immediately called her to find out what happened.

Ginny recounted to me that she had 2 at-home pregnancy tests. Both came out "Negative." It turned out she and her husband desired to have children as soon as they got married, unbeknownst to me. She threw the negative pregnancy tests in the trash can and said, "I don't receive these negative tests. GOD has given my friend, Elena, a dream that I am pregnant. I believe I am." Then, Ginny walked away.

15 minutes later, she felt led, as if GOD told her to go back to the trash can to get the pregnancy tests. She did, and when she picked them up to look, they showed "Positive."

Ginny was indeed pregnant!

I was humbled and in awe of how the GOD of the Universe chose to share with me the little secret before anyone in the entire world through a dream.

Ginny went on to give birth to a precious little girl named Ava (not her real name). Ava, shortly after birth, was diagnosed with one of the rarest forms of Leukemia that became a Medical School textbook case study. She was given 2 years maximum to live.

Throughout the season, battling and warring for Ava's life in faith and prayers without knowing the outcome, the only thing for certain was that "GOD is good," no matter what. That prophetic dream lent a sliver of hope and showed a glimpse of GOD's sovereignty to this family.

With our Miracle-Working GOD, Ava defied all odds and survived after going through chemotherapies and cancer treatments. Today, she is a beautiful, healthy, vibrant 11-year-old girl with a powerful story to tell.

Have you ever had prophetic dreams that display GOD's steadfast love?

If not, GOD can give you those dreams if you ask.

The word ישב Yashav Sit/Dwell in the Parashat Vayeshev title is to remind us to dwell, sit and remain in the peace of the Mashiach for His salvation. No matter what life brings, no matter how dim the future looks, we can count on GOD's goodness and good plans for us. Not only is Tamar declared "Righteous," but she is also among the very few in the Torah being called righteous, let alone for a woman. Her courageous act to do what is just and upright came with blessings through her twin boys. Because of her, kings and rulers, as well as the seed of the Mashiach, would come from the line of Judah.

**Let's pray:**

**Our Father in Heaven** אבינו שבשמימ,

Thank You for your unseen intervention in our lives. We trust that even when we don't see, You are very much present in our midst. When we surrender our will to Yours, Your sovereign will reigns beyond logic. LORD, teach us the kind of courage and fear of GOD that Tamar had, that we may dwell and remain in Your provision rather than strive to achieve our own plans. We thank You that You always work all things into good for those who love and serve You according to Your purposes.

B'Shem Yeshua HaMashiach בשם ישוע המשיח.

In Jesus' Name we pray. Amen.

# 9. TORAH TASTING

## *REFLECTION*

1. What is the word, picture or theme the LORD is highlighting to you in this chapter and Torah Portion?

2. Have you ever had a dream that pointed you to GOD or the things that He was saying to you?

3. Can you think of an example that GOD interfered with your plan, which in hindsight, you learned to appreciate that?

4. Tamar was and is still misunderstood by many, but yet she was declared more righteous than Jacob himself. Was there a time that you were misunderstood or smeared, yet you were confident in the truth, knowing GOD is your Defense?

# 10 י
# miketz
## (From the End)
מקץ

Genesis 41:1-44:17

Zechariah 2:14-4:7

Luke 24:13-29

---

This portion starts with Pharaoh having a dream the 2 full years after Joseph interpreted the dreams for the chief butler and the baker in prison in last week's portion. Then, the chief butler suddenly remembered Joseph, which prompted Pharaoh to summon Joseph. He interpreted the dreams. Joseph was promoted to execute the plan of saving 7 years' grains for the subsequent 7 years' famine. His interpretations and prophetic words came to pass. Jacob sent his sons to Egypt to buy grains. That is when the reunion and reconciliation between Joseph and his brothers begin to unfold.

> *Then it came to pass, at the end of (מקץ Miketz) two full years, that Pharaoh had a dream; and behold, he stood by the river.*
> **Genesis 41:1**

מקץ Miketz is the title of this Parasha, which means "at the end of." This Torah Portion is the beginning of the end of Joseph's dramatic story, particularly his miseries. Pharoah's dreams turned out to be his lifeline. GOD orchestrated the interpretation of Joseph's jail mates' dreams 2 years prior in order to set up for his deliverance. We can see Joseph mature over the course of his young adult life. He was humble and had a servant's heart. He knew where his strength came from. After the chief butler's dream interpretation came true and was set free, Joseph must have had his hopes up that the chief butler would remember to repay the favor, and liberation would not be far off. It did not happen for another 2 years. Sometimes we wonder about GOD's timing, but remember that He is all-knowing and He does have good plans for us. He sees beyond the current circumstances. Thank GOD!

Perhaps you are in a season that you are ready for it to end? Maybe the beginning of the end is lasting way longer than you'd expected. No worries, GOD knows the perfect timing for it to end. Rest and trust in His goodness over you.

Reading this Torah Portion, I cannot help but notice some striking similarities between Joseph and Moses, both are "Messianic figures" and types of the Mashiach.

## 10. MIKETZ / FROM THE END

| Joseph | Moses |
|---|---|
| (Name means "He increases") | (Name means "Out of Water") |
| Taken away from family at young age | Taken away from family at young age |
| Trained shepherd (family trade) | Trained (later in life with father-in-law) |
| As a late teen, raised in the Egyptian royal household | As a child, raised in the Egyptian royal palace |
| Married daughter of a priest of On | Married daughter of a priest of Midian |
| Wife Asenath was given to him after his dream interpretation, he saved them from other shepherds' as part of a reward | Wife Zipporah was given to him after<br>- he saved them from other shepherds'<br>- harassment, as part of a reward |
| 2 sons: Manasseh (Causing to forget all my toil and all my father's house) | 2 sons: Gershom (I have been a stranger in a foreign land) |
| Ephraim (GOD has caused me to be fruitful) | Eliezer (The GOD of my father is my help |
| Later delivered his own family from famine | Later delivered his own people from slavery |

It is as if someone had written the plots of these 2 great heroes' lives.

Transplanting is what comes to my mind in the stories of Joseph and Moses. Transplanting is when something or someone is taken out of their familiar environment to be re-planted or relocated in a different environment in order to maximize their growth. I would even say in order that their full potential would be reached and purpose would be accomplished to the fullest.

In my personal life, I have been transplanted several times. Leaving Metropolitan Hong Kong as a teenager to be placed in an Alabamian small town would be considered a major transplantation. Moving to the Nation's capital for a job offer the day after college graduation was another one. Being transplanted into a new place, new friends, with nothing familiar, having the "sink or swim" attitude by GOD's grace was the only way I strived. Paul and I moved out of Washington, D.C., to the Midwest for a job promotion after him living in D.C. for over 20 years. Paul was brought up in a New York Orthodox Jewish household but became secular as an adult. I was a self-proclaimed Christian, in name only, but still a good person.

As a new transplanted resident in Columbus, Ohio, on a particular Sunday morning, I "randomly" picked a small church to visit while Paul was at work. I remember the pastor said this about "big churches," "Well, those big churches are not where you need to be. Some of them ridiculously meet at movie theaters?! Don't just take my word for it. Go check it out for yourselves." His disdain for those modern and big churches was more than obvious. Well, that caught my attention. What? Church at a movie theater? Fun!

I wanted to visit one of those "ridiculous" big churches.

The Vineyard, Columbus... the first evangelical church I had ever visited... and I loved it. Of course, the LORD led me to a church where the pastor and the elders were all Jewish! They even had Saturday evening services for many Jewish people who are used to Saturdays (Shabbats) worship services. I came home and told Paul about it. He couldn't believe it and had to go see it for himself. That set us both on a spiritual journey seeking a genuine personal relationship with the LORD.

Paul often talks about his transplantation from New York to D.C., from D.C. to the Midwest with me, clearly was by GOD's hand. When we got to Ohio, we had only a handful of friends, mostly from his work. The LORD took him out of his familiar environment with family and friends on the East Coast to a place where it was just him and me. We only had each another. We sought GOD individually in our own ways while the LORD so intricately weaved our spiritual journeys together. We can see how GOD forever changed our lives through transplantation, much like He did with Joseph and Moses.

Do you have a GOD transplanting story? If so, share it with others. There is tremendous power in those testimonies.

I learned of a story from the Midrash about Joseph's wife, Asenath, that I found fascinating. The Midrash is a compilation of Torah commentaries and teachings by various rabbis. Some of these stories are legends. Nonetheless, they make good stories, perhaps like a theory explaining GOD's word. So, one of the stories tells us that after Jacob's daughter, Dinah, was raped by Shechem, she became pregnant and gave birth to a baby girl. Her brothers tried to kill the baby as she was the product of a heinous crime and would be a constant reminder of the violent act. But Jacob made an amulet, put it around the baby's little neck and sent her away. GOD's angel brought her to Egypt. She was found and raised by Potiphar's wife.

Sounds like the story of baby Moses, doesn't it?!

Later, when Joseph met Asenath, he saw her amulet (which was inscribed with the Holy Name of GOD or the House of Jacob, a clear sign to whom she belonged). He knew instantly she was not an Egyptian but rather a

Hebrew like himself. Therefore, he married her with the reassurance that she was not a pagan foreign woman. Whether that story is true or not, it is an interesting theory that Joseph's 2 sons, Manasseh and Ephraim, and later their tribes were Hebrews. Once again, this is another transplanting story, like Joseph and Moses, so that Asenath would fulfill her destiny. If this story were true, not only would it be significant for Joseph's lineage, it would also show that Dinah was not just another tragic helpless victim. The name Asenath means "belonging to goddess Neith," yet her legendary amulet would show that she really belonged to the GOD of Jacob.

What legacy Asenath's life would be for her mother, Dinah!

From the last Torah Portion, the pledge Tamar asked of Judah for her "service" is his signet, cord, and his staff.

> *And he (Jacob) said, "I will send a young goat from the flock."*
> *So she (Tamar) said, "Will you give me a **pledge** (ערבון Eravon) till you send it?"*
> *¹⁸ Then he said, "What **pledge** (ערבון Eravon) shall I give you?"*
> *So she said, "Your signet and cord, and your staff that is in your hand." <u>Then he gave them to her, and went in to her, and she conceived by him</u>…*
> *And Judah sent the young goat by the hand of his friend the Adullamite, to receive his **pledge** (ירבון Eravon) from the woman's hand, but he did not find her.*
> **Genesis 38:17-18,20**

Very interesting! After the pledge (a guarantee) is given, Tamar conceived.

Then, in this week's Torah Portion, Judah himself became a pledge to guarantee his brother Benjamin's safety when he was asked by Joseph to bring the youngest brother to Egypt so they could get more grains.

# 10. MIKETZ / FROM THE END

*Then Judah said to Israel his father, "Send the lad (Benjamin) with me, and we will arise and go, that we may live and not die, both we and you and also our little ones. <sup>9</sup> <u>I myself will be **surety/pledge** (ערב Arav) for him</u>; from my hand you shall require him. If I do not bring him back to you and set him before you, then let me bear the blame forever. <sup>10</sup> For if we had not lingered, surely by now we would have returned this second time."*
### Genesis 43:8-10

*<sup>32</sup> For your servant became **surety/pledge** (ערב Arav) for the lad to my father, saying, 'If I do not bring him back to you, then I shall bear the blame before my father forever.' <sup>33</sup> Now therefore, please let your servant remain instead of the lad as a slave to my lord, and let the lad go up with his brothers. <sup>34</sup> For how shall I go up to my father if the lad is not with me, lest perhaps I see the evil that would [c]come upon my father?"*
### Genesis 44:32-34

The ערב Arav surety/pledge mentioned in the above verse, in 5 instances, are the only times it is used in the entire Torah. The Hebrew root for Pledge/Guarantee is ערב Arav broken into 2 parts would be:

- ע Ayin — Eye to see
- רב Rav — Much

ערב Arav shows us that a pledge is the assurance that you will have much to see in the future. It is the guarantee of more to come.

Judah promised to pay the "prostitute," disguised by Tamar, a young goat from the flock. He gave her his signet ring, his cord, and his staff as a guarantee in exchange for her service. Later, Jacob did not want his sons to take his youngest son by Rachel, to Egypt with them. Judah became the pledge, using his own life to guarantee Benjamin's safety. It seems that Judah is the main character in both circumstances that the pledge is used.

The Messiah/Mashiach was prophesied to come from the lineage of Judah. The Mashiach would guarantee Israel's salvation with His own life. His life would be the pledge for our full redemption.

*¹³ In Him (Yeshua) you also trusted, after you heard the word of truth, the gospel of your salvation; in whom also, having believed, you were sealed with the Holy Spirit of promise, ¹⁴ who[d] is the **guarantee** of our inheritance until the redemption of the purchased possession, to the praise of His glory.*
**Ephesians 1:13-14**

The Mashiach, the Lion of Judah, would bring full redemption for GOD's people. The Spirit of the Living GOD given to us is the ערב Arav Pledge for the fullness of inheritance.

How magnificent!

Judah went away from his brothers (transplanted to an unfamiliar place to visit a man named Adullam), and there he married his wife and set into motion a series of events that led up to producing the kingly bloodline, that eventually, the Messiah would be brought forth. My transplantation story led us to the pledge/exchange of the encounter with GOD that Paul and I met our Mashiach. Paul received his Jewish Messiah, and I got to see the complete picture and understand the Hebrew heritage of my Christian faith as a Gentile. Baruch HaShem! Praise the Name of the LORD!

## 10. MIKETZ / FROM THE END

Let's pray:

**Our Father in Heaven** אבינו שבשמימ,

Thank You for divine transplantation that leads to maximize our growth and fulfillment of our destiny and purposes. Your transplantation often leads to a pledge, accomplishing Your will and revealing your good plans for us. LORD, please show us your perspective during the transplantation seasons, geographical or circumstantial, that we may appreciate it and trust You for the outcome to be for our best. We will never stop telling of Your goodness in our transplantation stories.

B'Shem Yeshua HaMashiach בשם ישוע המשיח.

In Jesus' Name we pray. Amen.

# 10. TORAH TASTING
## *REFLECTION*

1. What is the word, picture or theme the LORD is highlighting to you in this chapter and Torah Portion?

2. Transplanting can be an uncomfortable experience, and faith is necessary to minimize the initial pain. Do you recall a transplanting story of yourself or someone you know that brought forth GOD's amazing plans to be fulfilled?

3. After his dream interpretation, Joseph hoped someday he would be set free from prison, yet he had to wait 2 more years. Those 2 years were the beginning of the end of his suffering season. How does Joseph's story encourage you about hope during your beginning-of-the-end season that you had or perhaps are currently going through?

# 11 יא
# Vayigash
## (And He Came Near)
### ויגש

Genesis 44:18-47:27

Ezekiel 37:15-28

Luke 24:30-48

Parashat Vagyigash begins with Judah pleading for the release of his youngest brother, Benjamin. Then, the dramatic reveal of Joseph's true identity to his brother follows, as well as Jacob's migration to Egypt with his family settling in Goshen and the prophesied famine in Egypt. The title of this Parasha comes from its first verse:

*Then Judah came near (ויגש Nagash Draw Near/Approach) to him and <u>said</u>: "O my lord, please let your servant <u>speak</u> (Mouth) a word in my lord's <u>hearing</u> (Ears), and do not let your <u>anger burn</u> (Nose in Hebrew) against your servant; for you are even like Pharaoh.*
**Genesis 44:18**

Fascinating that in this verse, with Judah <u>approaching,</u> Joseph involves the mouth, the ears and the nose. Verbal communication, hearing and spiritual discernment are keys to being fully engaged in approaching the LORD, who has the authority to grant petitions.

**The Hebrew root for Vayigash is נגש Nagash Draw Near/Approach. The first time this word is used in the Torah is when Abraham approached GOD and pleaded to save Sodom and Gomorrah in Genesis 18:23:**

נגש Nagash Draw Near/Approach —

- נ Nun — Life/Activity
- ג Gimmel — Lift up, Pride
- ש Shin — Consume, Destroy

From its Hebrew root, you can see the essence of Approach and Draw Near to the LORD is an Activity that Destroys Pride. Abraham humbly drew near to GOD to plead for Sodom and Gomorrah, for GOD is the only One with the power to save the city. Judah drew near to Joseph, for he held the authority in Egypt as Pharoah.

**It gets more interesting when the 3 Hebrew letters in נגש Nagash Draw Near/Approach are scrambled. We get 2 other words:**

- גשן Goshen — Fertile
- נשג Nashag — Overtake

Drawing near to GOD in humility activates granting access to fertile ground that GOD's amazing promises and plans would then overtake us. The connection between this Torah Portion title Vayigash, נגש Nagash Draw Near and גשן Goshen is remarkable. Goshen is the land that Pharoah gifted Jacob and his family to settle during the remaining 5 years of famine (that famine lasted 7 years).

## 11. VAYIGASH / AND HE CAME NEAR

*Then Pharaoh spoke to Joseph, saying, "Your father and your brothers have come to you. ⁶ The land of Egypt is before you. Have your father and brothers dwell in <u>the best of the land</u>; let them dwell in the land of Goshen (גשן). And if you know any competent men among them, then make them chief herdsmen over my livestock."*
*²⁷ So Israel dwelt in the land of Egypt, in the country of <u>Goshen</u> (גשן); and they had possessions there and grew and multiplied exceedingly.*
**Genesis 47:5, 27**

גשן Goshen appears 9 times in this Parasha. 9 is the number for completeness and it also symbolizes the Mashiach for the finality He brings to accomplishing the ultimate restoration and salvation plan of GOD. גשן Goshen is where the LORD fulfilled His promises to Jacob.

*So Israel took his journey with all that he had, and came to Beersheba, and offered sacrifices to the God of his father Isaac. ² Then God spoke to Israel in the visions of the night, and said, "Jacob, Jacob." And he said, "Here I am." So He said, "I am God, the God of your father; <u>do not fear to go down to Egypt, for I will make of you a great nation there.</u> ⁴ I will go down with you to Egypt, and I will also surely bring you up again; and Joseph will put his hand on your eyes."*
**Genesis 46:1-4**

At the news of Joseph being alive, Jacob still hesitated to go to Egypt. Nonetheless, he set off on the journey to go and worshipped the LORD on the way to the "Unknown." It is at this point, in the same area, Jacob had the fateful encounter with the LORD (Genesis 28:10-16). GOD reaffirmed His promises He had made to Jacob. Jacob trusted the LORD's good plans for his family once more to go down to Egypt, walking by faith in the middle of severe famine. He could not have imagined the fertile land that GOD had been preparing for such a time as this.

Have you ever been in a season of "famine" that required a tremendous amount of faith to trust that the LORD had a provision in store for you on the other side? Jacob's Nagash/Goshen story should be a good reminder to all of us that GOD proves Himself over and over what an incredible Provider He is to us, being true to His words.

The Torah Portion opens with Judah's plea to his disguised brother, Joseph. He recounted what had happened on the trip returning home, how he convinced his father to allow him to bring his youngest brother Benjamin with him as commanded, and how he pledged Benjamin's safety with his own life.

Quite a speech of 16 verses!

Judah's speech triggered Joseph's emotions and that was the moment of the truth-disclosure.

> *³ Then Joseph said to his brothers, "I am Joseph; does my father still live?" But his brothers could not answer him, for they were dismayed in his presence. ⁴ And Joseph said to his brothers, "Please come near to me." So they came near. Then he said: "I am Joseph your brother, whom you sold into Egypt. ⁵ But now, do not therefore be grieved or angry with yourselves because you sold me here; for God sent me before you to preserve life.*
> **Genesis 45:3-5**

The big reveal, the dramatic reunion, and the reconciliation of forgiveness all happened here in this finale of Joseph's story. From the time Joseph was sold into slavery at age 17 to this point, the age of 39 (out of jail at age 30 + 7 plentiful years + 2 famine years), that is at least 21 years that Jacob thought his son was dead. There is a saying, "Perception is reality." What we see is what we perceive as "real." Reality can differ from yours and mine. Many factors play into it, such as worldviews, life experiences, biases, …, etc. Reality is not necessarily the truth. We see it now more than ever. I grew up in a time that if it is on the news, it must be real, and therefore it is true. It has come to light that reality can be manipulated to cause others to believe a certain projected reality. I remember once telling some friends something about current events; their response was, "If it is true, why haven't we heard it on the news?"

Jacob certainly believed a reality that was untrue. It was based on fabricated lies and evidence made up by his sons, with manufactured evidence of Joseph's multi-colored coat dipped in goat's blood. He believed the "reality" of Joseph being dead for over 21 years. Fake news existed even then. The revelation of Joseph being alive was so unbelievable to Jacob that his heart stopped a beat.

> [25] Then they went up out of Egypt, and came to the land of Canaan to Jacob their father. [26] And they told him, saying, "Joseph is still alive, and he is governor over all the land of Egypt." And <u>Jacob's heart stood still because he did not believe them</u>. [27] But when they told him all the words which Joseph had said to them, and <u>when he saw the carts which Joseph had sent to carry him, the spirit of Jacob their father revived</u>. [28] Then Israel said, "It is enough. Joseph my son is still alive. I will go and see him before I die
> **Genesis 45:25-28**

Not only Joseph was alive, but he was also the key to his family's survival during this famine. Isn't it just so like GOD that when He blesses us, He does it extravagantly!

My maternal grandmother grew up in Guangdong province in Southeastern China during the early 1900s when girls were not encouraged to be educated. She was the only child and her father spoiled her. He offered to hire a tutor to teach her to read, but she refused. She was incredibly smart but remained illiterate her entire life. We often joked that she could govern a nation like then U.K. Prime Minister Margaret Thatcher if only she could read. By the way, Grandma did have Thatcher's hairstyle. Her mother died when she was just a child. Her father remarried and his second wife died. He remarried again and his third wife died. This went on 7 times in total. His seventh wife was whom I knew as my great-grandmother. Great-grandfather later moved to (British) Hong Kong to live with some close relatives already there (long before the Communists took over China in the late 1940s). My grandmother got married and moved to Hong Kong as well. As a young mom with 6 children, life was tough. Many missionaries fled China into Hong Kong to escape Communists' persecution. They began holding church services and distributed food to the poor, drawing them to hear the Gospel. Grandma has told me that she went to church only for the free food. My mom recalls learning church hymns, memorizing Bible verses and receiving the LORD Jesus Christ into her life at age 8. Eternal life was a tremendous gift, and the free food and supplies were bonuses. One time she and her friends brought home big laundry bar soaps. They were so excited to wash their clothes with them. But when she began to rub them on the washboards with water, they were frustrated that soap suds were not produced no matter how hard they tried. It turns out that the big blocks they brought home were not laundry bar soap but cheese instead. She still laughs talking about it 'til this day.

My grandmother was a self-proclaimed Buddhist, like many Chinese people are. She went to the temple to offer prayers and sacrifices and to ask for blessings for her family. From time to time, she would go to church. You can imagine when her dying 90-year-old stepmother (remember? her father's 7th wife) told her she needed to see a pastor on her death bed; she was not happy. Grandma had an elaborate Buddhist funeral service planned. A typical Buddhist funeral involves lots of incense, fake paper money, and all necessities made of paper (cars, houses, maids,…, yes, even cell phones) burned for the deceased loved one to use in the afterlife. Monks would pray continuously with loud musical instruments like cymbals for hours. Great-grandma's request to see a pastor comes from visions she'd seen. She told her family that she saw her favorite dish, pork belly with pickled cabbage (a traditional Chinese peasant dish), in heaven. She could have all she wanted if she went to heaven. And the only way to go to heaven is accepting the LORD Jesus Christ. Grandma was livid and asked who had told her about Jesus. She could not believe it came from a vision, but indeed it was true. At Great-Grandma's persistent request, a pastor was brought in and prayed with her. Great-Grandma departed from this world peacefully into the arms of our LORD into Heaven. Several years later, Grandma's heart softened. She began going to church with her friends. Her change of heart was evident. She released many worries and concerns to the LORD. She and I had some amazing phone conversations about her prayers and how she was happier and more content. She told me she prayed for us often and spoke blessings over me and our children 8000 miles away. She even stopped going to the Buddhist temple, which was a big deal. At age 87, she professed her faith publicly by being baptized at her church. Many would have lost hope if they were waiting for their loved ones to receive the LORD in their late age. We didn't and neither should you. GOD is faithful!

*So don't lose hope.*
*I, the Lord, have spoken*
**Jeremiah 31:17**

*Let us hold fast the confession of our hope without wavering, for He who promised is faithful.*
**Hebrews 10:23**

You too, may have stories like that. GOD can revive a dream, a desire, a hope so dead that resurrection seems impossible. GOD can turn death into life. When Jacob was living in grief every day, thinking Joseph was dead, the truth is Joseph was living and ruling in Egypt that he would meet him at the appointed time. When they were worried in times of famine, the truth is that Joseph had been sent to Egypt and fertile land had been set aside for Jacob's family. The Haftorah portion for this Parasha is the second half of Ezekiel 37, about the dry bones becoming flesh. If GOD can revive an army from dry bones, bones so dead and dry to the point the last bit of life had been long gone... Nothing is impossible with GOD!

**Let's pray:**

**Our Father in Heaven** אבינו שבשמים,

Thank You for being a Death-Resurrector and Hope-Reviver! It is never too late for You to bring Your promises to pass. LORD, teach us to humbly draw near You every moment of our lives and know that fertile land is in store for us in times of famine. Please help us to fully engage as we trust in You and You alone and be able to discern between perceived reality and truth. As King David declared in Psalm 25:5,

"Lead me in Your truth and teach me,
For You are the God of my salvation;
On You I wait all the day."

B'Shem Yeshua HaMashiach בשם ישוע המשיח.

In Jesus' Name we pray. Amen.

# 11. TORAH TASTING

## *REFLECTION*

1. What is the word, picture or theme the LORD is highlighting to you in this chapter and Torah Portion?

2. This Torah Portion tells us Jacob's perception differs from reality and the truth. Was there a time when your perception of reality turned out to be untrue? What led you to see the truth?

3. The Word of GOD says the LORD never fails, and He always fulfills His promises. When you are still waiting for a promise to come to pass, how do you stay focused on GOD and remain encouraged?

# 12 יב
# Vayechi
## (And He Lived)
### ויחי

Genesis 47:28-50:26

1 Kings 2:1-12

John 13:1-19

Parasha Vayechi is the last Torah Portion in the Book of Genesis. It marks the end of an era in the lives of Israel's patriarchs, Abraham, Isaac and Jacob recorded. The Book of Genesis chronicles from how in the beginning, GOD created the heaven and the earth, many epic events and characters along the way, to finally, the "Homecoming Procession" of Jacob's family migrating back to the land of Canaan for his burial. This Parasha also provides closure to Joseph's remorseful brothers with great forgiveness. A big chunk of this portion also covers Jacob's prophetic blessings over his 12 sons and Joseph's 2 sons. Lastly, it is concluded with one more death and burial... Joseph's.

The title of this Parasha is taken from its first verse.

> *And Jacob lived* (ויחי יעקב *Vayechi Yaakov*) in Egypt seventeen years, and *the years of his life were a hundred and forty-seven*.
> **Genesis 47:28**

This verse echoes the beginning of another Torah Portion, חיי שרה Chayei Sarah, Sarah Lived.

> *Sarah lived* (חיי שרה *Chayei Sarah*) to be *a hundred and twenty-seven years old*.
> **Genesis 23:1**

When a person dies, it is his/her life that is celebrated. GOD is the Life-Giver and Life-Sustainer.

On every major Jewish holiday and special occasion, a specific blessing is recited —

### שהחינו Shehecheyanu (Who has granted/given us life)

ברוך אתה יי Baruch atah Adonai / Blessed are You, LORD

אלהנו מלך העלם Elohenu Melekh Ha'olam / Our GOD, King of the Universe

שהחינו וקימנו Shehecheyanu vekiymanu / Who has given/granted us life and sustained us

והגיענו לזמן הזה Vehigi'anu lazman hazeh / and allowed/let us (to) arrive at this time (season)

שהחינו The Shehecheyanu Blessing has been recited for over 1500 years. It is recited at every Bar/Bar Mitzvah, Jewish wedding, and feast of the LORD, as well as Hanukkah. It is GOD's will that His people live and fulfill the purposes which they were created for. This blessing reminds us that no matter the season, the LORD is blessed. He rules the world

## 12. VAYECHI / AND HE LIVED

around us. He gives life and it is His will that we have come into the time we are in; that in itself is a gift.

"And Jacob lived (ויחי יעקב Vayechi Yaakov) ..., and the years of his life were a hundred and forty-seven," 147, and "Sarah lived (חיי שרה Chayei Sarah) to be a hundred and twenty-seven years old," 127. Both begin with the verb "live," and then the years the person has lived. As the reader reads it, it is as if the days of the person in those years are flashing before our eyes.

How would our attitude toward life be different if we were truly thankful to GOD for life and mindful of our every breath being the gift of GOD, celebrating life as intended every single day? Like they were recorded in the Book of Life?

The only time the Book of Life is mentioned in the Old Testament is in Psalm 69.

*May they be blotted out of the book of life (הספר חיים HaSefer Chaiyim) and not be listed with the righteous.*
**Psalm 69:28**

The Book of Life lists the names of the righteous that they may live on. Here is a verse about the Book of Life in the New Testament.

*All inhabitants of the earth will worship the beast — all whose names have not been written in the **Lamb's book of life**, the Lamb who was slain from the creation of the world.*
**Revelation 13:8**

The 5 times the "Book of Life" appears in the Book of Revelation has to do with judgment and the eternal fate of the judged.

*For this is good and acceptable in the sight of God our Savior, <u>who desires all men to be saved</u> and to come to the knowledge of the truth.*
**1 Timothy 2:3-4**

GOD wants all the world to have their names written in the Book of life, that we may be saved and have eternal life.

On every Shabbat and special occasion, Jewish people raise their cup of wine and cheer "L'Chaim"/ לחיים To Life. That brings me to the blessing of the wine.

*Baruch ata Adonai, Elohenu Melech HaOlam, Boray P'ri Hagafen.*

*Blessed are You LORD, Our GOD King of the Universe, Who brought forth fruit from the vine.*

The wine or grape juice used is deep red, which is symbolic of blood. As followers of the Mashiach Yeshua Jesus Christ, we praise GOD for the bloodshed of the Mashiach that gave us life. The Blood of Yeshua cleanses us from sins. Through his death, we are resurrected from death to life spiritually.

*For <u>the life of the flesh is in the blood</u>, and I have given it to you upon the altar to make atonement for your souls; for it is **the blood that makes atonement for the soul**.*
**Leviticus 17:11**

*In Him we have redemption through **His blood**, **the forgiveness of sins**, according to the riches of His grace.*
**Ephesians 1:7**

The atonement of the Mashiach's blood gives us life. "Blood gives life" and "life is in the blood" display the close relationship between the blood and life. A covenant is made with the shedding of blood.

## 12. VAYECHI / AND HE LIVED

*So He (GOD) said to him, "Bring Me a three-year-old heifer, a three-year-old female goat, a three-year-old ram, a turtledove, and a young pigeon." <sup>10</sup> <u>Then he brought all these to Him and cut them in two, down the middle, and placed each piece opposite the other;</u> but he did not cut the birds in two... And it came to pass, when the sun went down and it was dark, that behold, there appeared a smoking oven and a burning torch that passeds between those pieces. On the same day, the Lord made a covenant with Abram, saying: To your descendants I have given this land...*
**Genesis 15:9,10,17,18**

*Likewise He also took the cup after supper, saying, "This cup is the new covenant in **My blood**, which is shed for you.*
**Luke 22:20**

When we acknowledge and receive the Blood of Yeshua, which the LORD accepted as an atonement for our sins, our end of the covenant being fulfilled with GOD, it is like us receiving a blood transfusion. Every time I raise a cup of wine/grape juice and thank the Father for Yeshua's bloodshed for me, I feel Him infusing life into my spiritual veins.

*The thief does not come except to steal, and to kill, and to destroy. <u>I (Yeshua Jesus) have come</u> that <u>they may have **life**, and that they may have it **more abundantly**</u>.*
**John 10:10**

I have life more abundantly in every possible way because I receive the blood sacrifice of Yeshua on my behalf.

Do you ever feel like something in your life needs life infused into it? Perhaps try accepting and acknowledging Yeshua's atonement wholeheartedly through His blood in full. Declare and thank the LORD that He has already given you life abundantly in every way while raising up a glass of red wine/grape juice to receive a spiritual blood transfusion.

## L'Chaim! To Life!

> *¹⁹ I call heaven and earth as witnesses today against you, that I have set before you life (חיים Chaim) and death, blessing and cursing; therefore choose life (חיים Chaim), that both you and your descendants may live (חיה Chayah-verb).*
> **Deuteronomy 30:19**

Every single day, we have a choice to make, choosing between life or death. Choose to see the life in everything the way GOD sees it. Life is beautiful as GOD intends.

One of my favorite songs is "Life Is Beautiful" by The Afters in the soundtrack of a movie titled "October Baby." Part of the chorus and tag goes like this:

> A father's love
> A wedding dance
> New Year's dreams
> A toast with friends
> A soldier coming home from war
> The faith the hope of so much more
> A brand new life, a mother's prayer
> Shooting stars, ocean air
> A lover's kiss, and hard goodbyes
> Fireworks, Christmas lights
>
> These are things that make us feel alive
> These are the times that make us realize
> Life is beautiful

Even in sadness and tragedy, if we look harder and more closely, we can somehow find life and beauty in it. I encourage you to prayerfully seek the LORD and see life and beauty in every situation.

## 12. VAYECHI / AND HE LIVED

The word קבר Qavar Bury appears over and over in this Parasha, totaling 11 times, starting in Genesis 47:29.

*When the time drew near (קרב Qarav Come Near/Approach) that Israel must die, he called his son Joseph and said to him, "Now if I have found favor in your sight, please put your hand under my thigh, and deal kindly and truly with me. Please do not bury (קבר Qavar Bury) me in Egypt...*
**Genesis 47:29**

When we scramble the 3 Hebrew letters in the root קבר Qavar Bury, we get קרב Qarav Come Near/Approach.

**It is remarkable that in the same verse (Genesis 47:29) found in this Torah Portion are these 2 words:**

- קבר Qavar Bury
- קרב Qarav Come Near/Approach

Here is the first time קרב Qarav Come Near/Approach found in the Torah:

*And it came to pass, when he (Abram) was close to (קרב Qarav Come Near/Approach) entering Egypt, that he said to Sarai his wife, "Indeed I know that you are a woman of beautiful countenance.*
**Genesis 12:11**

Fascinating that <u>entering Egypt</u> is mentioned in this verse as well with קרב Qarav Come Near/Approach, as is in Genesis 47:29 with קבר Qavar Bury when Jacob requested to be buried not in <u>Egypt</u>.

**The third outcome of scrambling the 3 letters in קבר Qavar Bury is:**

- קרב Q'Rav means Battle/War

> *Moreover I (Jacob) have given to you (<u>Joseph</u>) one portion above your brothers, which I took from the hand of the Amorite with my sword and my bow (<u>at battle</u>).*
> **Genesis 48:22**

The clue about battle in the word קרב Q'Rav is indicated in Jacob's word of giving Joseph an extra portion of inheritance above his brothers, which is the ridge of land Jacob gained through a battle.

When those 3 Hebrew letters scramble one more time, we have —

ברק Baraq means Lightning Flash, which we see in the Book of Exodus, the book that comes after Genesis.

> *Then it came to pass on the third day, in the morning, that there were thunder and **lightning flashes** (ברק Baraq), and a thick cloud on the mountain; and the sound of the trumpet was very loud, so that all the people who were in the camp trembled.*
> **Exodus 19:16**

The recurring theme of קבר **Qavar Bury** reminds us, over and over, that a season is coming to a close and something new is on the horizon.

I do not believe in coincidence, only Divine Providence. I believe somehow, all these little pieces of clues are connecting something for us.

This Torah Portion's title, ויחי And He Lived Vayechi, highlights "life," life after the burial. Abram once entered into Egypt and Jacob was to leave Egypt to be buried. After that, Israel (his descendants) will enter Egypt. Yes, battles are imminent, but the One True GOD, who is faithful to His people, would come like lightning flashes and bring deliverance to Israel from unexpected places in unimaginable ways.

**Another thing about the root word** קבר **Qavar Bury, it can be broken down into 2 parts:**

- ק Qoof — Following
- בר Bar — Son

Following the Son (the Son of GOD, the Mashiach, the Messiah) leads to deliverance and life.

One last remarkable thing in this Parasha is the theme of "last will be first, first will be last."

Joseph's sons: Ephraim and Manasseh —

> *But Israel reached out his right hand and put it on Ephraim's head, though he was the younger, and crossing his arms, he put his left hand on Manasseh's head, even though Manasseh was the firstborn... When Joseph saw his father placing his right hand on Ephraim's head, he was displeased; so he took hold of his father's hand to move it from Ephraim's head to Manasseh's head.* [18] *<u>Joseph said to him, "No, my father, this one is the firstborn; put your right hand on his head</u>. But his father refused and said, "I know, my son, I know. He too will become a people, and he too will become great. Nevertheless, <u>his younger brother will be greater than he</u>, and his descendants will become a group of nations."* [20] *He blessed them that day...*
> **Genesis 49:14,17,18,19,20**

Joseph, through his 2 sons, got the double portion of blessings though he was one of the youngest sons.

In the previous Torah Portions, there are a few similar incidents —

Tamar and Judah's sons: Perez and Zerah —

*When the time came for her to give birth, there were twin boys in her womb.* [28] *As she was giving birth, one of them put out his hand; so the midwife took a scarlet thread and tied it on his wrist and said, "This one came out first."* [29] *But when he drew back his hand, his brother came out, and she said, "So this is how you have broken out!" And he was named Perez.]30 Then his brother, who had the scarlet thread on his wrist, came out. And he was named Zerah.*
**Genesis 38:27-30**

Isaac's sons — Jacob and Esau, in Genesis 25-26

Jacob stole Esau's birthright and got the firstborn's birthright and blessings from his older brother.

The irony of "last will be first, first will be last" shows us the LORD is sovereign. We may not understand why, but we just need to trust GOD and His perfect will.

Yeshua Jesus told a parable regarding a landowner about the Kingdom of heaven:

*"For the kingdom of heaven is like a landowner who went out early in the morning to hire workers for his vineyard.* [2] *He agreed to pay them a denarius for the day and sent them into his vineyard…But he answered one of them, 'I am not being unfair to you, friend. Didn't you agree to work for a denarius?* [14] *Take your pay and go. I want to give the one who was hired last the same as I gave you.* [15] *Don't I have the right to do what I want with my own money? Or are you envious because I am generous?'* <u>*So the last will be first, and the first will be last.*</u>*"*
**Matthew 20:1,2,13-16**

Sometimes, life seems to be unfair, but if we devote our hearts to the LORD and trust Him, we know He has good plans for us and those around us. His heart is that all will see Him and know His love. If we approach him in humility, knowing that we deserve nothing to begin with, everything we have is due to His grace and love. With a thankful and humble heart, we would never feel we got the short end of the stick.

The very last verse of the Book of Genesis and of this Torah Portion is:

> So <u>Joseph died at the age of a hundred and ten</u>. And after they embalmed him, he was placed in a coffin in Egypt.
> **Genesis 50:26**

Joseph died at age 110.

110 is the number for the word the Hebrew word עם Am meaning People. (ע Ayin — 70, מ Mem — 40).

How appropriate is that following the death of Joseph in the Book of Exodus is the growth of the nation of Israel and the unfolding of GOD's mighty hand in delivering His "people" from slavery and bondage? It seems that even the age of Joseph's death foretells the focus of what is to come, GOD's "People," a nation of GOD's people is about to be born!

ויחי Vayechi Torah Portion "And He Lived" shows us that Life perpetuates according to GOD's perfect will. Burying the dead leads to a new season of life. The last will be first, and the first will be last. Following the LORD always leads to life.

**Let's pray:**

**Our Father in Heaven** אבינו שבשמימ,

Thank You for being our Life-Giver and Life Sustainer! We have nothing and we are nothing apart from You. We need your spiritual blood transfusion into us daily as we give You thanks for the Mashiach's blood atonement for our sins. We ask and receive that You would breathe new life into us. LORD, teach us and remind us to draw near to You so that we can see what You see and find life and beauty in everything. Even in death, we would somehow see life awaiting to come forth on the other side.

B'Shem Yeshua HaMashiach בשם ישוע המשיח.

In Jesus' Name we pray. Amen.

## 12. TORAH TASTING

### *REFLECTION*

1. What is the word, picture or theme the LORD is highlighting to you in this chapter and Torah Portion?

2. Life is beautiful and precious. What are some of the ways you are intentional about living life with a purpose? And how would you encourage others to appreciate everyday life as a gift from GOD?

3. Have you ever said goodbye to a loved one(s), immersed in so much pain and grief, and somehow the LORD gave you encouragement and comfort? What and how would you like to remember your loved one(s) today?

# 13 יג
## shemot
**(Names)**

שמות

Exodus 1 — 6:1

Isaiah 27:6 — 28:13

Matthew 2:1 — 12

Shemot is the first Parasha of the Book of Exodus. It sets up the background of one of the most history-making miracles ever! It has many elements of a blockbuster movie, the birth of a national hero, a genocide committed by an evil tyrant, supernatural intervention of GOD's invisible hand, the burning bush moment, and the LORD's refusing every excuse Moses threw His way about the assigned mission, and so much more.

But here, we are going to focus on a few key points. I feel it is important to help understand the rest of Exodus from this moment forward.

*Now (And) these are (ואלה V'Eleh) the names of the children of Israel who came to Egypt; each man and his household came with Jacob…*
**Exodus 1:1**

The letter ו Vav is used as a conjunction. Oftentimes, it means "and." 12 out of over 50 Torah Portion titles begin with "ו /V'…", that is over 20%. This is quite remarkable. Here are the Hebrew titles of the Torah, the five books of Moses, and their beginning verses.

- בראשית Bereshit / Genesis — "In the beginning GOD created the heaven and the earth…"
- שמות Shemot / Exodus — "**And** these are the names of the sons of Israel…"
- ויקרא Vayikra / Leviticus — "**And** He (the LORD) called to (Moses)…"
- במדבר Bamidbar / Numbers — "**And** He (the LORD) spoke (to Moses)…"
- דברים Devarim Deuteronomy — "These are words that Moses spoke (to all Israel)…"

A new book or chapter typically does not begin with the word "And." However, the 2nd, 3rd and 4th books of the Torah each begins with "And," indicating continuation of the bigger story being told. Is it possible that the title words of each of these books together give us a glimpse of the LORD's great plan? —

<u>In the beginning GOD created</u> the world with the desire that His people would know Him, and the <u>names</u> of Israel's sons are listed as a start to unfold GOD's magnificent plan to show His love for each of them; the LORD initiates the <u>call</u> to Moses to lead His people into freedom; the LORD <u>spoke</u> His words, the living Word that gives and sustains life for His people; Then, GOD's chosen people are authorized to speak <u>words</u> inspired by the Spirit of the Living GOD from generation to generation.

This Torah Portion opens the book, Exodus, its English name, with a very appropriate Hebrew title "שמות Shemot, the names" for the dramatic exit of the Children of Israel walking away from the place they were enslaved for 400 years. Just the name itself makes our hearts skip a beat seeing the earth-shaking defeat of the villain, enemy of GOD and His people, as many are familiar with Charles Heston's movie, Exodus.

The Hebrew title of this Parasha is שמות Shemot Names, taken from its first verse. There is a saying that "people don't care what you know until they know that you care." What follows in this Parasha is GOD's plan of deliverance for His people. It would be revealed to them "help is on the way." Corporate salvation is key for Israel, but I believe personal salvation and reassurance of GOD's love and mercy for each individual is equally essential to drive out insecurity and fear in times of waiting for the help/delivery. Shemot lays out Israel's suffering and victory, bondage and deliberation as a nation. Millions would be walking on dry ground crossing the Red Sea, and yet, each person is reminded that he is known by his name.

Here is the prophecy GOD spoke to Abram (Abraham) in Genesis:

*⁵ Then He (GOD) brought him (Abram) outside and said, "Look now toward heaven, <u>and count the stars if you are able to number them</u>." And He said to him, "<u>So shall your descendants be</u>."*
**Genesis 15:5**

The following verse is the fulfillment of that prophecy to Abraham:

*Now there arose a new king over Egypt, who did not know Joseph. ⁹ And he said to his people, "Look, <u>the people of the children of Israel are more and mightier than we.</u>*
**Exodus 1:8-9**

The Hebrew title of the book of Exodus שמות Shemot / Names highlights the names of the Children of Israel. The LORD told Abraham that his descendants would resemble the countless stars. GOD counts and knows every person by name, just as He counts and calls every star by name.

> *The Lord builds up Jerusalem;*
> *He gathers together the outcasts of Israel.*
> *³ He heals the brokenhearted*
> *And binds up their [b]wounds.*
> *He counts the number of the stars;*
> *He calls them all by name.*
> **Psalm 147:4**

You are not just a number or a minute part of a group. GOD loves you intimately and knows you by name. I can picture GOD taking Abram outside, looking up into that dark sky showing him the stars and beginning to name them each by name. I can envision GOD showing Abraham the corporate destiny of Israel as well as the individual's purpose being fulfilled by each of his descendants. Flaws and failures, triumphs and strengths, GOD loves His children, and Abraham would see it all through His eyes, gazing at the stars.

The first time the word שמות Shemot Names found in the Torah is in Genesis 2:

> *²⁰ So Adam gave names (שמות Shemot) to all cattle, to the birds of the air, and to every beast of the field. But for Adam there was not found a helper comparable to him.*
> **Genesis 2:20**

Adam was given full authority to rule over the earth at the time he was given the task to name every creature GOD had created. If "Every beast of the field" was named, can you imagine how valuable you are to GOD that He knows your name and your destiny? If you ever feel invisible and lost in a crowd, just close your eyes and imagine yourself with a spotlight pointed right at you. GOD notices you. He sees you.

## 13. SHEMOT / NAMES

*Now these are the **names** (שמות Shemot) of the children of Israel who came to Egypt; each man and his household came with Jacob: ²Reuben, Simeon, Levi, and Judah; ³Issachar, Zebulun, and Benjamin; ⁴Dan, Naphtali, Gad, and Asher. ⁵All those [a]who were descendants of Jacob were **seventy persons** (נפש Nefesh Souls) (for Joseph was in Egypt already). ⁶And Joseph died, all his brothers, and all that generation. ⁷But the children of Israel were fruitful and increased abundantly, **multiplied** and [c]grew exceedingly mighty; and the land was filled with them.*
**Genesis 1:1-7**

First comes the "Shemot/Names," then the number 70 souls, then multitudes filled the land. The Hebrew word translated as "persons" is נפש Nefesh Souls. נפש Nefesh has been used for creatures and life. It refers to something that has life in it. Have you ever met people that have no life in them? I mean, they go through the motion in life with no hope and no purpose, like a walking dead. It may be harsh to say, but many living that way do not even realize it. GOD intends for us to live with life as נפש Nefesh Souls because He has given us His spirit to reside within us for those who know the Mashiach. He came so that we can live life to the fullest, abundantly, as the Father designed for us to live.

*¹⁰The thief does not come except to steal, and to kill, and to destroy. I (Yeshua Jesus) have come that they may have life, and that they may have it more abundantly.*
**John 10:10**

Those 70 נפש Nefesh Souls are represented by the 12 sons of Jacob that are named. Then, they grew exceedingly. These 70 נפש Nefesh Souls, living beings and full of life, set up the backdrop for the epic story of Exodus. The LORD is about to show off His miracles like never before. His people would stand in awe of His might rooted in His love for them.

My husband's grandparents fled persecution from Eastern Europe before WWI. Jewish persecution had already been in full motion during the Pogrom in early 1900's Russia. Later during the Holocaust, one of the things inflicted on the Jews was tattooing a registration serial number on the prisoners of war. Many Holocaust survivors today have that tattooed number on their arms to retell their nightmares. That number was used to identity these prisoners and systematically track them like commodities and animals. It often is perceived as a form of humiliation. But, on the other hand, GOD has a way of redeeming what the adversary aims for harm and destruction. Believe it or not, you can be a number of significance. For example, in Judaism, a prayer minyan of 10 Jewish male adults (age 13 and up) is required to have a quorum to conduct certain religious obligations. 10 Jewish males form a community of Israel, according to the Talmud. Each person is equally important; without any one of the 10, a Jewish service cannot happen. At times, you being a number cannot be undermined for unseen heavenly purposes.

There are 3 extraordinary women that Moses owed his life to, Shifrah (Yochebed), Batya and Zipporah.

You may not be familiar with the first 2. Sages and rabbis throughout the ages have told stories through Jewish oral traditions that are not recorded in the written Torah. Some seem to be "far-fetched theories" explaining the Torah. Nonetheless, many are passed down from generation to generation to tell of GOD's faithfulness.

Let's start with Yochebed. There are countless people in the Torah. Some are mentioned by name; others are not. Those who are known by name are clearly to be noted of importance, especially women.

# 13. SHEMOT / NAMES

## 1. JOCHEBED/YOCHEBED –

*Now Amram took for himself Jochebed (יוכבד Yochebed), his father's sister, as wife; and she bore him Aaron and Moses. And the years of the life of Amram were one hundred and thirty-seven (137).*
**Exodus 6:20**

*The name of Amram's wife was Jochebed (יוכבד Yochebed), the daughter of Levi, who was born to Levi in Egypt; and to Amram she bore Aaron and Moses and their sister Miriam.*
**Numbers 26:59**

Some sages suggest that Shiphrah and Puah, the Hebrew midwives who did not kill the Hebrew baby boys as commanded, were Yochebed and her daughter Miriam. GOD rewarded the midwives for their courageous acts with families.

*Then the king of Egypt spoke to the <u>Hebrew midwives</u>, of whom the name of one was <u>Shiphrah</u> and the name of the other <u>Puah</u>;... Therefore God dealt well with the midwives, and the people multiplied and [f]grew very mighty. ²¹ And so it was, <u>because the midwives feared God, that He provided households (בתים Batim) for them</u>... And a man of the house of Levi went and took as wife a daughter of Levi. ² <u>So the woman conceived and bore a son.</u>*
**Exodus 1:15,20-21**

It was nothing short of remarkable that Yochebed, the rewarded midwife, gave birth to the 3 great prophets of Israel: Aaron, Miriam and Moses.

*<u>And when she (יוכבד Yochebed/ THE LORD IS GLORY) saw (ראה Ra'ah See) that he (Moses) was a beautiful (טוב Tov Good) child</u>, she hid him three months.*
**Exodus 2:2**

ראה Ra'ah See and טוב Tov Good appearing together points to another incident in Genesis 1, which is the first time these 2 Hebrew words appear in the Torah.

> *And God saw (ראה Ra'ah See) the light, that it was good (טוב Tov Good); and God divided the light from the darkness. [5] God called the light Day, and the darkness He called Night. So the evening and the morning were the first day.*
> **Genesis 1:4-5**

The name יוכבד Yochebed means THE LORD IS GLORY.

What if Exodus 2:2 reads like this: "Yochebed, THE LORD IS GLORY, saw that the baby boy is good?"

Could it be possible that Yochebed saw what GOD saw in Genesis 1, the light, and that the light in Moses is good, which carries the light and hope for Israel? Then she hid him for 3 months until the appointed time.

The enemy tried to extinguish the light GOD provided for redemption, but THE LORD, THE GLORY, preserved that light to bring liberty and life to His people. Yochebed somehow saw the goodness that the LORD saw. She risked her own life to save her baby boy without knowing that her act would be saving the entire nation someday.

Do you see what the LORD sees? Perhaps a sparkle of hope that would trigger the boldness in you to do something worth risking your life for? We can never underestimate the impact of seeing from the perspective of GOD's goodness and mercy.

## 2. BATYA —

*⁵ Then the daughter of Pharaoh came down to bathe at the river. And her maidens walked along the riverside; and when she saw the ark among the reeds, she sent her maid to get it. ⁶ And when she opened it, she saw the child, and behold, the baby wept. So <u>she had compassion (pity/spare) on him</u>, and said, "This is one of the Hebrews' children... And the child grew, and she brought him to Pharaoh's daughter, and he became her son. <u>So she called his name Moses</u>, saying, "<u>Because I drew him out of (משיתהו Mesitihu) the water</u>."*
**Exodus 2:5-6,10**

Today, in retelling the Passover story, some Jewish children's books depict Pharoah's daughter with outstretched arms fetching Moses out of the water. According to the Midrash in the Babylonian Talmud, her arms lengthened miraculously to reach the basket containing the baby flowing on the river from where she was on the bank of the river.

She named the baby Moshe משה from the way she saved him..."I drew him out of the water."

The phrase "outstretched arm" is used throughout the bible to show GOD's lovingkindness and mercy. Here are a couple of examples.

*Therefore say to the children of Israel: 'I am the Lord; I will bring you out from under the burdens of the Egyptians, I will rescue you from their bondage, and I will redeem you with an **outstretched arm** and with great judgments.*
**Exodus 6:6**

*With a strong hand, and with an **outstretched arm**, For His mercy endures forever.*
**Psalm 136:12**

The compassion of Pharoah's daughter led to rescuing the Hebrew baby with her supernaturally lengthened arms. Just like how GOD was moved by His people's outcry for help and raised up a deliverer to redeem them.

Did you know that Pharoah's daughter has a name?

Pharoah's daughter was presented a name, בתיה Batya, meaning "Daughter of GOD," for her heroic act of saving Moses, the future Deliverer of Israel. She is so revered and honored to be given a name like Batya, "Daughter of GOD."

I have always wondered how an Egyptian princess was allowed to bring a Hebrew male child, which her father had commanded to destroy, to be raised in the palace as her own son. A story from the Jewish oral traditions offers an intriguing explanation. Pharoah, Batya's father, felt that this Hebrew boy could possibly be a threat to his throne. He was advised to test him. Pharoah had 2 bowls placed in front of the little boy, one containing jewels and gold while the other containing burning coals. If he reached into the jewels, then it would be a sign that he had intents to usurp Pharoah's throne and, therefore, could not be trusted. By divine intervention, Moses reached into the burning coals and picked up one of the glowing coals. He brought it to his lips and burned his tongue. Legend has it that is the reason for Moses' speech impediment.

Quite a story!

> *Then Moses said to the Lord, "O my Lord, I am not eloquent, neither before nor since You have spoken to Your servant; but I am slow of speech and slow of tongue."*
> **Exodus 4:10**

Batya's "in the right place at the right time," along with her compassion for the Hebrew baby boy, is clear providence of GOD Almighty in the backdrop of the Exodus story.

## 3. ZIPPORAH —

> $^{24}$ *And it came to pass on the way, at the encampment, that the Lord met him and sought to kill him.* $^{25}$ *Then <u>Zipporah took a sharp stone and cut off the foreskin of her son and [c]cast it at [d]Moses' feet, and said, "Surely you are a husband of blood (חתן דמים Chatan Damim) to me!"</u>* $^{26}$ *So He let him go. Then she said, "You are a <u>husband of blood (חתן דמים Chatan Damim)!"</u> — because of the <u>circumcision (מולה Mulah).</u>*
> **Exodus 4:24-26**

This is one of the most puzzling passages in the Torah. And perhaps one of the least talked-about heroines in the Exodus story is Zipporah. Zipporah's fast thinking and an agile act of circumcising her son singlehandedly saved her husband's life. חתן דמים Chatan Damim Husband/Bridegroom of <u>Blood</u> alludes to a <u>covenant</u>, as well as <u>circumcision</u> being a sign of <u>covenant</u> instituted from Abraham's time. <u>Bridegroom</u> is a major part of the <u>marriage covenant</u>. Blood is required for sealing a covenant and circumcision is a covenantal sign. The word Blood here דמים Damim is in plural form, often translated as blood guiltiness, bloodshed or blood on a corporate or large scale. The Hebrew word used <u>מולה</u> Mulah for circumcision is the only time seen in the entire Torah! I get a sense that this circumcision is unlike any other. Knowing it or not, Zipporah's circumcision of her son on the spot, in her courage and wisdom, had a much larger implication of salvation. It was a crucial line drawn declaring this family's devotion to the LORD, and to Him alone! Moses' life was spared right before his mission of going to see his brother Aaron and he delivered GOD's word of hope to the Israelites. It cannot be overstated the role of Zipporah in Israel's deliverance!

There 3 national heroines of Israel, Yochebed, Batya and Zipporah, who demonstrate remarkable bravery in critical times, making monumental decisions on the spot that has changed the destiny of Israel forever! From an ordinary GOD-fearing Hebrew mother just loving her son, an Egyptian princess with such compassion and being blessed with the honor to be called "Daughter of GOD," to a Bride, sensitive to the will of

GOD, acknowledging her Bridegroom, sealing a covenant with a sign of covenant that would save her husband and then a nation. Compassion and GOD-fearing devotion drove these women to extraordinary acts of courage. GOD knows them each by name and the purposes they were destined to fulfill, just as GOD knows you by name and His divine call on your life.

**LET'S PRAY:**

Our Father in Heaven אבינו שבשמימ,

Thank You for knowing us by name, and at times we are marked by numbers for Your glory in order that Your sovereign will be accomplished. THE LORD OF GLORY always brings forth hope. LORD, remind us daily how You know us, which draws us to know You more. We are thankful beyond measure that You have sent the Mashiach into the world so that we may live life abundantly. Every day is a gift and has the potential to be extraordinary. Help us to see everyone and everything in Your perspective of goodness and mercy, changing the atmosphere and world around us one person at a time.

B'Shem Yeshua HaMashiach בשם ישוע המשיח.

In Jesus' Name we pray. Amen.

# 13. TORAH TASTING

## *REFLECTION*

1. What is the word, picture or theme the LORD is highlighting to you in this chapter and Torah Portion?

2. What is in a name? Do you know what your name means? If so, what is its meaning?

3. GOD knows every star by name. You are worth more than a star. You were called for a purpose by your Father in heaven. How does that truth help you see yourself and everything around you differently?

4. This chapter highlights 3 remarkable women. Which one of them stands out to you today? Any thoughts you would like to share about her story? Does it remind you of another story?

# 14 יד
# VA'ERA
## (And I Appeared)
## וארא

Exodus 6:2-9:35

Ezekiel 28:25-29:21

Luke 11:14-22

This week's Torah Portion title וארא Va'era derives from its second verse —

> ³ <u>And I appeared</u> to Abraham, to Isaac, and to Jacob, as God Almighty, but by My name Lord I was not known to them.
> **Exodus 6:3**

The word וארא Va'era is in Niphal/reflexive form, and its Hebrew root is ראה Ra'ah, "to see." The LORD was seen, appearing to Abraham, to Isaac and to Jacob, individually as אל שדי El Shaddai. Here are the very first 3 appearances of the GOD's name אל שדי El Shaddai in the Torah, as well as Jacob's reference of GOD with this name when speaking to Joseph.

GOD to Abram:

*When Abram was ninety-nine years old, the Lord appeared to Abram and said to him, "I am **Almighty God** (אל שדי *El Shaddai*); walk before Me and be blameless.*
**Genesis 17:1**

Isaac to Jacob:

*Then Isaac called Jacob and blessed him, and charged him, and said to him: "You shall not take a wife from the daughters of Canaan. ² Arise, go to Padan Aram, to the house of Bethuel your mother's father; and take yourself a wife from there of the daughters of Laban your mother's brother*

*"May **God Almighty** (אל שדי *El Shaddai*) bless you, And make you fruitful and multiply you, That you may be an assembly of peoples…*
**Genesis 28:1-3**

GOD to Jacob:

*Also God said to him (Jacob): "I am **God Almighty** (אל שדי *El Shaddai*). Be fruitful and multiply; a nation and a company of nations shall proceed from you, and kings shall come from your body. ¹² The land which I gave Abraham and Isaac I give to you; and to your descendants after you I give this land."*
**Genesis 35:11**

# 14. VA'ERA / AND I APPEARED

Jacob to Joseph:

*Then Jacob said to Joseph: "God Almighty (שדי אל El Shaddai) appeared to me at Luz in the land of Canaan and blessed me, ⁴ and said to me, 'Behold, I will make you fruitful and multiply you, and I will make of you a multitude of people, and give this land to your descendants after you as an everlasting possession.'*
**Genesis 48:3-4**

The LORD revealed Himself as **God Almighty (שדי אל El Shaddai)** to Abram, Isaac, Jacob and Jacob's 12 sons. GOD Almighty (שדי אל El Shaddai) seems to be connected to GOD's promises of physical blessings in the land and His covenant with His people in their fruitfulness and multiplying in numbers.

*And God spoke to Moses and said to him: "I am the Lord. ³ I appeared to Abraham, to Isaac, and to Jacob, as God Almighty, but by My name Lord. I was not known to them. ⁴ <u>I have also established My covenant with them, to give them the land of Canaan, the land of their pilgrimage, in which they were strangers.</u> ⁵<u>And I have also heard the groaning of the children of Israel whom the Egyptians keep in bondage, and I have remembered My covenant.</u>*
**Exodus 6:2-5**

This Parasha opens with GOD telling Moses, "I AM The LORD," אני יהוה Ani Adonai. Though He has said the exact words to Abram when they first met, the essence of this Name of GOD was not yet revealed then. Now, GOD is about to unveil it to Moses after his unsuccessful petition meeting with Pharoah.

*So Moses returned to the Lord and said, "Lord, why have You brought trouble on this people? Why is it You have sent me? ²³ For since I came to Pharaoh to speak in Your name, he has done evil to this people; neither have You delivered Your people at all."*
**Exodus 5:22-23**

The LORD never promised that this mission would be easy. The length of time from Moses' encounter with GOD at the burning bush, the 10 plagues and crossing the Red Sea could be around 5 months to a year. Going back and forth to Pharoah and witnessing the LORD's mighty wonders at work must have been exhausting physically, mentally, and spiritually. Wouldn't you agree?

> *⁶ Therefore say to the children of Israel: <u>'I am the Lord; I will bring you out from under the burdens of the Egyptians, I will rescue you from their bondage, and I will redeem you with an outstretched arm and with great judgments.</u> <u>⁷I will take you as My people, and I will be your God. Then you shall know that I am the Lord your God who brings you out from under the burdens of the Egyptians.</u> <u>⁸And I will bring you into the land which I swore to give to Abraham, Isaac, and Jacob; and I will give it to you as a heritage: I am the Lord.'"*
> **Exodus 6:5-8**

The LORD reveals who He is: "I AM The LORD," אני יהוה Ani Adonai, to His people beyond earthly blessings in Exodus 6:5-8. In the above verses, "I AM The LORD," אני יהוה Ani Adonai is the beginning and the end, bookending the 7 things the LORD will do for His people, as well as right in the middle being His vows to Israel.

Here's what I mean:

<u>I AM THE LORD יהוה Ani Adonai</u>

1. **I will bring you out** (יצא Yatsa Bring) from under the burdens of the Egyptians,
2. **I will rescue you** (נצל Natzal Rescue) from their bondage, and
3. **I will redeem you** (גאל Gaal Redeem) with an outstretched arm and with great judgments.
4. **I will take you** (לקח Laqach Take) as My people, and

5. **I will be** (היה **Hayah Be**) **your** God. Then you shall know that <u>I am the Lord (יהוה Ani Adonai)</u> your God who brings you out from under the burdens of the Egyptians.
6. **I will bring** (בוא **Bo Come/Bring**) **you** into the land which I swore to give to Abraham, Isaac, and Jacob; and
7. **I will give** (נתן **Natan Give**) **it to you** as a heritage

<u>I AM THE LORD</u> יהוה Ani Adonai

7 is the number for perfection. Creation was created in 7 days with a day of rest. GOD's promises are perfect and complete. Indeed, the LORD is the beginning and the end, the First and the Last, and all that is in between. He is our all in all.

> *Who has performed and done it, calling the generations from the beginning? '<u>I, the Lord, am the first</u>; and with <u>the last I am He</u>.'…*
> **Isaiah 41:4**

> *"Thus says the Lord, the King of Israel, and his Redeemer, the Lord of hosts: '<u>I am the First</u> and <u>I am the Last</u>; besides Me there is no God…*
> **Isaiah 44:6**

> *"Listen to Me, O Jacob, and Israel, My called: I am He, <u>I am the First</u>, <u>I am also the Last</u>…*
> **Isaiah 48:12**

If Mount Sinai's Ten-Commandment moment is compared to a wedding ceremony, this occasion (Exodus 6:6-8) would be the marriage proposal and engagement with Moses as the matchmaker. Try to reread the above 7 promises envisioning a princess trapped in a tower by an evil witch and that Prince-Charming had his messenger deliver this marriage proposal message to his beloved for what he is about to do in order to win her over and make her his bride. The tale is as old as time. Every girl dreams of being rescued by her prince, and every little boy dreams of righting the wrongs with some superpower as the superhero. Ecclesiastes 1:9 says, "There is nothing new under the sun."

This Parasha's affirmation of GOD's Word for His people is monumental because the LORD is personal to each generation and to each person. Moses and the Israelites knew of GOD's promises, but GOD wanted to visit them intimately so that they would know HIM firsthand. "I AM THE LORD יהוה Ani Adonai" is all we need as a pledge for the promises while we wait for their fulfillment.

When we say to the LORD, "YOU ARE THE LORD אתה יהוה Ata Adonai," we are affirming and receiving all that He says to be true; not only is He willing, but He wants to do everything to show Himself and His love to us. He is putting everything on the table to win the heart of His Bride. He does nothing to trick us. He does not inflict illness on us for any reason. He is the LORD, not that I am His servant, but His pursuit is to have a relationship with us and we would reciprocate His love. Sounds simple, doesn't it? It really is simple love. We often complicate this pure love of the Creator.

Those 7 engagement vows in Exodus 6:6-8 remind me of the last verses in Psalm 91.

<u>Because he loves me</u>," says the Lord,

1. "I will rescue him;
2. I will protect him, <u>for he acknowledges my name</u>.
3. He will call on me, and I will answer him;
4. I will be with him in trouble,
5. I will deliver him and
6. honor him.
7. With long life I will satisfy him and show him my salvation."

**Psalm 91:14-16**

## 14. VA'ERA / AND I APPEARED

Many speculate that Moses penned Psalm 91. It was written for the Shabbat day. Its wording and theme are profoundly similar to the beginning of Parashat Va'era.

| | |
|---|---|
| Psalm 91:1 — GOD **Shaddai** (שדי) | Exodus 6:3b — as God Almighty (שדי Shaddai) |
| Psalm 91:2 — I will say of the Lord (יהוה Adonai), "He is my refuge and my fortress, my God, in whom I trust." | Exodus 6:2 "I AM THE LORD יהוה Ani Adonai" |
| Psalm 91:9 — "YOU ARE THE LORD אתה יהוה Ata Adonai" | |
| Psalm 91:14 — Because he has known **my Name**. | Exodus 6:3b — but by My name Lord I was not known to them |

You can think of Exodus 6:6-8 and Psalm 91 as a duet. The LORD sings, "I AM THE LORD," and we sing in response, "YOU ARE THE LORD." What follows are the 7 vows of promises by the LORD because we love Him, know and acknowledge His Name. In the mode of rest, as in on a Shabbat Day, meditating on the goodness of GOD, we declare to Him, "YOU ARE THE LORD!" and receive every promise He has made to us.

Psalm 91 covers every single thing a person ever needs to live a prosperous and abundant life provided by the GOD MOST HIGH, lacking no good thing!

*The young lions lack and suffer hunger; but those who seek the Lord <u>shall not lack any good thing</u>.*
**Psalm 34:10**

*For the Lord God is a sun and shield; The Lord will give grace and glory; <u>No good thing will He withhold</u> from those who walk uprightly.*
## Psalm 84:11

In a world full of uncertainty with the future unpredictable, the only safety and security we can ever have is in the Presence of the LORD. He made His Name known to us so that we can receive all that He is. Knowing He is somehow working in our midst and He has a rescue plan in place gives us a peaceful feeling. Anxiety comes from worrying about the "what if's" in the future.

Ezekiel 28:25-26 is the Haftorah for this Parasha, the matching portion in the Prophets' writing. There are 7 things the LORD said would happen when He has gathered His children back:

²⁵ 'Thus says the Lord God: "When I have gathered the house of Israel from the peoples among whom they are scattered, and am hallowed in them in the sight of the Gentiles, then

1. They will <u>dwell</u> (ישב Yashav Sit/Remain/Dwell) in their own land, which I gave to My servant Jacob.
2. And **they will <u>dwell</u>** (ישב Yashav Sit/Remain/Dwell) **safely** there,
3. **Build houses,**
4. And **plant vineyards**; yes,
5. They will <u>dwell</u> (ישב Yashav Sit/Remain/Dwell) securely/safely,
6. When **I execute judgments** on all those around them who despise them.
7. Then **they shall know that I am the Lord** their God

*"Coincidentally," the very first Hebrew word in Psalm 91 is ישב Yashav Sit/Remain/Dwell. He who dwells (ישב Yashav Sit/Remain/Dwell) in the secret place of the Most High shall abide under the shadow of the Almighty.*
## Psalm 91:1

It seems that ישב Yashav Sit/Remain/Dwell is the key to unlocking the sure promises of protection and provision of the LORD.

A few years ago, I was sitting in a waiting room worrying about a situation. I was so anxious and stressed to the point of restlessness and lack of peace. Then, I heard the voice of GOD in my spirit saying to me, "You are worrying for nothing!" At that moment, it was like I was awakened by an alarm of truth and prompted to just turn off my anxiety button and consciously chose to push the ישב Yashav Sit/Remain/Dwell button.

ישב Yashav Sit/Remain/Dwell is not an inaction. It actually takes more to sit, rest, and trust in GOD than to thrive on my own effort. The next day, I was led to a plaque in my living room that had been purchased for a gift that says, "Where GOD Guides, He Provides." It references Isaiah 58:11:

*The Lord will guide you continually, and satisfy your soul in drought, and strengthen your bones; You shall be like a watered garden, and like a spring of water, whose waters do not fail.*
**Isaiah 58:11**

Little did I know GOD meant that Word for me. About that situation that I was so anxious about, it turned out that I was really worried for nothing. Since that time, Father GOD reminded me over and over, "You are worrying for nothing." You know, I have learned not to waste a second of my life worrying for nothing. The LORD worked out situations beyond my understanding. When I ישב Yashav Sit/Remain/Dwell in His presence and know that when I surrender my will to His, I can be sure that He provides in every way for where I am, where He has guided me to.

Let's pray:

> Our Father in Heaven אבינו שבשמימ,
>
> YOU ARE THE LORD; YOU ARE LORD THE GLORY! Thank You for revealing to us what it means that You are THE LORD! Thank You for blessing us with every spiritual blessing in the heavenly places in Christ! We seek after You each day to know deeper what Your Name means to us so that we may walk in the fullness of all that You have provided for us. Teach us to ישב **Yashav Sit/Remain/Dwell** in Your presence, not strive on our own effort. We believe all that You have said that You do in our midst that You are indeed Our Provider and Protector in more ways than we can ever comprehend.
>
> B'Shem Yeshua HaMashiach בשם ישוע המשיח.
>
> In Jesus' Name we pray. Amen.

# 14. TORAH TASTING
## *REFLECTION*

1. What is the word, picture or theme the LORD is highlighting to you in this chapter and Torah Portion?

2. Fairy tales tell us Prince Charming rescues the Princess. What is your favorite Prince-Charming-rescuing-princess story/movie?

3. Have you ever been anxious in a situation and consumed by restlessness? What have you learned from how you handled it?

4. Psalm 91:1 says those who sit and remain in the LORD's secret place shall be under His protection. What are some things causing us anxiety that keeps us from resting in the LORD?

# 15 יה
## BO
## (Come)
### בא

Exodus 10:1-13:16

Jeremiah 46:13-28

John 19:13-28

Bo "Come" is the title of this week's Parasha. The title comes from the first verse of this Torah Portion.

*Now the Lord said to Moses, "Go in (בא Bo Come) to Pharaoh; for I have hardened his heart and the hearts of his servants, that I may show these signs of Mine before him, ² and that you may tell in the hearing of your son and your son's son the mighty things I have done in Egypt, and My signs which I have done among them, that you may know that I am the Lord."*
**Exodus 10:1-2**

This portion covers the last 3 of the 10 plagues in Egypt, the Passover story of Israel hastily leaving Egypt and their consecration of the Firstborn for the LORD.

After the back and forth of Moses petitioning to Pharoah, "Let my people go!" and the 10 plagues of GOD showing off His power, it is finally happening... Pharoah surrendered and let Moses have his way allowing the Hebrew slaves to go.

The first word the LORD said to Moses is בא Bo, that means come. It is translated in English as, "Go … to Pharoah…." There are other Hebrew words for "Go," but here בא Bo Come is used instead.

Why? "Come" is "Go"?

I know I have been told, "These are "just" words. Certain words are used in certain contexts for no particular reason. Don't read too much into it."

Over the years, I have learned that I am a literalist. I take GOD's Word literally. GOD is intentional in the words chosen to use in context, and I seek after Him and the messages He may have hidden to be found.

For one, when someone tells you, "Come!," they are already there. For example, when a father tells his toddler to come to him, he is inviting him to join him to be where he is. The LORD's words, "Come to Pharoah…" alludes to the fact that what GOD was telling Moses has already happened; he only needed to trust Him and follow. The LORD has already hardened Pharaoh's heart so that Moses later could tell his descendants the LORD's mighty work and they would know that He is the LORD.

If someone is in the middle of a struggle or crisis, hearing "Come" is like an invitation to get out of the current mess. Things are going to be ok.

## 15. BO / COME

*Now the Lord spoke to Moses and Aaron in the land of Egypt, saying, <sup>2</sup> "This month shall be your beginning of months; it shall be the <u>first month of the year</u> to you.*
**Exodus 12:1-3**

Happy New Year! The LORD instituted Passover as Israel's new year, freshly out of their desperation. I see some similarities between Chinese New Year and the Passover New Year, the Hebrew calendar New Year. As a child, I remember Chinese New Year being a big deal. Actually, it was the biggest "holiday" we observed, and still is today in Chinese communities around the world. My mom always bought my sister and me a new dress to wear for New Year. There are red lanterns, blessings written on red strips of paper hung on every wall and door. The 3 red wide stripes of blessings hung on every Chinese family's door post resemble the blood of the lamb GOD commanded His people to smear before the plague of the firstborns on the night of Passover.

*The Lord said to Moses and Aaron in Egypt, <sup>2</sup> "<u>This month is to be for you the first month, the first month of your year.</u> <sup>3</sup> Tell the whole community of Israel that on the tenth day of this month each man is to take a lamb[a] for his family, one for each household... Take care of them until the fourteenth day of the month, when all the members of the community of Israel must slaughter them at twilight. <sup>7</sup> <u>Then they are to take some of the blood and put it on the sides and tops of the doorframes of the houses where they eat the lambs</u>.*
**Exodus 12:1-3,6-7**

Although the origin of Chinese New Year is not necessarily biblical, the color red dominates everything... red clothing, red lanterns, red greetings,... . Red represents good luck and life. I suppose red is the color of blood, and life is in the blood. Only positive things and words of life are allowed out of our mouths. One year as an adult returning to Hong Kong to celebrate the New Year with my family, I came out of my room in a professional classic Navy-blue dress. It was my favorite dress. Mother greeted me in shock and horror. Her reaction to my dress might have given the impression that I'd just committed a capital crime. She was upset with me for days simply for wearing dark colors for New Year's. Times have changed a bit now about wearing dark colors. Nonetheless, there are many traditions we have come to expect and honor every Lunar New Year, like having a large feast at Grandmother's on Chinese New Year's Eve. Her cooking was better than any five-star restaurant, with delicacies even emperors would envy. Then, the next day, her place would be our first stop to visit to greet New Year's. We all spoke blessings over her. She gave us red packets (small envelopes stuffed with money) in exchange. I am not sure why she always had freshly fried cashews, along with other simple traditional dishes like rice congee, savory turnip cakes and fried chow mein noodles, ready for us. To this day, whenever I see or smell fried cashews, they remind me of New Year's at Grandmother's. The noise of festivity throughout the Chinese New Year probably matches the Hebrews' crossing the Red Sea.

Let me also paint the picture prior to the Chinese New Year, the most stressful time of the year. Many people try to make money, borrow money to provide abundance for the family for the New Year. I could really sense the anxiety in many around me up to the last day of the year. However, when the New year rolled around, being with family and friends, all stress and anxiety melted away. That brings me back to the invitation of "Come," this Parasha's title. Whatever the struggle, the LORD invites us to come to the other side where He awaits us. In the midst of challenges, we have the Hope of "Bo," Come, to know that there is a new beginning awaiting us on the other side.

Hardening of the Pharoah's heart is highlighted throughout Egypt's plagues.

> *Now the Lord said to Moses, "Go in (בא Bo Come) to Pharaoh; for I have hardened (כבד Kavad make heavy/weighty) his heart and the hearts of his servants, that I may show these signs of Mine before him…*
> **Exodus 10:1**

כבד Kavod translated as "harden" in this Torah Portion's first verse, means glory and honor. It is the weightiness of GOD in glory. This parasha begins with GOD telling Moses to come and reveal to him that Pharoah's heart had been made weighty, as if through Pharoah's hardened, weighted heart, the LORD is about to reveal His glory. The following verses further show that, indeed, the LORD would be honored through Pharoah's hardened heart.

A different Hebrew word is used in describing GOD's hardening of Pharaoh's heart.

> *Then I will harden (חזק Chazak Strengthen) Pharaoh's heart, so that he will pursue them; and I will gain honor (כבד Kavad make heavy/weighty /honor) over Pharaoh and over all his army, that the Egyptians may know that I am the Lord." And they did so...*
> *¹⁷ And I indeed will harden (חזק Chazak Strengthen) the hearts of the Egyptians, and they shall follow them. So I will gain honor (כבד Kavad make heavy/weighty /honor) over Pharaoh and over all his army, his chariots, and his horsemen. ¹⁸ Then the Egyptians shall know that I am the Lord, when I have gained honor (כבד Kavad make heavy/weighty/honor) for Myself over Pharaoh, his chariots, and his horsemen."*
> **Exodus 14:4,17,18**

חזק Chazak means strength and strengthen. The word for "hardening" of Pharoah's heart in the following verses is חזק Chazak, as well as depicting the Egyptians urging and strengthening the Israelites to leave the land.

> *²⁰ But the Lord hardened (חזק Chazak Strengthen) Pharaoh's heart, and he did not let the children of Israel go... But the Lord hardened (חזק Chazak) Pharaoh's heart, and he would not let them go... And the Egyptians urged (חזק Chazak Strengthen) the people, that they might send them out of the land in haste.*
> **Exodus 10:20, 27, 12:33**

The LORD had to first חזק Chazak Strengthen/Harden Pharoah's heart before His people become strengthened חזק Chazak. And, He had to make Pharoah's heart weighty כבד Kavad, in order that the weightiness of His glory be revealed.

חזק Chazak reminds me of a modern-day Jewish tradition. Whenever we have completed the reading of one of the five books in the Torah, according to the Torah Portion schedule, we, as a congregation, recite:

*חזק חזק ונתחזק*
*Chazak, chazak, v'nitchazek.*

*Be Strong, Be Strong, & Let us Strengthen Each Other.*

Jewish traditions tell us this practice originates from the words the LORD spoke to him when Joshua had completed reading the Torah with the Torah scroll in his hand:

> *⁶ Be strong (חזק Chazak) and courageous, because you will lead these people to inherit the land I swore to their ancestors to give them. "Be strong (חזק Chazak) and very courageous. Be careful to obey all the law my servant Moses gave you; do not turn from it to the right or to the left, that you may be successful wherever you go. ⁸ Keep this Book of the Law always on your lips; meditate on it day and night, so that you may be careful to do everything written in it. Then you will be prosperous and successful. Have I not commanded you? Be strong (חזק Chazak) and of good courage; do not be afraid, nor be dismayed, for the Lord your God is with you wherever you go.*
> **Joshua 1:6-9**

After reading GOD's Word, we should feel strong and strengthened. The word חזק Chazak is repeated 3 times as we loudly proclaim, "Be Strong, Be Strong, & Let us Strengthen Each Other" with GOD and with one another, just as the LORD commanded Joshua to be strong 3 times. It truly is a powerful declaration echoing the LORD's words. Every time we make that proclamation as a congregation in unison in the synagogue, I could feel the building shake with our conviction and profession of faith. Completing the reading of a book in the Torah and anticipating the reading of the next book makes us strong and provides us with the strength to impart to those around us too.

There is something fascinating in the 10th plague of the death of the firstborn.

*Then the Lord spoke to Moses, saying,* [2] *"Consecrate⁽ᵃ⁾ to Me all the firstborn, whatever opens the womb among the children of Israel, both of man and beast; it is Mine."*
**Exodus 13:1-2**

[15] *"Everything that first opens the womb of all flesh, which they bring to the Lord, whether man or beast, shall be yours; nevertheless the firstborn of man you shall surely redeem, and the firstborn of unclean animals you shall redeem.* [16] *And those redeemed of the devoted things you shall <u>redeem when one month old, according to your valuation, for five shekels of silver</u>, according to the shekel of the sanctuary, which is twenty gerahs.*
**Numbers 18:15-16**

The LORD bought life to His people with the death of the firstborn in Egypt. Then, He said that the firstborn of Israel, from animals to humans, belong to Him.

GOD did not want the sacrifice of our firstborns, but He asked for silver, deemed valuable to us, as redemption. Today, in certain sects of Judaism, there is a ritual called Pidyon HaBen, Redemption of the Son. Although we did not perform this ritual with our firstborn son, I learned that when preparing for Matthew's Bris, circumcision ceremony when he was a newborn. On the 31st day of the newborn, his/her parents present their newborn to the rabbi. According to the Torah, this newborn opening a womb, boy or girl, belongs to the LORD. The father then redeems/buys back his child from the LORD with 5 shekels of silver.

Spiritually speaking, all our children belong to the LORD. We are just given the privilege to raise them. I would not want to buy them back or remove them from the LORD because I need Him to raise them with me, something I can never do on my own. However, the ceremony signifies that our children belong to the LORD and their lives were bought for a price. We acknowledge GOD is our Deliverer. The LORD is the only One that gives and sustains life. We honor Him and publicly declare that He is the One that our firstborns belong to.

The ultimate redemption is that the LORD paid and redeemed for our eternal life with His own Firstborn, the Mashiach, our Messiah.

> *Also, I will make him My firstborn,*
> *The highest of the kings of the earth.*
> **Psalm 89:27**

> *He is the image of the invisible God, the firstborn over all creation.*
> **Colossians 1:15**

> [29] *For whom He foreknew, He also predestined to be conformed to the image of His Son, that He might be the firstborn among many brethren.*
> **Romans 8:29**

This life that GOD's firstborn redeemed for me is not own.

> [19] *Do you not know that your bodies are temples of the Holy Spirit, who is in you, whom you have received from God? You are not your own;* [20] *you were bought at a price. Therefore honor God with your bodies.*
> **1 Corinthians 6:19-20**

> [0] *I have been crucified with Christ; it is no longer I who live, but Christ lives in me; and the life which I now live in the flesh I live by faith in the Son of God, who loved me and gave Himself for me.*
> **Galatians 2:20**

## 15. BO / COME

When things seem worse that is supposed to get better, like the LORD's hardening Pharoah's heart in order to accomplish His plans, we need to trust the process even when it looks illogical. In the last 3 plagues, locusts, darkness and death of the firstborn seem to reflect Genesis 1's chaos, darkness and hope of birthing of light. We have a choice to make each day to see what GOD invites us to see. Let's accept His invitation of בו Bo "Come" and see what awaits us on the other side, the dawning of a new season, and anticipation of the joy that comes with the New Year.

Let's pray:

**Our Father in Heaven אבינו שבשמים,**

Thank You for Your invitation of Bo "Come" that we will go forth boldly partnering with You to do Your will. In reading and receiving Your Word, we are strong and able to strengthen those around us. You have good plans for us and we trust the process even if we do not understand. We are blessed that You have instituted the New Year and new seasons. LORD, teach us to not be anxious in challenging times at the end of the year but to know that joy is just right around the corner. Let Your Hope be the anchor to our souls.

B'Shem Yeshua HaMashiach בשם ישוע המשיח.

In Jesus' Name we pray. Amen.

# 15. TORAH TASTING
## *REFLECTION*

1. What is the word, picture or theme the LORD is highlighting to you in this chapter and Torah Portion?

2. What are some of your favorite memories of starting a new year, a new school year, or beginning a new year on your birthday?

3. How have you been encouraged at the dawning of a new season that brought about renewed hope?

4. When you feel mentally or spiritually weak, what are some things that may bring you strength and refreshment (i.e., call a friend, take a walk, listen to a particular song, ...)?

# 16 יו
# Beshalach
## (When He Sent)
## בשלח

Exodus 13:17 — 17:16

Judges 4:4 — 5:31

Matthew 14:22 — 33

This week's Parasha (Torah Portion) begins with, "When Pharaoh let the people go, GOD did not lead them by way of the land of the Philistines, although that was near… ". First of all, the word "beshalach" comes from the 3-letter Hebrew root שלח "Shalach," meaning to send. Pharaoh reluctantly "let" G-d's people go. To me, the underlining meaning is the people were sent out from the word שלח Shalach. Maybe not so much that Pharaoh "let" GOD's people go, but it is that GOD sent His people out.

This Parasha recounts the story of the Children of Israel leaving Egypt, being delivered out of the bondage of slavery, finally. Moses and GOD's people brought the bones of Joseph with him, as promised. One last epic miracle of the Exodus is the splitting of the Red Sea, as it was famously depicted in Charles Heston's movie of the Passover story. The Children of Israel arrived on the other side of the Red Sea while the Egyptian army was being drowned in the sea. The Hebrews then began to sing the Song of Moses in victory.

Wait a minute, we can safely assume that Moses wrote the Song of Moses, but how did everyone know the words to sing it in unison? I mean, we have modern technology today to project lyrics on a screen, but they did not.

Interesting thought!

Maybe the LORD gave Moses the words to write. And He also clued that in every person to sing along. Nonetheless, it is a long, triumphant song boasting of GOD's mighty works on Israel's behalf. There are only a few songs outside of the Book of Psalm recorded in the Bible, and this is one of them.

Fascinating… there is a song recorded in the coinciding Haftorah Portion with this Torah Portion. Judges 5:1-31 is a song of Victory by Deborah, prophetess and judge. This song was sung after the Israeli victory over the Canaanite army by Deborah and Barak. Again, Deborah might have prepped Barak of the lyrics before singing it together. Prior to their win in Judges 4, Deborah summoned Barak to fight and defeat Sisera, the Commander of the Canaanite army, saying,

> *"Has not the Lord, the God of Israel, commanded you, 'Go, gather your men at Mount Tabor, taking 10,000 from the people of Naphtali and the people of Zebulun. And I will draw out Sisera, the general of Jabin's army, to meet you by the river Kishon with his chariots and his troops, and I will <u>give him into your hand</u>'?."*
> **Judges 4:6-7**

But Barak's response to Deborah was,

> *"If you will go with me, I will go, but if you will not go with me, I will not go."*
> **Judges 4:8**

What a wimp! But this is where it gets good… with Deborah's response to Barak's lack of courage…

> "And she said, "I will surely go with you. Nevertheless, the road on which you are going will not lead to your glory, <u>for the Lord will sell Sisera into the hand of a woman."</u>
> **Judges 4:9**

Deborah responded with a prophetic word of what was to come. Jael was a Kenite woman, descendent of Jethro. Jethro/Yitro is Moses' father-in-law. I find this connection intriguing. Moses delivered the Children of Israel out of Egypt; and now his father-in-law's descendent… a woman… someone ordinary outside of the twelve tribes of Israel… would have more boldness and courage than an Israelite military leader and warrior to deliver Israel from the 20-year oppression of the Canaanites!

What a story!

> *When Ehud was dead, the children of Israel again did evil in the sight of the Lord. ² So the Lord sold them into the hand of Jabin king of Canaan, who reigned in Hazor. The commander of his army was* **Sisera***, who dwelt in* **Harosheth Hagoyim***. ³ And the children of Israel cried out to the Lord; for Jabin had nine hundred chariots of iron, and for twenty years he had harshly oppressed the children of Israel… And Barak called Zebulun and Naphtali to* **Kedesh***; he went up with ten thousand men under his command, and Deborah went up with him.*
> **Judges 4:1-3,10**

> *Now Heber the Kenite, of the children of Hobab the father-in-law of Moses, had separated himself from the Kenites and pitched his tent near the terebinth tree at Zaanaim, which is beside* **Kedesh***.*
> **Judges 4:11**

*And they reported to Sisera that Barak the son of Abinoam had gone up to Mount Tabor. <sup>13</sup> So Sisera gathered together all his chariots, nine hundred chariots of iron, and all the people who were with him, from* **Harosheth Hagoyim** *to the River* **Kishon**.
**Judges 4:12-13**

The names of the battle locations mentioned seem to hint at us the LORD's strategy for His people.

- Harosheth Hagoyim (Hebrew root חרש Charash/Jeweler or engraver) — Jeweler of the nations (goyim is nations others than Israel)
- Kedesh — (Hebrew root קדש Kodesh) Sacredness/Holiness
- Kishon — (Hebrew root קוש Qush) Lure/bait

Notice how these Hebrew words seem to have similar alphabets? Here's one more clue word with a similar connection tucked in the Song of Deborah…

*They chose new (חדשים Chadashim) gods; Then there was war in the gates; Not a shield or spear was seen among forty thousand in Israel.*
**Judges 5:8**

- Chadashim — (Hebrew root is חדש Chadash) New


Fascinating!

The LORD heard His people's cry for help. He brought the enemy (representing the nations) out of the place of treasures and gems (where jewelers gathered) and lured them into a new place, a place of sacredness and holiness. It is in this new place of holiness that the enemy is destroyed!

So, here is how the story goes… Barak pursued Sisera with 10,000 men to Harosheth-Hagoyim. All of Sisera's army was slaughtered, and not a man was left. On his way fleeing away from Barak, Jael invited Sisera, the Canaanite general, into her tent. He asked for water; then she gave him a noble's bowl of milk. When Sisera fell asleep, Jael took a tent peg and drove it into his temple and killed him. He died at her feet. Tikva Frymer-Kensky of Jewish Women's Archive paints a fascinating imagery: Jael offered Sisera milk. Milk signifies nurturing, something a mother would offer her child out of care. She served the milk in a noble's bowl, signifying honor. This deceptive tactic led to Sisera dropping his guard and his eventual horrific murder. Sisera died at her feet, a sinister parody of something that likens a childbirth (www.jwa.org, Jael-Bible). Jael's heroic act was nothing short of tremendous wisdom and strength, risking her own life to save Israel, a battle she just happened to stumble upon and won. Jael's killing Sisera not only brought defeat to the murdered military commander, but also humiliation to Israel's General Barack, who failed to carry out the mission. Without her knowledge, Jael's bravery fulfilled Deborah's prophetic word of Judges 4:9.

*So she said, "I will surely go with you; nevertheless there will be no glory for you in the journey you are taking, for the Lord will sell Sisera into the hand of a woman."*
**Judges 4:9**

But wait… there's more…

Deborah told Barak when charging him to fight Sisera that the LORD would <u>give him into his hand</u>. But when he wouldn't go without her, she prophesied,

"The road on which you are going will not lead to your glory, <u>for the Lord will **sell** Sisera into the hand of a woman.</u>"

With Barak's refusal to go boldly, the offer of the LORD's <u>giving</u> the enemy into his hand is now off. The LORD would now <u>sell</u> the enemy into a woman's hand. Deborah could've said "deliver" or "give" but instead, "sell"? The root word here is "מכר machar," as in Esau "מכר machar" / sold his birthright to Jacob, as in Joseph being "מכר machar" sold by his brothers. The word use of selling something in exchange for something is not to be overlooked. The selling/destruction of the enemy of Jael brought the gain or exchange for the victory of Israel, leading to the birth of the nation's new season after an oppressive era.

Jael was called "The Most Blessed of Women" in the Song of Deborah. That is the title of an unlikely national heroine!

> "<u>Most blessed among women is Jael,</u>
> The wife of Heber the Kenite;
> Blessed is she among women in tents.
> **Judges 5:24**

Deborah also concluded her song with a declaration,

> "*Thus let all Your enemies perish, O LORD! But let those who love Him be like the sun When it comes out in full strength." So the land had rest for forty years.*"
> **Judges 5:31**

All these came to be due to one ordinary woman's courage to destroy the enemy.

Now, let's talk about the Songs of Victory. We have the Song of Moses, the Song of Deborah, there is also a song of Victory that is found in the Book of Revelation.

> "*And I saw what appeared to be a sea of glass mingled with fire — and also <u>those who had conquered the beast and its image and the number of its name,</u> standing beside the sea of glass with harps of God in their hands. <u>And they sing the song of Moses, the servant of God, and the song of the Lamb</u>…*"
> **Revelation 15:2-3**

The third song of Victory is the Song of the Lamb, sung by those who have conquered the enemy in an epic battle in the Book of Revelation.

Wait…There is one more little song sung in the Torah, and it is in this Torah Portion. After Moses had sung the Song of Moses with the people of Israel, his prophetess sister, Miriam, led all the women singing with tambourines and dancing, praising the LORD of His triumphant deliverance.

> *"Sing to the Lord, for he has triumphed gloriously;*
> *the horse and his rider he has thrown into the sea."*
> **Exodus 15:21**

Miriam singing this short song of triumph after the Red Sea moment is an incredible thanksgiving praise of GOD fulfilling His deliverance promise. Her words were a response echoing her brother's words. Exodus 15:20 calls her "Miriam the prophetess, Aaron's sister." Jewish traditions, the Midrash, tell us that as a child, Miriam had prophesied that her mother would give birth to the future redeemer of Israel. Then, Miriam saw GOD providing a way to save her baby brother in Exodus 1. More than 80 years later, she finally witnessed GOD's faithfulness bringing the prophetic word to pass right before her eyes. That definitely would call for a huge celebration.

What happened next is nothing short of remarkable, the Israelites went into the wilderness of Shur and found no water, but they came to a place named Marah (which means bitter) because the water was bitter. Then, the LORD made the water sweet and drinkable.

> *So Moses brought Israel from the Red Sea; then they went out into the Wilderness of Shur. And they went three days in the wilderness and found no water. ²³ Now when they came to Marah, they could not drink the waters of Marah, for they were bitter. Therefore the name of it was called **Marah**… So he cried out to the Lord, and the Lord showed him a tree. When he cast it into the waters, the waters were made sweet.*
> **Exodus 15:22-23,25**

This incident happened right after Miriam's rejoicing of GOD's goodness. Jewish traditions connect Miriam with the water-provision in the wilderness. Consequentially, her death also led to the end of Israel's water supply.

> *In the first month, the whole Israelite community arrived at the Desert of Zin, and they stayed at Kadesh. There <u>Miriam died</u> and was buried. Now <u>there was no water</u> for the community, and the people gathered in opposition to Moses and Aaron.*
> **Numbers 20:1-2**

Miriam is the first woman with the title "prophetess" in the entire Torah. She was an influential leader throughout Israel's forty-year wilderness journey. Her witnessing and celebration of GOD's goodness brought forth GOD's provision. Deborah's godly leadership, Jael's fearless courage to Miriam's unwavering faith, singing words of triumph inspire GOD's people throughout generations.

> *Giving thanks always for all things to God the Father in the name of our Lord Jesus Christ*
> **Ephesians 5:20**

> *Rejoice always, $^{17}$ pray without ceasing, $^{18}$ in everything give thanks; for this is the will of God in Christ Jesus for you*
> **1 Thessalonians 5:16-18**

(Credit: jwa.org, Miriam Midrash and Aggadah. Torah.org, Chukas)

## 16. BESHALACH / WHEN HE SENT

Let's pray:

**Our Father in Heaven** אבינו שבשמימ,

We are thankful for Your written Word in the Torah. We ask You to open our eyes as we continue to seek You and Your righteousness. We ask You to inspire more Songs of Victory with Your miraculous work in our lives. LORD, give us courage, boldness, and strategy to further Your Kingdom, defeating the enemy as You have led Jael to do for Israel. Let us sing praises to Your Name that bitter water would turn sweet. Hearing and Obeying Your voice would bring wholeness and health to our lives when we declare, "You Are Our LORD, Our Healer."

B'Shem Yeshua HaMashiach בשם ישוע המשיח.

In Jesus' Name, we pray.

# 16. TORAH TASTING
## *REFLECTION*

1. What is the word, picture or theme the LORD is highlighting to you in this chapter and Torah Portion?

2. What stands out to you in the stories of Miriam, Deborah and Jael?

3. Can you think of an incident or story you have heard or experienced that GOD turned a bitter situation into a sweet one?

4. How can we rejoice and give thanks in the midst of a struggle? What are some practical ways that can help us do that?

# 17 יז
# YITRO
## (Jethro)
יתרו

Exodus 18:1 — 20:23

ISAIAH 6:1-7:6, 9:5-6

Matthew 19:16-26

The Ten Commandments are nicely tucked in the middle of this Parsha named Yitro. Yitro (Jethro) is Moses' Father-in-law that came with Moses' daughter, Zipporah, and their two sons to meet Moses after the Exodus in the wilderness at the mount of God. Yitro (a Midianite priest) was not an Israelite, but after hearing the miraculous deliverance of the LORD, he "became a believer"!

Exodus 18:11 describes Yitro's response after hearing the testimony of God's mighty hand for His people —

> *"Now I know that <u>the Lord is greater than all gods</u>, because in this affair they dealt arrogantly with the people." And Yitro, **Moses' father-in-law**, brought a burnt offering and sacrifices to God; and Aaron came with all the elders of Israel to eat bread with Moses' father-in-law before God."*

Yitro was a descendent of Midian, a son of Abraham from his second wife, Keturah. Midianites were later known to be idolaters. So, it was no small matter that a Midianite priest worshipped the LORD and declared His greatness after hearing all that GOD had done.

Here is the sequence of events in this Parasha:

1. Yitro, Moses' father-in-law, came and worshipped the LORD in response to HIS Goodness.
2. Yitro observed and advised Moses, "It is not good" to judge this way. Moses listened and executed new strategies of judging God's people. Yitro's job was done, and he departed.
3. Purification and sanctification of the Children of Israel as "the Bride" to prepare themselves to receive the gift of GOD's Word, the Commandments.
4. Another EPIC event in Jewish history… SHAVUOT — A Sacred Covenant, The Ultimate Wedding Event, exchanging of vows. "I will be YOUR GOD, and you will be my people!"

Do you see the interesting connection between these events? The introduction of Moses' father-in-law is as if the theme of <u>marriage</u> is ushering in the upcoming Wedding of all weddings in World history. This may seem random, but I do not believe in random. Please stay with me… Yitro saw how Moses worked ineffectively, and he exclaimed, "This is not good." This phrase echoes GOD's words when he had just made Adam, His masterpiece. The creation of Adam's wife, Eve, would make what was "not good" to be "good." It seems that GOD was about to make something "not good" good here too. A new system of leadership delegation was to be set up to judge GOD's people, which relieved Moses of a more important assignment. After Yitro did what he came to do, Moses was instructed by the LORD to tell the children of Israel to purify and sanctify themselves and be ready for the BIG event at the Mount of GOD, the defining moment in Jewish History. The Revelation at Mt. Sinai was a tumultuous awe-inspiring experience. The entire Universe, our Sages remarked, trembled with the piercing sound of the ram's horn. Thunder and lightning filled the skies. Then — Silence. Not a bird chirped. No creature spoke. The seas did not stir. Even the angels ceased to fly, as the voice was heard: "I am the L-rd your G-d..." In Exodus, his is the First Shavuot (means weeks) /Pentecost (50) / Feast of Weeks, 50 days after Passover. All creation became silent before the big moment (Shavuot). A prequel of the Spirit of the LORD was given in the upper room after Yeshua Jesus' resurrection and ascension well over a thousand years later.

At Mount Sinai, a Holy Nation, a Nation of priesthood was born. Some sects of Jews say they are married to the Law/Torah since the Law was given at this time. The LORD refers to His people as His Bride in Jeremiah 2:2 —

*"Go and shout this message to Jerusalem.*
*This is what the Lord says: 'I remember how eager you were to please me as <u>a young bride</u> long ago, how you loved me and followed me even through the barren wilderness.'"*

The LORD uses the metaphor of a Bride for Israel to describe His relationship with them/her. Since we, followers of Christ, have been grafted into the Olive Tree, we also share the intimate marriage relationship with The LORD.

While it is a covenant made between the LORD and His people corporately as one, it is significant to note that the Ten Commandments, as a whole, is quite a personal covenant between the LORD and each one of us, individually. Here is what I mean, the Ten Commandments are directed to each individual encountering the LORD, rather than a group.

For example, Exodus 20:2 says,

> *"I am the Lord <u>your</u> God,*
> *who brought <u>you</u> out of the land of Egypt,*
> *out of the house of slavery."*
> **Exodus 20:2**

The "your" and "you" in this verse and every verse in the Ten Commandments are in the second-person singular form. It is a covenant intimately established between two parties, much like the Ketubah (a Jewish wedding contract). Isn't that great to know that we do not get lost in a crowd? But instead, the Creator of the Universe wants to be Your personal GOD, Your Provider of every need, Your Protector from all harm?

This Parasha contains one of the most monumental moments in the Torah, and yet it isא given an ordinary title named after an ordinary Midian priest, Yitro? Why? …

When mentioning Yitro in the Torah, readers are repeatedly reminded of his role — "Moses' father-in-law" in setting up the Big Wedding event. I cannot help but wonder if even his name would give us some hints of the context being expressed. The name "Yitro" comes from the Hebrew root verb of "Yatar" (יתר), which means remain over, remaining, or remnant. Those, who stay with the LORD and would not give up on Him no matter what are often referred to as His remnant.

> "And it shall come to pass that <u>he who is left</u> in Zion and <u>remains</u>
> (הַנּוֹתָר) in Jerusalem will be called holy —
> everyone who is recorded among the living in Jerusalem.
> When the Lord has washed away the filth of the daughters of Zion,
> and purged the blood of Jerusalem from her midst,
> by the spirit of judgment and by the spirit of burning,
> then the Lord will create above every dwelling place of Mount Zion,
> and above her assemblies, a cloud and smoke by day and the shining
> of a flaming fire by night.
> For over all the glory there will be a covering.
> And there will be a tabernacle for shade in the daytime
> from the heat, for a place of refuge,
> and for a shelter from storm and rain.
> Isaiah 4:3-6

This is a prophetic picture of what GOD would do with the remnant, those who remain and have not left nor lost faith and hope in the LORD. They would be under GOD's supernatural protection, shielded from harm. The remnant who may seem ordinary, but yet extraordinary in the eyes of GOD!

Does the imagery described in those verses look familiar? Does it look like what we have seen the LORD provide for His people in the Wilderness? The cloud and smoke by day, fire by night, His glory as covering? These are visuals we see when the Post-Exodus Wilderness experience comes to mind. Also, "For over all the glory there will be a covering" in verse 5 reminds us of the Chuppah (canopy) at a Jewish wedding ceremony. It represents "GOD ABOVE" as well as His presence over the covenant marriage. Just like His Presence, the LORD's steadfast love is constant to His people.

Shavuot, the Feast of Weeks, also known as Pentecost, is one of the only 3 Feasts of the LORD commanded for the Jerusalem pilgrimage. It is a major feast, no doubt. From Passover counting up 7 weeks to Shavuot calls for "Counting the Omer."

> "'From the day after the Sabbath, the day you brought the sheaf of the wave offering, count off seven full weeks. ¹⁶ <u>Count off fifty days up to the day after the seventh Sabbath, and then present an offering of new grain to the Lord.</u> ¹⁷ From wherever you live, <u>bring two loaves made of two-tenths of an ephah of the finest flour, baked with yeast, as a wave offering of firstfruits to the Lord.</u> ¹⁸ Present with this bread seven male lambs, each a year old and without defect, one young bull and two rams. They will be a burnt offering to the Lord, together with their grain offerings and drink offerings — a food offering, an aroma pleasing to the Lord. ¹⁹ Then sacrifice one male goat for a sin offering and two lambs, each a year old, for a fellowship offering. ²⁰ The priest is to wave the two lambs before the Lord as a wave offering, together with the bread of the firstfruits. They are a sacred offering to the Lord for the priest. ²¹ On that same day you are to proclaim a sacred assembly and do no regular work. This is to be a lasting ordinance for the generations to come, wherever you live. "'When you reap the harvest of your land, do not reap to the very edges of your field or gather the gleanings of your harvest. Leave them for the poor and for the foreigner residing among you. I am the Lord your God.'"
> **Leviticus 23:15-22**

The last verse about leaving the gleanings of the harvest for the poor is the backdrop of a fascinating Redeemer story in the Book of Ruth. Nevertheless, the modern practice of counting the omer each day for 50 days is an act of thanksgiving for what GOD has done and of anticipation of what He is about to do during Shavuot. It is a special time for us to reawaken and strengthen our special relationship with The LORD. We can do so by rededicating ourselves to the observance and study of GOD's word. Pentecost/Shavuot Eve is devoted to the study of the Torah. Jewish traditions say that the Israelites slept in on the day that GOD gave the Law/Torah on Mt. Sinai. In order to make up for this, some Jewish people stay up all night studying the Torah. Shavuot can be seen as the wedding day of Israel to GOD, sealing the eternal covenant. Furthermore, every morning, we can renew our vows with the LORD as Our Bridegroom, receiving Him as our sole Provider and Protector in exchange for our wholehearted devotion to Him.

Many commentaries have been written on GOD's tremendous gift of the Ten Commandments in regard to Yitro. But here I would like to leave you with two points. It is vital to be in self-reflection and sanctification of solemnness when we ask and prepare to receive revelations from the LORD. When we ask Him for His Word and insights, do we approach with a pure heart, understanding the sacredness and honor to come before our FATHER GOD? Lastly, through the LORD Yeshua Jesus Christ, we are the remnant when we answer "the call" and say yes to His commission to go and make disciples of all nations (Matthew 28:19-20).

Let's never give up hope and never give in to adversity.

For WE ARE the Remnant!

**Let's pray:**

> **Our Father in Heaven אבינו שבשמימ,**
>
> Thank You for the Torah, a life-manual with instructions to live an abundant life. We are eternally grateful for the covenant You have made with us. We individually declare, "I am forever Yours, and You are forever mine." In times of stress, LORD, please help us with our unbelief so that we may stand firm on Your promises and not lose faith. We are the remnant and we will remain and stand to see Your incomparable Glory.
>
> B'Shem Yeshua HaMashiach בשם ישוע המשיח.
>
> In Jesus' Name we pray. Amen.

# 17. TORAH TASTING
## *REFLECTION*

1. What is the word, picture or theme the LORD is highlighting to you in this chapter and Torah Portion?

2. Moses needed help without even realizing it. GOD sent help through Yitro, his father-in-law. Have you ever received unexpected help that you were amazed at GOD's gracious Providence?

3. Yitro heard Moses' testimony of the Exodus from Egypt and worshipped GOD. Do you have a story to tell that would direct others to marvel at GOD's goodness?

4. There is a solemnness when approaching the Word of GOD, any practical suggestions we can be reminded of that?

5. Shavuot (Feast of Weeks) is in the spring harvest season, a time of Thanksgiving. What are you thankful for today? What are you bringing before the LORD anticipating and expecting him to show off his faithfulness?

# 18 יח
# mishpatim
## (Judgments)
משפטים

Exodus 21:1-24:18

Jeremiah 34:8-22

Matthew 26:20-30

Mishpatim, translated as judgment or laws, is the title of this Torah Portion. It comes from the first verse of this Parasha.

> *"These are the <u>laws</u> you are to set before them:...*
> **Exodus 21:1**

This portion covers the laws regarding slavery, violence, justice and property, as well as various religious practices. It also includes the feasts of the LORD, weekly Shabbats, Sabbatical Year and the covenant GOD made with His people.

Slavery has been around since ancient world civilizations. When we think about that wicked word, inhumane treatment and abuse come to mind. No one dares to defend slavery in our times. It is wrong, vile and evil.

Case closed!

Period!

It is a hard topic for GOD's Children to reconcile a merciful GOD to allowing slavery, and even mentioning it in the Torah when the Law was given. There may be a good explanation for that. I am going to attempt to explore this sensitive topic with an open mind and proper context.

עוד Eved (male), שפחה Shivchah (female) and Eved עוד were used as servants or maids in the Torah, even as referred to those who were not Hebrews. There is no specific word for slaves in Hebrew. They were referred to as servants. Genesis 16:1 calls Hagar, Abram and Sarai's Egyptian female servant (שפחה Shivchah). Eliezer, in Genesis 24, called himself Abraham's servant (עוד Eved).

We do see a little distinction in Exodus 1:13-14 describing the beginning of the Children of Israel being enslaved by the Egyptians as "the Egyptians made the sons of Israel serve (from עוד Eved) with rigor." In some English translations, this verse became "they were made into slaves." Then, in verse 14, "The Egyptians made their lives bitter with hard labor or service (from עוד Eved)." So, to set apart the harsh treatment of the Hebrews, words of rigor and bitter were used so that readers could see they were not mere servants. They were treated harshly.

This Parashat Mishpatim begins with the law, standards that GOD wanted to give His children to live by. Exodus 21:1,2,7:

## 18. MISHPATIM / JUDGMENTS

*"Now these are the rules (משפטים Mishpatim, judgments, ordinances) that you shall set before them. If you <u>buy a Hebrew servant</u> (עֶבֶד Eved), six years he shall serve: and <u>in the seventh he shall go out free for nothing</u>.... When a man sells his daughter as a slave/servant (אָמָה Amah), she shall not go out as the male slaves (from עֶבֶד Eved) do."*

In the days of Moses, people were bought and sold for labor in households. Is that moral? No. But that was what it was, a norm. Were slaves abused? Absolutely they were. But in the Torah, the LORD clearly commanded His people to be kind and fair to their servants, unlike their pagan neighbors. First of all, it is heart-wrenching to see a father selling his daughter to be a servant. Sadly, it is still happening today. Life must be so hard for a father for him to do that. But wait...

Let's look at how servanthood may be different in those days. Let's suppose someone has served a wealthy household for six years, then is set free. Would you think that he/she has learned skills and acquired knowledge that he/she would not have otherwise? Probably.

This person would be elevated to a higher status, start a business or work for someone else with acquired skills under their belt.

Fathers who sold their daughters as a servant knew they would have a better life. In addition, when a young girl serves in a rich household, she has a chance to marry up. Yes, possibly as one of the many wives or concubines. Moreover, their children would enjoy equal status with others' children in the households. The Torah offers many examples of such. The twelve tribes of Israel came from Jacob's wives and their servants. Jacob's sons, birthed by his servants, were given blessings and inheritance as his wives' sons were. However, modern-day slavery is not so.

Purchased servants/slaves were not meant to be owned for life, according to GOD's commandments. They were to be set free after six years. Exodus 21:5 gives us a scenario that when slaves were freed but chose to stay. They could stay forever with their master because they "love their master."

Now, that's a concept. Why would anyone in their right mind choose to remain a slave, given the opportunity to be free? Would life possibly be better as a slave than a free person?

The Apostle Paul mentioned the word "slave" 8 times in Romans 6. He said in verse 15:

*"Do you not know that if you present yourselves to anyone* as obedient slaves, you are slaves of the one whom you obey, either of sin, which leads to death, or of obedience, which leads to righteousness?" *We are either slaves to sin or slaves to righteousness. When we proclaim the LORD Yeshua Jesus as our Savior, we become slaves to righteousness from slaves to sin.* "But now that you have been set free from sin and have become slaves of God, the fruit you get leads to sanctification and its end, eternal life."
**Romans 6:22**

The Good news is being slaves/servants to righteousness and to GOD has the benefit of eternal life. And He is a Good Master.

Everyone believes in something; even atheists do. They believe that there is no god, or some of them believe in science, just like worshiping a god. We all live by a set of beliefs. Those of us that believe in the LORD, we try to live by His Word. We serve to please Him. We believe it when He tells us that He is our Provider, and we are blessed as we trust in Him, … etc. Even atheists are guided by certain beliefs. Some of them believe in the Big Bang Theory or hold the humanistic point of view. They make decisions, process thoughts and ideas through the viewpoint that has been introduced, tried and adopted. Whether we like it, know it or care to admit it, we all serve a Master. Some serve the LORD, others material things. This is what Yeshua Jesus talked about serving a Master:

> *"No one can serve two masters, for either he will hate the one and love the other, or he will be devoted to the one and despise the other. You cannot serve God and money."*
> **Matthew 6:24**

We serve the Best Master, who wants the best for us. He has called us friends and His children.

My mom used to have a few businesses in Mainland China, that include a small hotel and a few restaurants. The dormitory was provided for her employees, who were servers and cooks. Most of her employees came from faraway towns seeking employment, with families miles and miles away. Mom treated them like they were her own children. She developed and mentored them. A few met their future mates while working for Mom. Some are now married for many years with grown children. A few went on to become entrepreneurs themselves. Many years later, now and then, when Mom goes to visit them, they still reminisce about her kindness from years before. They now repay Mom with gratitude for her motherly love by refusing to take money for her patronage. I witnessed firsthand how Mom cared for her employees many times, not as servants but as children and friends.

> *"No longer do I call you servants, for the servant does not know what his master is doing; but I have called you friends, for all that I have heard from my Father I have made known to you."*
> **John 15:15**

> *"The Spirit himself bears witness with our spirit that we are children of God, and if children, then heirs — heirs of God and fellow heirs with Christ, provided we suffer with him in order that we may also be glorified with him."*
> **Romans 8:16**

Not only the LORD turned us from servants into His friends and children, He also made us co-heirs to rule and reign with Him, alongside

Yeshua Jesus. That is some Crazy Love out of this world that the World does not understand.

Let's pray:

**Our Father in Heaven אבינו שבשמימ,**

Thank You for Your Torah and instructions for us to live by, that we may choose life in everything we say and do. We are grateful that You have called us out of sin into righteousness through Your Son Yeshua HaMashiach. You are a Good Master. You are a Good Friend and Father. LORD, please teach us Your ways as we seek Your Word, and that the world may know You as their Good Father too.

B'Shem Yeshua HaMashiach בשם ישוע המשיח.

In Jesus' Name we pray. Amen.

# 18. TORAH TASTING
## *REFLECTION*

1. What is the word, picture or theme the LORD is highlighting to you in this chapter and Torah Portion?

2. Slavery is an ugly subject. Some are enslaved mentally that no one can see on the outside. What are some things that people can be enslaved by, spiritually or mentally? What are some real-life examples you can think of that people found freedom in GOD and were set free from enslavement?

3. We all have masters we serve, and what you devote your love, time, and resources to rules you (ex., money, job, addiction, children, etc.). Who/what is your master(s)? How is serving money or other little gods different from serving GOD? Do you have any personal stories that come to mind?

# 19 יט
## TERUMAH
## (Heave Offering)
### תרומה

Exodus 25:1-27:19

Kings 5:26-6:13

Mark 12:35-44

---

Parashat Terumah begins with, "And the LORD spoke to Moses, saying, "Speak to the Children of Israel, they bring me an offering. From everyone who gives it willingly with his heart, you shall take My offering. The Hebrew word Terumah (תרומה) means offering/to be lifted up. The Maker of heaven and earth, who owns all things seen and unseen, is more than capable to make His Sanctuary/Dwelling place all by Himself, with no help from mere humans. Yet, He chose to ask for an offering from His people in building The Tent of Meeting, the Tabernacle המשכן HaMishkan, the dwelling place.

Why?

As a parent, I know a thing or two about teaching our children a lesson by involving them being a part of what I do. Oftentimes, it is easier to accomplish a task all by myself rather than involve them. For example, I once asked our children to prepare a fish meal. We brought a whole fish home. That was our homeschool Home-Economics lesson of the day. I gave our son Matthew the job of scaling the fish, a dirty job, and it had to be done thoroughly. No one wants to eat fish with scales still attached to the skin. I showed our daughter Mollie how to fillet the fish and later make broth with the fish bones. The whole process took hours. It would've taken me, at most, half the time by myself. However, it was a fun learning experience for our children. The kids learned about the cooking process of preparing a meal, what goes in the dishes and why. We laughed at their mistakes. Was the fish prepared perfectly? No. Was it a mess? Sure, cleanup was not fun. But the process was a joy! In Parashat Terumah, the LORD detailed every component that would go into the building of the Tabernacle/Dwelling (HaMishkan) — the Outer Court, the Inner Court, and the Holy of Holies. The Tabernacle HaMishkan had to be mobile. The Israelites would need to break it down and take it up during those 40 years in the Wilderness. GOD's blueprint was painstakingly detailed, leaving none to chances or speculation. Measurements, colors, materials, positions, placements, and directions to face were described in such detail, leaving no room for questions. I believe the whole plan of the Tabernacle HaMishkan, from every element to its measurement, has spiritual significance, which deserves a complete study on. They are not just numbers and things that we should gloss over. There are plenty of insightful studies on the subject. What fascinates me is how the LORD first asked His children to give for this project and then showed them how to build it, that He would dwell in it. When you have "skin in the game," you'd feel more invested in it. Therefore, you would have a different attitude toward taking care of it than someone who had not done so.

The Mishkan Tabernacle is the physical structure and ultimate symbol of "GOD WITH US" (Emanu-EL). The GOD of Israel is in the midst of His people. There would be no separation. Wherever the LORD leads, His people follow. In a similar way that I instructed our children in preparing a meal with me and enjoying the process of working with them, I feel that the LORD delighted in having His children giving their hearts and efforts in building something they would enjoy being together. The Mishkan and later the Temple built by King Solomon are the earthly representation, like no other, of the ONE TRUE GOD indwelling with His people. The rituals of ceremonies, like washing and sacrifice-offering, were of tremendous spiritual significance and impact.

**These are some of the components of the Mishkan that stand out:**

- The Ark of the Testimony (hosting the two tablets of the Ten Commandments)
- The Mercy Seat
- The Menorah (Lamp Stand of 7 branches) of pure gold
- Ten curtains of fine woven linen and blue and purple and scarlet threads
- Bronze Pegs

The ark of the testimony hosting the Ten Commandments likens the Ketubah, the marriage contract, a covenant made between GOD/the Bridegroom and His Bride/His people. The Mercy Seat (where GOD meets with His people in the Holy of Holies) comes from the Hebrew word כפרת Kaporet, which means Propitiatory and has the power to atone. The Menorah is my favorite. To me, it is the ultimate symbol of the LORD's — the Everlasting Light presenting His perpetuating Presence with us. The ten curtains of fine woven linens and blue and purple and scarlet threads point to the separation between the Holy and the Holy of Holies. That costly separation one day would be torn to pieces to make a way for our redemption. The Bronze pegs are the strong support of the structure of the Mishkan, which point us to the judgment of the LORD instead of avoiding that. We have a different perspective about it — it indeed is a gift giving us strength; because with GOD's grace and His provided atonement, Judgment is now placed on the One that we put our faith and trust in!

*(Credit: www.bible-history.com/backd2/bronze.html)*

Bronze, naturally, is used in Scripture as the symbol of what is firm, stubborn, strong and enduring. People can be referred to as strong as bronze, yet GOD is more powerful.

*For **He has broken the gates of bronze**, and cut the bars of iron in two.*
**Psalm 107:16**

*"Arise and thresh, O daughter of Zion; for I will make your horn iron, and **I will make your hooves bronze**; You shall beat in pieces many peoples; I will consecrate their gain to the Lord, and their substance to the Lord of the whole earth.*
**Micah 4:13**

Bronze is also mentioned as GOD's judgment:

*And **your heavens which are over your head shall be bronze**, and the earth which is under you shall be iron. ²⁴ The Lord will change the rain of your land to powder and dust; from the heaven it shall come down on you **until you are destroyed**.*
**Deuteronomy 28:23-24**

When Moses raised the bronze serpent on a pole, it displayed the serpent's power as being judged through the raising of the Son of GOD, being represented by the bronze serpent:

*So Moses made a bronze serpent, and put it on a pole; and so it was, if a serpent had bitten anyone, when he looked at the bronze serpent, he lived.*
**Numbers 21:9**

*For He made Him who knew no sin to be sin for us, that we might become the righteousness of God in Him.*
**2 Corinthians 5:21**

# 19. TERUMAH / HEAVE OFFERING

*Now from the sixth hour until the ninth hour there was darkness over all the land.* [46] *And about the ninth hour Jesus cried out with a loud voice, saying, "Eli, Eli, lama sabachthani?" that is, "My God, My God, why have You forsaken Me?*
**Matthew 28:25-26**

*"Speak to the children of Israel, that they bring Me an offering. From everyone who gives it willingly with his heart you shall take My offering."*
**Exodus 25:2**

The Hebrew word כפרת Kaporet for offering also means to be lifted up, just like this Portion's title Terumah. Very interesting that the LORD asks His children to bring Him an offering, willingly with their hearts, that the priest takes the LORD's offering. I find that intriguing that when we make an offering to Him, essentially, it is "His" offering. All that we have belongs to GOD to begin with. He just wants to see if our devotion was to Him. Much like the Provision of a ram in place of Isaac when Abraham was asked to sacrifice his son, the Provision of Yeshua Jesus the Mashiach provided His own life to give us LIFE.

The offering we lift up is a small price we willingly give to the LORD to be a part of a grander project of community and in communion with Him and with others. Though it is not our aim, the reward of atonement, restoration and redemption outweighs anything we could ever give Our Father.

Picture this with me...

You have contributed your precious possessions: gold, exquisite fabrics, and threads, and now you are part of the ultimate building project. Yes, there are skillful workmen, plenty of them trained their whole life for this. But you have a part in this too with your family. Seeing this bit by bit, precisely put together and every element intricately and exactly positioned according to the instructed plan of a building that will house GOD's Presence and will be His dwelling place.

What a sight! What an honor to be a witness and a participant!

You and Your GOD, the One that has delivered you out of darkness into light and freedom. Together again! He did not say, "Good luck and Goodbye. Have a good life." He promised to be forever Your GOD, and forever you and your family, His people. Every time you pass by the completed Mishkan/Tabernacle, you are reminded that the GOD you worship and serve is unlike any other gods you've seen worshiped. He does not want your children sacrificed in the fire. He does not desire immoral acts committed for His entertainment to earn His favor and provision. He simply asks for your heart to desire Him and reciprocate His love for you. He gave you the Torah (Law/Instructions) to live by, not because He is a controlling tyrant, but because He wants you on the path leading to life. Idolatry and immorality lead to death and destruction. We have a Father in Heaven that wants to give us life, an infinite GOD who chose to come into our dimension to dwell among us, to have a relationship with Him. To borrow from a pastor from California, Francis Chan… "That is some Crazy Love"! We will spend eternity trying to comprehend the incomprehensible love!

# 19. TERUMAH / HEAVE OFFERING

Let's pray:

### Our Father in Heaven אבינו שבשמימ,

Thank You for bringing Yourself down to be near us. You have provided us the offering that You simply ask us to give back to You to be a part of the Master Plan. You did not need us, still don't, but You chose to have us partner with You. I know every detail of Your plan is by design. If we just pay attention and look, there is so much mystery hidden away just to be discovered. Help us, LORD, to unite our hearts and fear Your Name, that we do not miss the work You are doing in our midst.

B'Shem Yeshua HaMashiach בשם ישוע המשיח.

In Jesus' Name we pray. Amen.

# 19. TORAH TASTING
## *REFLECTION*

1. What is the word, picture or theme the LORD is highlighting to you in this chapter and Torah Portion?

2. The concept of the immortal GOD choosing to live in a physical building is mind-boggling. Reading about the building of the Tabernacle in this Torah Portion, what are some of its elements that draw your attention? And why?

3. Whether you are a parent or a teacher, can you think of a time teaching a lesson by having your students' direct involvement and interaction? Investing in their learning process in any way you can, what might have impacted the outcome to be different from their learning without their involvement?

4. GOD owns everything in the world, yet what is something of value to you that He would be pleased in you offering that to him, and why?

# 20 כ
# Tetzaveh
## (He Shall Command)
תצוה

Exodus 27:20-30:10

Ezekiel 43:10-27

Matthew 5:13-20

Tetzaveh begins with, "You shall command the people of Israel that they bring to you pure beaten olive oil for the light, that a lamp may regularly be set up to burn."

GOD has given these specific instructions of what the Children of Israel about the Olives they would bring for the light…

- Pure — unblemished
- Beaten — tried and refined
- Oil — source of light

The first time we see "olive" mentioned is in Genesis 8:11.

*And the dove came back to him in the evening, and behold, in her mouth was a freshly plucked olive leaf. So Noah knew that the waters had subsided from the earth.*
**Genesis 8:11**

The olive tree dates back over 6000 years of Near East ancient civilization. They are some of the oldest trees in the world. Some that still produce fruits today are dated to be over 2000 years old! They are some of the strongest trees and are almost indestructible. Much like the Evergreen trees, the olive trees can survive droughts, as well as floods. Some argue they even survived the worldwide flood and produced fruits afterwards. That is how the dove found an olive leaf to bring back to Noah.

The olive tree is majestic. It has become a symbol of peace and hope. From Genesis 8:11, we see that it is a sign of life and prosperity. Partnering with the dove, Noah was shown after the flood that "Everything is going to be okay. Fear no more. The wait for peace is over. You are finally here!" Being in the ark for forty days and forty nights with all the animals and family, it must have felt like forever. Noah and his family must have wondered, "When is this going to end?"

The Messiah is referred to as שר שלום Sar Shalom Commander/Prince of Peace, as the olive tree is a symbol for peace. Also, I somehow cannot help but see a connection between the instructions regarding the olive oil, Yeshua Jesus the Mashiach and us. The words of instructions relating to the olives and what they insinuate are too much of a coincidence. "Pure" — unblemished, "Beaten" — tried and refined, "Oil" — source of light. Our Mashiach is Pure & Unblemished, Beaten & Tried/Refined, and is the Source of all lights. He has modeled for us what it means to bring forth the Light.

*"And you shall command the children of Israel that they bring you pure oil of pressed olives for the light, to cause the lamp to [a]burn continually (Ner Tamid נר תמיד).*
**Exodus 27:20**

Ner Tamid נר תמיד is a "lamp may regularly be set up" — the Eternal/Perpetual Light. The Menorah (seven-branch lamp stand/candelabra) in the Tabernacle (Mishkan) and later the Temple is Ner Tamid נר תמיד. It has become the ultimate symbol of GOD's Presence and His provision for Israel.

Over the centuries and even millennials, many have attempted to take out the Light and destroy the Light within GOD's people.

*Again Jesus spoke to them, saying, "I am the light of the world. Whoever follows me will not walk in darkness, but will have the light of life."*
**John 8:12**

Yeshua Jesus is the Light of the world, and He has called us to follow Him to be the light too.

The Hanukkah legend tells the story that there was only enough oil to light the Temple Menorah for one day, but it lasted 8 days supernaturally while more pure oil was being refined during those 8 days. This miracle of oil reminds us of the faith and devotion we need to aspire to have in honoring the LORD, stewarding His presence, not for ourselves, but for worshiping Him and for all to see His Glory.

During Hanukkah, we are to light the Hanukkiah (a nine-branch lamp stand) for eight nights. The center candle is called the Shamash, the Servant Candle. Every one of the eight lights can only be lit by the Shamash, the Servant Candle, their light source. Isn't this a beautiful picture of our dependence on the Mashiach to give us light? The victorious Hanukkah story shows how the LORD delivered His people from a powerful enemy. The adversary attempted to defile and destroy GOD's temple. When GOD's people (Maccabees and friends) defeated the powerful enemy against all odds, their first action was to clean out the temple and light the Menorah to remind themselves that the LORD is the inextinguishable LIGHT! No one could eradicate GOD's presence from among His people. Therefore, for generations after that until now and going forth, GOD's children light the Hanukkiah to show the LIGHT of the world.

Not only is there a strong correlation of Yeshua being the light and His calling us to be light, He is also what the olive points to as being pure, unblemished and a source of light. In a similar manner, we (GOD's children) are compared with the olive tree as well.

> *But I am like a green olive tree*
> *in the house of God.*
> *I trust in the steadfast love of God*
> *forever and ever.*
> **Psalm 52:8**

*The Lord once called you 'a green olive tree, beautiful with good fruit.'*
**Jeremiah 11:16**

*The Emblem of the State Israel is an olive wreath and a menorah.*
*Here's a couple of references of two symbols —*
*And he said to me, "What do you see?" I said, "I see, and behold, a lampstand all of gold, with a bowl on the top of it, and seven lamps on it, with seven lips on each of the lamps that are on the top of it. ³ And there are two olive trees by it, one on the right of the bowl and the other on its left."*
**Zechariah 4:2-3**

*These are the two olive trees and the two lampstands that stand before the Lord of the earth. ⁵ And if anyone would harm them, fire pours from their mouth and consumes their foes. If anyone would harm them, this is how he is doomed to be killed.*
**Revelation 4:4-5**

The close-knitted connection between the olive and the menorah is remarkable.

This is where it gets interesting —

Genesis 1 tells us GOD created light on Day 1. Then, He created grass, herbs and trees on Day 3. But the sun was created later on Day 4. That means it was GOD's light that provided for the plants, even before the sun was created. Then…

> *It shone with the glory of God,*
> *and its brilliance was like that of a very precious jewel, like a jasper, clear as crystal.*
> **Revelation 21:11**

We see here the LORD's light (the glory of GOD) shines in the beginning and the end, Genesis and Revelation (the first book in the Old Testament and the last book in the New Testament). He is the Perpetual Light! נר תמיד Ner Tamid!

נר תמיד Ner Tamid is the sanctuary lamp in every Jewish synagogue as a reminder that GOD is ever-present.

This year, we experienced a widespread power outage due to a winter storm. We don't realize how much we take things for granted until we lose it. For 3 days, we lived with no power at single-digit outdoor temperatures. With sunlight during the day having some candles burning for warmth, it was bearable. However, at sundown, not only did the temperature drop rapidly, we lived in utter darkness until we scrambled for a few flashlights in the dark. There was nothing much we could do but go to bed around 9 p.m., early bedtime for our family. We, modern people, have no idea what it is like to live with no light at nighttime. Therefore, the menorah shining brightly in the Tabernacle (HaMishkan) and the Temple (HaMikdash) must have brought safety, comfort and hope.

> <u>You are the light of the world</u>.
> *A city set on a hill cannot be hidden.*
> *Nor do people light a lamp and put it under a basket,*
> *but on a stand, and it gives light to all in the house.*
> *In the same way, let your light shine before others,*
> *so that they may see your good works*
> *and <u>give glory to your Father</u> who is in heaven.*
> **Matthew 5:14-16**

Yeshua Jesus proclaimed that you and I are the LIGHT OF THE WORLD! And we are to shine our light before others that Our Father in Heaven would be glorified! This is powerful! It is not we try to be the light, but we truly, verily, emphatically the LIGHT as our LORD is the Light! Are you shining your light today?

Now it got me thinking, "Could there be a connection between the instructions for the Menorah and the instructions for the priestly garments that are stated in this Parasha? It is thought-provoking that these two subjects are mentioned together, right?

Revelation 21:11 mentions that the brilliance of the glory of GOD was like Jasper and Crystal. Guess what? These are the two stones found on the priest's breastplate as parts of the twelve stones.

> *The fourth row a beryl, an onyx, and a **jasper**.*
> *They shall be set in gold filigree.*
> **Exodus 28:22**

Some sources say one of the stones, jasper, was **crystal** on the priest's breastplate. Crystals reflect the light source. GOD shows us that He is the olive and source of light, the Eternal Light, and has called us to be light and to follow Him as our Light source. The LORD has chosen the priests to minister to Him and serve His people.

We are His Royal Priesthood —

# 20. TETZAVEH / HE SHALL COMMAND

*But you are a chosen race, a royal priesthood, a holy nation,*
*a people for his own possession, that you may proclaim the excellencies*
*of him who called you out of darkness into his marvelous light.*
**1 Peter 2:9**

The priest's garment, with GOD's brilliant light, is what we put on to serve the LORD and His people. Do you see the partnership again? The Master of the Universe can do it all, not needing us. Yet, we are to glean from His Light, as commanded by the LORD and to show the world His light. GOD's נר תמיד Ner Tamid, Continuously-burning Lamp, is the symbol of His perpetual, never-failing hope and presence for us.

This Parasha highlights the Menorah and the Priestly garment. Menorah comes from the word Ner (נר), candle or lamp. The priestly garment is something one would put on and wear to perform a duty to serve. When a fireman puts on his uniform, his mindset and his attitude are focused and ready with the courage he has been prepared for the assignment. Even the stones on the priestly breastplate of judgment give us a glimpse of the brilliance of GOD's glory, which He has imparted to the priests. And while the LORD judged the twelve tribes of Israel (represented by the twelve stones on the ephod) when the priest went before Him, He has already provided the atonement for redemption and remission of their sins through His brilliant glory. Our part is to put on the priestly garment, turn on the lamp, light that candle with Yeshua, the source (all has been provided by our LORD), and step into the role He has for us, not only to remind ourselves of the tremendous gift and authority given to us but also of being Ambassador of the Kingdom of GOD and invite the world to receive the One that has created all things and has loved them from before the foundation of the earth.

Did you turn on the lamp today? Did you put on your Priestly garment?

**Let's pray:**

**Our Father in Heaven** אבינו שבשמימ,

Thank You for sending Yeshua, our Maschiach, to model for us what it is like to be the Light and how to walk in His Light. LORD, teach us and remind us to put on our priestly garment each day that we are to minister to You first, then to serve Your people. We are eternally grateful that the atonement for our sins has already been provided for through Yeshua Jesus. Please help us fulfill the commandment of bringing the pure beaten olive oil by acknowledging that it is the Mashiach within us who provides the oil for the Perpetual Light. Let us embody the image of the dove with an olive leaf in its beak returning to Noah, by the prompting of the Holy Spirit, that we may bring hope message to the hopeless around us.

B'Shem Yeshua HaMashiach בשם ישוע המשיח.

In Jesus' Name we pray. Amen.

# 20. TORAH TASTING
## *REFLECTION*

1. What is the word, picture or theme the LORD is highlighting to you in this chapter and Torah Portion?

2. GOD's presence is represented by the menorah in the Temple. Whether we are aware or not, the LORD is ever-present with us. Are you constantly aware of the LORD being with you? If not, what are some practical ways you can be reminded of that truth?

3. Shining GOD's light can come in various forms and look different with different people. It can depend on someone's personality and their spiritual gifts. How would you shine GOD's light in your everyday life? Any practical examples?

# 21כא
# ki tisa
## (When You Take)
### כי תשא

Exodus 30:11-34:35

1 Kings 18:1-39

Mark 9:1-10

Ki Tisa is the title of this Parasha, taken from its second verse.

> "When you **take the census** of the children of Israel for their number, then every man shall give a ransom for himself to the Lord, when you number them, that there may be no plague among them when you number them.
> **Exodus 30:12**

כי תשא Ki Tisa means when you lift up. It is essentially lifting a head to take a head count in this context. This Portion gives instructions on taking a census and further instructions on the Tabernacles and Shabbat; also, it tells the golden calf incident and GOD's renewing His covenant with His people.

This Torah Portion consists of the 3 heroes, <u>Moses</u> in the Torah, <u>Elijah</u> in the Haftorah portion, and both of them appeared with Yeshua Jesus in the Brit Chadasha (New Testament) portion in Mark 9:1-10 —

And He said to them, "Assuredly, I say to you that there are some standing here who will not taste death till they see the kingdom of GOD present with power." Now after six days Jesus took Peter, James, and John, and led them up on a high mountain apart by themselves; and He was transfigured before them. ³ His clothes became shining, exceedingly white, like snow, such as no launderer on earth can whiten them. ⁴ And Elijah appeared to them with Moses, and they were talking with Jesus. ⁵ Then Peter answered and said to Jesus, "Rabbi, it is good for us to be here; and let us make three tabernacles: one for You, one for Moses, and one for Elijah" — ⁶ because he did not know what to say, for they were greatly afraid.

Moses and Elijah remind me of a few famous patriots in ancient Chinese history. They felt alone at times, hopelessly loving their country to the point of death. One of them is 屈原 Qu Yuan, who was a poet and court minister in the 3rd century B.C. China. He had conflicts with the Emperor's advisors when the nation was facing many clear and present danger threats from outside the kingdom. 內憂外患 (literally means "internal worries external troubles") is a term describing troubles from the outside, as well as from within the Emperor's "trusted" powerful reigning circle. 屈原 Qu Yuan was falsely accused of treason by corrupt palace officials and driven to exile. He is considered the first patriotic poet in ancient Chinese history. He was in such despair that he threw himself with rocks tied to his feet into the river, with no desire to be saved. Legend tells us that villagers heard about it and attempted to find his body but failed. They then rowed boats on the river throwing rice into the river, as well as beating drums and splashing water with the paddles to keep fish and evil spirits from approaching and corrupting his body. This led to an annual commemoration for 屈原 Qu Yuan's death and his love for his nation at the 端午節 Duan Wu Jie, Dragon Boat Festival. It is celebrated on the 5$^{th}$ day of the 5$^{th}$ month on the Chinese Lunar Calendar, around mid-June on the Gregorian calendar. It is still a tradition today for Chinese people around the world to eat rice dumplings steamed in banana leaf (resembling Mexican Tamales), leaf-packets stuffed with rice, and have dragon-boat races beating drums.

The reason I tell you the story of Qu Yuan is because the emotions of despair were so overwhelming that it must have been what it was like for Moses and Elijah, their similar sentiments for Israel. For Moses, he was born with the mission to deliver the Children of Israel for the LORD. He devoted his whole life to GOD and His people. GOD's people were not only unappreciative of him at times, but they were also stiff-necked and just outright unbearable. Yet, he was focused on the mission for GOD, and he was determined to see to its completion. He was brave and had to think on his feet... He may even have shed a few tears of grief but still persevered and pleaded with the LORD for the sake of His people, remembering the covenant. Elijah faced persecution by the king and queen of Israel, fleeing for his life hopelessly, and asked GOD to take his life (1 Kings 19:3-4).

After the most epic events of Passover, parting the Red Sea and the LORD giving His people the Ten Commandments in the "vow-exchanging" ceremony ("I will be your GOD, and you will be My people"), while Moses was still conversing with the LORD, the LORD informed him His people had just turned on Him and worshipped a golden calf. The Israelites were impatient. They could not wait for Moses to return. They needed to make an idol to worship, which is what GOD had commanded them NOT to do.

*And the Lord said to Moses, "I have seen this people, and indeed it is a stiff-necked people!* [10] <u>*Now therefore, let Me alone, that My wrath may burn hot against them and I may consume them.*</u> *And I will make of you a great nation."*
**Exodus 32:9-10**

The next day Moses said to the people:

> *"You have sinned a great sin. And now I will go up to the Lord; perhaps I can make atonement for your sin."*
> *So Moses returned to the Lord and said, "Alas, this people has sinned a great sin. They have made for themselves gods of gold. But now, if you will forgive their sin — but if not, please blot me out of your book that you have written."*
> *But the Lord said to Moses, "Whoever has sinned against me, I will blot out of my book. But now go, lead the people to the place about which I have spoken to you; behold, my angel shall go before you. Nevertheless, in the day when I visit, I will visit their sin upon them."*
> **Exodus 32:30-34**

The LORD could not tolerate the faith-wavering people any longer. He offered Moses a very sweet deal. He would destroy the Children of Israel and make a nation of Moses to start over.

His response —

"No Deal!"

He would rather have his own existence blotted out than take this deal, for the sake of saving GOD's people, much like a selfless Messianic figure… a foreshadow of the Mashiach. I find that interesting in Exodus 32:9, the Hebrew word הניחה Hanichah (leave me alone) is used when GOD told Moses, "Leave me alone," and then told him He would get very angry and consume the stiff-necked people.

The LORD basically told Moses, "Leave me alone; I'm going to destroy Israel and make you a new nation…

Almost like GOD was setting up for a negotiation session.

Do you think He knew Moses' character that he would not take the deal? Perhaps.

Do you think GOD had a Second-Chance Plan for His people? I think so.

Our GOD is a GOD that is "slow to anger" (Psalm 103:8).

Back to the Hebrew word הניחה Hanichah, its root verb is ינח Yanach, it means cast down, lay down, let alone, remain, etc. This exact form of the word only appears twice in the entire Torah. Besides Exodus 32:9, the only other time we see הניחה Hanichah is in Judges 16:26-27 near the end of Samson's life…

And Samson said to the young man who held him by the hand,

*"Let me (הניחה Hanichah) feel the pillars on which the house rests, that I may lean against them." Now the house was full of men and women.*

The הניחה Hanichah here <u>led to</u> Samson's hands to feel the pillars that supported the house where the Philistines gathered, worshipped and sacrificed to their god, Dagon. The הניחה Hanichah eventually <u>led to</u> the destruction of Dagon's house and 3000 of Samson's enemies.

The הניחה Hanichah in Exodus 32:9 was when GOD told Moses to leave Him alone so that His anger would consume and destroy the Children of Israel.

But…

*And the Lord relented from the disaster that he had spoken of bringing on his people.*
**Exodus 32:14**

In the 2 appearances of the word הניחה Hanichah in the Torah, both were meant to lead to destruction. We see 2 different outcomes. One concluded with the display of GOD's mercy and the other GOD's judgment.

Then, with the two tablets of testimony in his hand, Moses found the Israelites dancing around the golden calf. Exodus 32:20-

> He took <u>the calf</u> that they had made and <u>burned it with fire</u> and <u>ground it to powder</u> and <u>scattered it on the water</u> and <u>made the people of Israel drink it</u>.
> **Exodus 32:20**

The Talmud (Jewish Traditions) compares the golden calf incident to Numbers 5:24-28 when a woman suspected of the crime of adultery, the water of bitterness would be given to her to see if she was guilty or not.

> *And he shall make the woman drink the bitter water that brings a curse, and the water that brings the curse shall enter her to become bitter.* [25] *Then the priest shall take the grain offering of jealousy from the woman's hand, shall wave the offering before the Lord, and bring it to the altar;* [26] *and the priest shall take <u>a handful of the offering</u>, as its memorial portion, <u>burn it on the altar, and afterward make the woman drink the water</u>.* [27] *When he has made her drink the water, then it shall be, if she has defiled herself and behaved unfaithfully toward her husband, that the water that brings a curse will enter her and become bitter, and her belly will swell, her thigh will rot, and the woman will become a curse among her people.* [28] *But if the woman has not defiled herself, and is clean, then she shall be free and may conceive children.*
> **Numbers 5:24-28**

Could the golden calf powder water that the Israelites were made to drink in Exodus 32:20 be another guilt test, much like the one used in Numbers 5:24-28 that helped the sons of Levi know if the accused adulterer was guilty or not?

Very Possibly.

*And the sons of Levi did according to the word of Moses. And that day about three thousand men of the people fell.*
**Exodus 32:28**

Judges 16:26-27 recorded that 3000 Philistines (<u>worshipers of Dagon, a Philistine god</u>) were killed at the hand of Samson after his הניחה Hanichah moment, and Exodus 32 recorded that 3000 people (<u>worshipers of the golden calf</u>) were struck for their sins in after the LORD's הניחה Hanichah moment.

Both incidents had 3000 idol-worshipers killed after their respective חניחה Hanichah moments? Coincidence? Not a chance.

Samson's הניחה Hanichah moment brought deliverance to Israel. The Exodus הניחה Hanichah moment brought salvation to Israel instead of the judgment that they deserved.

*But now go, **lead** (ינח Yanach, root word of הניחה Hanichah) the people to the place about which I have spoken to you; behold, my angel shall go before you.*
**Exodus 32:34**

The same Hebrew root word ינח Yanach used in Exodus 32:9 and Judges 16:26 that intended to bring about destruction is also used here in Exodus 32:34 that brought about GOD's mercy…

*The Lord said to Moses, "Depart; go up from here, you and the people whom you have brought up out of the land of Egypt, to the land of which I swore to Abraham, Isaac, and Jacob, saying, 'To your offspring I will give it.' ² I will send an angel before you, and I will drive out the Canaanites, the Amorites, the Hittites, the Perizzites, the Hivites, and the Jebusites. ³ Go up to a land flowing with milk and honey; but I will not go up among you, lest I consume you on the way, for you are a stiff-necked people."*
**Exodus 33:1-4**

... That also brought forth confirmation of GOD's tremendous promises made to Abraham, Isaac, and Jacob. He reaffirmed to His children that He would drive out their enemies and they would enter the Promise Land.

First, GOD told Moses הניחה Hanichah (ינח Yanach — its Hebrew root) , to leave Him alone — that His wrath could destroy Israel, but when GOD was moved by Moses' selfless devotion for GOD's people, He then told Moses to נחה Nachah (Command/Imperative form of the root verb ינח Yanach) <u>lead</u> his people, though first with a plague as punishment for their worshiping the golden calf, eventually to GOD relenting from destroying His people and reaffirming His promises. The Children of Israel were given a second chance. They then mourned and repented for their sins.

> *Or do you presume on the riches of his kindness and forbearance and patience, not knowing that God's kindness is meant to lead you to repentance?*
> **Romans 2:4**

GOD's kindness indeed leads to repentance. I believe GOD's Word is the absolute truth. Because of one person's intercession, the whole nation was saved. Elijah thought he was the only one prophet left in Israel (1 Kings 18:22). Even after the showdown with the prophets of Baal, defeating them gloriously, he still lived in despair, being chased after by Ahab and Jezebel feeling alone and desperate (1 Kings 19:10). The LORD let Elijah know that He had set aside 7000 that had not bowed to Baal (1 Kings 19:18). He was not alone.

> *Then Elijah said to the people,*
> *"I, even I only, am left a prophet of the Lord, but Baal's prophets are 450 men.*
> **1 Kings 18:22**

## 21. KI TISA / WHEN YOU TAKE

*He said, "I have been very jealous for the Lord, the God of hosts. For the people of Israel have forsaken your covenant, thrown down your altars, and killed your prophets with the sword, and I, even I only, am left, and they seek my life, to take it away."*
**1 Kings 19:10**

*Yet I will leave seven thousand in Israel, all the knees that have not bowed to Baal, and every mouth that has not kissed him.*
**1 Kings 19:18**

Have you ever felt that your devotion to the LORD, your family, your friends, and your country is just not enough? Not only are you unappreciated, but your intention also gets distorted, quite like the great Chinese patriotic poet, 屈原 Qu Yuan? Let me tell you, my friend, you are NOT ALONE, and never are! GOD's mercy tells you, "You are not alone." Anguish and hopelessness led to 屈原 Qu Yuan's death. However, unlike 屈原 Qu Yuan, faithful servants like Moses and Samson knew where their hope lay. Moses, as one person with his הניחה Hanichah moment with the LORD, changed the course of a nation. Samson, as one person, despite of his past mistakes with הניחה Hanichah moment, delivered Israel from their biggest adversary.

Do you recognize your הניחה Hanichah moment? That you would not leave GOD alone, but He is moved by your devotion to Him and to His people, and ultimately, His mercy is brought forth. Or perhaps you are still waiting for your הניחה Hanichah moment? You are not alone and never will be. You are more than enough as one person when GOD is with you and you with Him. Great things are bound to happen when you trust Him and keep the faith.

**Let's pray:**

**Our Father in Heaven** אבינו שבשמימ,

Thank You for showing us the two חניחה Hanichah moments in your Word that show us Your mercy and the plan of salvation for Your people. Just as Moses and Elijah devoted their lives to partner with You for Your glory, help us to see and know that You are always with us. We would never leave You alone but, instead, go wherever You lead. LORD, help us to never live in despair but be filled with hope in faith through the Messiah You've provided, walking by faith and not by sight.

B'Shem Yeshua HaMashiach בשם ישוע המשיח.

In Jesus' Name we pray. Amen.

# 21. TORAH TASTING
## *REFLECTION*

1. What is the word, picture or theme the LORD is highlighting to you in this chapter and Torah Portion?

2. Do you recall an example that your (or someone else's) devotion and effort not only was unappreciated but was also misconstrued and intention distorted?

3. Even though the LORD was disappointed in Israel to the point of wanting to destroy the whole nation, He ultimately chose otherwise. GOD is merciful and full of grace. Have you ever experienced GOD's mercy and grace that you did not deserve?

# 22 כב
# Vayakhel/Pekudei
## (He Gathered/Countings)
### פקודי / ויקהל

Exodus 35:1-40:38

Ezekiel 45:16-46:18

John 13:1-19, Luke 16:1-13

In certain years, these two Torah Portions, Vayakhel and Pekudei, are scheduled to be read on the same Shabbat, which makes this week's reading a double portion. The title of Torah Portion Vayakhel comes from the first verse in this portion in Exodus 35:1, "Moses <u>assembled/gathered</u> all the congregation of the people of Israel." It covers how the people of Israel were gathered to build the Tabernacle, and many details of the building of the Tabernacle are laid out.

The title of Parashat Pekudei comes from the first verse in this portion in Exodus 38:21, "These are the <u>records</u> (<u>counted</u> items/things) of the Tabernacle, the Tabernacle of the testimony, as they were recorded at the commandment of Moses…." It records how the funds were used for the Tabernacle-building project, its completion and the glory of GOD entering the Tabernacle.

We see in Exodus 35:1 Moses <u>gathered together</u> קהל kahal the Children of the LORD to hear what the LORD had commanded them to do. The word for <u>recorded</u> or <u>counted</u> here is פקד pakad, meaning to attend, visit or appoint. The first time this word, פקד pakad, appears in the Torah is in Gen. 21:1, "The LORD visited Sarah as he had said, and the LORD did to Sarah as he had promised." The New American Standard Bible translates the word as "<u>Took note</u>." The first time a Hebrew word appears in the Torah gives us a clue to the essence of the word. Notice when the Lord <u>took note</u> of Sarah, his promise was fulfilled. The inventory of items that go into the Tabernacle are not just random things. The Lord took note of each item of the Tabernacle, details are important to Him, and therefore they should be to us.

In regards to the Shabbat commandments, the LORD specifically said in Exodus 35:3,

*"You shall kindle no fire in all your dwelling places on the Sabbath day."*

Fire brings light, food from cooking and warmth to our dwelling places. We find comfort in light and warmth, but on the seventh day, we are not to kindle a fire in where we live. Perhaps, kindling fire would be allowed in the LORD's dwelling like the Lighting of the Menorah/lamp stand and burning of altar sacrifices and altar incense? In other words, while His people rest on Shabbat, the only place they would find comfort, warmth and light is in the Presence of GOD, His Dwelling Place. It may be a wild theory, but perhaps just when GOD's people lose sight of who their true Provider is and find comfort and peace in anything other than GOD, then once a week on Shabbat, GOD's people are reminded that true rest and ultimate provision of Light and Warmth is found in the LORD's Presence.

Now let's explore the order of Tabernacle items laid out in this Parasha. The LORD is the GOD of order. I sense that there is a significant purpose in how GOD arranged the sequence of the Mishkan Tabernacle construction. Before any mention of the construction of the Mishkan Tabernacle, GOD wanted to make sure His Children are <u>gathered together</u> to understand the importance of the SHABBAT REST. Without rest, all the work to follow would be meaningless. I have always been intrigued by the fact that a Jewish day begins at sundown. Imagine in ancient times, people got up early in the dark before sunrise to work and retreated at sundown when it was getting dark. According to the Jewish faith, at sundown, a new day begins when we go to rest. The LORD literally prepares our new day during our rest, laying there being relaxed, and inactive.

Can you imagine waking up refreshed in the morning with the thought, "Everything I need for today has been provided for?" What peace would we have? Even when a curveball is thrown our way, we know, "Everything I needed for today has been provided for." None of the commands of work would mean anything if the commandment of Rest is not understood and fulfilled first. Therefore, resting must go before working. After the Children of Israel were gathered to understand the commandment of Shabbat, then the Mishkan inventory items were taken note. So, a proper perspective is established.

The first three verses on Shabbat sets up the backdrop for the rest of the double Torah Portions.

> *Then Moses gathered all the congregation of the children of Israel together, and said to them, "These are the words which the Lord has commanded you to do: ² Work shall be done for six days, but the seventh day shall be a holy day for you, a Sabbath of rest to the Lord. Whoever does any work on it shall be put to death. ³ You shall kindle no fire throughout your dwellings on the Sabbath day."*
> **Exodus 35:1-3**

Then, we see people bringing in gold, silver and bronze with a generous heart as well as many materials for the Mishka Tabernacle fabrics needed.

The building of the Mishkan is followed as instructed: The making of the Ark of the covenant, the Mercy Seat, the Table of Showbread, the Menorah/lamp stand, the Altar of Incense, the Altar of Burnt Offering, the Bronze Basin, the Court, the Priestly Garments, the Tabernacle is then erected. This Mishkan construction begins from the core — from within — from the heart, starting with the Holy of Holies and then moving outward to the Court. Constructing the dwelling place of the LORD starts from the heart. Resting in the LORD has to begin from the heart.

Here is what Yeshua Jesus taught about defilement comes from within, from the heart,

*There is nothing that enters a man from outside which can defile him; but the things which come out of him, those are the things that defile a man.*
**Mark 7:15**

In the same way, I believe that true Rest has to come from the heart. Physical rest cannot happen without spiritual and mental rest. Have you tried to go to sleep when worries were overtaking your mind, leaving your spirit restless? Even though your body was laying still, not working, not doing anything? Rest and falling asleep was an utter struggle, wasn't it? We can try to rest physically all we want, but if our mind is unsettled, the commandment of Shabbat cannot be accomplished.

Lastly, these double Portions end with the magnificent display of the glory of the LORD.

*Then the cloud covered the tent of meeting, and the glory of the LORD filled the tabernacle.*
**Exodus 40:34**

What a sight this must have been to have GOD's glory encompassing the Mishkan, as well as infilling it. The work of the LORD's dwelling place is sandwiched by Him instituting the SHABBAT REST and the

## 22. VAYAKHEL/PEKUDEI // AND HE GATHERED / COUNTINGS

COVERING & INFILLING of HIS GLORY. Notice that GOD fulfilled a promise when He took note of Sarah. In the same way, the promise of the LORD's goodness for us is fulfilled when we enter into His SHABBAT Rest, complete rest in every way, then go about to work on building Him a dwelling place wherever we are, in whatever we do. When every part of the Mishkan that we construct is <u>TAKEN NOTE</u> פקד pakad in honoring Him starting from the heart, GOD's glory shows up! And the fulfillment of Glory infills us.

This Parasha concludes with the Greatest and Ultimate Blessing, the very Presence of the LORD among us.

*For the cloud of the Lord was on the tabernacle by day,*
*and fire was in it by night,*
*in the sight of all the house of Israel*
*throughout all their journeys.*
**Exodus 40:38**

**Let's pray:**

**Our Father in Heaven אבינו שבשמימ,**

Thank You for giving us the commandment of Rest, as well as the promise and blessing when we fulfill this commandment. We confess and repent to You for the times that we did not rest physically or spiritually due to distractions, lack of belief, faith, devotion, or for any other reasons. We ask You to forgive us and teach us what True Shabbat looks like, resting from within. As Yeshua Jesus taught, defilement comes from within, and rest starts from within as well. We desire to rest in You in every way possible and in every area of our lives. We long to see Your Glory to cover and infill us and guide us through all our journeys as we are reminded at least one day a week that You are the only place we find true comfort and Light. Let the way we rest in You draw others to see Your Presence and Your Glory that they may find true rest in You too.

B'Shem Yeshua HaMashiach בשם ישוע המשיח.

In Jesus' Name we pray. Amen.

## 22. TORAH TASTING
### *REFLECTION*

1. What is the word, picture or theme the LORD is highlighting to you in this chapter and Torah Portion?

2. This week, our focus is rest. Children love recess in school. We like taking breaks. Then why is it such a challenge for modern people to take a break one day a week? Do you personally find it hard to take a day off once a week? And if so, why?

3. What are some creative ideas you can think of to start resting once a week (any day of the week) and perhaps encourage our family and friends to join you? What are some benefits of rest (physical, emotional, and spiritual) you have found from your own experience?

4. GOD's Commandment of rest refers not only to physical rest but also mental and spiritual rest. Any examples that you or others do for complete rest? Think of the consequence of going on days without sleep or physical rest and what that does to the body and the mind. What are some of the outcomes of a lack of mental and spiritual rest?

# 23 כג
# VAYIKRA
## (And He Called)
ויקרא

Leviticus 1-5

Isaiah 43:21-44:23

Matthew 5:23-30

Parashat Vayikra opens up the Book of Leviticus. This second book of the Torah is jam-packed with laws regarding sacrificial rituals and duties to be performed by the LORD's priests. This book details how GOD's people are to be holy as He is holy, set apart.

Here's the last verse of the Book of Exodus and the first verse of the Book of Leviticus.

> *For the cloud of the LORD was above the tabernacle by day,*
> *and fire was over it by night,*
> *in the sight of all the house of Israel,*
> *throughout all their journeys.*
> **Exodus 40:38**

*And the LORD called unto Moses, and spoke unto him out of the tent of meeting, saying,*
**Leviticus 1:1**

After the Mishkan Tabernacle construction had been completed, the LORD filled the Tabernacle of meeting with His glory. His presence was constantly reassured with the sight of the cloud by day and fire by night for all of Israel to see. They would not move unless the cloud moved. By this point, the Israelites were made clear of the <u>Promise</u> that the LORD is their GOD, who provides their every need.

Understand, when we declare and proclaim who GOD is to us, it means that we acknowledge —

He is the One True GOD, Maker of Heaven and earth, Master of everything — with Whom and in Whom we have no lack nor wants. Period.

*And the Lord <u>called</u> (קרא Qara Call) to Moses, and spoke to him from the tabernacle of meeting, saying, "Speak to the children of Israel, and say to them: 'When any one of you brings an offering (קרבן Korban Sacrifice) to the Lord, you shall bring your offering (קרבן Korban Sacrifice) of the livestock — of the herd and of the flock. 'If his offering is <u>a burnt sacrifice</u> (עלה Olah) of the herd…*
**Leviticus 1:1-3**

Not only is Vayikra the Hebrew name for the Book of Leviticus, it is also the name of this Book's first Torah Portion. The word Vayikra is ויקרא (meaning "And he called"). The book begins with a conjunction "And," which tells us what is about to happen is linked to what just happened. The Glory of the LORD and the Assurance of His Presence and Provision are closely linked to the "<u>Calling</u>" (קרא Qara). So, what does that mean? Let's look at what follows after the "Calling." The Glory of the LORD is so magnificent that Moses could not enter the Tabernacle of Meeting. GOD spoke from inside the Tabernacle. The first thing He told Moses to tell the children of Israel was about bringing their offering for a burnt

## 23. VAYIKRA / AND HE CALLED

offering. I feel that these are not random pieces. They somehow are all connected to something significant...

The Hebrew word for sacrificial offering is קרבן Korban, which has a root קרב Karav meaning come near or approach. Many see sacrifice as giving up or losing something, but in fact, the sacrifice that GOD intends for us to give Him will draw us closer to Him. There are many sacrificial offerings and rituals mentioned in Leviticus, but the very first one commanded of us is the burnt offering עלה Olah. It is a whole burnt offering to be burnt and consumed completely, none to be eaten by the priest of the people. The word for burnt offering עלה Olah comes from the root is עלה Alah to go up. Not only when we give our burnt offering to the LORD, we will be closer to Him, but we will ascend, and go up to higher places.

The first time the word Vayikra ויקרא "And he called" used in the Torah is —

> *"And God <u>called</u> the light Day"*
> **Genesis 1:5**

The Hebrew root for call is קרא Qara, to call and to proclaim. I believe that the LORD, Who is the original "Caller" and "Proclaimer;" when He called something, it came to be. It has a strong prophetic connotation. To me, Vayikra also reminds me of one of my favorite songs by Steve McConnell, "Vayikra Sh'mo," meaning "His Name shall be called." It is taken straight from the Book of Isaiah.

> *For to us a child is born, to us a son is given;*
> *and the government shall be upon his shoulder,*
> *and <u>**His name shall be called**</u>*
> *Wonderful Counselor, Mighty God,*
> *Everlasting Father, Prince of Peace.*
> **Isaiah 9:6**

To some, this verse is a prophetic statement pointing to Yeshua HaMashiach, Jesus Christ, that came and fulfilled that prophecy. To others in the Jewish community, this prophetic declaration of the LORD's promises through Isaiah have been fulfilled in King Hezekiah. Nonetheless, whatever the LORD calls and proclaims, it is fulfilled every time.

> *So shall <u>My word be that goes forth from My mouth</u>; It shall <u>not return to Me void</u>, But <u>it shall accomplish</u> <u>what I please</u>, and it shall prosper in the thing for which I sent it.*
> **Isaiah 55:11**

GOD called the light day, and it came to be.

I don't know about you, but there is a certain solemn sentiment that goes with the Highest office of the land like the Office of the U.S. Presidency. Politics aside, if someone hands me the phone and said, "The President of the United States just called for you," I would be shaking, feeling nervous but yet excited to take the call and find out what he has to say to me. The call has a purpose. The call ushers in the will of the President that follows. A call is a prompting, initiating something else to be said or done. A call is also a proclamation of something into being. Similarly, the word קרא Qara was often used as naming something or someone.

For example, Genesis 2:19 says,

> *"And whatever Adam <u>called</u> each living creature, that was its name."*

And Genesis 4:25 says,

> *"And Adam knew his wife again, and she bore a son and named him Seth. "For God has appointed another seed for me instead of Abel, whom Cain killed."*

## 23. VAYIKRA / AND HE CALLED

Adam was saying, "This is what you are," when he was naming each creature. Just like the above examples, as GOD called the dry land earth in Genesis 1:10, He called forth a destiny in naming them. When GOD calls you and me, there's a destiny He is placing inside each one of us.

Writing this book is a call that I have ignored for many years. I was not willing to make the <u>sacrifice</u>, to give a <u>whole burnt offering</u> (holding back nothing) for the "call." I was held back by "I don't know," "I am not qualified to write such a book and I have not learned enough," "I don't have the time," "this is just not the right season," and "Many people are smarter and know more than I do"….

But you see, the Vayikra "And He called" moment has already happened long ago. He called me when He made me. He has already provided the gifts necessary for the call/calling. The sacrifices the LORD has asked of me are "קרבן Korban" that will draw me closer to Him and that I will "go up" higher in the knowledge of Him. I only need to do my part, answer the call, and offer Him my sacrifices.

*For the gifts and the calling of God are irrevocable.*
**Romans 11:29**

So, what has the LORD called you to be? The call that He cannot and will not take back.

The call placed on you can only be fulfilled by you. What has GOD been calling you to bring to the altar for the first burnt sacrifice? Do you see the sacrifices necessary for the call has already been provided for? All you have to do is to place them on the altar, <u>whole</u>, with nothing left behind, nothing held back.

*Then the priest shall bring it all and burn it on the altar;*
*it is a burnt sacrifice, an offering made by fire,*
*a sweet aroma to the Lord.*
**Leviticus 1:13**

The whole burnt offering produces a sweet aroma to the LORD, not only is it sweet to the LORD, I believe that sweet aroma will stir others to devote themselves to the LORD whole-heartedly as well.

Let's pray:

**Our Father in Heaven** אבינו שבשמימ,

We thank You for Your glory so brilliantly displayed for Your children to know that the promise of Your Presence and Provision is always there. Like the Israelites, we do not want to move unless You move. We only want to go where You lead. Your call to us has prepared us to bring our sacrificial offerings to You. Please help us step up in this season to answer and step into the calling You have placed on us the moment you created us. So that our Korbanot (sacrifices) will bring us closer to us, go up higher in knowing You, and produce a sweet aroma for You.

B'Shem Yeshua HaMashiach בשם ישוע המשיח.

In Jesus' Name we pray. Amen.

## 23. TORAH TASTING
### *REFLECTION*

1. What is the word, picture or theme the LORD is highlighting to you in this chapter and Torah Portion?

2. What are you good at doing, your gift and strength? What do you enjoy doing? Have you ever asked the LORD what He has called you to do (life purpose)?

3. Some calls (divine assignments) in life are seasonal, while others are for a lifetime. Can you share one of those calls in your life? Or would you like to ask GOD what He has created you to do?

4. GOD showed up in his glory in the Tabernacle and then called his children to bring Him offerings. His glory has left his children in awe. All that the LORD has asked them was a sacrifice that He had already provided for. What has GOD called you to do that you may be holding back from stepping forward to do? What are the sacrifices you may be hesitant to make in an order to answer the call?

# 24 כד
# tzav

## (Command)

צו

Leviticus 6:1-8:36

Jeremiah 7:21-8:3, 9:22-23

Matthew 9:10-17

The name of Parashat Tzav comes from Leviticus 6:8 —

*Then the Lord spoke to Moses, saying,*
*"Command (צו Tzav) Aaron and his sons, saying,*
*'This is the law of the burnt offering: The burnt offering shall be on the*
*hearth upon the altar all night until morning,*
*and the fire of the altar shall be kept burning on it.*

This Parasha reiterates the sacrificial offerings mentioned in the last Parasha, as well as the consecration of the priests. The word צו Tzav comes from the root צוה Tzava, which is made up of three Hebrew letters.

- צ Tsade — Desire or need
- ו Vav — Nail or secure
- ה Hay — Reveal

I believe the essence of the word צו Tzav (imperative/command form) "Command" is something that will secure/anchor our need and desire. Ultimately, it is for our own good. We often think of a command as something forced upon us to obey without choice, but if we think of the authority behind the command as our best intention — it changes everything. If a father commands his child, who has a knife in his hand, to put down the knife. The child has his own agenda with the knife, and he does not want to obey his dad because he does not understand or comprehend his parent's intent for his good.

Perhaps he is thinking, "Dad just does not want me to have fun. He doesn't understand that I just want to play with it. Why would he want to take that fun away from me? Doesn't he see what I want? I really need it!"

The following may help explain this scenario a little better.

The first time צוה Tzavah appears in the Torah is in Genesis 2:16 —

> *And the Lord God **commanded** (צוה Tzavah) the man,*
> *saying, "Of every tree of the garden you may freely eat;*
> *but of the tree of the knowledge of good and evil*
> *you shall not eat, for in the day that you eat of it you shall surely die."*

You see, the intention of the LORD's command is to freely eat any tree in the garden, except for the tree of the knowledge of good and evil. It is for Adam's good.

צוה Tzava appears in this Parasha 15 times! According to Biblestudy.org, the number 15 represents REST in the Bible.

"The number 15 in the Bible pictures **REST**, which comes after deliverance, represented by fourteen. The 15th day of the first Hebrew month (Nisan) is the first day **of the Feast of Unleavened Bread**, a day of rest for the children of Israel (and for Christians). The 15th day of the 7th Hebrew month (Tishri) begins the **Feast of Tabernacles**, also a day of rest.

GOD told Abraham in a vision, just as the sun was setting to begin **Nisan 15** on the Hebrew calendar, that his descendants would end up as slaves in a foreign country (Egypt). They would, however, eventually be set free (Genesis 15:12 — 16).

Many years later, in Egypt, GOD miraculously delivered Israel's firstborn from the death angel just as Passover began after sunset (Nisan 14). Then, 24 hours later (just as the sun was setting to begin Nisan 15), the children of Israel began to leave Egypt (Exodus 12:40 — 41). This night is referred to as the 'night to be much observed' (Exodus 12:40 — 42, Deuteronomy 16:1). GOD's prophecy of freedom, given to Abraham on Nisan 15, was fulfilled years later on the exact same day."

*(Credit: Biblestudy.org, meaning of numbers)*

This is very interesting that Nissan 15 is the beginning of the Feast of Unleavened Bread (GOD's deliverance of His people from slavery) and Tishri 15 is the beginning of the Feast of Tabernacles/Sukkot (GOD's provision during the Israelites' wilderness years and His dwelling among them). Both represent a time of rest and giving thanks for the LORD's supernatural providence.

What if every time we see or hear the LORD command us to do something, our response is to rest in His goodness and sovereign will for our well-being, with anticipation and expectancy of His provision and deliverance? What if instead of second-guessing and trying to figure out the why's behind the command, we rest and trust in the best plans GOD has for us?

Regarding to the burnt offering, Leviticus 6:13 says,

> *A fire <u>shall always be</u> burning on the altar;*
> *it shall never go out.*
> **Leviticus 6:13**

The phrase "Shall always be" can also be translated as continually or perpetually. I don't know about you, but "always," "forever," and "eternal" are overwhelming concepts; our minds have difficulty grasping infinity. The Hebrew Word here is תמיד Tamid means continually or perpetually, that is, day after day after day, day in and day out. We can understand consistency, one day at a time, focusing on each and every single day.

There is security in knowing something happens consistently and perpetually. When GOD's Word says in Lamentations 3:22-23,

> *The steadfast love of the Lord never ceases;*
> *his mercies never come to an end;*
> *they are new every morning;*
> *great is your faithfulness.*
> **Lamentations 3:22-23**

How reassuring is that to know that GOD's faithfulness is dependable EVERY morning?

GOD's steadfast love NEVER STOPS, and His mercies have NO END! PERPETUALLY!

GOD is a BIG, BIG GOD, and His mercies are FOREVER, but He sometimes has to break it down for us in order that we relate to His BIGNESS.

The Law of Burnt Offering mentioned in Leviticus 6:8-13 gives us a visual that the fire will not go out for all to see, אש תמיד Esh Tamid, <u>a perpetual</u>

fire burning on the altar that shall never go out. It is a constant reminder of GOD's light, warmth and provision.

The idea of a perpetual fire reminds me of the yahrzeit candle we burned for my father-in-law, Solly, several years ago. Solly, everyone called him Sol, came and lived with us after my mother-in-law, Millie, had passed away. Sol spent his last years watching our firstborn son grow from being an infant into a toddler and seeing our daughter's birth. Even after he moved into a retirement home, Sol was at our house for every one of our children's birthday parties.

I remember this incident like it was yesterday… After coming home in March from Sol's memorial service in New York, we burned a yahrzeit candle in remembrance of Sol. By the way, burning yahrzeit candles is a Jewish Tradition after a loved one's passing and on their anniversary for the memorial. We placed this candle on our kitchen window sill, lit the candle, and let it burn. The yahrzeit candle we burned was in a 15oz. glass. In Jewish Traditions, we do not blow out the candle; it is to be left alone to burn out on its own. However, our yahrzeit candle burned on… the fire in the candle kept on burning day after day, day after day, … . I noticed it hardly burned down after a few weeks. I looked at it every now and then. Not giving it much thought, I left it alone. That little fire was **perpetual**. Every time I passed by the kitchen window, the fire was burning, going strong… It was my first time burning a yahrzeit candle. I had no idea whether a candle burning for days and days was normal. Both our children were born around Passover in April. Much like every other year, we hosted our children's birthday party in April. But this year was different! Grandpa was not with us. Friends came and left, celebrating with us. The day after the party, I noticed something… something quite different. I looked up at the kitchen window, at the window sill. There stood the candle glass, but this time the fire went out. Finally… after six weeks of **burning perpetually**!!! Suddenly, a thought dawned on me, not in any weird, superstitious ways, but somehow the LORD provided this miraculous sign for us to see how much He loves us.

Yes, we missed Grandpa, but the supernatural and perpetual fire was a reminder of GOD comforting us. Even though Grandpa was not physically with us, he was somehow with us, perhaps thinking of us from heaven.

I will never forget this family's perpetual fire that the LORD once blessed us with.

The last thing to note about Parashat Tzav is the verse of Romans 12:1-2.

> *I appeal to you therefore, brothers, by **the mercies of God**,*
> *to present your bodies as **a living sacrifice**,*
> *holy and acceptable to God, which is your spiritual worship.*
> **Romans 12:1**

The mercies of GOD are forever, eternal and everlasting, and we are to present our bodies, to live our lives as a living sacrifice, burning perpetually, day by day, to be our spiritual worship, honoring the Eternal King. If you are like me, sometimes "forever" is too big and overwhelming to process. It needs to be broken down into bite sizes, into day-by-day pieces to see and comprehend. Are you presenting your life to the LORD as a living sacrifice? Is there something you need to lay down on the altar? Something you have a hard time letting go of? In addition, you must tend the altar fire and never let it burn out. Do you realize the perpetual burning fire in your living sacrifice will inspire others to take notice? Your faithful service tending the perpetual fire will become a living banner raised up on high for the world to see the KING Who is worthy to be praised. Your acknowledgement and declaration of the Eternal GOD's faithfulness and your testament of His goodness in your life will be a perpetual reminder and encouragement to those whose flame is beginning to dim, that they may be able to perpetuate the burning fire of their living sacrifice.

Let's pray:

**Our Father in Heaven** אבינו שבשמימ,

Thank You for being the Eternal GOD. Thank You for Your Commandments that give life and sustain life. Help us to respond to whatever You have commanded us with complete obedience and self-abandonment. Let our lives be the perpetual fire that never goes out in ministering to You in a Worship Lifestyle, display to the world Your everlasting faithfulness and continual everyday goodness.

B'Shem Yeshua HaMashiach בשם ישוע המשיח.

In Jesus' Name we pray. Amen.

# 24. TORAH TASTING
## *REFLECTION*

1. What is the word, picture or theme the LORD is highlighting to you in this chapter and Torah Portion?

2. Ner Tamid, perpetual light in the Tabernacle, represents GOD's ever-presence. Is there anything you devote your time and effort to that keeps the flame (GOD's light) continuously to be seen and experienced? Perhaps, you feel the urge to start rekindling the fire and commit to tending to the fire, helping you feel GOD's presence more?

3. This Torah Portion mentions the whole-offering sacrifice. The LORD asks for wholehearted offerings. Sometimes even holding onto pain and shame is a twisted form of comfort, which we are not meant to keep once GOD has healed us and redeemed us from. What is an area, if there is any, that you have a difficult time submitting/surrendering to the LORD wholeheartedly?

# כה 25
# shemini
## (Eighth)
## שמיני

Leviticus 9:1-11:47

2 Samuel 6:1-7:17

Matthew 3:11-17

Shemini is the title of this Torah Portion. It comes from its first verse —

*On the eighth day Moses called Aaron and his sons and the elders of Israel.*
**Leviticus 9:1**

Shemini שמיני means eighth. This Parasha is comprised of further instructions for sacrificial offerings. Then detailed dietary laws follow. Words like "clean," "unclean," "detestable", "holy" and "consecrate" fill this portion. Creation lasted six days; then the LORD rested on the seventh day.

Here's what comes after the seventh day in Genesis 2:2-3:

*And on the seventh day God finished his work that he had done, and he rested on the seventh day from all his work that he had done. 3 So God blessed the seventh day and made it holy, because on it God rested from all his work that he had done in creation.*

The LORD made the seventh day holy. That's what He did after He rested on the seventh day. And on the eighth day, GOD blessed and sanctified (made holy) the seventh day. Consecration means making or declaring something holy. That's what the eighth day is about. The theme of consecration is mentioned throughout this Torah Portion. Blood was seen spilled, thrown, and poured from the sacrifices of animals. The price of cleansing and consecration is enormous, and the costly bloodshed of animal sacrifice is a powerful reminder of the extent of what is to be done for consecration, to be made holy as the LORD is holy.

Today, consecration or holiness is an "outdated" term used mostly in religious settings. It would sound strange if you asked someone, "Would you like to be consecrated?" or "What do you think you need to do to achieve holiness?" How do we relate to this concept in our world and everyday living? Consecration and holiness means being set apart, not partially set apart, but fully. I don't believe it means that we need to isolate ourselves from "the world." How are we to be light to the world if we hide from the world? We would be no effect to darkness as light. The dietary law is one example of the LORD commanding His children to be set apart to be "clean." That is just one element of consecration. Outward cleanliness does not mean the person is truly clean. When confronted by the Pharisees about his disciples being unclean by not washing their hands in Matthew 15, Yeshua responded to them this way —

*Not what goes into the mouth defiles a man; but what comes out of the mouth, this defiles a man.*
**Matthew 15:11**

I understand this verse refers to handwashing, but the principle is that someone can follow the law "perfectly," but if his heart is evil and unkind, no amount of handwashing or clean food he eats would make him clean and righteous. Kosher dietary law can be controversial in the religious community, Jewish, Christian, Messianic, …. . I am not engaging in this debate here. However, I do believe humility goes before honor. It is stated in the Good Book. According to the Cambridge dictionary, one of the definitions for the word humility is "the feeling or attitude that you have no special importance that makes you better than others. Essentially, it is thinking less of oneself than others."

**Here's my story relevant to this topic-**

Many years ago, on my first trip back to Hong Kong (after 4 years of not seeing my family), as a new believer following Jewish traditions, I had just stopped eating pork and shellfish with my Jewish husband, as instructed in the Book of Leviticus. Guess what the main ingredients is in the Hong Kong Cantonese cuisine?

You got it, pork and seafood.

The "newly-over-zealous"-convert-me was ready to teach my family something about living a life of holiness by following the biblical dietary law. After all, they are Christians and ought to follow the Word of GOD. Didn't they read in the Bible that pork and certain seafood is forbidden? My mother was forewarned of my newly adopted diet prior to my arrival.

However, while preparing for one of the authentic and yummy dinners, my new conviction slipped Mom's mind and cooked a delicious dish with pork. I "politely" rejected the meal that she had spent hours preparing for me. Mom is one of the best cooks in the world, but I would not take even one bite of that dish because it would be against the Law. At restaurants with family and friends, my refusal to eat those traditional Chinese delicacies drew some attention. No, I was not condemned. I was "set apart" by not touching those "unclean" foods. I could sense some hurt and confusion from my loved ones by me being "clean" and "holy," superseding family relationships and my own culture and heritage.

Later while sharing with a wise friend about this, she wisely quoted the following scriptures:

*If one of the unbelievers invites you and you want to go, eat anything that is set before you without asking questions for the sake of conscience.*
**1 Corinthians 10:27**

*Jesus said, "Whenever you enter a town and they receive you, eat what is set before you."*
**Luke 10:8**

Thinking back, my "holier-than-thou attitude was appalling and annoying. I was immature and prideful, which was not my intention at all. My sweet friend saw the situation with clarity and spoke truth into me. She reminded me love supersedes the law. That is what Yeshua Jesus came to show us from the Father's heart.

Let me reiterate here. I am not debating about the dietary law. I am just sharing my personal experience with you. Even as I am writing this now, I am feeling the sadness and regrets convicting my heart for dishonoring my mother, someone who loves me more than life itself. Pride is such a dangerous thing; it blinds us from seeing anything or anyone but ourselves. Unfortunately, the desire to achieve righteousness ends up becoming self-righteousness.

Humility goes before honor, and pride goes before the fall (or dishonor, dishonoring others and oneself). Once again, this is not a debate about dietary law. I simply use it as an example to drive the point of what makes us holy. Yes, the LORD has commanded us to live by the law to be holy.

*And though I have the gift of prophecy, and understand all mysteries and all knowledge, and though I have all faith, so that I could remove mountains, but have not <u>love</u>, I am nothing.*
**1 Corinthians 13:2**

*Let no debt remain outstanding, except the continuing debt to love one another, for whoever loves others has fulfilled the law. The commandments, "You shall not commit adultery," "You shall not murder," "You shall not steal," "You shall not covet," and whatever other command there may be, are summed up in this one command: "Love your neighbor as yourself." Love does no harm to a neighbor. Therefore <u>love</u> is the fulfillment of the law.*
**Romans 13:8-13**

Consecration is from the heart. Sacrifices that are brought and set on the altar, provided from the heart, with love for the LORD and for His people, those around us.

Do we want to be known as "the religious ones" or "he/she is authentic in his/her faith, helping the needy and serving family and friends without ulterior motives," to even non-believers? To me, being set apart is when others don't know the LORD but are puzzled at how you are happy or at peace; even in situations most people would be losing it. My career prior to homeschooling and raising our children was in hotel management and in sales. At one hotel, I had co-workers that often went to Happy Hours and partied on weekends, in which I chose not to participate. I had never said one word of disdain. I talked about praying for them in love and encouraging them with daily motivational quotes in kindness. From time to time, I was approached with questions about GOD out of curiosity. They found my optimism and positive attitude appealing. My favorite co-worker was John (not his real name). John and I could laugh all day long. His cubicle was across from mine. We loved one another as close friends. Going to work was fun. John had a "colorful" lifestyle, not necessarily biblical. I could speak into him in ways that he might not receive and accept from others. One day, I said to John, "Jesus loves the sinners, but He hates the sin." John was speechless for a moment.

Then he said, "That's brilliant! Did you just make that up?"

I said, "No."

John added, "Say it one more time." John quickly grabbed a piece of scrap paper; he wrote it down and pinned it on his wall.

Another time returning to the office right after my OB-Gyn appointment, my comment of "I don't know how anyone can think this is not a life and thinks aborting the baby is okay when I could hear my son's heartbeat" really upset John, so much that he said he would not have overlooked it if it was someone other than me. He was so distraught about my comment and said he would've reported the "controversial" comment to Human Resources for a hostile work environment if it was not me that'd said it. Of course, John got over it, and we were still friends in the office.

After giving birth to our firstborn and leaving my career behind, John and I didn't stay in touch, but I know in faith that GOD had planted seeds with me there. The words of truth in grace and boldness shone a light in dark places. Controversial subjects people avoid in the workplace were discussed there because I first displayed my love for GOD in authentic ways. Being set apart and holy is what GOD intends for us in the midst of unholiness. Only in the presence of darkness can light shine through.

Every now and then, I check my motive for action. I ask myself this, "Am I doing this so I would look good? Or so Father GOD would be glorified?" The same good deeds may look the same from the outside, but the intent of the heart can make the world's difference. If my heart is not in the right place, I'd rather not do it at all.

> *But the Lord said to Samuel, "Do not look at his appearance or at his physical stature, because I have [c]refused him. For[d] the Lord does not see as man sees; for man looks at the outward appearance, but the Lord looks at the heart."*
> **1 Samuel 16:7**

Now, let's look at what Aaron's sons offered up to the LORD-

## 25. SHEMINI / EIGHTH

*Then Nadab and Abihu, the sons of Aaron, each took his censer and put fire in it, put incense on it, and offered profane (strange) fire before the Lord, which He had not commanded them.*
**Leviticus 10:1**

The Hebrew root word for profane or strange used for the fire is זור Zur. It means strange, as in foreign. The fire used by Aaron's sons were strange, foreign, not normal or usual according to what they had been commanded. The result was GOD sent fire and instantly consumed them. Romans 6:23 says-

*For the wages of sin is death, but the gift of GOD is eternal life in Christ Jesus our Lord.*

While it may seem harsh to kill Aaron's sons for using "strange" fire on the altar, I don't think we actually understand the crime. It was so severe that GOD had to deal with it instantly, even though they were Aaron's sons and Moses' nephews. Serving the LORD is a privilege and a life-long calling. There are many examples in the Bible of priests despising that office or even abusing it, like Eli's sons in Prophet Samuel's days.

*But you are a chosen generation, a royal priesthood, a holy nation, His own special people, that you may proclaim the praises of Him who called you out of darkness into His marvelous light... having your conduct honorable among the Gentiles (unbelievers), that when they speak against you as evildoers, they may, by your good works which they observe, glorify God in the day of visitation.*
**1 Peter 2:9, 12**

We bear a responsibility of self-consecration in the ministry serving the LORD. In serving GOD, living a life of holiness, set apart, whether following the biblical dietary law or loving others in GOD's grace, the world will see the light shine through from within us. In 1 Peter 2:12, it says when the unbelievers speak evil against us, they will see our good works and glorify GOD when He visits them. Our acts of kindness and gentle words deflect unbelievers' evil words in the "Day of visitation?" Is it possible that if our works invite GOD to come to visit them, that they would glorify GOD?

*Let your light so shine before men, that they may see your good works and glorify your Father in heaven.*
**Matthew 5:16**

Light pierces into darkness just like we set ourselves in our deeds, words and thoughts aligning with GOD's will. We allow GOD's light to shine, notice that we let His light shine, not manipulate it or create a "strange" fire that is not commanded for?

The eighth day after creation is about consecration. The eighth day in Parashat Shemini is about the consecration of our sacrificial offerings to the LORD. The ultimate goal of consecration is our hearts to be made right with the LORD in humility, that we would be set apart, holy as a light shining into darkness, which allows others to see our good works and glorify our Father in heaven.

# 25. SHEMINI / EIGHTH

Let's pray:

### Our Father in Heaven אבינו שבשמימ,

We thank You for first setting us apart as Your children that You have rescued from darkness into Your marvelous light and then giving us the mantle of the royal priesthood to serve You and draw others close to You. We repent for the times that we have put our self-righteousness before You and before loving others. LORD, thank You for forgiving us when we confess to You and ask for forgiveness that You promise that You would cleanse us from all unrighteousness. Please help us to love beyond just following the commandments. Commandments without love are meaningless, not Your intention at all. We don't want legalism nor religion. We desire You and follow Your will that Your light may shine through us to draw others to glorify You!

B'Shem Yeshua HaMashiach בשם ישוע המשיח.

In Jesus' Name we pray. Amen.

# 25. TORAH TASTING
## *REFLECTION*

1. What is the word, picture or theme the LORD is highlighting to you in this chapter and Torah Portion?

2. We are called to be in the world but not of the world. What are some practical ways we can be friends with the world, yet stay true to who we are in the LORD and follow his commandments that lead to life?

3. Is there any part of the "cleanliness comes from the heart, not what we do on the outside" that resonates with you?

# 26 כו
# Tazria / Metzora
## (She Will Conceive / Leper)

תזריע

מצירע

Leviticus 12:1-13:59 / 14:1-15:33

2 Kings 7:3-20

Luke 2:22-35; Mark 1:35-45

---

Tazria and Metzora are Double Portions for this week that are often read on the same Shabbat, except in Jewish leap years. Tazria, meaning "She Will Conceive"; Parashat Tazria talks about women's purification laws after childbirth and various types of leprosy and protocols. Parashat Metzora discusses cleansing rituals for lepers and leprous homes, as well as cleansing rituals from bodily emissions. These are topics that are not often discussed.

The week's Double Torah Portions are very special to me. Both our children were born around Passover, with 2 years apart. Both went through the Bar and Bat Mitzvah program. Bar/Bat Mitzvah means Son/Daughter of the Law. In Jewish Traditions, children are taught

Jewish studies and Jewish history, along with Biblical Hebrew. At age 13, Jewish children celebrate their accomplishments at their Bar/Bat Mitzvah ceremony, marking the season they will begin taking responsibility for GOD's Word and His Commandments, with which they have been equipped for life. It is a rite of passage for Jewish children.

Since the day Matthew, our firstborn son, was born, I have imagined the day of his Bar Mitzvah, like every Jewish mother. My husband, Paul, had his Bar Mitzvah at age 13, so did his brother Michael. Girls did not have Bat Mitzvah in their Orthodox community at that time. Nonetheless, this wonderful tradition has been going on for generations, L'dor V'dor ל׳דור ודור (meaning from generation to generation). The Jewish faith is full of rich traditions, Bar/Bat Mitzvah is one of them. Each synagogue has its own training and requirements for completing the B'nei Mitzvah program. After 2 years of Biblical Hebrew, 2 years of Jewish studies and many hours of Torah reading, lots of practice and preparations, Matthew canted (reading with melody, like singing) his Torah Portion, Metzora, at his Bar Mitzvah ceremony. He presented a mini-sermon, a short commentary of what he felt Parashat Metzora meant to him. We hosted a reception with "Speak Life" as the theme of the occasion. My amazing Jewish husband, Chef Paul, catered the event, best food ever for his son's monumental event. It was a glorious day!

Our daughter, Mollie, went through the same rigorous training. Her Torah Portion was also this Double Portion, Tazria/Metzora. She had her Bat Mitzvah ceremony 2 years after her brother's. Mollie, too, canted her Portion directly from the Kosher Torah scroll.

Luke 4:16-19 recorded Yeshua Jesus reading from the Haftorah of the Yesha'yahu (Isaiah) scroll in the synagogue on a Shabbat —

So He came to Nazareth, where He had been brought up. And as His custom was, He went into the synagogue on the Sabbath day and stood up to read. And He was handed the Book of the prophet Isaiah. And when He had opened the book, He found the place where it was written:

> "The Spirit of the Lord is upon Me,
> Because He has anointed Me
> To preach the gospel to the poor;
> He has sent Me to heal the brokenhearted,
> To proclaim liberty to the captives
> And recovery of sight to the blind,
> To set at liberty those who are oppressed;
> To proclaim the acceptable year of the Lord."
> **Luke 4:16-19**

The Torah reading on every Shabbat service reminds me of this scene of Yeshua Jesus walking up to the front and reading the Book of Isaiah.

Quite a powerful scene of this prophecy fulfilled right before the audience's eyes!

In addition to the Torah reading, a beautiful Blessing, Shehecheyanu (Who has granted us life), was recited and sung over the occasions at our children's Bar/Bat Mitzvahs, as it is recited on every special Jewish occasion.

*Ba-ruch A-tah A-do-noi E-loi-hei-nu*
*Me-lech ha-o-lam she-he-chee-ya-nu v'ki-yi-ma-nu*
*vi-hi-gi-ya-nu liz-man ha-zeh.*

*Translation:*
*Blessed are You, L-rd our G-d,*
*King of the Universe,*
***Who has granted us life**, sustained us*
*And enabled us to reach this occasion.*

It was a magnificent day for our family both times. Our children's Bar/Mitzvahs have been monumental events for our family. Matthew and Mollie have been raised up to read the Word of GOD (both in Hebrew and in English), seeking and growing in the LORD in prayers and Torah studies, individually and corporately in a community. There is no word that can describe the sight of seeing them reading the Torah scroll publicly, speaking of the Torah Portions they had just read, expressing their gratitude to the LORD and to all who had helped them reach this point of their faith walk, appreciating our friends and family that were instrumental in shaping them to be the young man and young woman they have become thus far. Hundreds of believers in the LORD witnessing, encouraging and supporting our children at the milestone moments of their life journey was beyond awe-inspiring!

Having gone through 2 Bar/Bat Mitzvahs of these Double Portions, I think I have read Tazria and Metzora more than a few times. To be honest, one can be envious of those Bar/Bat Mitzvah kids that had Portions like the Genesis creation story, Noah's ark, and the Israelites' Wilderness adventures. Tazria/Metzora portions are filled with instructions and laws on purification after childbirth, women's menstrual cycles, bodily discharges, skin spots, and yes, scary leprosy. It is not something we get excited thinking or talking about, let alone for children. However, if we see beyond the surface, there may just be amazing revelations to be discovered.

The word Hebrew תזריע Tazria means "She Will Conceive," which comes from Leviticus 12:2-

> *Then the Lord spoke to Moses, saying, "Speak to the children of Israel, saying: 'If a woman has **conceived** (actual meaning conceives), and borne <u>**a male child** (זכר Zachar)</u>, then she shall be unclean seven days;*
> *as in the days of her customary impurity she shall be unclean.*
> *And on the eighth day the flesh of his foreskin shall be circumcised. She shall then continue in the blood of her purification thirty-three days. She shall not touch any hallowed thing, nor come into the sanctuary until the days of her purification are fulfilled.*
> **Leviticus 12:1-4**

The Hebrew word מצירע Metzora means Leper or the one who is diseased, which the portion begins in Leviticus 13 detailing the law regarding leprosy. What is interesting in the portion is the titles of these Double

Portions, Tazria/Metzora. Translating the Hebrew words put together, we have — "She Will Conceive a Leper." Before we dig deeper into this, I would like to point out what a woman would conceive according to Leviticus 12:1… "if she conceives and borne <u>a male child</u>." The Hebrew word used for "**male child**" is זכר Zachar, as in **Genesis 1:27**, "So GOD created man in his own image, in the image of GOD He created him; <u>male and female</u> He created them."

This is the <u>very first time</u> זכר Zachar is used in the Torah.

Subsequently, the "male and female" reference of Zachar זכר is also seen in **Genesis 5:2, 6:19, 7:3, 7:9 and 7:16.**, totaling 7 times.

Then, Zachar זכר (male) is used when the LORD established his covenant with Abraham through circumcision in **Genesis 17:10**.

What follows is fascinating, Zachar (male) appears 7 times total in **Genesis 17:10, 17:12, 17:14, 17:23, 34:15, 34:22, 34:24** in relation to the circumcision of Abraham's **male** descendants.

7 is a number for perfection and completion, as in 7 days of creation being perfect, and Circumcision is a sign of GOD's everlasting covenant with His people, GOD's covenant with His people being perfect.

In addition, זכר Zachar, as a Hebrew root verb, means Remember.

This is remarkable!

Let me bring in one more element, and we will put the whole picture together.

Have you heard of the concept of a Suffering Messiah or Leper Messiah (Tza'arat HaMashiach)?

The idea of the Messiah (Jewish Savior) being both King and Leper, King Messiah and Tza'arat HaMashiach/Leper Messiah, is found in Jewish

Traditions. Some say this concept came from when the rabbis wrestled with Isaiah 53. Christians believe Isaiah 53 is a Messianic prophecy, while Jews see it as a reference to Israel.

> *Surely He has borne our griefs and carried our [h]sorrows;*
> *Yet we esteemed Him stricken, Smitten by God, and afflicted.*
> *⁵ But He was wounded for our transgressions, He was bruised for our iniquities; The chastisement for our peace was upon Him, and by His stripe we are healed. ⁶ All we like sheep have gone astray; We have turned, every one, to his own way; And the Lord has laid on Him the iniquity of us all. He was oppressed and He was afflicted, Yet He opened not His mouth; He was led as a lamb to the slaughter, And as a sheep before its shearers is silent, so He opened not His mouth.*
> **Isaiah 53:4-7**

According to the Babylonian Talmud, it is said, "The Rabbis say, The Leper Scholar, as it is said, surely he has borne our griefs and carried our sorrows: yet we did esteem him a leper, smitten of God and afflicted..." (Sanhedrin 98b).

Chaim.org has an insightful commentary on the topic:

The Talmud also "records" a supposed discourse between the great Rabbi Joshua ben Levi and the prophet Elijah. The rabbi asks, "When will the Messiah come?" And "By what sign may I recognize him?" Elijah tells the rabbi to go to the gate of the city, where he will find the Messiah sitting among the poor lepers. The Messiah, says the prophet, sits bandaging his leprous sores one at a time, unlike the rest of the sufferers, who bandage them all at once. Why? Because he might be needed at any time and would not want to be delayed. Elijah says he will come "Today, if you will listen to his voice." (Sanhedrin 98a).

There is a strange story about the Baal Shem Tov, the founder of the Hasidic movement. One day the rabbi was riding with a young student. He stopped his wagon at the hut of an old leper, horribly affected by the disease. The rabbi climbed down and spent a great deal of time with the poor man. When he returned to the wagon and recommenced his journey, the puzzled student asked the rabbi who it was that the rabbi had visited with. The rabbi replied that in every generation, there is a Messiah who will reveal himself if the generation is worthy. The leper he had been meeting with was that Messiah, but the generation was not worthy, so the Messiah would depart. (Quoted in The Messiah Texts, by Raphael Patai, page 31.)

> "Where did this "Leper Messiah" idea come from? This odd concept must have arisen from the rabbis as they struggled with Isaiah 53. They either saw the Messiah's sufferings as leprosy or split the Messiah in two, one a sufferer and one a conqueror. (See the section on the <u>Suffering Messiah and the Two-Messiahs theory.</u>) The Hebrew words in Isaiah 53:4, stricken (nagua) and smitten (mukkay) are interpreted as referring to a leprous condition. Either word can refer to being stricken with a disease, yet they need not be understood in that way, much like our English work "stricken" can refer to stricken with disease or just simply stricken, as with a fist. Either way, Jesus was stricken. He was certainly made sick by the Roman floggings and beatings and the tortuous ordeal of crucifixion. He was certainly stricken with the Roman lash. As a leper was despised and rejected by men, so also was the Messiah despised and rejected. And still today, there are many who see Jesus as being as repugnant as leprosy and his followers as those who should be isolated and shunned".

"To the followers of the Suffering One, his afflictions, described in Isaiah 53, are the agonies of one dying to provide atonement. The lamb being led to slaughter envisioned by Isaiah is described as one punished in the place of his people. Jesus, the true Messiah, came as the "Lamb of God who takes away the sin of the world." His crucifixion provided a substitutionary sacrifice adequate to fulfill the punishment we all deserve. Let us praise the God of Israel, our Redeemer, who has provided his Messiah to take the just punishment for his people so that we might be forgiven our sins!"

*(www.chaim.org/leper-messiah)*

I do not believe in coincidence. There is only Divine Providence. Let's look at these Double Portions' titles again, "She Will Conceive a Leper."

Who is this male leper that she will conceive?

**Let's review the points discussed so far —**

- זכר Zachar "Male" used 7 times in the "male and female" phrase point to GOD's original intent in creating man, male and female.
- …7 times — meaning Completion/Perfection
- Then, זכר Zachar "Male" used 7 times in the context of the circumcision, a sign of GOD's covenant with Abraham to be his GOD, as well as Abraham and his descendants as GOD's people.
- … 7 times — meaning Completion/Perfection
- זכר Zachar as a root also means Remember.
- Leper — a Leper Messiah

I believe these clues speak of a woman conceiving and giving birth to a male child, a leper. A leper that would be stricken and rejected, shamed, and despised. And this would be a sign of the covenant.

The word זכר Zachar/Remember calls for us to remember the circumcision sign of GOD's everlasting covenant so that we would remember GOD's perfect original plan. Moreover, GOD remembers His covenant, and so should we. The LORD's original plan is perfect, and His covenant plan is complete. He always holds up to his end of the bargain. Though the Leper is to be despised and rejected, and yet His affliction is the perfect redemption plan to bring us salvation and deliverance. I feel that with GOD, Plan B is His Plan A. Unlike us, He is not surprised by Plan A not working out. Plan B usually routes back to Plan A.

## 26. TAZRIA/METZORA // SHE WILL CONCEIVE / LEPER

It is noteworthy how specific GOD is about the protocol of cleansing of the disease, detailing to which toe and thumb the priest is to use in these rituals.

> *The priest shall take some of the blood of the trespass offering, and the priest shall put it on the tip of the right ear of him who is to be cleansed, on the thumb of his right hand, and on the big toe of his right foot. And the priest shall take some of the log of oil and pour it into the palm of his own left hand.*
> **Leviticus 14:14-15**

The LORD thought of EVERYTHING, even down to if someone who is poor and not able to afford certain burnt offerings.

> *But <u>if he is poor</u> and cannot afford it, then he shall take one male lamb as a trespass offering to be waved, to make atonement for him, one-tenth of an ephah of fine flour mixed with oil as a grain offering, a log of oil...*
> **Leviticus 14:21**

Healing has been provided. The only question is whether the diseased wants to be healed?

> *Then the Lord spoke to Moses, saying, "This shall be the law of the leper for the day of his cleansing: He shall be brought to the priest. And the priest shall go out of the camp, and the priest shall examine him; ... He who is to be cleansed shall wash his clothes, shave off all his hair, and wash himself in water, that he may be clean. After that he shall come into the camp, and shall stay outside his tent seven days.*
> **Leviticus 14:2-3, 8**

> *When Jesus saw him lying there, and knew that he already had been in that condition a long time, He said to him, "Do you want to be made well?"*
> **John 5:6**

The LORD does not force wholeness and healing on anyone. He offers the plan. The diseased have to desire healing and go to the priest to be cleansed.

Tazria and Metzora Torah Portions lay out details of cleansing rituals for after childbirth, leprosy on skin, clothing, and houses. Isn't that interesting that a disease would grow on garments and houses? Some argue it was some sort of mold. However, many Jewish rabbis agree that this skin disease is a result of sins, such as gossiping or the Evil Tongue (לשון הרע Lashon Ha'Ra).

> *Then Miriam and Aaron spoke against Moses because of the Ethiopian woman whom he had married; for he had married an Ethiopian woman.*
> *So they said, "Has the Lord indeed spoken only through Moses? Has He not spoken through us also?" And the Lord heard it…*
> *So the anger of the Lord was aroused against them, and He departed. And when the cloud departed from above the tabernacle, suddenly Miriam became **leprous** (צרעת Tz'arat), as white as snow. Then Aaron turned toward Miriam, and there she was, a leper.*
> **Numbers 12:1-2, 9-10**

Miriam became leprous due to her unkind words against Moses' Ethiopian wife. צרעת Tza'arat (with same root as Metzora) is translated as leprosy. The word נגע Nega (Plague/affliction) is translated as plague or sore or mark. However, many believe the disease is not simply a physical disease but rather a spiritual one. There is a close relationship between צרעת Tza'arat Leprosy and נגע Nega Plague/affliction.

> *When a man shall have in the skin of his flesh a rising, a scab, or bright spot, and it be in the skin of his flesh like the **plague** (נגע Nega) of leprosy (צרעת Tz'arat),.*
> **Leviticus 13:2**

The first time we see the word נגע Nega (Plague/affliction) used is in Genesis 12:17 when the LORD struck Pharaoh of Egypt and his household because Sarai was taken into his house for her beauty, a <u>result of wrongdoing</u>.

> *But the Lord <u>plagued</u> (נגע Nega) Pharaoh and his house with great plagues (נגע Nega) because of Sarai, Abram's wife.*
> **Genesis 12:17**

The second time נגע Nega (Plague/affliction) is used in Exodus when the LORD finished his plan of deliverance of His people at the last plague. This final and LAST blow of killing the firstborn in Egypt would finally release the Children of Israel from bondage, once and for all. What a <u>Redemption</u> Plague for GOD's people!

> *And the Lord said to Moses,*
> *"I will bring one more <u>plague</u> (נגע Nega) on Pharaoh and on Egypt. Afterward he will let you go from here. When he lets you go, he will surely drive you out of here altogether.*
> **Exodus 11:1**

Then, coincidentally,

the third time נגע Nega (Plague/affliction) appears in Leviticus 13:2, referring to the plague/affliction/mark of leprosy on a <u>man's skin</u>. In Leviticus 13:47, the leprous plague also grows in garment. The leprous plague even grows on walls, referenced in Leviticus 14:33-34, 44.

> *Also, if a garment has a leprous plague (נגע Nega) in it, whether it is a woolen <u>garment</u> or a linen <u>garment</u>,*
> **Leviticus 13:47**

*And the Lord spoke to Moses and Aaron, saying: "When you have come into the land of Canaan, which I give you as a possession, and I put the leprous <u>plague</u> (נגע Nega) <u>in a house</u> in the land of your possession..."*
**Leviticus 14:33-34**

*Then the priest shall come and look; and indeed if the <u>plague (נגע Nega) has spread in the house</u>, it is an active <u>leprosy</u> in the house. It is unclean.*
**Leviticus 14:44**

*And he shall look on the plague, and, behold, if <u>the plague (נגע Nega) be in the walls of the house</u> with hollow strakes, greenish or reddish, which in sight are lower than the wall;*
**Leviticus 14:37**

1 Kings 8 demonstrates **plague (נגע Nega)** as more than a physical disease.

*Whatever prayer, whatever supplication is made by anyone, or by all Your people Israel, when each one knows <u>the plague (נגע Nega) of his own heart,</u> and spreads out his hands toward this temple…*
*that Your eyes may be open to the supplication of Your servant and the supplication of Your people Israel, to listen to them whenever they call to You.*
*For You separated them from among all the peoples of the earth to be Your inheritance, as You spoke by Your servant Moses, when You brought our fathers out of Egypt, O Lord God.*
**1 Kings 8:37, 52**

Spiritual diseases are manifested in physical forms, as on skin, clothing, and even houses…. . 1 Kings 8:37, 52 speaks about when a person who knows **the plague of his own heart** and comes to the LORD humbly, GOD would be open to his prayers and listen to him.

Leprosy is just an example of a disease that needs to be healed by spiritual means. The sick had to seek healing from the priest, the one who was given the authority to make them whole.

Yeshua Jesus is the High Priest that we can seek healing from any type of sickness and afflictions, whether it be physical, emotional, spiritual, or in any form.

## 26. TAZRIA/METZORA // SHE WILL CONCEIVE / LEPER

*Where <u>Jesus</u> has entered as a forerunner for us, having <u>become a high priest forever</u> according to the order of Melchizedek.*
**Hebrews 6:20**

*For <u>He healed</u> many, so that as many as had afflictions pressed about Him to touch Him. And the unclean spirits, whenever they saw Him, fell down before Him and cried out, saying, "You are the Son of God."*
**Mark 3:10-11**

The duality of spiritual sickness surfacing and displaying in the physical manifestation of the disease show that leprosy discussed in these Double Portions is more than a mere physical illness. The fact that it spreads to garments and walls of houses is an interesting phenomenon.

You will see how the Double Portions are summed up here —

תזריע Tazria (She will conceive) comes from the Hebrew root זרע Zara, meaning sowing seed. A **woman conceives/sows a seed to** — **a Leper** / a diseased one, the **Leper Messiah,** One that would be rejected and shunned.

**She will conceive a Leper,** a Suffering/Leper Messiah, to bring Redemption and life for GOD's children, which has always been GOD's Original Plan, His Plan A. It's a Restoration Plan. **That male seed** sown will come to fruition as our Redemption in the reality and truth in the duality of the Leper Messiah and King Messiah.

Have you given up on Plan A, and tried to think up Plan B, Plan C, .... ?

Recently, I heard an amazing testimony of my friend's "prodigal son" returning home. His parents have been praying and crying tears of desperation for many years. Their son lived in the agony of drug addiction and on the path of destruction. On the day of having been released from jail, he met a kind stranger who gave him clean clothes and offered him a place to get cleaned up. The son just wanted to call his mother and let her know he wanted to come home.

Can you imagine the surprise of the phone call and the joy of hearing her son is okay, not having heard from him for 2 years? That day, that stranger "randomly" showed up on the prodigal son's path and led him to receive the Love of Yeshua Jesus.

His parents never gave up on GOD's Plan A, GOD's Plan A of redemption and restoration for their son.

Were there heartbreaks in the detours and disappointments? Sure.

But GOD's faithfulness endures forever.

Let's pray:

**Our Father in Heaven** אבינו שבשמימ,

Thank You for Your plans for us. Your steadfast love endures forever, and Your faithfulness is renewed every morning. LORD, please help us to trust in Your perfect plan. Help us remember the covenant promises You have made with us and for us when we forget. Guide us to walk by faith and not by sight, for things seen are temporal, but things unseen are eternal. And, we declare through Yeshua Jesus that we are set on the path to Restoration and Redemption, to GOD's original perfect plan.

B'Shem Yeshua HaMashiach בשם ישוע המשיח.

In Jesus' Name we pray. Amen.

# 26. TORAH TASTING

## *REFLECTION*

1. What is the word, picture or theme the LORD is highlighting to you in this chapter and Torah Portion?

2. Leper Messiah, the king and the pauper are mentioned in this chapter. The concept of the Messiah being both king and leper is in Jewish Traditions. Yeshua Jesus humbled himself to be incarnated in human form to bring us redemption. He came in a form that was not recognized as King Messiah. Matthew 25:37 tells us the deeds that we do to help the poor and needy; we do it for the Messiah. What are some things we can do to serve the LORD by helping the poor and needy?

3. In this Torah Portion, I shared about our children's Bar and Bat Mitzvah as the rite of passage as Jews. Is there anything in your family or have you witnessed in friends about their traditions of rite of passage preparing a young person for adulthood, specifically in the spiritual area?

# 27 כז
# Acharei Mot / Kedoshim
## (After the Death / Holy)

אחרי מות

קדושים

Leviticus 16:1-18:30 / 19:1-20:27

Ezekiel 22:1-19 / Amos 9:7-15

Matthew 15:10-20; Mark 12:28-34 / Mark 12:28-34

We have a Double Portion again this week with Parashat Acharei Mot אחרי מות (After the Death) and Parashat Kedoshim (Holy). We will focus on Parashat Acharei Mot אחרי מות (After the Death), which begins with-

*The LORD spoke to Moses after the death of the two sons of Aaron, when they drew near before the LORD and died.*
**Leviticus 16:1**

What follows are the rituals commanded for the Day of Atonement, Yom Kippur. It consists of the bull offering, ram offering, goat offering and a goat of atonement to be released into the wilderness. The word Blood appears 13 times in this portion concerning Yom Kippur in Leviticus 16:14, 14, 15, 15, 15, 15, 18, 18,19, 27, 17:4, 4, 6.

Blood is required to atone for our sins.

Without blood, sins cannot be atoned for. Period.

There is no substitution.

Each Hebrew alphabet is associated with a number. Is it a coincidence that the sum of the four numbers coinciding with the four Hebrew letters of the word אהבה Love Ahava is 13? In the same way, the Hebrew words אחד Echad One and אבי Av My Father also sum up to be 13.

Is it possible that the 13 Blood-mentions of the altar sacrifice point to the Love of our Father, the One True GOD?

The number 13 usually is known as an unlucky or haunted number. And yet we see the number 13 connects with the Father's Love?

What if 13 is GOD's Redemption plan with Yeshua Jesus the Messiah, Yeshua HaMashiach's Blood to show our Father's Love (the One True GOD) for His Children?

What if 13 is the 12 Tribes of Israel + 1 True Covenant GOD (13 = 12+1) to complete the Divinely Ordained Family?

What if 13 is the 12 Disciples + 1 The Great Rabbi Yeshua (13 = 12+1) to bring Light to the Dark world to execute the Final Kingdom Restoration Mission?

What if 13 is not an unlucky number but instead a Powerful Display of GOD's Restoration Strategy of Justice and His Love for His Children?

What if the thing that GOD intended to be good, the enemy has distorted it?

Here are a few scriptures demonstrating the devil being the father of lies and deceiving GOD's people to lead them astray —

*You are of your father the devil, and your will is to do your father's desires. He was a murderer from the beginning, and does not stand in the truth, because there is no truth in him. When he lies, he speaks out of his own character, for he is a liar and the father of lies.*
**John 8:44**

*And the great dragon was thrown down, that ancient serpent, who is called the devil and Satan, the deceiver of the whole world — he was thrown down to the earth, and his angels were thrown down with him.*
**Revelation 12:9**

*In their case the god of this world has blinded the minds of the unbelievers, to keep them from seeing the light of the gospel of the glory of Christ, who is the image of God.*
**2 Corinthians 4:4**

Oftentimes, the Adversary, Satan, distorts the Truth and good plans the LORD has intended for us.

The provision of sin atonement on Yom Kippur stems from the Father's Love. No doubt. It is fascinating that right after the instructions for atonement involving 13 appearances of the word Blood, in Leviticus 17:10-13, God specifically speaks against eating blood.

*'And whatever man of the house of Israel, or of the strangers who dwell among you, who eats any blood, <u>I will set My face against that person</u> who eats blood, <u>and will cut him off from among his people.</u> For the life (**soul**) of the flesh is in the blood, and I have given it to you upon the altar to make atonement for your **souls**; for it is the blood that makes atonement for the **soul**.'... for it is the life (soul) of all flesh. Its blood sustains its life (soul). Therefore I said to the children of Israel, 'You shall not eat the blood of any flesh, for the life (soul) of all flesh is its blood. Whoever eats it shall <u>be cut off</u>.'*
**Leviticus 17:12, 14**

The consequence of eating blood of any flesh is that the LORD will set His face against that person and that he will be cut off from among his people. When GOD sets His face on us, there is salvation.

*Restore us, O LORD God of hosts; Cause Your face to shine (on us), And we shall be saved!*
**Psalm 80:19**

*Thus I establish My covenant with you: Never again shall all flesh <u>be cut off</u> (כרת Karat/ cease, destroy, kill) by the waters of the flood; never again shall there be a flood to destroy the earth."*
**Genesis 9:11**

The word כרת Karat means to cut off, kill or destroy. The punishment for eating blood is that the LORD will turn away and that ultimately leads to destruction and death.

To understand the possible reasons for the severity of this punishment, we need to read deeper into Leviticus 17. Leviticus 17:14 says of Blood, "for it is the life of all flesh. Its blood sustains its life." The word translated for life is from the Hebrew word נפש Nefesh, meaning Soul and Life. Every human has a human soul. According to Leviticus 17:12, GOD gave us the Blood (the soul of the flesh in the Blood) to make atonement for the soul. It is very clear that the Blood was given to us for one purpose, and one purpose only — Atonement.

GOD clearly warned us against consuming any blood because of the detrimental spiritual significance. What did ancient people know about the power of blood? Blood was and is still a major part of the occult world. Those who practice black magic, witchcraft, spells and such have been incorporating blood into their rituals for thousands of years. The blood of human and animals contain life source and can provide tremendous power to these practitioners. Characters in movies and books have been portrayed as drinking blood to obtain supernatural power from the dark side.

What a blatant mockery of the commandment of the LORD against consuming of blood!

The Word <u>Blood</u> in Hebrew דם Dam. The letter ד Dalet means door or opening. The letter מ Mem means <u>water.</u> דם Dam Blood is Door to the flowing of water. Life depends on water. That is what blood is — our life source, physical and spiritual.

> *Then Pharaoh commanded all his people,*
> *"Every son that is born to the Hebrews you shall cast into the Nile,*
> *but you shall let every daughter live."*
> **Exodus 1:22**

Pharaoh ordered to have every Hebrew newborn boy thrown into the Nile River. The water was to be filled with Hebrew babies' blood. The Egyptian god Hapi was depicted as a water bearer and worshipped as the god of the Nile River. The first plague the LORD displayed His might by turning the Nile River water into blood. Again, we are seeing the blood and water connection here. The Nile River was Egyptians' life source. Is it possible that during the time Hebrew babies were being thrown into the River, Egyptians continued to consume the water from the River? And perhaps turning the Nile River water into blood was to show the

LORD's supreme power over the Hapi god, as well as cutting off the very life source for the Egyptians?

In recent years, certain companies have marketed drinking the blood of the young to restore youthful vitality. Medical clinicians have offered cures to various illnesses with blood consumption. These are supposed to have nothing to do with the supernatural of the dark side, so they claim. We already see that blood indeed contains the life of a person or an animal. Outside of the atonement rituals, consuming it would lead to devastating consequences.

About the destructive sin of eating Blood… GOD intended for Blood to atone for our sins by having the priest sprinkle blood on His people. The mere ritual of being covered in sacrificial blood, along with the altar offering of the sacrifice, would lead to the cleansing of people's sins. But …

What if Eating Blood is about warning against Defiance; the rebellious ones say — "GOD says sprinkling blood and covering with blood brings atonement, BUT I say drinking/consuming it in order that I would have that atoning power within me, perhaps I would be the entity to bring forth the atoning power then?"

Does that sound familiar? In Genesis 3:1, the serpent said, "<u>Has GOD indeed said</u>, 'You shall not eat of every tree of the garden'?"

> *And Samuel said, "Has the Lord as great delight in burnt offerings and sacrifices, as in obeying the voice of the Lord?*
> *Behold, <u>to obey is better than sacrifice</u>, and to listen than the fat of rams.*
> **1 Samuel 15:22**

GOD cares more about our genuine obedience from the heart than our sacrifices. My theory is Eating Blood is not so much about the destructive consequences eating blood leads to (i.e., Witchcraft and black magic practices), but even more so, it is about mocking GOD's perfect Atonement Plan.

## 27. ACHAREI MOT/KEDOSHIM // AFTER THE DEATH / HOLY

One More thing about the Blood...

The word for Mankind in Hebrew is אדמ Adam, the name of the first created man. It consists of the Hebrew letter א Aleph and then the word דמ Dam, meaning Blood. The letter א Aleph is a silent letter and, the first of all letters believed to represent GOD. אדמ Mankind is designed to have GOD (א Aleph) leading the physical body (דמ Dam Blood) and as the main component of our living. Apart from Him, we are nothing and have no good.

*I am the vine; you are the branches. Whoever abides in me and I in him, he it is that bears much fruit, for apart from me you can do nothing.*
**John 15:5**

*I say to the LORD, "You are my Lord; I have no good apart from you."*
**Psalm 16:2**

Demonic forces can stir up fear and fright, but as children of the Living GOD, who is the All-Powerful Ruler of the Universe, do we have any doubt the dark side is nothing next to our GOD Most High? No human or animal blood sacrifice can ever compare to the Blood sacrifice of the Mashiach Yeshua Jesus!

*For the bodies of those animals whose blood is brought into the holy places by the high priest as a sacrifice for sin are burned outside the camp. So Jesus also suffered outside the gate in order to sanctify the people through his own blood.*
**Hebrews 13:11-12**

Do we, as children of GOD and followers of our Mashiach Yeshua, truly understand the Unsurpassable Power of the Blood of Yeshua Jesus?

My friends, Bob and Maureen, have lived in Indonesia for several years. They made some wonderful missionary friends in the region. One of them was an 18-year-old evangelist named Joy from New Zealand. Joy had a charismatic personality and made friends everywhere she went. She even learned the local language and loved sharing the Good News of Yeshua Jesus with everyone. One time while being on the beautiful island of Bali, a place filled with Hindus, Joy was invited by a young Hindu friend to go to the temple. Being young and naive, Joy had no idea what she was walking into. Once inside the temple, the service began, and things quickly turned dark and scary. Joy witnessed demonic manifestations around her. Objects were flying over her head. At that moment, she realized she should not have been there. All she could do was squat down and bow her head with her hands covering her head to protect flying objects from hurting her. She then instinctively said these words, "I ask the Blood of Jesus to cover and protect me." Moments later, a Hindu woman took a look at Joy, horrified, screaming, "I see Blood! I see Blood!" Eventually, Joy was rescued from the temple and brought to a safe place. Joy asked to be covered with the Blood of Jesus spiritually, and the supernatural protection was seen by a woman's physical eyes. What an incredible display of the power of the Blood of the LORD Yeshua Jesus!

Needless to say, this experience became a great faith-builder for Joy. It strengthened her faith and emboldened her to move forward to testify of the power of the Messiah with many people!

*And the Lord said, "What have you done? The voice of your brother's blood is crying to me from the ground.*
**Genesis 4:10**

*He is clothed in a robe dipped in blood, and the name by which he is called is The Word of God.*
**Revelation 19:13**

The first time Blood appears in the Torah is when Cain murders his brother, Abel. Abel's blood cried out from the ground. This incident shows us the first violent crime of murder committed, and Abel's blood cried out for justice. However, the last time Blood appears in the Bible is when Yeshua Jesus, our Messiah, returns with his robe dipped in blood, bringing salvation to the world. Yeshua Jesus brought Justice to the world.

*Then I saw heaven opened, and behold, a white horse! The one sitting on it is called Faithful and True, and in righteousness he judges and makes war.*
**Revelations 19:11**

*Truly, truly, I say to you, whoever hears my word and believes him who sent me has eternal life. He does not come into judgment, but has passed from death to life.*
**John 5:24**

The LORD judges us for our sins, but we are declared righteous by the atonement of our Mashiach Yeshua. He has carried our sins upon Himself and washed away our iniquities by His Blood sacrifice. This Torah Portion titled אחרי מות Acharei Mot/After The Death begins with mentioning of death, then we see the Blood-atoning power in remission of sins, that provides life for us instead of death, which we deserve.

Abel's Blood cried out for justice out of his brother's sin committed against him. Yet, Yeshua's Blood executed justice and brought that to completion with the ultimate atonement for all who receive and believe Him.

**Let's pray:**

**Our Father in Heaven אבינו שבשמימ,**

We thank You for giving us life; blood flowing through our veins is Your amazing, intelligent design. You specifically mention blood containing life and soul, which holds power, but how much more is the power of our LORD Yeshua Jesus, who has shed His Blood so we can have eternal life? For that, we are eternally grateful. LORD, please continue to reveal to us how we are secure and provided for under the Blood of Yeshua Jesus. When we declare the Blood of Jesus over ourselves and our families, no power can come against us. We do not need any physical blood covering but only the spiritual covering of the LORD. In faith, we know dark powers have to flee at the Name of Yeshua and at the sight of the proclamation of the Blood of Jesus!

B'Shem Yeshua HaMashiach בשם ישוע המשיח.

In Jesus' Name we pray. Amen.

## 27. TORAH TASTING
### *REFLECTION*

1. What is the word, picture or theme the LORD is highlighting to you in this chapter and Torah Portion?

2. Blood is not seen on the outside. It is inside our veins, yet it holds the power of life. No one can live without blood. It is unseen yet life-sustaining, much like the Messiah in our lives. We have to trust in faith that He provides us with abundant life. Any characteristics of blood that stands out to you in this chapter that is applicable in understanding its atoning power?

3. Have you witnessed the amazing power of the Blood of Yeshua Jesus or any stories that you've heard that helped you understand its power?

4. Many believe the number 13 is unlucky. Oftentimes superstitions instill fear in people. Do you have any superstitions that you believed were busted by GOD before?

5. Perhaps right now you feel like it is time you surrender certain superstitions to GOD in exchange for having faith in Him, no more fear. What would they be?

# 28 כח
# EMOR
## (Say)
## אמור

Leviticus 21:1-24:23

Ezekiel 44:15-31

Matthew 26:56-66

This week's Torah Portion begins with instructions to the priests, Aaron's sons to stay holy and pure for the LORD. The rest of the Parasha covers the Biblical feasts and appointed times commanded to observe. The Torah Portion's title, אמר Emor, comes from the first verse.

*And the Lord **said** to Moses, "**Speak** to the priests, the sons of Aaron, and say to them, No one shall make himself unclean for the dead among his people...*
**Leviticus 21:1**

The Hebrew word for Say/Speak/Amar אמר is used more than 10 times in this Parasha.

The 10th mention of this word in this Torah Portion is-

*The Lord spoke (דבר D'var) to Moses, saying (אמר Amar), "Command the people of Israel to bring you pure oil from beaten olives for the lamp, that a light may be kept burning regularly.*
**Leviticus 24:1**

Additionally, there is another Hebrew word for דבר Say/Speak/D'var. It appears 17 times in this Torah Portion.

The first time the word אמר Amar is used in the Torah is found at the beginning of Creation in Genesis 1. And it is subsequently used 11 times in the Book of Genesis relating to the Creation Story.

*Then God said (אמר Amar), "Let there be light,"; and there was light.*
**Genesis 1:3**

Then, the first time דבר D'var shows up in the Torah is in Genesis 8.

*Then God said (דבר D'var) to Noah, "Go out from the ark, you and your wife, and your sons and your sons' wives with you. ¹⁷ Bring out with you every living thing that is with you of all flesh — birds and animals and every creeping thing that creeps on the earth — that they may swarm on the earth, and be fruitful and multiply on the earth."*
**Genesis 8:15-17**

Here, Genesis 8 opens up the scene showing the end of the Great Flood and water having subsided. It is finally safe for Noah and his family to come out of the Ark. The LORD then said to Noah to come out with his family and all the animals, that they may be fruitful and multiply.

Does that sound familiar?

Yes? Well, it is because the "Be fruitful and multiply" charge for the sea and land creatures is also found in Genesis 1:22.

## 28. EMOR / SAY

I find it interesting the two words (דבר D'var and אמר Amar) for saying or speaking have the "Creation" and "Life-giving" themes in common.

Genesis 1 tells us that GOD created the world by speaking out words. Jewish Traditions even go as far as GOD spoke Hebrew words; creation was formed from each of the Hebrew alphabets in the words, as each of the Hebrew letters came into existence.

What a powerful visual! Can you imagine those Hebrew alphabets floating around in the spiritual realm as the LORD spoke them and creation came to be manifested in the physical form?

No matter your theory, we can all agree that GOD's Word carries tremendous power, spoken or written. The verse of Genesis 1:3, "Then GOD said, 'Let there be light'; and there was light," displays the magnificent creative power of GOD's spoken words.

אמר Amar is the Hebrew root of Emor (Imperative/Command form — Speak!...), which is the title of this Torah Portion, "And the LORD said to Moses, '<u>Speak</u> to the priests, the sons of Aaron, and say to them…'", with instructions to stay clean and holy. The first time אמר Emor (Command form) used is in Genesis 45:17 when Pharoah told Joseph to tell his brothers to pack up their household and move to a place of abundance.

> *And Pharaoh said (אמר Emor, Hebrew root of אמר Amar) to Joseph, "Say (אמר Emor, Hebrew root of אמר Amar) to your brothers, 'Do this: load your beasts and go back to the land of Canaan, and take your father and your households, and come to me, and I will give you the best of the land of Egypt, and you shall eat the fat of the land.'…"*
> **Genesis 45:17**

The instructions for Aaron's sons to stay holy and clean have the underlining intention of life-sustaining. Unholiness and uncleanliness lead to death. Therefore, I sense that the אמר Emor reference in Leviticus 21:1 insinuates Life.

And, of course, the first time we see the אמר Emor, the Command form of אמר Amar, used is when rich provision had been made by Pharoah for Joseph and his family that they would have abundant living in Goshen. The only other time אמר Say/Amar is used in this Torah Portion is in Leviticus 24:1, referring to the Menorah, the light of the lamp is to be burnt continually.

> *Then the Lord spoke (דבר D'var) to Moses, saying (אמר Emor):* ²
> *"Command the children of Israel that they bring to you pure oil of pressed olives for the light, to make the lamps burn continually.*
> **Leviticus 24:1**

Menorah represents the LORD's perpetual presence among us, with His warmth and light. Now, do you recognize the Life-sustaining theme here? Just as the very first time the LORD spoke (Amar) in the Torah was to speak Light into existence. Light is somewhat synonymous with Life. For example, when something goes dark, life goes out. GOD's Word is weighted with His Glory and Power. His spoken words carry creative power, bringing Light into darkness.

> *Then God said, "Let us make man in our image, after our likeness. And let them have dominion over the fish of the sea and over the birds of the heavens and over the livestock and over all the earth and over every creeping thing that creeps on the earth."*
> **Genesis 1:26**

Since we are made in GOD's image and after His likeness, we are like GOD. We resemble Him. People take one look at us, and we should remind them of our Creator. We make them think about Our Father in Heaven.

So if our Father in Heaven is invisible, then in what way can we resemble Him?

Well, of course, His character: His kindness, His love, … . Others recognize our resemblance to our Father when we walk in His kindness and His love.

What if I told you when we have been redeemed through the Blood of Yeshua Jesus, our spoken words transmit His weight of Glory?

What's more? They even possess creative power?

No, it is not some mystical concept. It is indeed biblical.

> *Death and life are in the power of the tongue,*
> *and those who love it will eat its fruits.*
> **Proverbs 18:21**

> *For by your words you will be justified, and by your words you will be condemned.*
> **Matthew 12:37**

> *There is one whose rash words are like sword thrusts,*
> *but the tongue of the wise brings healing.*
> **Proverbs 12:18**

> *By the word of the Lord the heavens were made,*
> *and by the breath of his mouth all their host.*
> **Psalm 33:6**

Those are just a few examples of scriptures demonstrating the mighty force of our spoken words. Have I convinced you that our words are powerful yet?

What if the words we speak give life in power that the hearers recognize the source behind that life and glorify our Father in Heaven?

A few years ago, on a trip to the City of Los Angeles, my daughter and I shared a Lyft ride with other passengers. One of our "Lyft-mates" was a man named Harold. On our way to Hollywood, the driver made a stop, and Harold hopped on. He picked up on the conversation I had just been having with the driver about praying for his family.

Harold said with curiosity, "So, you are a Christian?"

I replied, "Yes, I am."

He then said with excitement, "I believe in god too. "Pointing to a big "statement" necklace / a thick gold chain he had around his neck with the oversized medallion-sized charms of symbols representing different religions, and proceeded to tell me all the different gods/entities he believed in. One of the charms was a big gold cross.

I said to the LORD in my head, "Father, I can't have a religious debate in this car. And I don't know what to say."

I felt that the LORD prompted me to pray for him.

So, I responded to Harold, "Man, you really don't discriminate, do you?" (meaning he gave "equal opportunity" for the many different deities.)

He shrugged his shoulders and said, "Nope."

I complimented him, "I am glad you are seeking after the Truth. The Bible says the LORD will be found when you seek after Him. Harold, is there anything I could pray for you?"

Harold then told me some personal things that he could really use some prayers for.

Well, I began to pray with him. I made sure to end every other sentence with the words, "In Jesus' Name!" to clarify and emphasize the GOD we were praying to, the One True GOD. The LORD showed me things to pray for Harold, which caused him to interrupt me a few times and ask me if I was a psychic.

He would say, "I don't think I told you those things. Are you sure you are not a psychic? How do you know those things to pray for me?"

I replied confidently, "No, I am not a psychic. The LORD knows you intimately, and He led me to pray for you. He loves you, Harold!" Harold was very much encouraged by our prayer time during our ride to Hollywood. At his destination, upon getting out of the car, he said to me, "I really appreciate you praying for me. And for that, I will honor the Name of Jesus Today!"

Wow! The LORD BE THE GLORY!

I know GOD worked with and through me that day. I don't know where Harold is now. But I know that the LORD has met him then and continued to pursue his heart.

You see, our words are just one way people see GOD's likeness and His image in us. I believe when they see GOD's likeness and get touched by His Glory, their lives are impacted in ways beyond our imaginations or expectations. Speaking life does not always come naturally to us. It takes conscious awareness and consistent practice and effort.

When someone says, "I am so bad with names." They are stating a fact with a helpless sentiment, nothing can be done. But if they say instead, "I sometimes forget people's names, but I am getting better at it," or "GOD made me good with names; this is just so unlike me!" Can you see the difference in the tone and attitude? That directly affects our thinking and therefore changes everything.

In desperate situations, we can either choose to say hopeless words like "I don't know how we can get out of this situation. Man, it looks like this is getting worse. I hope it won't, but I don't know…" or instead faith-filled words like "This situation looks bad, but with GOD all things are possible. He always provides for us. I trust Him!"

*I call heaven and earth to witness against you today,*
*that I have set before you life and death, blessing and curse.*
*Therefore choose life, that you and your offspring may live,*
**Deuteronomy 30:19**

So, what do you say? Are you ready to speak as if what you say will come into existence? Like the LORD spoke creation into existence? Would you start imagining your words carry weight in the unseen realm when you put your faith in the LORD Yeshua our Messiah? I believe when you begin to speak Life and Light into people and situations, you can and will see yourself partnering with the Creator of the Universe to bring hope and light into the places that you speak into.

Let's pray:

**Our Father in Heaven אבינו שבשמימ,**

Thank You for the creative power of Your spoken words, and therefore we have the same power to speak life as Your children. Will You open our eyes to see how our words matter and that they can either lead to life or death? LORD, help us choose to speak life and not death. Through the LORD Yeshua Jesus, we diffuse the knowledge of the Living GOD and Hope of Glory wherever you send us, that the world will see Your likeness and Your image in us, then glorify and worship You.

B'Shem Yeshua HaMashiach בשם ישוע המשיח.

In Jesus' Name we pray. Amen.

# 28. TORAH TASTING
## *REFLECTION*

1. What is the word, picture or theme the LORD is highlighting to you in this chapter and Torah Portion?

2. This Torah Portion highlights "The LORD speaks" and how His word brings life. In what way does life and light in GOD's word resonate with you? Is there an area in your life that you're speaking life into?

3. Have you experienced someone speaking words of love and kindness into you that caused something to shift and change? Perhaps an incident in that you spoke hope into someone changed their perspective and even the outcome of a situation?

4. The LORD said life and death is set before us and tells us to choose life. What are the reasons why people speak death rather than life over themselves or their loved ones? What are some practical ways that we can practice speaking life more?

# 29 כט
# Behar / Bechukotai
## (On the Mountain / In My Statutes)

בהר

בחקותי

Behar / Bechukotai

Leviticus 25-27

Jeremiah 16:19-17:14

Luke 4:14-22, Matthew 16:20-28

---

This week's Torah Portion is a Double portion of the readings of Behar and Bechukotai. The title of Behar / In The Mountains is taken from the first verse in Leviticus 25.

> *The Lord then spoke to Moses **on Mount** Sinai, saying,*
> *"Speak to the sons of Israel and say to them,*
> *'When you come into the land which I am going to give you,*
> *then the land shall have a Sabbath to the Lord.*
> **Leviticus 25:1-2**

This portion lays out the laws regarding Sabbatical Years and the Years of Jubilee, as well as instructions for redemption. Meanwhile, Bechukotai / In My Statutes (Leviticus 26:3-27:34)

covers the blessings for obeying GOD's instructions and curses in detail as a result of breaking GOD's commandments.

Again, each Torah Portion covers a variety of topics, filled with many hidden treasures to be discovered. As we study and meditate on GOD's Word, certain things are highlighted to us. They may be different for you and me. The Word of GOD is living and powerful. We can read the same portion several times. The LORD can and often does give us new revelations. For this week's Portion, I would like to talk about the idea of "Redemption" embedded throughout this Parasha.

Redemption is a word we don't often use. It is not common to have "redeem" or "redemption" come up in daily conversations outside of religious settings. However, I learned the concept of redemption as a child in the context of soda-drinking. When purchasing a glass bottle of soda, an amount of deposit is built into the purchase price. For example, if I pay $1.00 for a bottle of soda, 5 cents out of the dollar is the deposit. Therefore, when I have finished drinking the soda, I can then "redeem" the 5-cents deposit back when returning the empty glass bottle. Only by giving back the bottle, the deposit can then be returned to the consumer.

Believe it or not, this is still in practice today.

Redemption is available for all, but not all receive redemption.

You see, the deposit of 5 cents is mine and belongs to me, but if I don't bring back the bottle, there is NO Redemption.

In ancient times, it was not uncommon to sell properties and even oneself as a servant during hard times. In China, even up to the early 1900's, families would sell their children as servants to wealthy families in order to have a better life for their children. Some of these servants either stay for life with their masters or redeem themselves with an agreed contracted price.

It is hard for us modern people to imagine doing that. The closest thing may be selling something in a pawn shop for a period of time for some quick and desperately-needed cash. Within a certain window of time, the owner could come back and redeem or buy back the item.

Redemption means to claim back or buy back. The idea is returning to claim back something that used to belong to me for a price that was given up for a time by an agreement.

The Hebrew word for "Redeem" is גאל Gaal. The Hebrew root גאל Gaal is used 22 times in this Double Portion! The first time of Gaal גאל's appearance in the Torah is in Genesis 48.

> *And he (Jacob) **blessed Joseph, and said:***
> *"God, before whom my fathers Abraham and Isaac walked, The God who has fed me all my life long to this day,* [16] *The Angel who **has redeemed** (גאל Gaal) me from all evil, Bless the lads;*
> *Let my name be named upon them, And the name of my fathers Abraham and Isaac;*
> *And let them grow into a multitude in the midst of the earth."*
> **Genesis 48:15-16**

The Law of First is the first time a Hebrew word appears in the Torah, offering clues to the essence of the word. Through the Law of First here in Genesis 48:15-16, we can see blessings are attached to the redemption גאל Gaal concept. The first mention of redeeming something is at Jacob's dying moment. He blessed Joseph, Joseph's children and their descendants. He pointed out that it is GOD that shepherded and fed him his whole life and "has redeemed" him from ALL EVIL. Jacob blessed them. The LORD made some incredible promises to Abraham and his descendants. After many drama-worthy ups and downs in Jacob's life, with all twelve children by his deathbed, he was content to declare that he had been redeemed from all evil. That indicates that at one point, he was taken by the evil one, and GOD was his Redeemer. I have learned that GOD always has a redemption plan. The Adversary can attempt to rob us of the blessings that have been promised to us; in the end, GOD's redemption plan trumps any evil schemes. We only need to be patient and willing to trust Him.

As Shavuot/The Feast of Weeks/Pentecost is fast approaching, counting the Omer each day, the Book of Ruth is on my mind. Biblical Shavuot is a festival that celebrates the first fruits of the wheat harvest.

> *And you shall celebrate the **Feast of Weeks**,*
> *that is, **the first fruits of the wheat harvest**,*
> *and the **Feast of Ingathering** at the turn of the year.*
> **Exodus 34:22**

Later, the rabbinic Shavuot became a time to celebrate the giving of the Torah. The Greek word Pentecost (meaning 50) has come to be known as the Giving of the Holy Spirit in The Book of Acts.

> *When **the day of Pentecost** had come, they were all together in one place.*
> *And suddenly, a noise like a violent rushing wind came from heaven, and it filled the whole house where they were sitting. And tongues that looked like fire appeared to them, distributing themselves, and a tongue rested on each one of them.*
> *And they were all filled with the **Holy Spirit** and began to speak with different tongues, as the Spirit was giving them the ability to speak out.*
> **Acts 2: 2-4**

It is customary to read the Book of Ruth during the Shavuot observance.

## 29. BEHAR/BECHUKOTAI // ON THE MOUNTAIN / IN MY STATUTES

*So Naomi returned, and with her Ruth the Moabitess, her daughter-in-law, who returned from the land of Moab. And they came to Bethlehem at the beginning of barley harvest.*
**Ruth 1:22**

*So she stayed close by the young women of Boaz, to glean until the end of barley harvest and wheat harvest; and she dwelt with her mother-in-law.*
**Ruth 2:23**

Amazingly, aside from Spring Harvest being the major backdrop of the story, the redemption theme in the Book of Ruth is one of the strongest in the entire Bible. It illustrates a family that had sold their land and moved to Moab, a foreign land. After some time, the wife Naomi lost her husband and two sons, which were her everything. Her last hope was to return to Bethlehem, her hometown. Ruth, her daughter-in-law, unwilling to leave her side, insisted on returning to Bethlehem with Naomi. If you've read the book, you know about the happy ending. A hero named Boaz came to the rescue in the form of a kinsman-redeemer. Here is the tie-in that gets interesting. The redemption law laid out in Leviticus 25 (in this Double portion of בהר Behar/In The Mountains and בחקתי Bechukotai/In My Statutes) gives the instructions of what needs to be done for Naomi to reclaim her land for her dead husband and sons.

25 "*If your brother becomes poor and sells part of his property, then his <u>nearest redeemer</u> shall come and redeem what his brother has sold...*
"*If a man sells a dwelling house in a walled city, he may redeem it within a year of its sale. For a full year he shall have the right of redemption. If it is not redeemed within a full year, then the house in the walled city shall belong in perpetuity to the buyer, throughout his generations; it shall not be released in the jubilee...*
"*If a stranger or sojourner with you becomes rich, and your brother beside him becomes poor and sells himself to the stranger or sojourner with you or to a member of the stranger's clan,* 48 *then after he is sold he may be redeemed. One of his brothers may redeem him, or his uncle or his cousin may redeem him, or a close relative from his clan may redeem him. Or if he grows rich he may redeem himself.*
**Leviticus 25:25, 29-31, 47-49**

"*If brothers dwell together, and one of them dies and has no son, the wife of the dead man shall not be married outside the family to a stranger. Her husband's brother shall go into her and take her as his wife and perform the duty of a husband's brother to her. And the first son whom she bears shall succeed to the name of his dead brother, that his name may not be blotted out of Israel. And if the man does not wish to take his brother's wife, then his brother's wife shall go up to the gate to the elders and say, 'My husband's brother refuses to perpetuate his brother's name in Israel; he will not perform the duty of a husband's brother to me.' Then the elders of his city shall call him and speak to him, and if he persists, saying, 'I do not wish to take her,' then his brother's wife shall go up to him in the presence of the elders and pull his sandal off his foot and spit in his face. And she shall answer and say, 'So shall it be done to the man who does not build up his brother's house.' And the name of his house shall be called in Israel, '<u>The house of him who had his sandal pulled off.</u>'*
**Deuteronomy 25:5-10**

The characters in the Book of Ruth followed the law fulfilling a family obligation —

> *Now this was the custom in former times in Israel concerning the redemption and the exchange of land to confirm any matter: a man removed his sandal and gave it to another; and this was the way of confirmation in Israel.* <u>*So the redeemer said to Boaz, "Buy it for yourself." And he removed his sandal.*</u> *Then Boaz said to the elders and all the people, "You are witnesses today that I have bought from the hand of Naomi all that belonged to Elimelech and all that belonged to Chilion and Mahlon.*
> **Ruth 4:7-9**

Don't you love that GOD always provides a plan of Restoration? The "taking off sandal" part is humorous to some, but the situation is a serious matter. I can't help but think there is interesting significance. The kinsman refuses to redeem the land. He then takes off his sandal. Could that be a symbolism he can no longer claim the land he treads on, giving up his right to redeem the land? Boaz's act of taking up the role of the Kinsman Redeemer not only restored the land for Naomi and her family but his firstborn with Ruth would also perpetuate the name of her dead husband and partake Boaz's own inheritance as well. Remember early on, we saw Jacob's blessings closely tied to GOD's redemption of him? Well, here we have the consequence of tremendous blessings from Naomi's redemption of the land.

**Let's read on —**

> So Boaz took Ruth, and she became his wife, and he had relations with her. And the Lord enabled her to conceive, and <u>she gave birth to a son</u>. Then <u>the women said to Naomi, "Blessed is the Lord who has not left you without a redeemer today, and may his name become famous in Israel</u>. ¹⁵ May he also be to you one who restores life and sustains your old age; for your daughter-in-law, who loves you and is better to you than seven sons, has given birth to him."
> ¹⁶ Then Naomi took the child and laid him in her lap, and became his nurse. ¹⁷ And the neighbor women gave him a name, saying, "A son has been born to Naomi!" So they named him Obed. He is the father of Jesse, the father of David.
> ¹⁸ Now these are the generations of Perez: Perez fathered Hezron, ¹⁹ Hezron fathered Ram, and Ram fathered Amminadab, ²⁰ and Amminadab fathered Nahshon, and Nahshon fathered Salmon, ²¹ and Salmon fathered Boaz, and Boaz fathered Obed, ²² and Obed fathered Jesse, and Jesse fathered David.
> Ruth 4:13-22

The ending to this story is SO SWEET!

How Naomi went from being **bitter** (Ruth 1:20: "But she said to them, "Do not call me Naomi; call me Mara, for the Almighty has dealt very **bitter**ly with me.) to "**sweet**."

It is incredible that Naomi was blessed in her old age, and the Greatest King of Israel would later come from her lineage.

Do you know what else I find interesting?

While we proclaim, "Blessed is the LORD who is our Redeemer and His Great Name becomes famous in the land," we are blessed in the process. GOD is blessed; therefore we are blessed. When we say to Him, "We bless You, LORD." He says, "Therefore, you are blessed also." Our being blessed is a natural by-product of us blessing GOD!

ISN'T THAT SO GOOD?

Hebrew alphabets are fascinating. In these 3 letters of the word גאל **Gaal** ג-א-ל, we see 2 components — Gimel ג (the alphabet Gimel) and אל EL. אל EL is a word for God, and the letter ג Gimel means to lift up or pride. My theory is that "Redeeming" something (returning something to the rightful owner for a purchase price) would lift up אל EL GOD and lead to His Pride? Aren't we His Pride and Joy?

> *Looking only at Jesus, the originator and perfecter of the faith, who for the joy set before Him endured the cross, despising the shame, and has sat down at the right hand of the throne of God.*
> **Hebrews 12:2**

I believe so. I believe we are that Pride and Joy that was set before Yeshua Jesus when He paid the ultimate price for our lives to claim us back to Him and our Father in Heaven.

The LORD Yeshua Jesus Christ paid the ultimate price, laying down his own life with his body broken and blood shed so that we can be redeemed and our eternal life restored.

> *If you address as Father the One who impartially judges according to each one's work, conduct yourselves in fear during the time of your stay on earth; <u>knowing that you were not redeemed with perishable things like silver or gold</u> from your futile way of life inherited from your forefathers, <u>but with precious blood, as of a lamb unblemished and spotless, the blood of Christ.</u>*
> **1 Peter 1:17-19**

Do you realize we are living in a time of Harvest?

The harvest of souls that the LORD talked about in the Old and the New Testaments.

> *You have multiplied the nation; you have increased its joy; they rejoice before you as with joy at **the harvest**, as they are glad when they divide the spoil.*
> **Isaiah 9:3**

> *Then he said to his disciples, "The harvest is plentiful, but the laborers are few; therefore pray earnestly to the Lord of the harvest to send out laborers into **his harvest**."*
> **Matthew 9:37-38**

Yeshua the Mashiach Jesus the LORD is GOEL GADOL גאל גדול The Great Redeemer of souls for the Harvest!!

He is our Ultimate Kinsman Redeemer (the One who has the right to make the redemption through our Heavenly Father). He gave us His all, so we can have it all. Through His redemption comes the most amazing blessings in our reconciliation with the Father and the gift of life through salvation.

We are living in the time of Harvest, with GOD's Redemption Plan through Yeshua Jesus.

We are blessed beyond measure.

⁸ *'And you shall count seven sabbaths of years for yourself, seven times seven years; and the time of the seven sabbaths of years shall be to you forty-nine years. ⁹ Then you shall cause the <u>trumpet of the Jubilee to sound</u> on the tenth day of the seventh month; on the Day of Atonement you shall make the trumpet to sound throughout all your land. ¹⁰ And you shall <u>consecrate the fiftieth year, and proclaim liberty throughout all the land</u> to all its inhabitants. It shall be a Jubilee for you; and each of you shall return to his possession, and each of you shall return to his family...*
²⁸ <u>*But if he is not able to have it restored to himself,*</u> *then what was sold shall remain in the hand of him who bought it until the Year of Jubilee;* <u>*and in the Jubilee it shall be released, and he shall return to his possession...*</u>
³⁹ *'And if one of your brethren who dwells by you becomes poor, and sells himself to you, you shall not compel him to serve as a slave. ⁴⁰ As a hired servant and a sojourner he shall be with you, and shall serve you until the Year of Jubilee. ⁴¹ And then he shall depart from you — he and his children with him — and shall return to his own family. He shall return to the possession of his fathers.*
**Leviticus 25:8-10, 28, 39-41**

This Double Portion bears the good news of the Year of Jubilee: debts are forgiven, possessions are restored and slaves are liberated. In Leviticus 25:1-2, the LORD told Moses on the mountain that His people would enter into the Promise Land and the land would rest for the LORD.

Do you feel like you've been robbed? Not just physical possessions but spiritual ones as well, blessings, relationships, health, … or perhaps spiritual territories that the enemy has taken ground? I have good news for you! Rest in the LORD and His promises for you. We have The Great Redeemer that has not refused to do what a Kinsman Redeemer is to do but also has agreed and paid the price to redeem, claim back and buy back what the Father has meant to give us to have eternal life and a relationship with Him.

**Let's pray:**

**Our Father in Heaven** אבינו שבשמימ,

Thank You for providing a Restoration Plan. You always come through according to Your perfect will. Thank You for the Ultimate Kinsman Redeemer, to claim back what belongs to You, us as Your Children. As Our Redeemer has acted, we declare and claim back physical territory and spiritual territory for the Kingdom of GOD. We do not seek after blessings, but how sweet it is that You bless us enormously as a result of Your Redemption of us. LORD, open our eyes to see the Harvest around us and bring the good news of redemption to the lost, that they too would be redeemed and brought back to Your heart.

B'Shem Yeshua HaMashiach בשם ישוע המשיח.

In Jesus' Name we pray. Amen.

## 29. TORAH TASTING
### *REFLECTION*

1. -What is the word, picture or theme the LORD is highlighting to you in this chapter and Torah Portion?

2. -This Torah Portion discusses the topic of redemption. It is buying back, returning something like property in a Sabbatical year or the Year of Jubilee. What are some things, physical or spiritual, that have been taken from you that you need to claim back? Have you been in a situation that you felt stuck, perhaps even right now, that you need to be set free from?

3. -Whenever GOD redeems, He also blesses. Receiving GOD's redemption unlocks many blessings. Have you seen any real-life examples of that?

# 30 ל
# BEMIDBAR
## (In the Wilderness)
### במדבר

Numbers 1:1-4:20

Hosea 2:1-22

Matthew 4:1-7

This week's Parasha opens up the Book of Numbers, "In the Wilderness" במדבר Bemidbar. This portion begins with GOD commanding Moses to number all the men of military age (at and over the age of twenty). The title "In the Wilderness" במדבר Bemidbar is taken from the first verse in this portion.

> *The Lord spoke to Moses **in the wilderness** (במדבר Bemidbar) of Sinai, in the tent of meeting, on the first day of the second month, in the second year after they had come out of the land of Egypt, saying, "Take a census of all the congregation of the people of Israel, by clans, by fathers' houses, according to the number of names, every male, head by head.*
> **Numbers 1:1-2**

What is noteworthy is that the focus of last week's Double Portion was בהר Behar On the Mountain. "The Lord then spoke to Moses **on Mount** Sinai…" (Leviticus 25:1). This week, it's about The LORD speaking to Moses **in the wilderness** (desert) of Sinai. The LORD spoke about redemption on the Mountain, and the LORD here spoke about the numbering of the Children of Israel and their encampment positions surrounding the Tabernacle, the Levites' duties, as well as redemption of the Firstborn. The LORD can speak on the mountain, as well in the wilderness. He sometimes calls us to go up higher to meet Him. Other times, He simply meets us where we are. I believe the instructions He gave Moses are for specific purposes, not random. We may not fully comprehend those purposes, but we need to trust in the LORD.

This Torah Portion starts out with lots of numbers and positioning of each tribe of Israel. That sounds like a military strategy, lots of organization in preparation of something to come. One of my favorite Bible scholars, Dr. Michael Heiser and author of many books such as "The Unseen Realm," says of the Wilderness as a place filled with wild beasts and unclean spirits. That is a very interesting observation. On the way to the Promise Land, Moses led GOD's people through the Wilderness/ the desert. Through their time in the desert, we see that in the second Book of the Torah, Leviticus ויקרא Vayikra And He called, the LORD gave lots of instructions on purification and sacrificial offering rituals. Why? That may have to do with them being in the Wilderness? Is that possible that they were entering into enemy territory, staying "clean" and being marked as "GOD's people" is key for them to be protected and untouched? While some brush over the book of Leviticus for its complexity, it may very well be the Lifeline for GOD's people.

What does "Numbering" have to do with being "In the Wilderness"?

Census was done once before for poll tax purposes in Exodus 38.

## 30. BEMIDBAR / IN THE WILDERNESS

*A bekah for each man (that is, half a shekel, according to the shekel of the sanctuary), for everyone included in the **numbering** (פקד F'kad) from twenty years old and above, for six hundred and three thousand, five hundred and fifty men (603,550).*
**Exodus 38:26**

I believe the key lies in the word פקד F'kad "number" used here. In Exodus 38:26, the Hebrew used is פקד F'kad, which means muster or call together (troops). In Numbers 1:2, the Hebrew words used are שאו את ראש כל עדת בני ישראל. It literally means "Lift up the head of all the congregation of the children of Israel". שאו את ראש (Su et rosh) is translated as the phrase "Take the sum." The Hebrew root for the word שאו Su is Nasa נשא means to lift up, carry or take. Here, it is translated as "sum up" or "count" in English. What follows provides us with the purpose of the "counting" or "lifting up" of these men.

*From twenty years old and upward, all in Israel who are able to go to war, you and Aaron shall **list** (פקד F'kad) them, company by company.*
**Numbers 1:3**

Now, I understand linguists and scholars may argue that those are simply random words being used, "Don't read too much into it." That's just how the language was being applied. To me, I think GOD is intentional in certain words being used. We may disagree; however, I cannot help but see certain words being used for specific purposes.

*All who were numbered were six hundred and three thousand five hundred and fifty (603,550).*
**Numbers 1:26**

The word "number" (פקד F'kad) in Exodus 38 has a military connotation in numbering for poll tax purposes. The purpose of summing up Israel's men was to prepare for future warfare. In both counting incidents, the concluded number is 603,550. In Numbers 1:3, when they were counting these military-age men, they had to lift up the head (literally what the

Hebrew words say). They were not just numbers, counting heads one by one; faces are seen with their heads lifted. "Lift up the head" may be the phrase "Sum up" all the congregation of the children of Israel. These men were counted individually, but collectively they are one, one nation.

Now, going back to the Numbering and Wilderness connection, I'd like to suggest that even though going into the Wilderness can be scary, with lots of unknown, unfriendly entities awaiting with unkind intentions, the LORD has equipped us for this process. Getting through the desert is a necessary path into the Promise Land. However, GOD has a plan. He always does. Never undermine the preparation (Leviticus' sacrificial offering and purification rituals)!

Do not underestimate the power of numbering, lifting up the head, and taking inventory of our resources in preparation for battle.

While war is inevitable, the LORD has promised and reassured victory throughout the Torah.

> *Moses answered the people, "Do not be afraid. Stand firm and you will see the deliverance the Lord will bring you today. The Egyptians you see today you will never see again. The Lord will fight for you; you need only to be still."*
> **Exodus 14:13-14**

I think the saying, "There is madness to the method," is so appropriate to GOD's strategies. Sometimes, we see madness like the command for the Children of Israel to march around Jericho city walls once each day for 6 days, then 7 times on the $7^{th}$ day in Joshua 6. That seems like madness to the logical human mind, but the walls crumbled down, and Israel captured the city of Jericho. That is just one of many examples of the methods of madness deployed in the Bible. GOD uses a variety of methods. Oftentimes, they seem outright "crazy." Even in the ways Yeshua Jesus the Mashiach performed miracles, He did not do the same thing. There is no set formula. We just need to believe.

## 30. BEMIDBAR / IN THE WILDERNESS

The military strategies adopted in this Parasha are numbering of military-age men, positioning of the 12 tribes, the redemption of the 22,273 Firstborn males and instructions of priestly duties.

Have you heard of the phrase "Don't put GOD in a box?" We get discouraged because we have certain expectations and perspectives for a situation and how GOD would work it through. What if we shift that a bit? When things are not going the way we anticipated, we declare, "LORD, You are greater, and Your way is higher than ours. I repent for limiting You and how You resolve situations. Will You please forgive me for my stubbornness and small-mindedness? I declare and decree that You are All-Powerful, and I invite You to intervene in a way only the Master of the Universe can." Then… Wait… Listen… and Obey.… .

Stepping out of our comfort zone can be daunting. I believe there are times we know the direction we are being led to for GOD's purpose, but we resist, then ultimately, we know it is the right way to go (because it's GOD's way). It requires courage. It takes guts. It feels right and we feel at peace about it going forward, even when those around us think we are out of our minds. Remember, the LORD will call us higher and take us to unchartered waters. He does meet us where we are, taking our hand gently to leave, away from the status quo.

There are many numbers strategically placed in the Bemidbar / Book of Numbers. There are ample commentaries on their meanings. But for people, we are not merely numbers. You are never just a number. The LORD sees us. He sees you as unique. Just like counting people one by one in this Torah Portion, lifting each head is necessary and strategic in this military operation. Do you believe that? How does Yeshua Jesus spot someone in need in a crowd? He sees him as a precious son. He sees her as a cherished daughter. He sees what others do not see.

As we continue to explore the rest of the portions in the Bemidbar / Book of Numbers, let's keep in mind that numbers are not just random numbers. What treasure will we uncover if we see every word, every number, with the idea that GOD may have intentional and strategic purposes in mind?

Very exciting! Let's go!

Let's pray:

> **Our Father in Heaven אבינו שבשמים,**
>
> We are thankful for You, the All-Knowing, All-Powerful Creator of the Universe. We thank You for being purposeful in everything that You do. Help us, with the finite mind, to get a glimpse of Your Master Plan. We know You desire to have us partner with You in Kingdom business. We are honored that when we answer Your call and are willing, You unveil to us Your strategies. During our times in the Wilderness / the desert, teach us to have confidence that we have nothing to fear when we have the Fear of GOD, clinging onto You as our Lifeline. There are no wild beasts that can harm us. We are completely and utterly protected and provided for in every way because we declare, "You are Our Refuge and Yeshua Jesus is Our LORD!"
>
> B'Shem Yeshua HaMashiach בשם ישוע המשיח.
>
> In Jesus' Name we pray. Amen.

# 30. TORAH TASTING

## *REFLECTION*

1. What is the word, picture or theme the LORD is highlighting to you in this chapter and Torah Portion?

2. Sometimes GOD uses unlikely ways to bring about victory? Have you been in the Wilderness season when GOD gave you unusual strategies in preparation for a waiting season or a breakthrough moment? Perhaps those strategies even seemed silly at the time?

3. Have you ever felt you were just a number, lost in a crowd? How does the Hebrew phrase "lift up their heads" used in counting the people encourage you to see things differently from GOD's perspective, seeing you as more than just a number?

# 31 לא
# naso
# (Take Up)
## נשא

Numbers 4:21-7:89

Judges 13:2-5

Luke 1:11-20

This Torah Portion starts with taking a census of Gershon's sons, from age 30 to age 50, that would serve in the Tabernacle.

The title of Parashat Naso comes from the word נשא Nasa, which we discussed in the previous parasha. The exact words used in Numbers 4:22 in Hebrew are:

נשא את ראש בני גרשון

They are literally translated as "Lift up the heads of Gershon's sons."

Fascinating how this phrase is used again about counting Gershon's family members, who would perform duties in the Tabernacle.

Then, the Torah Portion goes on to cover the law of jealousy, the laws of the Nazirite vows, the Aaronic Benediction (Priestly Blessing), and lastly, the offerings of the leaders of Israel's twelve tribes for the dedication of the altar. The birth of Samson is the Haftorah portion, as he was a Nazirite, as the Nazirite laws are discussed in this Torah Portion.

Numbering people was first mentioned for poll tax purposes in Exodus 38:26, then later for military purposes in Numbers 1:3, and now for Tabernacle duties purposes in Numbers 4.

*The Lord spoke to Moses and Aaron, saying, "Take a census of the sons of Kohath from among the sons of Levi, by their clans and their fathers' houses, from thirty years old up to fifty years old, all who can come on duty, to do the work in the tent of meeting. This is the service of the sons of Kohath in the tent of meeting: the most holy things.*
**Numbers 4:1-4**

I see the numbering purposes pose an interesting pattern… from giving toward the Tabernacle-building project, preparation for battles to now worship service duties… It is as if the numbering commandment is not a random request by GOD but instead has a purpose.

Think of this in spiritual terms, in order to serve the LORD and be ready for what He has in store for us, our hearts first need to be pure. Giving of our earthly possessions require some sacrifice; yes, some can give reluctantly or out of obligation, but the LORD gives His blessings freely and joyously to us, and we are to reciprocate in the same way. With a pure heart, aligning our will to GOD's, victory is a surety in battles. Then, serving with our gifts and time is something we would do so naturally in response to knowing who the LORD is to us, not just what He has and can do for us.

The vows of a Nazirite are about consecration. The shaving of the head and the refrainment from wine are signs of a lifelong dedication to the

LORD, setting the Nazirites apart for GOD. Much like priesthood, the Levites were set apart for serving the LORD. Immediately following the Nazirite laws is the infamous Aaronic Benediction. The Priestly Blessing is the LORD commanding Aaron and his sons to bless His people.

> The Lord spoke to Moses, saying, "Speak to Aaron and his sons, saying, Thus you shall bless the people of Israel: you shall say to them,
> The Lord <u>bless</u> you and <u>keep you</u>;
> the Lord <u>make his face to shine</u> upon you and <u>be gracious</u> to you;
> the Lord <u>lift up his countenance</u> upon you and <u>give you</u> (put on you) peace. "So shall they <u>put My name upon</u> the people of Israel, and I will bless them."
> **Numbers 6:22-27**

This is the only time in the Torah that the LORD specifically instructed Moses to tell Aaron and his sons to bless His people with the above exact words. In Hebrew, these 3 verses are laid out in 3 words, 5 words and then 7 words, as if the LORD Himself was building these blessings into a climax.

יברכך יהוה וישמרך
יאר יהוה פניו אליך ויחנך
ישא יהוה פניו אליך וישם לך שלום

First of all, the three verses show clearly who is the One doing the blessing. Adonai HaShem the LORD יהוה is the subject, initiating the act of blessing and conducting the blessing in each one of these three verses. No question about it.

Next, the object, the one receiving the blessing, is in singular form ("you" in singular form). Some say it is because Israel is referred to as one body, and as a whole. That makes sense, but we can also look at this as the LORD personally bless us individually as an intimate and personal promise of His blessings.

This Blessing of all blessings is filled with so much richness. It begins with the phrase, "The LORD bless you and keep you." The LORD bless… is a load of words already, a tremendous concept. The KING of the Universe desires to bless and adorn over us with every goodness. Then, He further elaborates on what that means for us. "Keep" is keeping us from harm, keeping us safe, keeping and watching over us to make sure we are provided for. It is about our physical needs being provided for, and the physical blessings given to us are more than anything we can ever ask or imagine.

The LORD is our Keeper, our Provider, and our Protector! He is our All in All!

*And my God will supply every need of yours according to his riches in glory in Christ Jesus.*
**Philippians 4:19**

The second verse of this Blessing uses יאר Yaer <u>Light</u> and חן Chen <u>Grace (Favor)</u> as verbs toward us. He causes His Face to "Light" us up and places Grace and Favor upon us. Lighting up can also allude to enlightenment. We would be enlightened to know Him, His Favor and Grace. Can you imagine what that does to us? The LORD is the only source of Light and Grace/Favor. He bestows that on us that we may have it too, simply because He wants to impart to us who He is. GOD's words of Blessing spoken over us give us that light, which opens us up to understanding. With His Light, we can see the Truth, that the LORD is the Only One that can save. His light is closely linked to salvation for us. Father GOD places on us salvation and Grace/Favor, which is unmerited and un-earnable, the spiritual blessings we simply can never work to attain.

*The unfolding of your words gives light; it gives understanding to the simple.*
**Psalm 119:130**

> *The LORD is my light and my salvation — whom shall I fear?*
> *The LORD is the stronghold of my life — of whom shall I be afraid?*
> **Psalm 27:1**

The third verse is the crescendo of the Blessing... the LORD lifting up His Face upon/toward us and put on us PEACE.

Here are a couple of examples of the LORD's Face shining leads to salvation.

> *O Lord God of hosts, restore us;*
> *Cause <u>Your face to shine upon us</u>, and we will be <u>saved</u>.*
> **Psalm 80:19**

> *Make <u>Your face to shine</u> upon Your servant;*
> *<u>Save</u> me in Your lovingkindness.*
> **Psalm 31:16**

Following are two verses of distress and even destruction as a result of the LORD's Face hidden.

> *Answer me quickly, O Lord, my spirit fails;*
> *<u>Do not hide Your face</u> from me,*
> *Or I will become like <u>those who go down to the pit</u>.*
> **Psalm 143:7**

> *O Lord, by Your favor You have made my mountain to stand strong;*
> *<u>You hid Your face</u>, I was <u>dismayed</u>.*
> **Psalm 30:7**

The Hebrew word for Face is פני Penai. It is by nature in plural form, as in "faces." Its root is פנה Panah meaning to turn. Turning is a movement, therefore, Face is the noun of a turning movement; almost like when GOD shines His Face on us, He shines/focuses His moving Face to project His Mercy and Grace on us.

Can you imagine the Master of the Universe stopping everything, and turns His Face toward you just to be present with you?

The LORD lights up and lifts up His Face upon us. Then He puts on us PEACE. The LORD's Face is the essence of who He is. I find that fascinating that this Blessing concludes with the word Nasa נשא lift up like it echoes the beginning of this Torah Portion. Could it possibly be a reminder of the lifting up the heads (numbering) of the Gershonites for Tabernacle service? Lifting up the heads of GOD's people to be counted and also to be blessed? A "priestly" connection?

Lifting up and lighting His Face on us for the purpose of setting us apart? Then, "He puts on us PEACE." The Hebrew word used here is שום Soom to put on, like someone placing something or putting a garment on someone. שום Soom is also translated as to establish, to appoint or to mark.

*So Abraham rose early in the morning and took bread and a skin of water and gave them to Hagar, putting them on (שום Soom) her shoulder, and gave her the boy, and sent her away.*
*And she departed and wandered about in the wilderness of Beersheba.*
**Genesis 21:14**

*Blessed be the Lord your God, who has delighted in you and set you on the throne of Israel! Because the Lord loved Israel forever, he has made (appointed/established) you king, that you may execute justice and righteousness."*
**1 Kings 10:9**

The best part of the Blessing is that the LORD puts on us PEACE, as in enveloping us with PEACE; we are wrapped in and completely covered in His PEACE. May I also point out that the word שום Soom "Put On" with the Hebrew letter ל Lamed added to it becomes שלום SHALOM PEACE? The Shalom that means Completeness, Wholeness, Nothing-lacking, that kind of PEACE! שלומ SHALOM PEACE and שומ Soom consist of the same 3 letters, except for the additional Lamed ל in שלומ SHALOM. Is this a coincidence? But then again, I don't believe in Mere Coincidence but Divine Providence. The additional Hebrew alphabet Lamed ל, in שלומ SHALOM PEACE, is in the shape of a shepherd's staff, which means control, authority or tongue. The LORD puts on us His PEACE, with us allowing Him as authority and control over us. With GOD, do we need anything else? No matter what life brings, His PEACE covers it all, we have no lack and we have no other desire.

Yeshua Jesus the Mashiach is referred to as שר שלומ Sar Shalom PRINCE OF PEACE, the Commander of Peace.

*Peace I leave with you, My peace I give to you;*
*not as the world gives do I give to you. Let not your heart be troubled,*
*neither let it be afraid.*
**John 14:27**

*Be anxious for nothing, but in everything by prayer and supplication,*
*with thanksgiving, let your requests be made known to God; and the*
*peace of God, which surpasses all understanding, will guard your*
*hearts and minds through Christ Jesus.*
**Philippians 4:7**

But wait… there's a bonus blessing that was added to this Blessing in the following verse —

*"So shall they <u>put My name upon</u> the people of Israel, and I will*
*bless them."*
**Numbers 6:27**

After the words of the Blessing, the LORD said that the priests would put HIS NAME on His people, and He would personally bless them. For one, this is the only place we are told that the LORD put His Name on someone. Secondly, Numbers 6:22-27 starts with "The LORD BLESS"

His people and ends with "The LORD BLESS" His people. When The LORD repeats something, it is significant, like it is being underlined and highlighted.

What if we are to wear the LORD's Name as we wear clothing because He put it on us, that we carry His Name with reverence as the priests wore GOD's Name with reverence? GOD put His Name on us to seal the Blessing.

> "You shall make a plate of pure gold and engrave on it, like the engraving of a signet,
> 'Holy to the Lord.' And you <u>shall fasten it</u> (Soom שום put on) on the turban by a cord of blue.
> It shall be **on the front of the turban.**
> It shall be **on Aaron's forehead,**
> and Aaron shall <u>bear</u> (Nasa נשא carry/lift up/bear) any guilt from the holy things that the people of Israel consecrate as their holy gifts.
> It shall **regularly be on his forehead**, that they may be accepted before the Lord.
> **Exodus 28:36**

As the priests were given the honor to wear GOD's Name in the priestly garment, the LORD placed His Name on us that we may be covered with His PEACE and completely sealed in His Blessing. We are marked eternally as His.

The third of the Ten Commandment is this —

לא <u>תשא</u> את־שם־יהוה אלהיך לשוא
כי לא ינקה יהוה את אשר־ישא את־שמו לשוא

> "You shall not take (Nasa נשא lift up/carry/bear) *the name of the Lord your God in vain,* for the Lord will not hold him guiltless who takes his name in vain.
> **Exodus 20:7**

This commandment speaks of not lifting up/carrying the LORD's Name in vain. The word שוא Shav "in vain," also means falsehood, worthlessness and emptiness. Carrying, Lifting up the LORD's Name is a Huge Honor as well as a Huge Responsibility.

The LORD's Blessing is the seal of His Love over us. He wants to give us all that He has, His Face, His Name, His essence, His everything.

What if we wake up every morning being intentionally aware of the tremendous privilege of being GOD's children carrying His Name on us, wearing it continually like Aaron the High Priest?

What if we consciously make ourselves aware of the weight bearing GOD's Name on us with the Yeshua Jesus the Mashiach within us, and live our lives by the Spirit of the Living GOD for the incredible Blessing He so placed on us, with the Perfect PEACE covering us that we need nothing else this world has to offer? Nothing else!

Would you say that would be a powerful life we would lead?

**I want to leave you with the powerful words of the song** *"We Could Change the World"* **by Matt Redman** —

Could we live like Your grace is stronger
Than all our faults and failures?
Could we live like Your love
Is deeper than our hearts can fathom
Could we live like this?

Could we live like Your name is higher
Than every other power?
Could we live like Your ways
Are wiser than our understanding?
Could we live like this?

Yes, our God is all He says, all He says He is
Jesus, in Your name we could change the world
We stand in Your love, in Your power
And all You say we are
Jesus, in Your name we could change the world

**Let's pray:**

### Our Father in Heaven אבינו שבשמימ,

Thank You for the Ultimate Blessing that You have invoked over us, with Everything we ever need and desire, all physical and spiritual blessings. LORD, help us know and realize every morning the tremendous honor and responsibility of wearing and carrying Your Name. As the Nazirites and Aaron were consecrated and set apart, let us be set apart as a symbol of our dedication to You and You alone. Let us reflect the Light You have put on us, that the world will see our good deeds and glorify You, our Father in heaven. We are eternally grateful that You have commanded the Priestly Blessing to be declared and proclaimed over us. Please show us how we can also declare and proclaim Your Blessing over those around us, that they too may know You and Your Love for them.

B'Shem Yeshua HaMashiach בשם ישוע המשיח.

In Jesus' Name we pray. Amen.

# 31. TORAH TASTING

## *REFLECTION*

1. What is the word, picture or theme the LORD is highlighting to you in this chapter and Torah Portion?

2. How does the concept/truth of "GOD wants to bless you" encourage you today? What insight does the picture of the LORD making his face to shine on you that is needed regarding a circumstance or situation that is on your heart right now?

3. Wearing GOD's name like clothing is a huge responsibility. How does that thought affect the way you shine and interact with others on a daily basis?

# 32 לב
# Beha'alotecha
## (When You Cause to Ascend)
בהעלתך

Numbers 8:1-12:15

Zechariah 2:14-4:7

Matthew 14:14-21

This week's Torah Portion is Beha'alotecha. The title comes from the first two verses of this portion.

*And the Lord spoke to Moses, saying:* [2] *"Speak to Aaron, and say to him, 'When you **arrange** the lamps, the seven lamps shall give light in front of the lampstand.'"*
**Numbers 8:1-2**

The word "arrange" translated is בהעלתך Beha'alotecha When You Cause to Ascend/Go Up or Bring Up. Essentially, it is when Aaron causes to go up in order to clean and light the lamps. After the instructions of making and lighting the seven lamps, the first Passover happened a year after the Exodus from Egypt. Then, there was the making of the silver trumpets, leaving Sinai, Israelites' complaints, Israel's 70 elders being appointed, and some of them even prophesied and Joshua's disapproval of it, the provision of quails to Israel as meat, and lastly, the Aaron-Miriam's ill-speaking of Moses' wife.

**That is a lot packed into five chapters in this Parasha. What stood out to me are a few things —**

1. Lighting the lamps requires going up.
2. Setting out and Resting is key to seeing the enemy scatter
3. Recognizing the Help provided behind Greatness

The first one involves the three words used in the instructions about serving in the Tabernacle regarding the lampstand, ניר Nir Lamp/Candle, מנורה Menorah/Lampstand, and אר Or Light. Of course, we know and acknowledge that we ourselves cannot light anything. The LORD is the Source of Light and the Creator of Light. Obviously, there is tremendous significance to having the Lamps perpetually lit in the Tabernacle. We have touched on some of that in the previous Parashiot (Torah Portions). This Parasha sets off the Israelites' journey leaving Sinai after celebrating their first Passover in the Wilderness. Although the LORD is the source of Light, He commanded Aaron to be the one to bring forth the light in the Lampstand. The Light is not only essential, but also it is a way of survival for directions, along with the Cloud of the LORD provided, as the timing of the setting out and resting. The word Beha'alotecha is used only once in the Torah and the entire Tanakh (Old Testament), and it is in this Parasha. It is safe to say that the phrase בהעלתך Beha'alotecha When You Cause to Ascend/Go Up or Bring Up (the light in the lamps) instruction is a perfect opening to unfold the rest of the Torah Portion.

As the Children of Israel set out on their journey in groups, the LORD guided them every step of the way. The repetition of the word נסע Nasa Set Out is noteworthy. The word Nasa means to set out or journey. On this journey, what is highlighted is the LORD set out before them.

## 32. BEHA'ALOTECHA / WHEN YOU CAME TO ASCEND

*So they departed from the mountain of the Lord on a journey of three days; <u>and the ark of the covenant of the Lord went</u> (נסע Nasa Set out/Journey) before them for the three days' journey, to search out a resting place for them. ³⁴ And the cloud of the Lord was above them by day when they went out from the camp.*
*So it was, whenever the ark **set out** (נסע Nasa Set out/Journey), that Moses said:*
*"Rise up, O Lord! Let Your enemies be scattered,*
*And let those who hate You flee before You." And when it **rested** (נוח Nuach Rest), he said: "Return, O Lord,*
*To the many thousands of Israel."*
**Numbers 10:33-36**

The Children of Israel never traveled alone nor felt alone. I find it intriguing — it is the Ark of the Covenant of the LORD that went and journeyed before them to prepare the way. The Ark does not move on its own. I feel that either this is a metaphor of the LORD remembering His covenant and promises for and with His people, the Ark symbolizing the Covenant, or the Ark moved supernaturally and traveled ahead of Israel to display that the LORD is their PROVIDER and GUIDE. Either way, it is an amazing visual for us to know that the LORD knows the way, and He is ready to lead us on the path to Life and Great Promises. He shows us where and when to pick up and go. Not only He provides for the Journeying, but He also provides the Resting.

Numbers 10:33-36 is a profound picture of recognizing who GOD is. Crying out, "Rise up, O Lord," leads to us witnessing the enemies being scattered. When Israel was led to a resting place, Moses proclaimed, "Return, O LORD, to many thousands of Israel."

When you feel like you are journeying toward unfriendly territory, do you cry for help in fear or proclaim who GOD is as Moses did, "Rise up, O Lord! Let Your enemies be scattered, and let those who hate You flee before You." I believe this is a powerful example of what happens when the LORD is magnified, called and acknowledged to arise. Instead of focusing on what's hostile to us, it is completely and utterly vital to focus on GOD, agreeing with His Greatness rather than the adversary's illusional might. Even in the LORD's resting, there is tremendous power. The first time the word נוח **Nuach Rest** being used is in Genesis 8:4.

> *Then the ark rested (נוח **Nuach Rest**), in the seventh month, the seventeenth day of the month,*
> *on the mountains of Ararat.*
> **Genesis 8:4**

Of course, this scene is in the context of after the catastrophic worldwide flood, Noah's Ark rested. Noah's name נוח means rest. Interesting, before the concept of rest/settle, is minted in Genesis 8, Noah was introduced. On a side note, in Genesis 2:2, when GOD rested on the seventh day after the six days of creation, the word used there is שבת Shavat Rest/Cease as in Shabbat. It is a different word and a different fascinating topic to discover.

Immediately following the powerful visual of the LORD being the ultimate Guide and Covenant-Keeper GOD, the Israelites complained of adversity…

> *Now when the people complained, it displeased the Lord;*
> *for the Lord heard it,*
> *and His anger was aroused.*
> *So the fire of the Lord burned among them, and consumed some in the outskirts of the camp.*
> **Numbers 11:1**

We think of the Israelites as stiff-necked, suffering from short-term memory. They complained often and forgot all the miracles of the LORD they'd witnessed firsthand. Yet, many of us at one point praise the LORD for being faithful and loving, and yet at another, we become fearful at the moment of uncertainty or circumstances going against expectations. No wonder the LORD constantly reminds us of His faithfulness in His Word and tells us to meditate on His goodness. Otherwise, we forget.

## 32. BEHA'ALOTECHA / WHEN YOU CAME TO ASCEND

The last thing I would like to highlight in this Parasha is the Zipporah-connections. There is a popular saying, "Behind every successful man, there stands a woman." In this case, I would venture to say, "Behind the Greatest prophet ever lived, there stands a woman and her family."

I don't know about you. I wonder about Moses' wife sometimes when studying the Torah. Zipporah, in Hebrew, is Tzipporah (meaning a bird), was a reward for Moses' bravery in saving her and her siblings from some bullying shepherds. According to Exodus 2:14-21, after Moses fled from Pharoah. Tzipporah's father, Reuel (meaning Friend of GOD, a Midianite), gave her to Moses as a wife. I wonder if there were other daughters that the father could have chosen, and why Tzipporah. Little was mentioned about Tzipporah. As a matter of fact, the only time she spoke in the Torah was when she saved Moses' life. Remember in Exodus 4:25? Tzipporah circumcised Moses' son and said, "Surely you are a husband of blood to me!". That was quite a dramatic scene. Jethro, Moses' father-in-law, entered the scene in Exodus 18:2 when he brought Tzipporah back to Moses after the grand miraculous epic event of the Exodus. He came at a time when Moses needed help. He gave timely and valuable advice to Moses about delegation. Then in this Parasha, the Midianite family displays yet another one of GOD's incredible provisions.

> *And Moses said to <u>Hobab the son of Reuel</u> the Midianite, Moses' father-in-law, "We are setting out (נסע Nasa Set out/Journey) for the place of which the LORD said, 'I will give it to you.' Come with us, and we will do good to you, for the LORD has promised good to Israel." But he said to him, "I will not go. I will depart to my own land and to my kindred." And he said, "Please do not leave us, for you know where we should camp in the wilderness, and you will serve as eyes for us.*
> *And if you do go with us, whatever good the LORD will do to us, the same will we do to you." So they set out (נסע Nasa Set out/Journey) from the mount of the LORD three days' journey.*
> **Numbers 10:29-33**

Hobab, in this verse, can be seen as Moses' brother-in-law (son of Reuel). However, in Judges 4, Hobab is referred to as Moses' father-in-law.

*Now Heber the Kenite, of the children of <u>Hobab the father-in-law of Moses</u>, had separated himself from the Kenites and pitched his tent near the terebinth tree at Zaanaim, which is beside Kedesh.*
**Judges 4:11**

Either way, these guys were Moses' Midianite in-laws. In Numbers 10:29-33, Moses pled with Hobab not to go, for he had the wisdom to know where they should camp in the wilderness. Again, Moses would rely on his in-law's wise counsel regarding leadership and strategies. This short little encounter is inserted in the Torah Portion, which I believe is to show the significant Providence of the GOD of Israel at the appropriate time. Here, Hobab was there when Israel was setting out/journeying in the wilderness and Moses spotted his talent and asked him to stay. Although the name Midian מדין, stems from Madon מדון, meaning strife or contention, there was none of that evident in the in-law's dealings with Moses, quite the contrary.

I would like to propose this theory to you — the meaning of the names of Moses' wife and in-laws — Tzipporah (a Bird), Reuel (Friend of GOD), Jethro (Yatar, Remain Over, the rest) and Hobab (to Love) may very well give us insights into GOD's Provision.

GOD's Provision often comes swiftly as a bird, making us feel like we are not alone, but we have a friend indeed. He is what remains when everyone has left, with no other solutions, He is constant and present because HE LOVES US! That's how I see Moses' in-laws coming in and going out of the scenes. Those are the unsung heroes behind Moses, orchestrated by GOD.

I am not sure when in-laws started to get a bad reputation. We often get what we expect. I am beyond blessed to have the best in-laws in the world. From the moment my husband introduced me to his parents and his siblings, I fell in love with them. Though a guarded New Yorker by nature, Sol, my father-in-law, turned out to be a softie inside. Millie, my little 4-foot-tall Jewish mother-in-law, was the most affectionate and sweet-natured person I ever knew. Whenever I felt down, my husband would suggest to call his mother, that she would cheer me up and make me feel better. Sure enough, she did lift me up every time I called her. By the Grace of GOD, they both had encounters with their Jewish Mashiach Yeshua on earth before their journey into the arms of our Heavenly Father. My sisters-in-law, brother-in-law and I have a close relationship. I know that is not always the case with some people. I believe the LORD supplies what we need through friends, family, or in-laws at just the right time.

Have you ever been in a situation where you needed to be rescued, and someone somehow came "coincidentally" and "suddenly" to get you out of the sticky situation? While working in Washington, D.C., I had a personal issue needing attention and professional help. My Human Resources director and managers told me there was nothing they could do. I prayed. Shortly after that, our hotel was acquired by another company, and they sent an interim General Manager. Many called that temporary boss "a hitman." This person is often brought into the operation to "clean house," terminate key players and leave. I approached the new GM (General Manager) about my circumstance, and he agreed to resolve the situation WITHOUT HESITATION, overriding all the other managers' decisions. And yes, just like that, he was gone after that. 'Til this day, I cannot even recall his name. I remember him as a stern but friendly person in our brief conversation in the parking lot. I can tell you this much, I know he was not just there for me. I cannot help but wonder if the LORD brought him there to rescue me to get me out of a knot. Like Moses, his wife and in-laws were there at just the right time to resolve some mess. I believe we have a GOD that Always Provides! Do you believe?

**Let's pray:**

**Our Father in Heaven אבינו שבשמימ,**

We thank You that You always provide, whether it be our physical needs or spiritual needs, solutions to resolve a problem. You are always here. We are never alone, even at times we may feel that way. The Truth of You being Our Provider should override our own feelings that may say otherwise. LORD, we ask You to remind us of who You are when we forget. We ask You to strengthen our Faith in trusting in You, walking by Faith and not by sight in every situation.

At all times, whether we set out on a new journey or return to rest, we declare, "Rise up, O LORD, and let Your enemies be scattered"… and we watch Your enemies flee before Your Presence.

B'Shem Yeshua HaMashiach בשם ישוע המשיח.

In Jesus' Name we pray. Amen.

# 32. TORAH TASTING
## *REFLECTION*

1. What is the word, picture or theme the LORD is highlighting to you in this chapter and Torah Portion?

2. Do you remember a time when you or a friend were on a journey somewhere (physically or spiritually) that you were filled with uncertainty? Were you paralyzed by fear or chose to gather up the courage to choose to trust the good that was ahead of you?

3. When there seems to be no way, GOD makes a way. Do you have a story of how the solution was provided unexpectedly to get you out of a sticky situation?

# 33 לג
# shelach
## (Send)
## שלח

Numbers 13:1-15:41

Joshua 2:1-24

Matthew 10:1-14

---

This week's Torah Portion is Shelach. It derives from its first 2 verses.

*And the Lord spoke to Moses, saying,*
*"Send (שלח) men to spy out the land of Canaan, which I am giving to the children of Israel; from each tribe of their fathers you shall send a man, every one a leader among them."*
**Numbers 13:1-2**

This Torah Portion consists of the command of the LORD to Moses to send men to go spy out the Promise Land. Israel rebelled at the hearing of the disheartening report of the ten fearful spies and Moses interceded on their behalf. As a result, a whole generation of Israelites were to wander in the wilderness for forty years before some of them and their children were going to enter the Promise Land. Then, a man that has broken the Shabbat law by gathering sticks was stoned to death. Finally, tassels/fringes/tzitzis were commanded to be worn on the corners of garments to remind them of the LORD's commandments.

This Parasha begins with twelve spies who were sent to Canaan to scout out the land. They came back with two very different reports.

> *They brought back word to them and to all the congregation,*
> *and **showed them the fruit of the land.***
> *And they told him, "We came to the land to which you sent us.*
> *It flows with milk and honey, and this is its fruit.*
> *However, **the people who dwell in the land are strong,***
> ***and the cities are fortified and very large.** And besides, we saw the descendants of Anak there.*
> **Numbers 13:26-28**

Ten spies saw the luscious fruits but were overwhelmed with fear by the people and the cities.

> *But Caleb quieted the people before Moses and said,*
> *"Let us go up at once and occupy it, for we are well able to overcome it."…*
> *(Caleb and Joshua tore their clothes and said),*
> *"The land, which we passed through to spy it out, is an exceedingly good land.*
> *If the LORD delights in us, he will bring us into this land and give it to us, a land that flows with milk and honey.*
> *Only do not rebel against the LORD.*
> <u>*And do not fear the people of the land, for they are bread for us.*</u>
> <u>*Their protection is removed from them, and the LORD is with us; do not fear them."*</u>
> **Numbers 13:30, 14:7-9**

The two spies, Caleb and Joshua, instead saw the amazing provisions in the land that the LORD had promised. More importantly, they were confident; the LORD was bigger than the challenges, no matter how scary they seemed.

This Parasha reminds me of a story I heard years ago…

A shoe manufacturer sent two of their best salesmen to explore a new potential market, Africa. After having spent some time in Africa conducting market research, they returned with their reports. The first salesman reported in disappointment to his boss,

"Forget it! We will not sell any shoes in Africa. No one wears shoes there."

Then, the second salesman came in bursting with excitement,

"You won't believe this! The market is wide open. Let's gear up our production today! We are going to sell so many shoes. No one wears shoes there! Everyone is going to be our customer!"

Having GOD's perspective is seeing opportunities instead of despair!

Fear often paralyzes and blinds us from seeing possibilities and hope.

In each situation, we can choose to see either life or death, hope or despair.

The idea of "send" also insinuates readiness. When I send a package out, it is ready. When a student is being sent to school, the school is ready, and the student is ready, ideally. **When you are sent to the store, it is assumed that the store you are sent to has what you are sent there for, AND you have been prepared (i.e., with the money necessary) to complete the assignment or mission you've been sent to purchase.**

When the LORD commanded to send spies into Canaan, the Land was ready, and He was testing to see if His people were ready. Well, you know the story; they apparently needed forty more years before they were truly ready.

Readiness is a mindset. That's why our belief/faith is so important. As we make up our minds to be ready (it is a decision), the rest of our being has to come into alignment with that decision. That's why GOD's Word often reminds us to guard our hearts and our thoughts. There is a saying: "The Body is the Slave of the Mind."

How true is that?! Whatever our mind has decided, the rest of our body and emotions follow.

Did the Israelites need to be ready to slay their enemies in Canaan? Probably not, just needed the faith to know that the LORD was with them, and He was the One that would deliver victory, as Caleb and Joshua believed.

The word "Send" in Numbers 13:2, "**Send** men to spy out the land of Canaan," is שלח Sh'lach in imperative/command form, as in "You go send men…".

The first time the Command form of send Sh'lach seen in the Torah is in Exodus 4 in the conversation between Moses and the LORD at the burning bush. The LORD gave Moses a mission to lead His people out of Egypt/slavery, instructing him what to do with a rod if the Children of Israelites needed proof to know that he was indeed sent by the Living GOD.

*And He said, "Cast it on the ground."*
*So he cast it on the ground, and it became a serpent;*
*and Moses fled from it.*
Then the Lord said to Moses, "**Reach out** (שלח Sh'lach Send Out) your hand and take it by the tail" (and he reached out his hand and caught it, and it became a rod in his hand),
"that they may believe that the Lord God of their fathers, the God of Abraham, the God of Isaac, and the God of Jacob, has appeared to you."
**Exodus 4:3-4**

I believe the word שלח Shalach Send, according to the above scriptures, has an undertone of leading us to GOD's promises. The LORD sent His people to the Promise Land as well as preparing to lead His people out of slavery as promised to Abram in Genesis 15:13-14. Even in Exodus 4:4, Moses' taking hold of the serpent by the tail and its turning back into a rod is a visual of the LORD's mighty power of vanquishing the enemy, symbolized in a serpent.

His promises never fail.

And, one more note on the first episodes the word שלח Send makes its appearance in any form in Genesis —

> *Then the Lord God said, "Behold, the man has become like one of Us, to know good and evil. And now, lest he **put out** (שלח Sh'lach Send Out) his hand and take also of the tree of life, and eat, and live forever" — therefore the Lord God **sent** (שלח Sh'lach Send Out) him out of the garden of Eden to till the ground from which he was taken.*
> **Genesis 3:22-23**

> *Then he (Noah) **sent out** (שלח Sh'lach Send Out) a raven, which kept going to and fro until the waters had dried up from the earth. He also **sent out** (שלח Sh'lach Send Out) from himself a dove, to see if the waters had receded from the face of the ground. But the dove found no resting place for the sole of her foot, and she returned into the ark to him, for the waters were on the face of the whole earth. So he **put out** (שלח Sh'lach Send Out) his hand and took her, and drew her into the ark to himself.*
> **Genesis 8:7-9**

Again, the Promises of fulfillment being ready are on full display in these scriptures. Do you see it? Though Genesis 3:22 shows the fallen state of Adam and the Tree of Life provision of eternal life, which we know later, the LORD's redemption plan would be revealed in the Book of Revelation. How about Noah in Genesis 8 demonstrates at the end of the flood, he sent out a raven and a dove. The dove returned, but later in verses 10-12, after waiting seven days, Noah **sent out** the dove again, she returned with a freshly plucked olive leaf (signifying new life of the olive tree). After waiting yet another seven days, Noah **sent out** the dove again. This time she never returned (signifying she has found life in the land and settled).

All the Shalach's (Send/Send Out) give us recurring reminders that GOD's Promises always come to pass.

Moses, instructed by GOD, turned the serpent back into a rod, which the word שלח Shalach Send is used in Exodus 4:4. The word rod in Hebrew is מטה Mateh. Interestingly enough, it also means tribe, and it is also in this Torah Portion's opening.

*Then the Lord said to Moses, "Reach out (שלח Sh'lach Send Out) your hand and take it by the tail." and he reached out his hand and caught it, and it became a rod (מטה Mateh) in his hand, that they may believe that the Lord God of their fathers, the God of Abraham, the God of Isaac, and the God of Jacob, has appeared to you."*
**Exodus 4:3-4**

*"Send (שלח Sh'lach) men to spy out the land of Canaan, which I am giving to the children of Israel; from each tribe (מטה Mateh) of their fathers you shall send a man, every one a leader among them."*
**Numbers 13:1-2**

Are you making the connection yet? The promises of the LORD to redeem His people from slavery beginning with sending Moses to convince His people it was indeed their GOD that would bring them deliverance from bondage into freedom. He is the same GOD that would deliver them to occupy the Promise Land, as it has been promised long ago. The Rod GOD used to demonstrate His power and might is the same Rod that each tribe will be shown individually and corporately; the LORD that always keeps His promises.

## 33. SHELACH / SEND

The word שלח Shalach Send is something that encompasses life. It can be divided into 2 parts: של Shel and ח Chet. The first two letters form the word של Shel meaning Belonging /in Possession of. The letter ח Chet is associated with the number 8, that means new beginning, as in 8 people on Noah's ark and as in on the 8th day, the first day after the Seven days' Creation. Of course, the letter ח Chet forms the word Chai חי that means Life in Hebrew. Therefore, I believe the word Shalach שלח Send also means the act of sending that leads to life and new beginning.

Isn't that appropriate that, indeed, the references to the end of the Flood water subsiding outside Noah's ark and Moses' encounter with GOD about his mission of leading the Hebrews out of Egypt into the Promise Land all point to Life and New Beginning?

I sense that this Torah Portion is much more than the severe sin of unbelief of the 10 spies that nearly had the entire Israel annihilated as punishment....

The "Sending-out" (שלח Sh'lach) of the spies was a test of readiness and faith in trusting GOD. Noah's sending out of the dove would be the beginning of seeing GOD's promises unfold, but also a test to see if the land was ready for them to exit the ark. Moses' sending out/stretching out his hand to turn the serpent back into the rod was to help GOD's people to witness the LORD's mighty power and to shift from unbelief to belief.

At the crown of the year 2021, the LORD gave me the Bible verse in John 20:21.

> *So Jesus said to them again, "Peace to you!*
> *<u>As the Father has sent Me, I also send you.</u>"*

I had a strong sense of the LORD sending us out. For the mission He sends us out for, we have been well-equipped and trained with gifts and experiences. The World needs to know and receive hope and life. That's what we are sent to do, to reveal the Hope of Glory and the Living GOD to everyone around us.

The mission leads to seeing GOD's promises being fulfilled. This mission leads to Life and New beginning, not just for us but also for those the mission is involved with. This mission is not only for the year 2021. It will continue well beyond that.

Don't worry… When GOD sends you out on a mission, He knows and is confident that you are ready. The question is — Do you believe you are ready to witness GOD's power and might and that He is the One that will defeat the enemies in bringing forth the fulfillment of His promises… No matter what the circumstances look like?

## 33. SHELACH / SEND

Let's pray:

**Our Father in Heaven** אבינו שבשמימ,

We thank You for You are a GOD of Promises-Made Promises-Kept, now and through eternity, in this Age and the Age to come. Where we have doubts, LORD, please help us to believe, like You sent Moses to show Your people with the rod turning into a serpent and the serpent back into a rod. Help us to have eyes to see as Caleb and Joshua did, the Land flowing with milk and honey was far greater than any challenges the enemy presented. Remind us daily to choose life and hope.

Thank You for Your Sending-Out's always lead to life and new beginnings.

As Yeshua Jesus our Mashiach has been sent, He also has sent us.

We have made up our mind to trust in You and Your promises, and the rest of our being will align with that decision and determination.

We are ready, in Your Name and for Your Glory.

B'Shem Yeshua HaMashiach בשם ישוע המשיח.

In Jesus' Name we pray. Amen.

# 33. TORAH TASTING
## *REFLECTION*

1. What is the word, picture or theme the LORD is highlighting to you in this chapter and Torah Portion?

2. Can you think of a time when you were sent to do something which you felt you were not ready for? Beginning a new season of starting a new school, a new job or even becoming a new parent can make us feel unready. Do you have any of the examples like those that you later realized you had been equipped by GOD for the task all along?

3. Seeing the glass half full rather than half empty takes effort and faith. What are some practical ways that you can remind yourself and others to see things from GOD's hope-filled perspective?

# 34 לד
# korach
## (Korah)
### כורח

Numbers 16:1-18:32

1 Samuel 11:14-12:22

John 19:1-17

Parasha Korach begins with some movie-worthy drama of Korach and his group confronting Moses and Aaron, then climaxes to the epic scene of GOD's action as a result of the Korahites' uprising. The LORD further solidifies Aaron's role of priesthood. Then, we see the budding of Aaron's rod, as well as the detailed layout of the responsibility and portion of priests and Levites. The Parasha title "Korach" comes from the first verse of the name of the rebels' leader.

> Now **Korah** the son of Izhar, the son of Kohath, the son of Levi, with Dathan and Abiram the sons of Eliab, and On the son of Peleth, sons of Reuben, took men; and they rose up before Moses with some of the children of Israel, two hundred and fifty leaders of the congregation, representatives of the congregation, men of renown.
> **Numbers 16:1-2**

There are four concepts in this Torah Portion that we will discuss:

1. Rise Up/Establish
2. Separate/Set Apart
3. Swallow Down/Cast Down
4. Put Forth/Shine


## 1 – RISE UP – ESTABLISH

> And they **rose up** (קוּם Koom) before Moses with some of the children of Israel, two hundred and fifty leaders of the congregation, representatives of the congregation, men of renown.
> **Numbers 16:2**

This word קוּם Koom Rise Up/Stand Up/Establish in Numbers 16:2 first appeared in the Torah in Genesis 4 prior to the first murder ever committed.

> Now Cain talked with Abel his brother; and it came to pass, when they were in the field, that Cain **rose up** (קוּם Koom) against Abel his brother and killed him.
> **Genesis 4:8**

Cain rose up against Abel and killed him. The rising up of Cain was filled with envy, as in the case of Korah and his followers.

While the first murderer in history rose up in jealousy, committing a crime out of self-centeredness, many references of the word קוּם Koom

Stand Up/Establish after that are initiated by the LORD to rise up and establish His covenant with His people in order to begin a relationship that He would be their Provider and Protector.

*And behold, I Myself am bringing floodwaters on the earth, to destroy from under heaven all flesh in which is the breath of life; everything that is on the earth shall die. But **I will establish** (קוּמ Koom) My covenant with you; and you shall go into the ark — you, your sons, your wife, and your sons' wives with you.*
**Genesis 6:17-18**

Then God spoke to Noah and to his sons with him, saying:

*"And as for Me, behold, **I establish** (קוּמ Koom) My covenant with you and with your descendants after you, and with every living creature that is with you: the birds, the cattle, and every beast of the earth with you, of all that go out of the ark, every beast of the earth. Thus **I establish** (קוּמ Koom) My covenant with you: Never again shall all flesh be cut off by the waters of the flood; never again shall there be a flood to destroy the earth."*
**Genesis 9:8-11**

The sin of envy and jealousy is a sin against our own soul and leads to self-destruction; and it often destroys those around us too. We see that happen in the first family in history. Cain rose up (קוּמ Koom) against his own brother, Abel, sinning against Abel, GOD and his own soul. His jealousy destroyed the path GOD had intended for him. Nonetheless, GOD's intention for **rising up** is to **establish** His covenant with us, which has redemptive and life-creating power. When GOD (קוּמ Koom) **establishes** a covenant, it brings life and promises.

## 2 – SEPARATE – HOLY / SET APART

The whole premise of Korah's complaint was that Moses and Aaron were not the only ones who were holy, as all of Israel, everyone was made holy by GOD.

They gathered together against Moses and Aaron, and said to them,

*"You take too much upon yourselves, **for all the congregation is** holy, every one of them, and the Lord is among them. Why then do you exalt yourselves above the assembly of the Lord?"*
**Numbers 16:3**

The word בדל Badal/Separate is used first in Genesis to separate light from darkness in GOD's Creation.

*And God saw the light, that it was good; and God **separated/divided** (בדל Badal) the light from the darkness. GOD called the light Day, and the darkness He called Night. So the evening and the morning were the first day... Thus GOD made the firmament, and **separated/divided** (בדל Badal) the waters which were under the firmament from the waters which were above the firmament; and it was so.*
**Genesis 1:4,5,7**

*You must **distinguish** (בדל Badal) between what is sacred and what is common, between what is ceremonially unclean and what is clean.*
**Leviticus 10:10**

*By these instructions you will **know** (בדל Badal) what is unclean and clean, and which animals may be eaten and which may not be eaten.*
**Leviticus 11:47**

Korah & Company claimed that there were just as holy as Moses and Aaron. Being holy is to be set apart for the LORD.

> *Then Moses said to Korah, "Hear now, you sons of Levi:*
> *Is it a small thing to you that the <u>God of Israel has separated</u> (בדל*
> *Badal) <u>you</u> from the congregation of Israel, to bring you near to*
> *Himself, to do the work of the tabernacle of the Lord,*
> *and to stand before the congregation to serve them;*
> *and that He has brought you near to Himself,*
> *you and all your brethren, the sons of Levi, with you? And are you*
> *seeking the priesthood also?*
> **Numbers 16:8-9**

Moses reminded Korah that, indeed the LORD had separated him for Himself to serve in His presence, but Korah was not content. He was not content with what the LORD had given him. He was jealous of Moses, and he wanted more…

> *And the Lord spoke to Moses and Aaron, saying, "Separate (בדל*
> *Badal) yourselves from among this congregation, that I may consume*
> *them in a moment."*
> **Numbers 16:20-21**

Throughout the Torah, GOD separated the holy from the unholy, clean from the unclean. How ironic that Korah's group demanded their "holy" status be equal as Moses and Aaron, then to have the LORD "separate" them from the rest of the Israelites to be consumed. It is no accident that the LORD used the word בדל Badal/Separate to make the case of the ungrateful attitude and envy in Korah & Company that led to their own demise.

## 3 – SWALLOW DOWN

The uprising of Korah and his followers brought the unprecedented consequence to themselves. Never had the earth opened and swallowed people up prior to this incident, nor did it since. Following are references retelling this very incident in other parts of the Bible.

> "Who is like You, O Lord, among the gods?
> Who is like You, glorious in holiness,
> Fearful in praises, doing wonders?
> You stretched out Your right hand;
> The earth <u>swallowed</u> them.
> Exodus 15:11-12

*When they envied Moses in the camp, and Aaron the saint of the Lord,
The earth opened up and <u>swallowed</u> Dathan, and covered the faction of Abiram.*
Psalm 106:16-17

The LORD is clear about what He does with the humble and the wicked.

> *The Lord **lifts up** the humble;
> He **casts** the wicked **down** to the ground.*
> Psalm 147:6-8

Notice the humble does not rise up on their own; he is lifted up by the LORD.

There are TWO Rebellions in this Parasha; the second one happened the day after Korah's group was destroyed.

**FIRST REBELLION — 250 men died with Korah, Dathan, Abiram and their families**

<u>A sign of remembrance of the consequence for the First rebellion against GOD</u> —

## 34. KORACH / KORAH

*Then the Lord spoke to Moses, saying: "Tell Eleazar, the son of Aaron the priest, to pick up the censers out of the blaze, for they are holy, and scatter the fire some distance away.*
*The censers of these <u>men who sinned against their own souls</u>, let them be made into hammered plates as a covering for the altar. Because they presented them before the Lord, therefore they are holy; and <u>they shall be a sign to the children of Israel</u>."*
*<u>So Eleazar the priest took the bronze censers</u>, which those who were burned up had presented, and they were <u>hammered out as a covering on the altar, to be a memorial to the children of Israel that no outsider, who is not a descendant of Aaron, should come near to offer incense before the Lord, that he might not become like Korah and his companions</u>,*
*just as the Lord had said to him through Moses.*
**Numbers 16:36-40**

The LORD told Eleazar, the priest, to use the censers of Korah's group to make a covering for the altar as a sign that only Aaron and his descendants were allowed to offer incense for the LORD.

### SECOND REBELLION — 14,700 died in a plague

*On the next day <u>all the congregation of the children of Israel complained</u> against Moses and Aaron, saying, "You have killed the people of the Lord."*
*Now it happened, when the congregation had gathered against Moses and Aaron, that they turned toward the tabernacle of meeting; and suddenly the cloud covered it, and the glory of the Lord appeared. Then Moses and Aaron came before the tabernacle of meeting.*
**Numbers 16:41-43**

> *So Moses said to Aaron,*
> *"Take a censer and put fire in it from the altar, put incense on it, and take it quickly to the congregation and make atonement for them; for wrath has gone out from the Lord. The plague has begun."*
> *Then Aaron took it as Moses commanded, and ran into the midst of the assembly; and already the plague had begun among the people. So he put in the incense and made atonement for the people. <u>And he stood between the dead and the living; so the plague was stopped.</u>*
> **Numbers 17:46-47**

Fascinating that it was Aaron, the High Priest, that made atonement with the incense for the people. "He stood between the dead and the living; so the plague was stopped" — Aaron saved many from death by standing between the dead and the living. You can say that's a literal description and a depiction of the High Priest, the Messiah standing in the gap for us, in the unseen spiritual realm. I'd say that's a pretty cool Superhero Deliverance, wouldn't you?

## 4 – PUT FORTH/GO FORTH/SHINE IN AARON'S ROD

A sign of remembrance of the consequence for the Second rebellion against GOD —

> *Now it came to pass on the next day that Moses went into the tabernacle of witness, and behold, <u>the rod of Aaron</u>, of the house of Levi, <u>had sprouted</u> and <u>put forth buds</u>, had <u>produced blossoms</u> and <u>yielded ripe almonds</u>. Then Moses brought out all the rods from before the Lord to all the children of Israel; and they looked, and each man took his rod. And the Lord said to Moses, "Bring Aaron's rod back before the Testimony, to be kept <u>as a sign against the rebels, that you may put their complaints away from Me, lest they die.</u>" Thus did Moses; just as the Lord had commanded him, so he did.*
> **Numbers 17:8-11**

Aaron's Rod was to be a sign of the salvation the LORD brought through Aaron. The verse says this of the Rod: it <u>sprouted</u>, put forth (go forth/bring forth) <u>buds</u>, <u>produced</u> (shine/sparkle) blossoms and <u>yielded</u> (abundantly with) ripe almonds. First of all, this is a supernatural phenomenon. Aaron's rod is the only one out of the 12 tribes' rods that came to life from death — a rod, dead stick that started sprouting, blossoming, and bearing fruit. This is a physical confirmation of Aaron and his descendants being called by the LORD into priesthood.

There is a saying, "All roads lead to Rome," but I say in regards to the Torah, the Word of GOD, "All roads lead to the Mashiach (Messiah)." Whether it be Moses, Joseph, Aaron and many others being the foreshadowing and Messianic figures, prophetic portraits of the Mashiach are to be, or the wicked plans of polluting the gene pool of the Mashiach to be born of, … , the Torah is full of such glimpses reminding us of the Mashiach. I believe the four elements highlighted in this Parasha point to the Mashiach.

**RISE UP/ESTABLISH – SEPARATE/SET APART – SWALLOW DOWN – PUT FORTH/SHINE –**

The Mashiach **rose up and established** His Kingdom and Dominion forever. He is Holy as the Divine King, **separate and set apart** from the rest. The Mashiach is to **be swallowed down** into the grave, atoning sins of the world unto death. Aaron, as the foreshadowing of the Mashiach standing between the dead and the living, what a perfect depiction of our Ultimate Deliverance who has brought life in this age and the age to come for us. As supernatural as Aaron's Rod, the Mashiach is to resurrect from death, come back to life, being **brought forth** to bear fruit for us all.

Parashat Korach is more than a rebellion story. It is a lesson of envy and jealousy, a lesson of a group of people who were not content with what they've been given, time after time. Nonetheless, the LORD's original plan has always been to provide redemption for His people. Even with Cain rising up to commit an unspoken crime against his own brother and GOD, the LORD's intent was to establish His covenant with His Children to bring about redemption through the Mashiach.

Oh, one more note about Aaron's Rod blossoming and bearing fruits into almonds…

> *Moreover the word of the Lord came to me, saying,*
> *"<u>Jeremiah, what do you see?</u>"*
> *And I said, "I see <u>a branch of an almond tree</u>."*
> *Then the Lord said to me, "<u>You have seen well</u>, <u>for I am ready to perform My word</u>."*
> *Jeremiah 1:11-12*

Isn't that just like GOD the MOST HIGH to use almonds as a sign of fulfilling all His promises, as referenced in Jeremiah 1:11-12? Isn't the Mashiach the fulfillment of what the LORD promised His people long ago to bring forth deliverance, salvation, and LIFE?

Let's pray:

> **Our Father in Heaven** אבינו שבשמימ,
>
> Thank You for the promises of Your plans of deliverance through the Mashiach! Truly, Your Word brings life. Even through the stories of the Korah rebellion, we see how You always have a redemption plan in mind for us. LORD, help us to see our role individually in your plans instead of being envious of others. Just like the almonds on Aaron's Rod, let us see You as a promise-fulfilling GOD that You are. You will certainly carry out all Your plans — Your good plans for us!
>
> B'Shem Yeshua HaMashiach בשם ישוע המשיח.
>
> In Jesus' Name we pray. Amen.

# 34. TORAH TASTING
## *REFLECTION*

1. What is the word, picture or theme the LORD is highlighting to you in this chapter and Torah Portion?

2. The priests were set apart to be holy for GOD. What are some ways that we can set ourselves apart, leading others to desire to draw close to GOD?

3. Messiah came to save us. He established a Kingdom that has no end. Our Redeemer lives, and He is our very present help in time of need! He is our help when we need help, no matter how big or small. Do you have anything that you are crying out for help with at this moment?

# 35 לה
# chukat
## (Statute)
חקת

Numbers 19:1-22:1

Judges 11:1-33

John 19:38-42

Parashat Chukat got its name from its second verse.

> *Now the Lord spoke to Moses and Aaron, saying,*
> *"This is the **statute/ordinance** (חקת chukat) of the law which the Lord has commanded, saying:*
> *'Speak to the children of Israel, that they bring you a **red heifer** (פרה אדמה Farah Adumah) without blemish, in which there is no defect and on which a yoke has never come.*
> **Numbers 19:1-2**

It is interesting how the Torah Portion titles were chosen.

Oftentimes, it comes from the first verse of the portion. In this case, it could have been Red Heifer, perhaps. Even though titles of the Torah Portions and the chapter/verse divisions are assigned by man, I do believe the LORD can direct them to fit His purposes. I have said it many times. There is No Coincidence, only Divine Providence.

This Parasha consists of the ceremony of removing defilement with a red heifer after being in contact with the dead, the death of Miriam, Moses striking a rock instead of speaking to it that disallowed him to enter into the Promise Land, Edom refusing Israel's passage, death of Aaron, salvation by looking up at the bronze serpent and Israel's song of the well. Lots of major events are packed into this Torah Portion.

While I would like to talk about the infamous episode of the plot-turning event of Moses striking the rock or the miraculous and ironic healing of the bronze serpent from fiery serpent bites, I sense the LORD is directing us to look at the Red Heifer. You see, the title of this Parasha is חקת Chukat Statute, so I would think that is a subtle little clue to a main theme of this Portion. I do not know much about farming or animals. Cows don't pick my interest. It's fascinating that this Torah Portion opens with the statute involving a Red Heifer.

Hmmm... okay... The reference of heifer is also in several other places within the Torah. However, "Red Heifer" is only mentioned in this Portion throughout the entire Tanakh (Old Testament).

Now. That caught my attention.

What's even more interesting...

*And the one who gathers the ashes of the **heifer** shall wash his clothes, and be unclean until evening. It shall be a **statute forever** (חקת עולם Chukat Olam) to the children of Israel and to the stranger who dwells among them.*
**Numbers 19:10**

## 35. CHUKAT / STATUTE

*It shall be a perpetual statute (חקת עולמ Chukat Olam) for them. He who sprinkles the water of purification shall wash his clothes; and he who touches the water of purification shall be unclean until evening.*
**Numbers 19:21**

The beginning of the Torah discusses the detailed removal of defilement by dead body, which requires a red heifer. At the same time, the red heifer ritual is a forever statute (חקת עולמ Chukat Olam). I have found the exact phrase of חקת עולמ Chukat Olam forever/eternal statute mentioned 19 times in the Torah:

Ex. 27:21, 28:43, 29:9, Lev. 3:17, 7:36, 10:9, 16:29, 16:31, 17:7, 23:14, 23:21, 23:31, 23:41, 24:3, Numbers 10:8, 15:15, 18:23, 19:10, 19:21.

The Hebrew word עולמ Olam is translated as ages, forever, perpetual, continual, eternal, everlasting, …, basically infinite, no end… .

That is, if we draw a dot representing our lifetime, in comparison, Olam/forever is a line that goes on infinitely with no stopping. That is an overwhelming concept! So, חקת עולמ Chukat Olam is a statute that has no finality. Its effect is continual and perpetual with no end. This ordinance or law or statute or command does not and will not change for eternity.

Now, the Red Heifer has to be without blemish nor defect. The Red Heifer would take away the defilement of death?

### Check this out —

*For if the blood of bulls and goats and the ashes of a <u>heifer</u>, sprinkling the unclean, sanctifies for the purifying of the flesh, how much more shall the blood of Christ, who through the <u>eternal</u> Spirit offered Himself **without spot** to God, cleanse your conscience from dead works to serve the living God?*
**Hebrews 9:13-14**

Do you see the connection in this verse with the Red Heifer we have been discussing? Yes, this reference points to Yeshua HaMashiach Jesus Christ as the One without blemish nor defect that would take away our defilement of the dead. I venture to say this is the only verse in the New Testament comprising the words "heifer" and "eternal," as in the Torah Portion verse mentioned earlier.

Not every statute mentioned in the Torah is forever עָלוּם Olam, but those that carry significant weight to what GOD has purposed for us.

This forever statute of Red Heifer is unique in the Bible. Many believe there are prophetic implications for what is to come in GOD's plans.

I do too.

The Hebrew word for Red is אדמ Edom, the same letters that make Adam אדמ, mankind, man. Red represents the Blood; the Hebrew word for Red has the mankind connection. The Deliverer of the world is the one that would have His Blood shed, carrying the sins of mankind onto Himself.

Ok. If you're not convinced of the connections yet, here's one more.

This Parasha inserted a little episode of Edom refusing to allow Israel to pass through their territory, right between Moses striking the rock and the death of Aaron. The significance of the order of events cannot be overlooked. In these 8 short verses, the king of Edom refused to let Israelites pass through, even with much pleading. A curious mind may wonder why this may be worthy of mentioning… That's exactly my thought.

**Well, let's look at the origin of Edom —**

> *So when her (Rebekah's) days were fulfilled for her to give birth, indeed there were twins in her womb. And the first came out **red** (Hebrew root אדם Adom). He was like a hairy garment all over; so they called his name Esau…*

## 35. CHUKAT / STATUTE

*Now Jacob cooked a stew; and Esau came in from the field, and he was weary. And Esau said to Jacob, "Please feed me with that same red stew, for I am weary."*
*Therefore his name was called Edom (Hebrew root אדם Adom).*
**Genesis 25:24-25, ... 29-30**

Edomites come from Edom אדם, which is the name of Esau, meaning red, for the color Esau was born in (perhaps covered in blood and hair) and the color of the stew with which he sold his birthright to Jacob.

Is that a coincidence that Edom is casually mentioned in this Portion, or is it there as a clue to confirm the Red Heifer?

Hmmm…

Let's talk more about this little episode. After Edom refused the Israelites to go through their land, Aaron passed his baton onto his son Eleazer as his successor and died on the mountaintop. Israel then defeated King Arad of the Canaanites, King Sihon of the Amorites and King Og of Bashan. During that time, despite their grumpy complaints and fiery serpents coming out to bite them, the LORD provided miraculous healing through looking at the Bronze Serpent. Even though they were not allowed to pass through the Edomite territory and had to go through a detour, the detour led Israel to see defeats of their enemies and witness miraculous healings.

Detours sometimes prevent us from harm. There are times detours lead us to unexpected blessings. We get upset when we see a "DETOUR" sign on the road because now we have to take a different route to the destination. It is not part of the plan! It takes longer than expected.

What we don't realize is that sometimes the detours can take us to places we have not planned to go, which may be for our good.

Have you ever failed a class and had to take it again? Who did you meet in this new class, and what new things have you learned there?

Have you ever come to a closed path and had to take a different route only to find amazing sceneries like a hidden waterfall, which you would've missed if things had gone as planned?

Have you ever had a flight that was delayed? Very frustrating! You now had to rethink the plans, but perhaps blessings are just right around the corner of the detour?

*And we know that all things work together for good to those who love God, to those who are the called according to His purpose.*
**Romans 8:28**

I believe the LORD is highlighting the Red Heifer as an eternal statute (חקת עולמ Chukat Olam)

and forever sign for the provision of His salvation through the Mashiach. GOD weaves His everlasting mercy and steadfast love throughout the Torah.

"Forever" is an incomprehensible concept, yet, the lesson of what our daily-life detours can bring eternal triumphs and blessings is so apparent in this Parasha.

# 35. CHUKAT / STATUTE

**Let's pray:**

**Our Father in Heaven** אבינו שבשמימ,

Thank You for being Eternal. You are so beyond space and time. We ask You to reveal to us the magnificent purposes of the perpetual statutes and teach us to appreciate them and see them in ways as You have destined them to be appreciated. You have placed countless foreshadows of the Mashiach throughout the Torah in people and circumstances. Give us understanding and wisdom to see each one in deeper ways. Just like the surprises the Israelites saw on their detours, LORD, please help us appreciate the outcome of circumstances that were unexpected and unplanned.

B'Shem Yeshua HaMashiach בשם ישוע המשיח.

In Jesus' Name we pray. Amen.

## 35. TORAH TASTING
### *REFLECTION*

1. What is the word, picture or theme the LORD is highlighting to you in this chapter and Torah Portion?

2. GOD is eternal and the concept of us living eternally with Him is beyond our understanding. How does this eternality concept affect the way we live life each day?

3. Have you had an experience where things did not go as planned or you were led to a detour, which turned out to be a blessing in disguise? What have you learned looking back at it in hindsight?

# 36 לוֹ
# Balak
## (Balak)
## בלק

Numbers 22:2-25:9

Micah 5:6-6:8

Matthew 21:1-11

This Parasha opens with the entry of a Moabite king named Balak. There are only a handful of Torah Portions that are named after a person, such as Yitro (a Midianite priest and Moses' father-in-law), Korah (a Levite challenging Moses' leadership) and Pinchas (Aaron's heroic grandson). In this list, there are heroes and enemies of Israel. The character of Balak is highlighted as, in the title, someone significant is being brought onto the surface.

In this Parasha, Balak draws some parallels to the Exodus Story. He was a son of Zippor (male bird) (Numbers 22:2), and the name of Moses' wife is Zipporah (a bird). Parashat Balak states in Numbers 22:3, "And Moab was in great dread of the people because they were many. Moab was overcome with fear of the people of Israel."

This reminds us of this-

*Now there arose a new king over Egypt, who did not know Joseph. And he said to his people,
"Look, the people of the children of Israel are more and <u>mightier than we</u>; come, let us deal shrewdly with them, lest they multiply, and it happen, in the event of war, that they also join our enemies and fight against us, and so go up out of the land." …
And <u>they were in dread of the children of Israel</u>.*
Exodus 1:8-10,12b

While the Egyptian king Pharoah enslaved and killed GOD's people (causing physical harm), the Moabite king Balak, learning how powerful Israel was destroying the Amorites, intended to curse Israel (inflicting spiritual casualty). Both kings felt threatened by the strength of Israel and her GOD.

The name of Balak comes from the Hebrew word Balak בלק, meaning lay waste or devastate. Therefore, Balak's name means "Devastator" for this Moabite king. It seems that the backdrop of the story is a Devastator being fearful of Israel, without realizing the mighty power behind this terrifying group of people is the LORD.

Do we dare to think after GOD liberating His people and bringing them out of Egypt, He will yet save them from devastation again?

Absolutely!

The word Balak בלק Devastate/Lay waste is only used twice in the Torah, Isaiah 24:1 and Nahum 2:10 —

*Behold, the Lord makes the earth <u>empty</u> and **makes it waste (בלק Balak),***
Isaiah 24:1

## 36. BALAK / BALAK

*And it will be said in that day:*
*"Behold, this is our God;*
*We have waited for Him, and He will save us.*
*This is the Lord;*
*We have waited for Him;*
*We will be glad and rejoice in His salvation."*
*¹⁰ For on this mountain the hand of the Lord will rest,*
*And <u>Moab shall be trampled down under Him,</u>*
*As straw is trampled down for the refuse heap.*
**Isaiah 25:9-10**

Note that the first usage of **laying waste** (בלק **Balak**) describes the beginning of the devastation of GOD's enemy (Isaiah 24:1), but ends with gladness, salvation and <u>Moab</u> being defeated and destroyed (Isaiah 25:9-10).

*She (Nineveh) is <u>empty</u>, desolate, and waste (בלק **Balak**)!*
*The heart melts, and the knees shake;*
*Much pain is in every side,*
*And all their faces are drained of color… All who hear news of you*
*(Nineveh's devastation)*
*Will <u>clap their hands</u> over you.*
**Nahum 2:10, 3:19**

The second time the word of בלק **Balak** used echoes the first one. The devastation of GOD's enemy concludes with joy (clapping of hands).

Isn't this the resounding theme of the work of GOD?

His enemies intend to destroy and devastate Him and His people always end up in destruction and their own defeat!

Who is Balaam that possibly changed the course of the fate of Israel in this epic story?

Balaam was the son of Beor (the "burning") at Pethor, which is near the River in the land of <u>the sons of his **people**</u>.

> *So the elders of Moab and the elders of Midian departed*
> *with the diviner's fee in their hand, and they came to Balaam*
> *and spoke to him the words of Balak.*
> **Numbers 22:7**

Balaam was a diviner. Obviously a well-known and a well-sought-after one that the king of Moab had to seek him out to accomplish this tremendous task of cursing Israel, who had just defeated the Amorites. Their victory preceded them and brought terror to Moab.

> *And God said to Balaam, "You shall not go with them; you shall not curse the people, for they are blessed."*
> **Numbers 22:12**

> *So Balaam rose in the morning and said to the princes of Balak, "Go back to your land, <u>for the Lord has refused to give me permission</u> to go with you."*
> **Numbers 22:13**

> *For I (Balak) will <u>certainly honor you greatly</u>,*
> *and <u>I will do whatever you say to me</u>.*
> *Therefore please come, curse this people for me.'*
> *Then Balaam answered and said to the servants of Balak,*
> *"Though Balak were to give me his house full of silver and gold,*
> *<u>I could not go beyond the word of **the Lord** my God</u>, to do less or more.*
> **Numbers 22:17**

Balak kept sending Moabite princes to convince Balaam to curse Israel. That indicates how effective and powerful the curses of Balaam had been, and yet He needed the permission of "the LORD my GOD" to curse His people. Interestingly, even a diviner/sorcerer, who called the LORD "my GOD," is subject to His Word!

How would you like the assignment of cursing the Un-cursable?

Balaam was taken up to the high places of Baal, where the pagans worshiped at the instruction of Balak, the Moabite king, promising earthly riches. Instead of being blinded by the bribe, Balaam blessed GOD's people at the sight of GOD's mighty power in His people.

In **Balaam's 4 prophesies**, he blessed GOD's people 3 different times (Numbers 24:10) and spoke a Messianic promise.

<u>First prophecy</u> — Numbers 23:7-10

> *"How shall I curse whom God has not cursed?*
> *And how shall I denounce whom the Lord has not denounced?"*
> **Numbers 23:8**

— GOD's blessed people are "un-curse-able".

<u>Second prophecy</u> — Numbers 23:18-24

> *Behold, I have received a command to bless;*
> *He has blessed, and I cannot reverse it.*
> **Numbers 23:10**

— GOD cannot lie, and his blessings are irreversible.

<u>Third prophecy</u> — Numbers 24:3-7

> *"How lovely are your tents, O Jacob!*
> *Your dwellings, O Israel!...*
> *"God brings him out of Egypt;*
> *He has strength like a wild ox;...*
> *"Blessed is he who blesses you,*
> *And cursed is he who curses you."*
> **Numbers 24:5,...,8,9**

— Whatever is spoken over Israel would be boomeranged back to the speaker, blessing or cursing!

<u>Fourth prophecy</u> — Numbers 24:17-24

> *A Star shall come out of Jacob;*
> *A Scepter shall rise out of Israel, …*
> *Out of Jacob One shall have dominion,*
> *And destroy the remains of the city.*
> **Numbers 24:17,19**

— The Star and the Scepter in this verse are of Messianic reference, as well as "Out of Jacob" and "One shall have dominion." The Messiah King is prophesied here, just as in Genesis 49.

> *The scepter shall not depart from Judah,*
> *Nor a lawgiver from between his feet,*
> *Until Shiloh comes;*
> *And to Him shall be the obedience of the people.*
> **Genesis 49:10**

At each of the 3 intended curses turning out to be blessings, Balak had Balaam build 7 **altars** sacrificing 7 <u>bulls</u> and 7 <u>rams</u>.

The 7 altars were meant to be built to make a sacrifice for cursing Israel. Certainly, the receiving end of the sacrifice was meant for the LORD, but Balaam knew he could only do the LORD's bidding. The Fear of GOD fell upon him that led him to speak words of blessings over Israel. No matter how Balak changed the setting, the outcome was the same. GOD's love and mercy for His people was not going to change.

The very first <u>ram sacrifice</u> in the Torah was made when the LORD established <u>a covenant with Abram</u> (Genesis 15:9-12). The first <u>bull sacrifice</u> in the Torah is a peace offering for the <u>atonement of sins</u>. (Ex. 29:1).

The 7 in the 7 altars is a number for completeness and perfection. GOD created the world in 7 days. The 3 of the 3 blessings also has the significance of completeness. Israel has 3 patriarchs, Abraham, Isaac and Jacob. The Hebrew Bible is comprised of the Torah, Prophets and Writing. It seems even the elements of the sacrifice set up the backdrop of what the LORD meant for completeness in His blessings over Israel. His promise to Abram and his descendants and the provision of atonement of sins for Israel are seen through the ram and bull sacrifice, as well as the words of the blessings and the Messianic prophecy.

Balaam, though a foreign diviner, had a tremendous impact in Israel's history. His prophetic words in this Torah Portion cannot be understated. He reinforced the covenant between the LORD and Abram with 3 blessings. Even the Moabite king said this of him in Numbers 22-

> *Therefore please come at once, curse this people for me, for they are too mighty for me. Perhaps I shall be able to defeat them and drive them out of the land, for I know that he **whom you (Balaam) bless is blessed**, and he whom you curse is cursed.*
> **Numbers 22:6**

What Balak said of Balaam is remarkable! While he acknowledged how powerful Balaam's spoken words were, what he did not realize was that GOD had blessed Israel. No amount of curses can be spoken that can un-bless GOD's people!

> *I (GOD) will bless those who bless you, And I will curse him who curses you; And in you all the families of the earth shall be blessed."*
> **Genesis 12:3**

Those <u>who blessed Abram</u> were blessed, and those <u>whom Balaam blessed</u> would be blessed.

Balaam's Messianic prophecy (Numbers 24 in the fourth prophecy) reaffirmed Jacob's last words to his sons. It might have taken a talking donkey to intercept his journey to Balak; Balaam's words declared over Israel overlooking GOD's people continue to be echoed in every synagogue on every Shabbat, even to this day.

מה-טבו אהליך יעקב משכנתיך ישראל
ואני ברב חסדך אבוא ביתך אשתחוה אל-היכל-קדשך ביראתך

"Ma tovu ohalekha Ya'akov, mishk'notekha Yisra'el. Va'ani b'rov hasd'kha, avo veytekha, eshtahaveh el heikhal kodsh'kha b'yir'atekha. And in thy great compassion, I will come into Your house. There I will bow, there I will fear, Thy Holiness, O GOD."
How lovely are your tents, Jacob, your dwelling places, Israel! As for me, through Your abundant kindness I will enter Your house; I will prostrate myself toward Your Holy Sanctuary in awe of You. O LORD, I love the House where You dwell, and the place where Your glory tabernacles. I shall prostrate myself and bow; I shall kneel before the LORD my Maker. As for me, may my prayer to You, LORD, be at a favorable time; O God, in Your abundant kindness, answer me with the truth of Your salvation!
Numbers 24:5, Psalm 5:7,8, 26:8, 95:6 and 69:14.

How many times have we heard, "GOD can use anyone?" Anyone and Anything? Even someone that was paid to speak curses on His people. Even a talking donkey? By the way, the animation movie Shrek's talking donkey character is not an original concept.

Then <u>the Lord opened the mouth of the donkey</u>, and she said to Balaam, "What have I done to you, that you have struck me these three times?"
**Numbers 22:28**

The Devastator King "got a taste of his own medicine." Not only did he not get what he'd paid for, but Israel's blessings were also further solidified, and the coming Messiah and His power were decreed and declared, confirming the words of Israel's patriarch.

This Parasha did sadly end (Numbers 25:1-9) with some of Israel's men committing harlotry with Moabite women and worshipping their gods, which resulted in a plague killing 24,000 people. The plague was stopped due to the heroic act of Phinehas, son of Eleazar and grandson of Aaron. Nonetheless, what we have learned is that at the end of their wilderness journey, before entering the Promise Land, Israel's enemy attempted yet again to destroy them to no avail. During the time when their enemy (Balak, the Moabite king) sought to curse Israel to eternal damnation, the LORD battled against him through Balaam's blessings over Israel. When Israel camped in the land of Moab, being oblivious to the epic spiritual battle for their very survival, the GOD of the Universe was strategizing and moving on their behalf. It truly was an incredible, unseen battle for Israel.

Destiny had it that Balak, The Devastator Moabite king met Balaam (his name, "Bala-am," means "Lord of the people" or "Not the People" in different languages). It really was not Balaam that this king was encountering, but the LORD of the people, GOD of Israel.

The LORD Our GOD Most High is Almighty, Supreme and Omnipotent. No king on earth or anywhere else can come close to His wisdom, power, and knowledge, but most of all, His love for His people. Time and time again, the LORD turned what was meant for devastation for His people into life and gladness. He confirmed and reaffirmed His promises to us beyond our realization. He provided salvation, even through a talking donkey, a debatable and unlikely heroic foreign diviner, as well as Aaron's grandson's sudden and decisive act ending a fatal plague among His people.

Many times when "bad" things happen, I'd say, "I have no idea what the LORD has saved me from. It could've been a lot worse," whether it be our son falling out of a second-floor window resulting with only a few scratches, a canceled connecting flight returning home after traveling for 24 hours, or a minor car accident that interrupted our day. Every time I hear or recite MA TOVU (How Lovely…), I try to envision what Balaam saw in GOD's people looking down from the mountain top, declaring what GOD told him to speak, no more, no less.

We are GOD's people. He is our GOD! The unseen war is waging in our midst against us, but the LORD's defense for us is constant and resolute, whether we realize it or not. We only need to give thanks in all circumstances and trust in His goodness. No matter what happens, the LORD has been and is working in our midst for our good.

We are Blessed and Un-curse-able!

Do we dare to live as this being the ABSOLUTE TRUTH?!

Let's pray:

### Our Father in Heaven אבינו שבשמימ,

Thank You for Your good plans for us. Your promises are eternal. As the Apostle Paul advised us, we are to give You thanks always, in every situation, at the hearing of good news and moments of disappointment because we know Your Provision and Defense for us is constant, and we can always count on no matter what we see in the physical realm. LORD, help us to agree with Your plans and to walk by faith. We ask You to help us understand deeper the blessings You spoke through Balaam, that not only You had not changed your mind about loving Your people, but You also reassured the promise in the Messiah to bring salvation and hope for us. Thank You, Father!

B'Shem Yeshua HaMashiach בשם ישוע המשיח.

In Jesus' Name we pray. Amen.

# 36. TORAH TASTING
## *REFLECTION*

1. What is the word, picture or theme the LORD is highlighting to you in this chapter and Torah Portion?

2. If GOD can open the mouth of a donkey to deliver a message, He can use anything. Have you ever heard a story or experienced a time that GOD spoke or confirmed to you through an unlikely person or an unexpected circumstance?

3. Can you recall a time that something bad happened that could have been worse, with the realization that GOD saved you from what could have been catastrophic?

# 37 לז
# pinchas
## (Phinehas)
## פנחס

Numbers 25:10-30:1

1 Kings 18:46-19:21

John 2:13-22

Parashat Pinchas is titled after Aaron's grandson, who heroically killed Zimri, an Israelite, and Cozbi, a Midianite woman, for their adulterous act. Thus, it ended the plague. Pinchas is translated as Phinehas in English. This Torah Portion begins with the details of how Pinchas' jealousy for GOD stopped the plague, then the LORD's call for a census for the new generation, Zelophechad's daughters' request for an inheritance, Joshua being named as Moses' successor and instructions of offerings at various appointed times.

From Pinchas' courageous act rewarded with the Covenant of Peace, Joshua taking over Moses' "Baton," to Zelophechad's daughters making their request about their inheritance, I sense "Posterity" being the major theme here.

Here is a famous quote by President Ronald Reagan —

"Freedom is never more than one generation away from extinction. We didn't pass it to our children in the bloodstream. It must be fought for, protected, and handed on for them to do the same, or one day we will spend our sunset years telling our children and our children's children what it was once like in the United States, where men were free."

Anything that we have, physical possessions or spiritual heritage, it cannot be assumed that they would be passed onto our children without intentionally safeguarding and instilling it into the next generation. How many times have we heard some wealthy tycoons' children waste away their inheritance? How often do we see godly people's children or grandchildren lose their faith? There is a Chinese proverb that says, "It is hard to build a business, but it is harder to keep it," 創業難, 守業更難 (chuang ye nan, shou ye geng nan). It specifically speaks of the challenge the next generation has in guarding and keeping an established business.

> *And what great nation is there that has such statutes and righteous judgments as are in all this law which I set before you this day? Only take heed to yourself, and <u>diligently keep yourself</u>, lest you forget the things your eyes have seen, and lest they depart from your heart all the days of your life. And <u>teach them to your children and your grandchildren</u>.*
> **Deuteronomy 4:8-9**

Children learn mostly from observation; lessons learned are caught, not taught. As the saying goes, "Monkey see, Monkey do." That's why the LORD instructed Israel to diligently keep the statutes themselves, then to teach them to their children and their grandchildren.

My husband and I grew up on opposite sides of the globe, respectively, New York City and Hong Kong. Yet, our childhood experiences may be more similar than couples coming from within the same state. We both remember going to the market with our grandmothers, where they shopped daily for fresh meat and produce. 'Til this day, we can still picture our grandmothers picking out the "best" live chicken (of course, Kosher for Paul's Bubbe, Jewish Grandmother) and had them butchered right there on the street. We lived in high-rise buildings throughout our childhoods, walking and taking a few bus-routes to get to school. (FYI, Paul, as a child, was way naughtier than I was).

Before leaving Hong Kong to come to the U.S. for high school, my mother often reminded me, "No matter where you are and what happens, take pride in who GOD has made you to be, a HongKongese, representing the Chinese honoring heritage and the sophistication of British-influenced upbringing. People may not know you as a person, but they will say, "that girl from Hong Kong is respectful or otherwise." "You may be the only HongKongese girl they ever meet." Because of that, I do not ever feel ashamed that I am not good enough because I am Chinese, if anything, I am proud of my culture and history…

4000+ years of Chinese history and the 4 Great Inventions in ancient human civilization that changed the world: compass, gunpowder, paper, and printing technology… and many more other achievements from the Chinese civilization.

Paul, on the other hand, recalls his mother's admonition, "Paul, always remember that you are a Jew, no matter what others say. You will always be a Jew." Paul did not continue to practice the very strict Orthodox Judaism after leaving New York. When he received Yeshua Jesus as LORD, he was secure in knowing he is a Jew and always a Jew, despite the lie, "You can be a Buddhist Jew, an atheist Jew, but you are no longer a Jew when accepting Yeshua Jesus."

O, the Power of a mother's words!

Similarly, passing on what we were taught, we teach our children from a young age that they are both Chinese and Jewish. Many even remark to them how blessed they are of the 2 smartest and richest civilizations in world history. Learning simultaneously the languages of Chinese and Hebrew and being immersed in both cultures have been part of life since birth for them. Admiration, not shame, is associated to the identity of who GOD has made them to be.

Posterity is very important to the LORD. L'dor v'dor לדר ודר From Generation to Generation is a recurring theme in the Torah. Just as stated in Deuteronomy 4:9, "And teach them to your children and your grandchildren." The very survival of the Jewish people hinged upon L'dor v'dor לדר ודר. The precious Word of GOD, Jewish traditions, and cultures in the faith that we have today triumphed over countless attempts of annihilation, which attribute to GOD's commandment of L'dor v'dor לדר ודר.

Some of us came to know the LORD as an adult. Nonetheless, we wish for our children to have their faith secure in the LORD at a young age, serving and loving Yeshua wholeheartedly to avoid some of the hard roads in life that we have experienced. We want our ceiling to be our children's floor to build upon, that their faith will go further than we can ever imagine.

In Parashat Pinchas, there are 3 major lessons of courage and boldness we can learn about teaching our children and our grandchildren L'dor v'dor לדר ודר From Generation to Generation.

1. Pinchas — Dare to do the right thing out of zeal for the LORD can bring salvation to the whole nation at a decisive moment and be rewarded for generations to come. Dare to stand up for righteousness, not being clouded by emotions.

> *Then the Lord spoke to Moses, saying: "Pinchas (Phinehas) the son of Eleazar, the son of Aaron the priest, has turned back My wrath from the children of Israel, because <u>he was zealous with My zeal among them</u>, so that I did not consume the children of Israel in My zeal. Therefore say, 'Behold, I give to him <u>My covenant of peace</u>; and it shall be to him and his descendants after him <u>a covenant of an everlasting priesthood</u>, because <u>he was zealous for his God</u>, and made atonement for the children of Israel."*
>
> **Numbers 25:10-13**

The Hebrew word used for zeal is קנא Kanah. It also means jealousy. Pinchas could not stand the adultery committed by Israel against the LORD. It was utterly unjust, given what the LORD had done and was doing for His people.

An incredible "coincidence" I found is the sum of the 3 numbers associated with each the 3 Hebrew letters in קנא Kanah is 151. The sum of the letters in the word for נקא N'keh Pure/Clean is also 151.

נקא N'keh Pure/Clean is when you flip the last 2 letters in קנא Kanah Zeal. נקא N'keh Pure/Clean is only used once in the entire Tanakh (Old Testament). It is in Daniel 7, describing GOD as the Ancient of Days, Who alone is pure and clean.

> *I watched till thrones were put in place,*
> *And the Ancient of Days was seated;*
> *His garment was white as snow,*
> *And the hair of His head was like **pure (נקא N'keh) wool**.*
> *His throne was a fiery flame,*
> *Its wheels a burning fire;*
>
> **Daniel 7:9**

The Hebrew letter א Aleph, known as the GOD letter, the first of the Hebrew alphabet and yet a silent one. The LORD is always present, being our Head leading the way.

- Kanah קנא Zeal
- N'keh נקא Pure/Clean

So, we see Pinchas <u>zealous</u> for the LORD, honoring Him as the Head and consumed with the <u>pure and clean zeal</u>, he acted decisively, slaying the adulterous couple, and the plague ended. He and his descendants were rewarded by GOD with a covenant of peace, a covenant of an everlasting priesthood.

Our love for GOD ought to be like Pinchas' (no, I'm not talking about killing the sinners). Our zeal for the LORD needs to be clean and pure. It ought to consume our thoughts, deeds and words, yet with grace. It is vital to teach our children to stand up and speak the truth in all circumstances, having their motive pure for the love of GOD.

> *Then Phinehas stood up and intervened, And the plague was stopped.*
> **Psalm 106:30**

Our zealous words and deeds may or may not have national impact, but I can assure you they are like a pebble thrown into the water, having ripple effects with impact beyond our knowledge and understanding.

> *And indeed, one of the children of Israel came and presented to his brethren a Midianite woman in the sight of Moses <u>and in the sight of all the congregation of the children of Israel, who were weeping at the door of the tabernacle of meeting</u>. Now when <u>Phinehas,</u> the son of Eleazar, the son of Aaron, the priest, saw it, he rose from among the congregation and <u>took a javelin in his hand; and he went after the man of Israel into the tent and thrust both of them through</u>, the man of Israel, and the woman through her body. So the plague was stopped among the children of Israel. And those who died in the plague were twenty-four thousand.*
> **Numbers 25:6**

Pinchas saw everyone else weeping at the sight of the immoral couple, he picked up the javelin and killed the adulterers. His resoluteness was not tainted by emotions around him.

2. Joshua — Dare to believe, despite of being surrounded by the opposition of the majority, can bring GOD's promises to fruition.

Some of you are familiar with the story of Joshua in Numbers 14. He, with fellow spy Caleb, gave good reports about the Promise Land while the other 10 spies gave negative ones out of fear and lack of faith. Joshua had the audacity to believe the LORD being greater than any giants and challenges ahead. He simply trusted in GOD's promises and who GOD is, no more, no less. And because of him, Israel took possession of the Promise Land, and the rest is history.

Do we have the same audacity to believe in the Word of GOD? Do we live as if GOD is bigger than any "problems" in life? Our children watch what we say and do. The world may spew fears every day, in every way it can. It cannot hold a candle to the reassurance of the Greatness of GOD in His Word:

*Fear not, for I am with you; be not dismayed, for I am your God; I will strengthen you, I will help you, I will uphold you with my righteous right hand.*
**Isaiah 41:10**

*Trust in the Lord with all your heart, and do not lean on your own understanding. In all your ways acknowledge him, and he will make straight your paths.*
**Proverbs 3:5-6**

*Cast your burden on the Lord, and he will sustain you; he will never permit the righteous to be moved.*
**Psalm 55:22**

> *I can do all things through him (the Messiah) who strengthens me.*
> **Philippians 4:13**

Above are only a handful of verses in the Bible that we can live by, knowing the LORD is BIGGER! Dare to believe GOD's promises bring salvation and deliverance, as in Joshua's name, יהושע Yehoshua, "The LORD is Salvation." Salvation seems like a big word to us modern-day people. It truly is a big concept to be given eternal life, to live forever and ever. Bringing down to earthly terms, we can be set free from sticky situations. Sometimes, circumstances may not seem to change on the outside, but it is monumental when we look to the LORD for His protection and His provision, His Perfect Peace covering us transcends our mindset and therefore shifts our perspective… and that… changes everything.

Seeing GOD bigger than the challenges like Joshua did, rather than the challenges bigger than GOD like the 10 other spies, moved the LORD's heart. Thus, He deemed Joshua worthy to be Moses' successor and entrusted him to take His children into the Promise Land.

There is power in our Faith, believing in the All-powerful GOD, that can and will move mountains on our behalf.

Praying and declaring GOD's Word. Saying things like, "Diseases? No problem!", "Plans got interrupted? GOD has better ones!" "With GOD all things are possible, my child." This will help instill truth in our children that Our-GOD-is-limitless!

This kind of Joshua-like faith, my friend, is worth everything, to pass onto our children and our grandchildren.

3. Zelophehad's 5 daughters — Dare to speak up boldly and make a request for posterity preservation.

## 37. PINCHAS / PINHAS

*Then came the daughters of Zelophehad, the son of Hepher, the son of Gilead, the son of Machir, the son of Manasseh, from the families of Manasseh the son of Joseph;*
*and these were the names of his daughters: Mahlah, Noah, Hoglah, Milcah, and Tirzah.*
*And they stood before Moses, before Eleazar the priest,*
*and before the leaders and all the congregation, by the doorway of the tabernacle of meeting, saying: "Our father died in the wilderness; but he was not in the company of those who gathered together against the Lord, in company with Korah, but he died in his own sin;*
*and he had no sons. <u>Why should the name of our father be removed from among his family</u>*
*because he had no son? Give us a possession among our father's brothers."*
### Numbers 27:1-4

You want to look for "Girl-power" examples in the Torah? Look no further. These 5 "chicks" had the nerve to go before Moses and all the leaders of Israel, challenging the status quo about their inheritance. They obviously knew who they were, Manasseh's Great-great-great-grand-daughters. Manasseh was Joseph's eldest son, and Joseph named Manasseh for GOD has made him forget his troubles. These young ladies were Joseph's Great-great-great-great-grand-daughters. Joseph was Jacob's favorite son (the Third of Israel's Patriarchs, with the nation named after him by GOD). Their genealogy was clearly laid out preceding their request to let us know they were not just some random girls stepping forward demanding something ridiculous.

Prior to this moment, women did not inherit the land. These young ladies came forward for the sake of their posterity, "Why should the name of our father be removed from among his family." It was a bold move for their future generations.

> *So Moses brought their case before the Lord: And the Lord spoke to Moses, saying:* <sup>7</sup> *"<u>The daughters of Zelophehad speak what is right</u>; you shall surely give them a possession of inheritance among their father's brothers, and cause the inheritance of their father to pass to them. And you shall speak to the children of Israel, saying: 'If a man dies and has no son, then you shall cause his inheritance to pass to his daughter. If he has no daughter, then you shall give his inheritance to his brothers. If he has no brothers, then you shall give his inheritance to his father's brothers. And if his father has no brothers, then you shall give his inheritance to the relative closest to him in his family, and he shall possess it" And <u>it shall be to the children of Israel a statute of judgment</u>, just as the Lord commanded Moses.*
> **Numbers 27:6-11**

WOW! What? Zelophehad's daughters requested for something that no one else had asked before. They gave sensible reasoning. The LORD agreed with them, and a new statute was established.

Here's what the book of James talks about asking —

> *Yet you do not have because you do not ask.*
> **James 4:2**

You don't get what you don't ask… Here is a funny little story:

On our daughter's 6<sup>th</sup> birthday, we were out and about that morning. Seeing a MacDonald's, Mollie asked me, "Mom, do you think they have a birthday present for me?" My response, prompted by the Holy Spirit, "I don't know. If you don't ask, you won't know. All they can say is 'no,' right?" So, we pulled into the parking lot. Mollie and I walked inside. The manager was standing at the cash register, ready for business.

**Here is the exchange:**

Mollie (with a smile): Today is my birthday…

The Manager (looking puzzled): Ok… Happy… Birthday?!...

Mollie: Do you have a present for me?

The Manager (still looking puzzled, paused a few seconds trying to think about what to say to this little girl's unprecedented request): Would you like a toy or ice-cream?

Mollie: A toy please…

The manager proceeded to bring out a basket full of toys for Mollie to choose from. We said "thank you" and left.

Then, we met some friends for lunch at a Chinese restaurant. While ordering food, Mollie tucked on my shirt and said, "Mom, do you think they have a birthday present for me?" My response again was, "I don't know. If you don't ask, you won't know. All they can say is 'no,' right?"

So, here is the exchange Mollie had with the cashier after ordering our food:

Mollie (with a smile): Today is my birthday…

The Cashier (looking puzzled): Okay…Happy… Birthday?!...

Mollie: Do you have a present for me?

The Cashier (still looking puzzled, paused a few seconds): I am so sorry. We don't have birthday presents, but you can buy a stuffed animal here.

Mollie (with a smile): That's okay. Thank you very much.

My daughter was not upset at all with the response. We then sat down with our friends to eat lunch. A few minutes later, the same sweet cashier walked over to our table and handed Mollie a mesh bag full of fortune cookies (a spontaneous DIY present), and said, "Happy Birthday!" Mollie's face lit up. She learned a valuable lesson of "you don't get what you don't ask."

She has not done that since then, and I am not promoting asking for free stuff everywhere you go. Another precious lesson our daughter learned from this is to not take things personally if someone said "no" when she asked.

One more story I'd like to share with you about making a request and having it granted.

On one of our weekly shopping trips to the grocery store, Mollie picked up a boxed macaroni & cheese in the Pasta Aisle and asked me, "Mom, can we buy this?"

I responded, "Wow, $2.00 for that? It's a bit more than I'd like to pay. Sometimes they have coupons; then it will be less. We can buy it another time."

About a minute later, Mollie came back to me with something in her little hand, "Is this a coupon of $1.00 off for the Mac & Cheese, Mom? I found that on a shelf at the end of the aisle."

When I saw that, I thought, "Wow! LORD, how cool are You?!" Indeed, it was a coupon for the particular brand of Mac & Cheese she'd just shown me.

I said to my daughter, "Well, I guess you get to have the Mac & Cheese today after all. What do you say?"

Mollie exclaimed with excitement, "Thank You, Jesus!"

My daughter was very polite and never felt entitled she deserved anything, just like Zelophechad's daughters when making a request to their leaders.

צלפחד Zelophechad (Tzelaph-echad) consists of 2 words, צלף Tsalaph and אחד Echad One. צלף Tsalaph, according to Nehemiah 3:30, is the father of one of the Jerusalem wall-builders. I know Nehemiah comes after Numbers, but would it be possible that the Oneness of GOD and the wall-builder theme is somehow in the צלפחד Zelophechad's daughters' story?

These 5 brave daughters of Zelophechad, Mahlah, Noah, Hoglah, Milcah, and Tirzah, are forever listed in GOD's word in changing a statute they had challenged. Passing the name and heritage onto the next generation is GOD's desire. The LORD is One, and wall-building takes more than a few people. These courageous daughters were ready to build a legacy for the name of their father!

A Grandson's Dare to act, a Spiritual Son's Dare to believe, 5 Daughters' Dare to ask are the 3 things I've learned from this Parasha in passing on spiritual inheritance to our children.

What are some spiritual lessons you wish to pass on from generation to generation for your family?

**Let's pray:**

**Our Father in Heaven** אבינו שבשמימ,

Thank You for teaching us to be strong and courageous, not be afraid nor discouraged, for You are with us (Joshua 1:9). LORD, remind us according to Your Word what we need to do to guard the faith and freedom You've given us, and how we can teach our children and our grandchildren Your way, that they will carry the precious treasures of spiritual blessings onto generations to come. Much like a marathon, the baton has to be passed onto the next person. President Reagan's words remind us to be diligent and intentional to teach our children what You have taught us and given to us. Help us to dare to act, dare to believe, and dare to ask when prompted by the Holy Spirit, L'dor v'dor לדר ודר From Generation to Generation.

B'Shem Yeshua HaMashiach בשם ישוע המשיח.

In Jesus' Name we pray. Amen.

## 37. TORAH TASTING

### *REFLECTION*

1. What is the word, picture or theme the LORD is highlighting to you in this chapter and Torah Portion?

2. The theme of courage is evident in this Torah Portion. In your personal experience or in those around you, have you witnessed how a bold action led to a rewarding payoff?

3. What are some spiritual lessons your parents, grandparents or mentors have passed onto you? What are some spiritual lessons you have passed or are passing onto your children and grandchildren?

# 38 לח
# mattot / massei
## (Tribes / Journey)

מטות

מסעי

Numbers 30:2-36:13

Jeremiah 2:4-28, 3:4

Luke 13:1-9, Matthew 11:12-23

This week's Double Portions are Mattot and Massei. Mattot comes from Numbers 30:1, "Then Moses spoke to the heads of the **tribes** (מטות Mattot) concerning the Children of Israel, saying, "This is the thing which the LORD has commanded…". Mattot covers the laws of oaths and vows, the war commanded by GOD to destroy Midian, and the dividing of war spoils. Also, it tells the account of the tribes of Reuben, of Gad and the half-tribe of Manasseh settling East of Jordan River after some negotiation with Moses.

With the exception of leap years in the Biblical calendar, Mattot is read with the subsequent Parashat Massei.

Torah Portion Massei comes from Numbers 33:1, "These are the journeys of the children of Israel…". The Hebrew word מסעי Massei means Journeys. Massei recounts the Historian Prophet Moses documenting Israel's journeys. It details the division of the land among the tribes and borders of Israel. The laws regarding the cities of refuge and inheritance for heiresses were discussed. Massei concludes the Book of Numbers.

While reading Mattot/Massei, I am reminded of Balaam and Zelophechad's 5 daughters from the previous Torah Portions, Balak and Pinchas. Balaam was the Midianite prophet that was hired to curse Israel but instead blessed Israel.

*They killed the kings of Midian with the rest of those who were killed — Evi, Rekem, Zur, Hur, and Reba, the five kings of Midian.* ***Balaam the son of Beor*** *they also killed with the sword.*
**Numbers 31:8**

*And Moses said to them: "Have you kept all the women alive? Look, these women caused the children of Israel, through* ***the counsel of Balaam****, to trespass against the Lord in the incident of Peor, and there was a plague among the congregation of the Lord.*
**Numbers 31:15-16**

Balaam was killed, along with the 5 kings of Midian, for his wicked counsel that led Israel to sin.

The Midianite women caused Israel to sin, committing adultery; adversely, after boldly speaking out, the Israelite women in the tribe of Manasseh were changing the inheritance laws for generations to come allowing daughters to be heirs.

## 38. MATTOT/MASSEI // TRIBES / JOURNEYS

*And they said: "The Lord commanded my lord Moses to give the land as an inheritance by lot to the children of Israel, and my lord was commanded by the Lord to give the inheritance of our brother Zelophehad to his daughters…*
*This is what the Lord commands concerning the daughters of Zelophehad, saying,*
*"Let them marry whom they think best, but they may marry only within the family of their father's tribe." So the inheritance of the children of Israel shall not change hands*
*from tribe to tribe, for every one of the children of Israel shall keep the inheritance of the tribe of his fathers.*
**Numbers 36:2, 6**

*Just as the Lord commanded Moses, so did the daughters of Zelophehad; for <u>Mahlah, Tirzah, Hoglah, Milcah, and Noah</u>, the daughters of Zelophehad, were married to the sons of their father's brothers.*
**Numbers 36:10**

These 5 daughters of Zelopheched are once again mentioned here near the end of Parashat Massei. Many feel that the Bible is full of leading men doing great things for GOD. While it may be true, there are many brave leading ladies like Sarah, Rebekah, Rachel, Miriam, Deborah, and many unnamed ones. The Book of Ruth is a prime example of a strong female-lead story. It is full of verbs in feminine plural forms. That is rare in the Torah.

Here's a little Hebrew Grammatical information: Every Hebrew verb has conjugation to indicate whether it is in perfect or imperfect tense, action completed or not yet completed, whether it be in singular or plural, male or female.

ותלכנה שתיהם עד באנה בית לחם ויהי כבאנה בית לחם ותהם כל העיר עליהן ותאמרנה הזאת נעמי:

*Now the two of them <u>went</u> until they came to Bethlehem.*

> *And it happened, when <u>they had come</u> to Bethlehem, that all the city was excited <u>because of them</u>; and the women <u>said</u>, "Is this Naomi?"*
> **Ruth 1:19**

4 verbs in feminine plural form are found in just this one verse, which is uncommon in the Torah and the rest of the Hebrew Bible. Last but not least, near the end of the chapter of the last book of Numbers comes the mention of Zelophechad's 5 daughters again.

> *This is what the Lord commands concerning the daughters of Zelophehad, saying,*
> *"Let them <u>marry</u> whom they <u>think</u> best,*
> *but they may <u>marry</u> only within the family of <u>their</u> father's tribe."*
> *So the inheritance of the children of Israel shall not change hands from tribe to tribe, for every one of the children of Israel shall keep the inheritance of the tribe of his fathers. And every daughter who possesses an inheritance in any tribe of the children of Israel shall be the wife of one of the family of her father's tribe, so that the children of Israel each may possess the inheritance of his fathers.*
> *Thus no inheritance shall change hands from one tribe to another, but every tribe of the children of Israel shall keep its own inheritance."*
> **Numbers 36:6-9**

The above verses show 4 verbs in the feminine plural form. Again, it is not common in the Torah. Zelophechard's 5 daughters' impact extended far beyond their family and their own tribe when they spoke out about passing on their father's name and legacy in Parashat Pinchas. In this Torah Portion, we see the leaders of the tribe of Manasseh brought up a concern about what to do in the case of the heiresses marrying outside their own tribe. A new amendment of marriage only within the heiresses' own tribe was added to the statute and applied to all of Israel, and generations to come.

## 38. MATTOT/MASSEI // TRIBES / JOURNEYS

Mattot/Massei has references of war, spoil, dividing the spoil and some strong female-focused themes in the laws of heiresses' inheritance. Somehow, this reminds me of a verse in Psalm 68.

> *The Lord gave the word;*
> *Great was <u>the company/army of those who proclaimed</u> (plural feminine form) it:*
> *"Kings of armies flee, they flee,*
> *And she who remains at home divides the spoil...*
> **Psalm 68:11-12**

The LORD never mentioned women being inferior or less than men. Women are just different. GOD created Adam and Eve differently, at different times, and for different purposes. Our anatomy is different. Our roles are different. Women have the privilege of carrying a child in the womb, then giving birth and nursing. Many rules have been made and limitations created for both genders, unintended by GOD. If we focus on the privileges and blessings the LORD has given to each of us, we feel thankful and content.

The word המבשרות Hamvasrot in Psalm 68:11 means "The women who proclaim/bring good tidings" in feminine plural form. The root verb for המבשרות Hamvasrot is בסר Basar, it means to bear tidings, to bring good news. I have always been intrigued by how the LORD chose a group of women to be the main characters in this psalm. Psalm 68 is a tremendously encouraging psalm. Verses 12-23 are what the bold group of women proclaimed, the WORD that the LORD had uttered. It begins with:

> *Let GOD arise, let His enemies be scattered... Let those who hate Him flee before Him The Lord gave the word; Great was <u>the company of those who proclaimed</u> (המבשרות Hamvasrot) it; Kings of armies flee, they flee And <u>she</u> (feminine singular form) who remains (נוח Naveh Abide) at home divides the spoil.*
> **Psalm 68:1,11-12**

What an incredible picture of a WORD of GOD proclaimed by Psalm 68 women in unity bearing good news, then the enemies fled. The woman that remained at home, not going to war, were the ones dividing the war spoils, getting the "goodies." The group of women declared GOD's WORD, yet it is up to the individual woman to abide and habituate to receive the spoil. That's some Good News! We often think of warriors, tired and weary from fighting in battles, distributing the war plunders in victory. Here, in the contrary, those who decide to remain, staying behind, abide, unmoved, didn't go to war, are dividing the war booty.

What a powerful group of women hearing the Word of GOD, proclaiming it unreservedly and receiving a reward! In this psalm by David, he painted a worshippers' procession that involved maidens and tribes of Israel. I do believe Psalm 68's reference to those bold women strongly resonates with Zelophechad's daughters. There are some valuable lessons in this connection.

The 5 daughters of Zelophechad have been mentioned 5 times in the Bible: Numbers 26, 27, 36, 1 Chronicles 7:5 and Joshua 17:3.

They are 5 generations down from Manasseh (Joseph's son, name of their tribe — Manasseh, Machir, Gilead, Hepher, Zelophechad). What's more?

Their father's name in Hebrew צלפחד Zelophechad has 5 letters. צל Tsel means shadow, פחד Pachad means fear, together mean shadow (protection) from fear.

5 is a number known for Grace in the Bible. The 5th Hebrew Alphabet is ה Hey, meaning to reveal.

The number 5 is seen in 3 instances here: 5 times in the Bible, 5 generations down from Manasseh, and צלפחד Zelophechad has 5 Hebrew letters.

When something is repeated 3 times, it is supposed to catch our attention. We should really look more closely.

What if the story of Zelophechad's daughters is to reveal GOD's Grace?

What if their act not only opened up the daughters of Israel the opportunity to inheritance but also their father's name Zelophechad "Protection From Fear," would be carried on? Protection From Fear would become their legacy, spiritual heritage to their children and their children's children?

What if these daughters intertwined in the war, fought for the continuation of their father's name, somehow are connected to the women in Psalm 68, marching in triumphant procession declaring the Strength and Greatness of GOD, which inspire us to see what seemingly insignificant women can accomplish for the LORD and those around them?

The word אחד Echad, meaning the number 1, is found in the name Zeloph<u>echad</u>. The 5 daughters petitioned to Moses and to GOD as One Voice. All 5 of the references of them in the Bible are "the 5 daughters of Zelophechad" as One Group. There is power in unity. Coincidentally, there is a sense of the voice of unison in the Psalm 68 women. Their proclamation was made together, like in a choir.

I believe the lesson we can learn from the Zelophechad's daughters and Psalm 68's WORD-proclaiming women is that instead of seeing themselves as the inferior gender, they dared to say otherwise. We see what the 5 daughters spoke, GOD agreed, and what GOD spoke, the Psalm 68 women agreed!

If willing, women can choose to answer GOD's call to be gracefully bold good-news-bearers. On the other hand, Balaam mentioned in this Torah Portion also shows us the irony of words spoken against GOD's will. Balaam was praised for his words of blessings over Israel instead of cursing in Parashat Balak; but later, his downfall is also his words, his wicked counsel (Numbers 31:16) that resulted in the sins of Israel and devastating plague in Peor.

Women can change the atmosphere we walk in, even change the course of history, by simply looking on the All-Powerful GOD, who is the source of All Strength and declaring His WORD in unison. Limitations are placed by people, but not our GOD, Who is limitless.

We have Protection From Fear. Do we dare to be courageous to pass it onto our children and their children as an inheritance?

What do you need GOD to agree with you about (as in the daughters of Zelophechad)?

Or what do you need to agree with GOD about (as in the Psalm 68 women)?

**Let's pray:**

> **Our Father in Heaven אבינו שבשמימ,**
>
> Thank You for the example of Zelophechad's daughters and the Psalm 68 women. You show us that when we look closely, there are many heroes and heroines that are less known but are just as inspiring. LORD, please teach us to be brave to challenge the status quo when necessary, in order that our children will know our limitless GOD. Everywhere we go, we want to be Good-News-bearers, proclaiming, "Arise O LORD, let Your enemies be scattered. Let those who hate You flee before You"!
>
> B'Shem Yeshua HaMashiach בשם ישוע המשיח.
>
> In Jesus' Name we pray. Amen.

# 38. TORAH TASTING

## *REFLECTION*

1. What is the word, picture or theme the LORD is highlighting to you in this chapter and Torah Portion?

2. There is power in unity. Can you think of a real-life example that demonstrates that truth?

3. How does Psalm 68 and this Double Torah Portion encourage you in the way GOD looks at the role of women? How is that Biblical perspective different from what society may be saying?

# 39 לט
# DEVARIM
## (Words)
### דברים

Deuteronomy 1:1-3:22

Isaiah 1:1-27

Matthew 24:1-22

This Torah Portion is the first in the Book of Deuteronomy. Deuteronomy is a Greek word, meaning "A Second Law." An ancient name for the book is משנה התורה Mishnah HaTorah from Deuteronomy 17:18, "he shall write for himself a copy of this law (משנה התורה Mishnah HaTorah) in a book." Mishnah means second, double or copy. Therefore, משנה התורה Mishnah HaTorah means repetition of the law. This Book's Hebrew title דברים Devarim, means words. Devarim is also the title of this Parasha, deriving from the first verse in this Book:

"These are the <u>words</u> which Moses spoke to all Israel."

This Torah Portion begins with Moses' farewell address to GOD's people before his death and their entry into the Promise Land. He retold the story of their journey from GOD's deliverance of their bondage in Egypt to their adventurous journeys in the Wilderness. You can say Moses gave some commentary on their experience and offered advice to look to GOD to guide Israel to the next chapter of their expedition.

Following are Moses' recounts of their original 11-day trip turning into a 40-year one…

> *"So we departed from Horeb, and went through all that great and terrible wilderness which you **saw** on the way to the mountains of the Amorites, as the Lord our God had commanded us. Then we came to Kadesh Barnea. And I said to you, 'You have come to the mountains of the Amorites, which the Lord our God is giving us. <u>Look/See</u>, the Lord your God has set the land before you; <u>**go up**</u> and possess it, as the Lord God of your fathers has spoken to you; <u>do not fear</u> or be discouraged.'*
> **Deuteronomy 1:19-21**

> *The Lord your God, who goes before you, He will fight for you, according to all He did for you in Egypt **before your eyes**, and in the wilderness where you **saw** how the Lord your God carried you, as a man carries his son, in all the way that you went until you came to this place.' Yet, for all that, <u>you did not believe</u> the Lord your God, who went in the way before you to **search out (Toor** תור**)** a place for you to pitch your tents, to show you the way you should go, in the fire by night and in the cloud by day…*
> *Surely not one of these men of this evil generation shall **see** that good land of which I swore to give to your fathers, except Caleb the son of Jephunneh; he shall **see** it, and to him and his children I am giving the land on which he walked, because he wholly followed the Lord.'*
> **Deuteronomy 1:30-33, 36**

The recurring idea in this Parasha's first verses is seeing. Moses kept repeating what they saw before and what they would see again if they believe.

## 39. DEVARIM / WORDS

**In Deuteronomy 1:19-21, he admonished them 3 things...**

1. To see (what GOD would have them see) the Land
2. To go up and possess it
3. Do not fear

More occurrences of the word "see" are found in Deuteronomy 1:30-33, 36. Along with them is the word search out (Toor תור ), as in seeing the LORD's way of searching out and what He has searched out.

Seeing in GOD's perspective in faith, follow Him and search Upward result in inheriting the Promise Land.

I believe תור **Toor Search** is GOD's perspective for us to see. תור **Toor** means to spy, search, that leads to His will, which is best for us. Its interconnection with "going up" is not to be undermined — Searching upwards as the LORD would have us do, as displayed in the Book of Numbers:

*And the Lord spoke to Moses, saying, "Send men **to spy out** (תור Toor) the land of Canaan, which I am giving to the children of Israel; from each tribe of their fathers you shall send a man, every one a leader among them."... Then Moses sent them **to spy out** (תור Toor) the land of Canaan, and said to them, "<u>Go up</u> this way into the South, and <u>go up</u> to the mountains... So they <u>went up</u> and spied out (תור Toor) the land from the Wilderness of Zin as far as Rehob, near the entrance of Hamath.*
**Numbers. 13:1, 17, 21**

Following is the very first appearance of תור Toor Search in the Torah.

Guess who did the searching?

*So they departed from the mountain of the Lord on a journey of three days; and the ark of the covenant of the Lord went before them for the three days' journey, **to search out (תור Toor)** a resting place for them. And the cloud of the Lord was above them by day when they went out from the camp.*
**Numbers 10:33**

You got it! The LORD searched out (תור Toor) a resting place for His people.

Can you feel His love and His desire to provide for His Children?

*One who is righteous is a **guide (root verb search out תור Toor)** to his neighbor, but the way of the wicked leads them astray.*
**Proverbs 12:26 (ESV)**

*And I applied my heart to **seek (תור Toor)** and to search out by wisdom all that is done under heaven.*
**Ecclesiastes 1:13**

GOD's way of searching-out leads to life. It is associated with going upward, by wisdom, with hope, and most of all, fearlessness.

Conversely, man's perspective of searching חפר Chapar is digging downward.

Digging what is hidden, as in digging a well.

*(Moses said,) "And every one of you came near to me and said, 'Let us send men before us, and let them **search out (חפר Chapar)** the land for us… Nevertheless you (Children of Israel) would <u>not go up</u>, but <u>rebelled</u> against the command of the Lord your God…*
**Deuteronomy 1:22, 26**

*And he (Abimelech to Abraham) said, "You will take these seven ewe lambs from my hand, that they may be my witness that I **have dug** (חפר Chapar) this well."*
**Genesis 21:30**

Search Downward, man's way leads to going down (not up), rebellion and unbelief. Man's way of searching apart from the LORD, is foolishness.

Notice that Moses in Deuteronomy 1:22 and 26 pointed out that even with all that the Israelites witnessed first-hand GOD's magnificent victory and miraculous provision, they still would not believe what GOD would do for them. Instead, they chose to be overcome by second-hand bad-news-bearers' reports!

Merriam-Webster's definition of Mirage is "A **mirage** is a sort of an optical illusion, a reflection of light that can trick the mind into interpreting the sight as an apparently solid thing."

Britannica defines the word as such, "**Mirage**, in optics, the deceptive appearance of a distant object or objects caused by the bending of light rays (refraction) in layers of air of varying density."

Think of mirage as the Fear that the Children of Israel saw resulted in the bending of Light (GOD), the distorted view of the LORD being not enough (not Strong enough, not Big enough) next to the Giants in the Promise Land. The Acronym of FEAR is False Evidence Appearing Real. Isn't that just what a mirage is?

What and how we see will determine the way we search out the Promise Land the LORD has in store for us. Searching upward with GOD leads to life and promises. On the other hand, searching downward in man's ways leads to death and forfeited promises.

Our eyes can deceive us. Sometimes our mind can be tricked into seeing what we want to see and steer us to act illogically.

When the LIGHT of the true character of the LORD is twisted, a MIRAGE of false hope or false fear can appear.

However, faith comes by hearing…

> *But they have not all obeyed the gospel. For Isaiah says, "Lord, who has believed our report?" So then <u>faith comes by hearing</u>, and hearing by <u>the word of God</u>.*
> **Romans 10:16**

> *How beautiful upon the mountains*
> *Are the feet of him who brings good news (בשר Basar Proclaim/Bring good news), Who proclaims (root verb- שמע Shama <u>Hear</u>) peace, Who brings glad tidings (בשר Basar Proclaim/Bring good news) of good things, Who proclaims (root verb- שמע Shama <u>Hear</u>) salvation, Who says to Zion, "Your God reigns!"…*
> *Your watchmen shall <u>lift up their voices</u> (as they believe), With their voices they shall sing together; For they shall <u>see eye to eye</u> When the Lord brings back Zion… The Lord has made bare His holy arm In the <u>eyes</u> of all the nations; And all the ends of the earth shall <u>see</u> The salvation of our God.*
> **Isaiah 52:7,8,10**

Isaiah 52 gives us a clear visual of hearing, believing and then seeing the LORD's salvation and good plans for His people. Note that seeing comes after hearing and believing here.

There is no coincidence here that the word בשר Basar Proclaim/Bring good news used in Isaiah 52 is the same word used for "proclaim" in the Psalm 68 women, discussed in the last Torah Portion Massei Journeys. The incredible power of proclaiming GOD's Word, the Good News, good tidings is once again highlighted in this Parasha.

Very interesting that בשר Basar also means flesh as in Genesis 2…

*And the Lord God caused a deep sleep to fall on Adam, and he slept; and He took one of his ribs, and closed up the flesh (בשר Basar) in its place... And Adam said, "This is now bone of my bones and flesh (בשר Basar) of my flesh (בשר Basar)...*
**Genesis 2:21,23**

Basar בשר also means meat as in Exodus 16...

*Also Moses said, "This shall be seen when the Lord gives you meat (בשר Basar) to eat in the evening, and in the morning bread to the full...*
**Exodus 16:8**

So, could there possibly be a connection between Proclaiming Good News, Flesh and Meat in the word בשר **Basar**?

I think so. There is no Mere Coincidence, only Majestic and Divine Providence.

The LORD used Adam's flesh to create Eve, providing him with a perfect companion. That is some good news to proclaim in GOD's perfect plan and provision for us.

The LORD's gift of meat for His Children sustained them in the Wilderness. Meat is referred to as substantial food for man in the Bible. Paul spoke of meat in 1 Corinthians 3:2, "I fed you with milk and not with solid food (meat); for until now you were not able to receive it, and even now you are still not able."

Meat is symbolic of spiritual food that takes maturity to process and digest in order to grow.

When we proclaim good news in the flesh, hearing it with our physical ears, I believe it will be like spiritual meat that gives us nutrients and grows our faith.

The conventional saying, "Seeing is Believing," is not quite accurate, in my opinion. Let's look at this verse…

> *And in the wilderness where you <u>saw</u> how the Lord your God carried you, as a man carries his son, in all the way that you went until you came to this place. Yet, for all that, <u>you did not believe</u> the Lord your God.*
> **Deuteronomy 1:31-32**

Moses used the analogy of the ultimate love and care in a father carrying his son. The Israelites "<u>saw</u> it," but yet they <u>did not believe</u>.

Oftentimes, our faith is strengthened by hearing a good report. The Bible provides ample examples of people's believing resulting from good reports. Inversely, people have lost faith from bad reports, as in this Torah Portion. Parashat Devarim's title means Words.

Here are a few examples of what good report/news can do —

> *The light of the eyes rejoices the heart,*
> *And a <u>good report</u> makes the bones healthy.*
> **Proverbs 15:30**

> *Like cold water to a weary soul, So is <u>good news</u> from a distant land.*
> **Proverbs 25:25**

> *Surely the righteous will never be shaken;*
> *they will be remembered forever.*
> *They will have <u>no fear of bad news</u>;*
> *their hearts are steadfast, trusting in the Lord.*
> **Psalm 112:6-7**

Words we hear can either give us faith or fear.

I have heard someone teach about the importance of speaking GOD's word out loud so that our faith will increase through hearing it from our own mouths. Much like the verses above in Isaiah 52, when we proclaim what we hear and hear what is proclaimed, then, Faith is the natural by-product.

Is our hearing more influential to the mind than our sight?

Think about how easy it is to not see something, just close your eyes effortlessly. On the other hand, it is not so with our hearing.

I hate horror movies! I cannot stand any suggestions of it, not radio horror storytelling, not haunted house music. When a horror movie commercial comes on tv, not only do I have to close my eyes, but I also have to plug my ears with my fingers with both hands, AND sing out loud "la la la la la" until my family says, "Mom, it's over. You can open your eyes now."

It takes more effort to shut out the bad report being blasted around us than to allow it in. It does take conscious effort to guard our faith.

What are you choosing to hear? What is coming out of your mouth that you are hearing? Because the reports and words you choose to hear or not hear will determine what you believe and set you on the path to what GOD intends for you or otherwise.

Are you allowing fear to enter your ears? Even the loved ones around you can speak bad reports. I had a beloved relative once say some mindless words, opposite of GOD's will for our family. Without confronting her, I immediately mouthed these words under my breath, "I cancel those words, In Yeshua/Jesus's Name. I do not receive them for our family. I believe the LORD has good plans for me, my husband, and our children."

No, I was not offended, but my words nullified and revoked those spoken words opposite to GOD's will for us; and I made a conscious choice to speak what I believe.

When our kids were younger, people would sometimes say (unintentionally, just repeating what they knew), "They are so cute now, wait until they are teenagers, and your nightmares will begin."

Wow. What a horrible prophecy! What a terrible curse over our children, but you probably have heard that too. A curse no one wants, but some speak it so carelessly with no ill intention.

Our natural response to that is fear, dreading the day these kiddos turn 13. Thankfully, we also have heard someone wise say, "Teenage years do not have to be horrible. They can be quite exciting seeing our children explore and grow to become what GOD has created them to be." Right then and there, I chose to believe this hopeful parent, who chose to hear, see, speak, and believe what GOD said about his teenagers. And so did I.

What are you hearing today? What do you choose to believe?

Because what you do by your conscious choice can have an eternal impact.

Let's pray:

> **Our Father in Heaven אבינו שבשמימ,**
>
> Thank You for searching out and providing us a place to rest in Your Presence and Your good plans for us and our children. Help us to search upward, see You in the Light that is unbent in truth, and to not fear. LORD, prompt us to hear good reports and cancel out bad ones; we may proclaim the good news that our faith may grow. What's more, is that those around us will also hear the words of Hope, be Strengthened and Believe in the good plans You have for them and their families too.
>
> B'Shem Yeshua HaMashiach בשם ישוע המשיח.
>
> In Jesus' Name we pray. Amen.

# 39. TORAH TASTING
## *REFLECTION*

1. What is the word, picture or theme the LORD is highlighting to you in this chapter and Torah Portion?

2. Faith comes from hearing. What are some things, positive or negative, that you consistently speak out loud or listen to that affect your faith? Any changes that you would like to help increase your faith?

3. Have your eyes been deceived like the mirage discussed in this chapter? Have you witnessed what you see is completely different from what others see? What do you think caused that? How can we see things in their true form in GOD's perspective?

# מ 40
# va'etchanan
## (And I Pleaded)

ואתחנן

Deuteronomy 3:23-7:11

Isaiah 40:1-26

Luke 3:2-15

This Torah Portion is titled V'etchanan, which means "I pleaded," as it appears in the first verse of this Portion in Deuteronomy 3:23, "I pleaded with the LORD at that time, saying…". Moses continued his admonition to GOD's Children to follow the LORD's instructions closely as they were entering the Promise Land. The Ten Commandments were reiterated here as well as highlighting the Greatest Commandment. He reminded them why the LORD had chosen Israel as His people.

The pattern of the repetition of the Hebrew words שמע Shama Hear and דבר Dvar Word is striking. שמע Shama Hear is repeated 23 times and דבר Dvar Word 15 times. The words of שמע Shama Hear and דבר Dvar Word/Thing used in the same context happen in 5 instances in just this one Torah Portion, as shown in the following.

*Only take heed to yourself, and diligently keep yourself, lest you forget the **things** (דבר **Dvar** Word/Thing) your eyes have seen, and lest they depart from your heart all the days of your life. And teach them to your children and your grandchildren, especially concerning the day you stood before the Lord your God in Horeb, when the Lord said to me, "Gather the people to Me, and I will let them hear My **words** (דבר **Dvar** Word/Thing), that they may learn to fear Me all the days they live on the earth, and that they may teach their children."*
Deuteronomy 4:9-10

*And the Lord spoke to you out of the midst of the fire. You **heard** (שמע **Shama** Hear) the <u>sound</u> (קול **Kol** Voice/Call) of the **words** (דבר **Dvar** Word/Thing), but saw no form; you only **heard** a <u>voice</u> (קול **Kol** Voice/Call).*
Deuteronomy 4:12

*Out of heaven He let you **hear** (שמע **Shama** Hear) His <u>voice</u> (קול **Kol** Voice/Call), that He might instruct you; on earth He showed you His great fire, and you heard His **words** (דבר **Dvar** Word/Thing) out of the midst of the fire.*
Deuteronomy 4:36

*Then the Lord **heard** (שמע **Shama** Hear) the <u>voice</u> (קול **Kol** Voice/Call) of your **words** (דבר **Dvar** Word/Thing) when you spoke to me, and the Lord said to me: 'I have **heard** (שמע **Shama** Hear) the <u>voice</u> (קול **Kol** Voice/Call) of the **words** (דבר **Dvar** Word/Thing) of this people which they have spoken to you. They are right in all that they have spoken.*
Deuteronomy 5:28

Now I am seeing something even more interesting, which is another common factor of קול (Kol Voice/Call) in this Parasha. Like in math, a common factor is the number that can be used to be divided by 2 or more numbers.

For example, both the numbers 2 and 4 are the common factors of the numbers 8 and 40:

- 2x4=8
- 2x4x5=40

So, as I dig deeper, the common factors of שמע Shama (Hear), Dvar דבר (Word/Thing) and קול Kol (Voice/Call) in this Portion become clearer. I do not believe in Mere Coincidence, only Majestic Divine Providence.

**In Parashat Va'etchanan — the following is noted:**

- שמע Shama Hear — 23 times
- דבר Dvar Word/Thing — 15 times
- קול Kol Voice/Call — 12 times
- The 5 instances that שמע Shama Hear and דבר Dvar Word are common factors.
- 4 of those involve קול Kol Voice/Call as the Third Common Factor!

What is going on? This is too much to ignore.

Let's see if the following verses will lend us any clues…

*The first time שמע Shama Hear used in the Torah is in Genesis 3- And they heard (שמע Shama Hear) the <u>sound</u> (קול Kol Voice/Call) of the Lord God walking in the garden in the cool of the day, and Adam and his wife hid themselves from the presence of the Lord God among the trees of the garden.*
**Genesis 3:8**

Adam and Eve heard שמע Shama, the sound/voice/call קול Kol of GOD, after disobeying GOD's <u>Word</u>.

*The first time דבר Dvar Word/Thing used in the Torah is in Genesis 11 — Now the whole earth had one language and one **speech** (דבר **Dvar**).*
**Genesis 11:1**

The First Time all 3 of those words being the common factors in the Torah is found in Genesis 21 —

*And Sarah saw the son of Hagar the Egyptian, whom she had borne to Abraham, scoffing. Therefore she said to Abraham, "Cast out this bondwoman and her son; for the son of this bondwoman shall not be heir with my son, namely with Isaac." And the **matter** (דבר **Dvar** Word/Thing) was very displeasing in Abraham's sight because of his son... But God said to Abraham, "Do not let it be displeasing in your sight because of the lad or because of your bondwoman. Whatever Sarah has said to you, **listen** (שמע **Shama** Hear) to her voice (קול **Kol** Voice/Call) for in Isaac your seed shall be **called** (קול **Kol** Voice/Call). Yet I will also make a nation of the son of the bondwoman, because he is your seed."*
**Genesis 21:9-10,12-13**

I see the following from the common factors in the above verses —

GOD's original intent is the use of One Language in the world, and His redemption plan is shown in Adam and Abraham, despite of Adam's disobedience and Abraham's lack of faith.

It is interesting how the LORD weaves His intended message for us to see from lesson to lesson.

Last week's Torah Portion shows these two verses being highlighted in the context of faith comes from hearing and believing the Word of GOD —

*But they have not all obeyed the gospel. For Isaiah says, "Lord, who has believed our report?" So then faith comes by <u>hearing</u>, and hearing by <u>the word of God</u>.*
**Romans 10:16**

> *Your watchmen shall lift up their voices (as they believe),*
> *With their voices they shall sing together; For they shall see eye to eye*
> *When the Lord brings back Zion...*
> **Isaiah 52:8**

And just so happens that the 3 Common-Factor words, Hear, Word and Voice, are once again being brought to attention this week.

שמע Shama Hear means hear, obey and understand. It is translated as such throughout the scriptures. שמע Shama Hear can be separated into 2 parts: the word שם Shem Name and the letter ע Ayin that represents the Eye.

Seeing is in the Hearing?

Jewish people today refer to the LORD as HaShem The NAME, for His Name is too holy to be pronounced and spoken. When we hear, obey, and understand the LORD, in essence, we can see HIM, The Name. We can see His Name, His nature and His character.

דבר Dvar Word is made up of 2 parts — the letter ד Dalet symbolizing the Door and the word בר Bar in Aramaic means Son. The Hebrew word בר Bar means Pure, Clean and Innocent. The Word of GOD is the Door as the Son to the FATHER. The Son of GOD, the Mashiach, is the WORD and the DOOR. The Mashiach is also the Door to a pure life. Through the Son of GOD, we are declared pure, clean, and innocent.

> *In the beginning was the Word, and the Word was with God, and the Word was God.*
> **John 1:1**

*Then Jesus said to them again, "Most assuredly, I say to you, I am the <u>door</u> of the sheep. All who ever came before Me are thieves and robbers, but the sheep did not hear them. I am the <u>door</u>. If anyone enters by Me, he will be saved, and will go in and out and find pasture. ¹⁰ The thief does not come except to steal, and to kill, and to destroy. I have come that they may have life, and that they may have it more abundantly.*
**John 10:7-10**

*Behold, I stand at the door and knock. If anyone hears My <u>voice</u> and opens the <u>door</u>, I will come in to him and dine with him, and he with Me.*
**Revelation 3:20**

The Mashiach (Messiah), Son of GOD, is unquestionably the One who is the Door to the LORD. He is the One that points us to life. The Mashiach is the Anointed One that leads GOD's people to Hope and Redemption.

*Serve the Lord with fear,*
*And rejoice with trembling.*
*<u>Kiss the Son</u>, lest He be angry,*
*And you perish in the way,*
*When His wrath is kindled but a little.*
*Blessed are all those who put their trust in Him.*
**Psalm 2:11-12**

We are saved when we put our trust in the SON, the One that has been sent to show us the Way and Salvation.

קול Kol Voice/Call is made up of the letters ק Kof symbolizing "Follow," the letter ו Vav meaning "Securing," the letter ל Lamed meaning "Authority" / "Shepherd's Staff." The Voice of GOD is what leads us to be secured when we follow His Authority and His "Shepherd's Staff."

שמע Shama Hear — דבר Dvar Word — קול Kol Voice/Call

## 40. VA'ETCHANAN / AND I PLEADED

GOD's original plan is that we would lift up our <u>voices</u> to HIM as ONE Speech, ONE Language, ONE <u>Word</u> in unity (Genesis 11:1), as well as following HIM, <u>hear</u>ing and obeying HIM, following HIM, our ONE TRUE GOD!

*(Yeshua Jesus said:) Blessed rather are those who hear the word of God and obey it.*
**Luke 11:28**

Hearing the Voice/Call of GOD's Word is the way to Life. The Ten Commandments in Hebrew is עשרת הדברימ Adseret HaDvarim. It literally means The Ten Words, words as in Devarim, the title of the Book of Deuteronomy. The LORD's commandments are Words that He gives us, offering life instructions. When we hear the sound, the call of His Word, and follow, we are led to life, away and far away from destruction.

Here is the LORD's warning about the destructive impact of idol-worshipping in Deuteronomy 4:15-40.

*Take careful heed to yourselves, for you saw no form when the Lord spoke to you at Horeb out of the midst of the fire, lest you act corruptly and make for yourselves a carved image in the form of any figure: the likeness of male or female, the likeness of any animal that is on the earth or the likeness of any winged bird that flies in the air, the likeness of anything that creeps on the ground or the likeness of any fish that is in the water beneath the earth...*
*When you beget children and grandchildren and have grown old in the land, and act corruptly and make a carved image in the form of anything, and do evil in the sight of the Lord your God to provoke Him to anger, I call heaven and earth to witness against you this day, that you will soon utterly perish from the land which you cross over the Jordan to possess; you will not prolong your days in it, but will be utterly destroyed.*
**Deuteronomy 4:15-18, 25, 26**

Carved images of idols, idolatry and making offerings to a variety of gods was a familiar thing to me as a child. I grew up in Hong Kong, which was a British colony until the year 1997. After the Communists took over China, Mainland China became an atheistic nation, a godless nation (that is, if you don't count idol-worshipping the Communist Party Chairman Mao as a religion). Most of the missionaries in China fled to Hong Kong after 1948.

People were free to choose whatever religion they'd like to practice in the British-Crown-reigned territory. Though Christians were a minority group, Christianity was a well-respected faith. The majority of Chinese people in Hong Kong were polytheists, worshiping many gods as Taoists or Buddhists. Not being an expert in world religions, I can only tell you about polytheism from a child's perspective, observing my grandmother and other polytheists around me. The spirit realm is as real as everything we can physically see, with which we were very much aware that we co-exist. Going to fortune-tellers and burning incense to gods was a common scene.

Grandma was very superstitious. After all, who would want to anger the spiritual beings, whom we could not see and had no power over whatsoever. I remember well when my little cousin Billy was just a toddler, we were in the countryside one day, like any little boy that needs to go use the bathroom urgently, Grandma took him by a tree, murmuring as if someone was standing near her, "Excuse me, please turn aside and allow my grandson to relieve himself." She told us if we didn't say anything, the offended little gods or beings could come after us. Also, the seventh month in the Chinese Lunar calendar is known to be a ghosts' month. The hungry pitiful spirits are free to come up into our realm from the deep places to be fed. Many people burn incense and "paper money"; some even put out actual meat and fruit to appease them. I was told not to go out at night during that month to avoid them. Fortunately, Grandmother found salvation in the Messiah Yeshua in her later years, that she received and realized the only True Peace she had ever known.

There were countless gods in the polytheistic society, kitchen god, sea god, river god, lake god, earth god, mountain god, sun god, moon god, ..., and yes, even money god. I think that's what Yeshua Jesus was talking about that we cannot serve GOD and Mammon (Money-god in Matthew 6:24). During the Chinese Lunar New Year, we greet one another with words of blessings. A common one is, "恭喜發財 Gong Xi Fa Cai, I wish you prosperity with lots of money and wealth this year." Like Santa Claus at Christmas time, a man would dress in an ancient-Chinese period costume as Money-god and appear in many New Year gatherings. He hands out make-believe gold-foil chocolate coins and make-believe ancient money currencies. Naturally, whenever the Money-god appears, many follow him wanting favor from him and have good luck with money for the upcoming year.

Buddha and other gods' favor is conditional — "I give you something in exchange for something I want from you." (Side note: If those gods were really that powerful, why would they need humans to burn them incense or any material things? More than any physical offerings, I believe it is our heart's devotion that gives them power.)

There was no caring relationship. No love. I had never heard that any of these gods care about us. Grandma was making offerings on a regular basis in exchange for family health, safety, provision, … .

Almost like giving the mafia money in exchange for peace and safety for your family. You dare not to comply.

There is no long-term genuine relationship between a master and his slave. A demon can destroy someone's life over a small mishap. Very scary stuff! Talk about walking on eggshells. There were many different gods, different rules, different territories, … . These little gods were easily provoked and never to be offended.

Fear of spiritual beings had tremendous power over us. They played with humans however they wished.

This comparison reminds me of the fairies in the comedic play by William Shakespeare, Midsummer Night's Dream. The gods I knew operated with childlike devious intents, as the fairies in this play. They were temperamental. Humans were helpless mortals, easily manipulated and controlled.

Don't get me wrong. There were "good" gods and demons, but their intent to help often comes from their end-goal of benefiting themselves in the next life or other self-serving motives. With all that said, I came across a book titled "Finding God in Ancient China" by Chan Kei Thong. Chan offered compelling historical and literary evidence for the Chinese emperors worshipping ONE GOD 2000 years ago and that One GOD had the same characteristics as the GOD in the Torah; the worship rituals were also similar to those in Moses' time. Looks like monotheism existed also in ancient China for the same GOD as in Israel.

I suppose by now you get the horrible picture of idol-worshipping from my childhood experience and observations. There is the ONE GOD that owns everything, Master of all, and can take care of all my needs. He is not temperamental. He gives His people clear instructions on how to live. He is full of love and compassion for His children.

*And my God shall supply all your need according to His riches in glory by Christ Jesus. Now to our God and Father be glory forever and ever. Amen.*
**Philippians 4:19**

This ONE TRUE GOD needs nothing from us except for our affection reciprocated toward Him, and that we would know and receive His love for us. That's it?! He supplies our every need. There is no need for a god for each thing. He is our all in all.

This is a huge paradigm shift!

After the warning about idolatry in Deuteronomy 4 and the retelling of the Ten Commandments in Deuteronomy 5, the LORD, through Moses, called for His Children's attention to the SHEMA- We simply cannot talk about this week's Torah Portion Va'etchanan without discussing the

## 40. VA'ETCHANAN / AND I PLEADED

SHEMA. The SHEMA is the central creed of the Jewish faith, thus our faith believing in the One True GOD. It is the first thing every Jewish father teaches his children. It is recited every morning and every night upon bedtime, declaring the Oneness of the LORD.

*<u>Hear</u> (SHEMA) Obey/Understand) O Israel: The Lord our God, the Lord is ONE!*
שמע ישראל יהוה אלהינו יהוה אחד
*(Shema, Yisrael Adonai Elohenu Adonai Echad)*
**Deuteronomy 6:4**

There are numerous teachings on the SHEMA. It is the foundation of Torah and the cornerstone of the Jewish faith throughout the ages. Its main idea is that The All-Powerful ONE GOD is calling for His children to hear and follow Him. In order to do that, they have to be near Him. It is hard to hear someone speak if we are far away. "The LORD our GOD" alludes to the truth that He is ours. The possessive pronoun suggests that He is a personal GOD. I rarely hear anyone refer to "My Buddha". The sound of "My GOD" and "Our GOD" instantly brings HIM closer to us.

He is ONE. Period. He holds all the power. Period.

We have the ONE GOD, unique, incomparable. He is all we need, and no one else.

"Hear O Israel: The Lord our God, the Lord is ONE!" is one of the most powerful statements in all faiths. No contest! Hands down!

No one dares to compete with the Creator and King of the Universe.

*(Prophet Samuel's Mother, Hannah's Prayer) —*
*No one is holy like the Lord,*
*For there is none besides You,*
*Nor is there any rock like our God.*
**1 Samuel 2:2**

> *I am the Lord, and there is no other;*
> *There is no God besides Me.*
> *I will gird you, though you have not known Me,*
> *That they may know from the rising of the sun to its setting*
> *That there is none besides Me.*
> *I am the Lord, and there is no other;*
> **Isaiah 45:5-6**

The SHEMA is immediately followed by the V'ahavta (meaning "And you shall love"), admonishing GOD's children to love Him with some details of how they could do that.

> *You shall <u>love</u> (V'ahavta) <u>the Lord</u> your God with all your heart (mind/will), with all your soul (desire/passion/emotion), and with all your strength (force/abundance/muchness).*
> *And these <u>words</u> which I command you today shall be in your heart. You shall teach them diligently to your children, and shall talk of them when you sit in your house, when you walk by the way, when you lie down, and when you rise up.*
> *You shall bind them as a sign on your hand, and they shall be as frontlets between your eyes.*
> *You shall write them on the doorposts of your house and on your gates.*
> **Deuteronomy 6:5-9**

I know no other god that commands his followers to love him.

Devotion? Sure. Love? No.

But you can see from the V'ahavta that it is important to the LORD that His children constantly remind themselves and teach their children about GOD and what He has done. The purpose is for our good, not for GOD's. Being apart from the LORD has consequences. Being close to Him has immeasurable benefits, as listed in GOD's Word.

The first time the word אהב Ahave LOVE is seen in the Torah is in Genesis 22, referring to the only son that Abraham "loved." The story displays Abraham's devotion and obedience to GOD to the point of releasing and giving his one and only son whom he loved, with his own life. It may sound radical, and the LORD did not intend for Abraham to actually sacrifice his own son, but I believe it is that kind of unreserved love GOD asks of us. He needs nothing from us, but when we are willing to give Him our all, He wants to and will give us His all!

I remember a story of a little girl with a toy pearl necklace. One day, her father asks her to give him her pearl necklace. She says, "Daddy, you know how much I love my necklace. I cannot give it to you." The next day, her father comes to her with the same request. Her reply was unchanged, "Daddy, this is really my favorite necklace. I really can't." After a few gentle requests, the little girl finally said to her father, "Alright, daddy, here it is. I love you so much! I want you to have it now." At this moment, her dad took her necklace and handed her a beautiful velvet box in exchange. To her surprise, when she opens the box, she sees a genuine and the most beautiful and exquisite pearl necklace. Her daddy had this necklace all along but was waiting patiently for her to give up her own first. This story reminds me what we have is beyond pale to what our FATHER GOD has for us. The LORD is gentle. He does have the best for us. Are we ready to give up the counterfeit, the temporal, to receive what truly matters and is eternal?

Parashat Va'etchanan concludes with this "mic-drop" Promise by the One True GOD —

> *Therefore know that the Lord your God,*
> *He is God, the faithful God who keeps covenant and mercy for a*
> *thousand generations*
> *with those who love Him and keep His commandments;*
> **Deuteronomy 7:9**

GOD's faithfulness lasts 1000 generations! That is a long time!

GOD has spoken. Are you ready to hear the voice of His WORD that you may receive His end of the Covenant? All that you ever need has already been provided for.

Let's pray:

**Our Father in Heaven אבינו שבשמימ,**

We are ready to hear, obey and understand Your Word, our ears are ready to hear and with eyes that we may see Your Name, Your Character and all that You are to us. Unlike the little gods controlling through fear, You draw us close to you through Your lovingkindness, Your faithful and steadfast love. Help us see Your Word as the Door in our Messiah Yeshua to Eternal Life and a life filled with Hope. LORD, teach us how to love You with all our heart, soul, and strength. We decree and declare that You are the ONE GOD that we ever need for everything in our lives. Help us to teach everyone around us this life-transforming truth, to live with that truth as our reality in everything we do and say for the next generation and the generations to come.

B'Shem Yeshua HaMashiach בשם ישוע המשיח.

In Jesus' Name we pray. Amen.

# 40. TORAH TASTING

## *REFLECTION*

1. What is the word, picture or theme the LORD is highlighting to you in this chapter and Torah Portion?

2. John 1:14's "The word became flesh" speaks of the Messiah. This chapter discusses the Hebrew word דבר D'var (word) which is made up of two parts, a door and a son. The Son of GOD as the door and the Living Word, He is the Door to the heavenly Father. How does this concept encourage you today? What has the Door, the Messiah, led you to? Hope? Restoration...?

3. Besides money being a god that people worship, what other gods have you seen people worship (devoting their time and life in), or perhaps you have seen the destruction as a result of worshiping other gods?

# 41 מא
# eikev
## (Because)
## עקב

Deuteronomy 7:12-11:25

Isaiah 49:14-51:3

Matthew 16:13-20

Parashat Eikev comes from the first verse in this portion, "Because you listen to these judgments…". Moses reminded the Children of Israel that the LORD had provided for them in the Wilderness and that He would continue to provide for them in the Promise Land if they hear and do His statutes and commandments. He told them that GOD gave them the Promise Land, not because of their own righteousness but instead for the wickedness of the nations and to confirm the word the LORD had sworn to their fathers, Abraham, Isaac, and Jacob (Deuteronomy 9:4-9). Moses then retold the LORD's giving of the Ten Commandments, the Golden Calf incident, a re-giving of the Commandments on new tablets. Lastly, he admonished them to love and serve the LORD, the V'Ahavta, "And You Shall Love" (as mentioned in the last Torah Portion).

The word עֵקֶב Eikev Because/Heel/End of has a connection with the name Jacob Yaakov יַעֲקֹב (the 3 letters in עֵקֶב Yaakov make עֵקֶב Eikev).

*Afterward his brother came out, and his hand took hold of Esau's heel (עָקֵב Eikev); so his name was called Jacob (יַעֲקֹב Yaakov).*
**Genesis 25:26**

The first time עֵקֶב Eikev Because/Heel/End show up in the Torah is in Genesis 22 when the LORD spoke to Abraham about His promises.

Because — Hear/Obey — Bless —

*In your seed all the nations of the earth shall be blessed, because you have obeyed (שָׁמַע Shama Hear) My voice.*
**Genesis 22:18**

All the nations from Abraham's seed would be blessed because of One Person hearing and obeying GOD's voice.

And, in this Parasha…

*Then it shall come to pass, because (עֵקֶב Eikev Because/Heel/End) you listen (שָׁמַע Shama Hear) to these judgments, and keep and do them, that the Lord your God will keep with you the covenant and the mercy which He swore to your fathers. And He will love you and bless you and multiply you…*
**Deuteronomy 7:12-13**

A strong connection is displayed between Hear/Obey and Blessings. It seems that blessings are the clear consequence and promise of Hearing GOD, an undisputable cause-and-effect principle.

Hear=Obedience => Overwhelming Blessings

## 41. EIKEV / BECAUSE

We should follow GOD and love Him from a genuine heart, not because we can get something out of Him, a pure-hearted love with no "hidden" agenda.

When I was studying Hebrew, one of my favorite words was L'ma'an למאן "In Order That." It is used 272 times in the Old Testament according to the Strong Concordance. Naturally, I came across this word quite a bit reading the Torah. And it is fun to say, L'ma'an למאן "In Order That," every time. Whenever I see this word, a cause-and-effect is happening. Something is being explained about what caused it or what this action will lead to, much like "because" (עקב Eikev Because).

For example, Abraham was blessed <u>because</u> he obeyed GOD's voice. And, The LORD told His Children to carefully observe His commandment <u>in order that/so that</u> they would multiply and possess the Promise Land (Deuteronomy 8:1).

Very interesting that the word למאן **L'ma'an** appears 10 times in this Torah Portion (Deuteronomy 8:1,2,3,16,16,18, 9:5, 11:8,9,21). 10 as in the Ten Commandments to be followed, to be SHAMA/Heard/Obeyed. The number 10 is represented by the Hebrew letter י Yod, the Hand. The stone tablets with the Ten Commandments given to Moses were written by the finger of GOD, His Hand! I believe that His commandments and statutes were given to us למאן **L'ma'an in order that** we have life.

If someone lays out all the benefits of an action — like no sickness, no lack of any kind, peace and prosperity, EVERY GOOD THING, the Whole Package, would you consider doing that? That is a pretty good deal. My question is then — Why do people not obey and follow when the consequences are so good?

We can go back to the Garden of Eden to see if we get some clues.

GOD the CREATOR laid out His Best Plan to Adam and Eve. They saw the best possible world for them. Between the Tree of Life and the Tree of Knowledge of Good and Evil, Adam and Eve chose the one that GOD had said not to.

Why?

To us, it appears to be a stupid choice and we can hardly comprehend their decision. However, I think there's more to it.

Life is full of choices. We wake up every morning. We choose whether to get up now or sleep in a little longer (for those snooze-button-hitters). Then, we choose whether we eat breakfast or not, have our coffee/tea or not, go to work or not. The choice-making is endless…

And every single choice we make, whether we think it, speak it or do it will lead us on a path that would alter something in our lives. Some are big shifts and others small.

Even a small choice which may not look like a big deal at the time, can cause ripple effects that lead to big consequences, good or bad.

The LORD talks a lot about making choices, life vs. death, blessing vs. cursing, going out to fight vs. staying in and rest, … .

> *By faith **Abraham obeyed when he was called** to go out to the place which he would receive as an inheritance. And **he went out, not knowing** where he was going.*
> **Hebrews 11:8**

There are many possible causes to the Fall of Adam in the Garden of Eden — Fear, Pride, Vanity… . Nonetheless, what we learn is instead of GOD laying out His perfect plan and telling His creations to follow, He gave them choices and freedom to choose. Without it, man would be mere robots with no free will to reciprocate a genuine love to the LORD on their own initiative. In the musical "Annie" about the story of an orphan named Annie, there is one scene that the Orphanage director Mrs.

Hannigan walking through the orphans' room inspecting the children. Each orphan stands up straight and robotically yells out, "I love you, Mrs. Hannigan!" because that is what Mrs. Hannigan demands to be said to her every day. No emotions necessary. Mere words. That's the opposite of what our Father GOD wants from us.

Free will is the greatest gift GOD gives to mankind. Without it, life is simply meaningless. As parents, we desire our children to make good choices, choices that lead to life. We want to rescue them from every mistake, fix it for them and save them from heartaches and pain. Unfortunately, they will never grow to maturity without owning their own choices and subsequent mistakes, living with the consequences of their own decisions.

I've been told by one of our children once, "Mom, can you just let me make my own choice, even if it's wrong?"

I wanted to scream, "NOOOOOOOOOO!!!!!"

But the Spirit of the Living GOD inside of me "convicted" me of my natural and immediate response. As parents, we do not know it all. We totally have to rely on the LORD and His grace. I ask for forgiveness from our kids when I do make a mistake. And that helps them to know we are human too, and it's okay to make mistakes and grow from them. Recently, I had a dilemma — one of the most difficult choices I had to make as an adult and as a parent. Either decision could lead to some serious consequences. I had a choice to make. Either outcome would require some much-needed grace. In the end, things worked out.

Thank GOD that His grace is sufficient for us, for His strength is made perfect in weakness (2 Corinthians 12:9).

If the freedom to choose is a gift, then so is answering the call when GOD calls. When Abraham was called to move, he responded immediately and moved without hesitation or questions, for which he was accounted righteousness. I liken hearing GOD's prompting to an alarm clock.

I am a big fan of the snooze button!

O, am I?!

The wonderful invention of the snooze button! I set my alarm clock 30 minutes before my wakeup time so that I can snooze the button until the time I absolutely have to get up. My poor husband is a much lighter sleeper than I am and not a big fan of the snooze button. He would be awakened by my alarm, heard me hit the snooze button over and over for 30 minutes and said, "Would you please get up already?" while I was enjoying my last resting moments, holding onto the ending of my sweet dream. "No, I am not ready yet!" is what I wanted to say. I have gotten better over time at being more considerate to my bedmate.

How often do we hit the "snooze button" on the LORD when He needs us to act NOW? We can miss a very important call, not answering it with a sense of urgency. The snooze button delaying the answer to "the call" can cost us in life, resulting in heartaches, pain, or worse. Like the Shulamite woman/the Bride in the Song of Solomon missing the Bridegroom's call because she did not feel like getting up when he knocked on the door. She responded, "not now, not my timing…".

*I (the Bride) sleep, but my heart is awake;*
*It is the voice of my beloved!*
<u>*He knocks, saying,*</u>
<u>*"Open for me, my sister, my love,*</u>
*My dove, my perfect one;*
*For my head is covered with dew,*
*My locks with the drops of the night."*
³<u>*I have taken off my robe;*</u>
<u>*How can I put it on again?*</u>
<u>*I have washed my feet;*</u>
<u>*How can I defile them?*</u>
⁴ *My beloved put his hand*
*By the latch of the door,*
*And my heart yearned for him.*
⁵ *I arose to open for my beloved,*
*And my hands dripped with myrrh,*
*My fingers with liquid myrrh,*
*On the handles of the lock.*
⁶<u>*I opened for my beloved,*</u>
<u>*But my beloved had turned away and was gone...*</u>
*The watchmen who went about the city found me.*
*They struck me, they wounded me;*
*The keepers of the walls*
*Took my veil away from me.*

**Song of Solomon 5:2-6**

Making a choice to hit the snooze button to delay answering a call is due to thinking that there is no consequence to that, the "I can wait..." and "I can do it later" mentality. There are tremendous blessings of answering the call immediately when called, choosing life and acting promptly. What would the outcome be had Adam and Eve chosen the Tree of Life? What would the result be had Abraham not heard and obeyed GOD's voice? There were even incidences when Yeshua Jesus called people and they responded with, "Lord, let me first go and bury my father." And another responded this way, "Lord, I will follow You, but let me first go and bid them farewell who are at my house." Yeshua Jesus' reply was pretty harsh, "No one, having put his hand to the plow, and looking back, is fit for the kingdom of God." (Luke 9:60-62). When called, one needs to jump on acting with no delay, no looking back. This shows there is a huge difference in the outcome between immediate and delayed obedience.

The phrase "Hear O Israel" (Shema Israel) is repeated 5 times in the Torah. This phrase is not uniquely attached to the Deuteronomy 6 SHEMA, Judaism's central creed from.

*And Moses called all Israel, and said to them:* "**Hear, O Israel**, *the statutes and judgments which I speak in your hearing today, that you may learn them and be careful to observe them.*
**Deuteronomy 5:1**

*Therefore* **hear, O Israel**, *and be careful to observe it, that it may be well with you, and that you may multiply greatly as the Lord God of your fathers has promised you — 'a land flowing with milk and honey.'*
**Deuteronomy 6:3**

*"***Hear, O Israel***: The Lord our God, the Lord is one!* ⁵ *You shall love the Lord your God with all your heart, with all your soul, and with all your strength.*
**Deuteronomy 6:4**

*"***Hear, O Israel***: You are to cross over the Jordan today, and go in to dispossess nations greater and mightier than yourself, cities great and fortified up to heaven,*
**Deuteronomy 9:1**

*And he shall say to them, '***Hear, O Israel***: Today you are on the verge of battle with your enemies. Do not let your heart faint, do not be afraid, and do not tremble or be terrified because of them;*
**Deuteronomy 20:3**

## 41. EIKEV / BECAUSE

Bonus in Brit Chadashah (New Testament):

> *Jesus answered him, "The first of all the commandments is: 'Hear, O Israel, the Lord our God, the Lord is one. And you shall love the Lord your God with all your heart, with all your soul, with all your mind, and with all your strength.' This is the first commandment.*
> **Mark 12:29-30**

"Hear O Israel" is as if GOD is saying, "Listen up... Hear what I have to say as follows... This is very important that you not only hear but also take it to heart, obey and do...".

Reading the above verses, does it make you feel some sense of the LORD's yearning for us to hear what He has to say, to connect with us, and also, what amazing things He has in store if we would just hear Him out and follow?

I believe the LORD is still saying to us today, "Hear Susie," "Listen up, Johnny!"

Years ago, a popular commercial had these questions repeated on the TV screen —

"Can you hear me?"... "Can you hear me now?"... "How about now?"

Can you sense the LORD asking you, "Can you hear me" trying to get your attention? When He tries to draw your attention to what He wants to say, He waits a little longer, moves to a different location and asks again, "Can you hear me now?"... "How about now?"...

He needs us to tune in to His voice each day as He calls. He offers us choices to respond now or later or never — to choose His Best Plan for us or not.

We certainly can learn many lessons from the choices of Adam & Eve, Abraham and many others that came before us. Ultimately, we each have choices to make each day. We can choose, for whatever choices presented to us, in faith, in trusting in the LORD, taking ourselves out, in acknowledging that our GOD is the Almighty GOD who knows and wants the Best for us, in choosing the Fear of GOD, not the Fear of man. The outcome of choosing GOD and answering His call promptly always results in blessings, perhaps even beyond what the eye can see! Just like the 2 components of שם SHEM Name and the Letter ע Ayin (symbolling the Eye) in the word שמע SHAMA Hear/Obey. In Hearing and Obeying the LORD, we can <u>see</u> the SUPREME <u>NAME</u> manifested, the invisible Master of the Universe, the Name above all the names, in the age and the age to come!

**Let's pray:**

Our Father in Heaven אבינו שבשמימ,

We thank You for the gift of Free Will. We thank You for the incredible blessings and promises that await us when we hear and obey Your Words and Commandments. Help us to be more attentive to Your voice when You speak and to respond promptly so that we will not miss a thing, any good thing that You have prepared for us. We say to You today, "LORD, we hear YOU. We want to do Your Commandments, NOW! Ruach HaKodesh, Holy Spirit, direct and guide us so that, (in order that) in our HEARING GOD, we SEE YOUR GREAT NAME.

B'Shem Yeshua HaMashiach בשם ישוע המשיח.

In Jesus' Name we pray. Amen.

## 41. TORAH TASTING

### *REFLECTION*

1. What is the word, picture or theme the LORD is highlighting to you in this chapter and Torah Portion?

2. In this season, do you sense something GOD is calling you to, but somehow you are delaying your response? If so, what is holding you back?

3. This chapter shows us hearing GOD leads to seeing GOD's name. Have you ever heard or obeyed GOD's word / His call, then you saw GOD's hand and His blessing as a result?

# 42 מב
# Re'eh
## (See)
## ראה

Deuteronomy 11:26-16:17

Isaiah 54:11-55:5

John 6:35-51

This week's Torah Portion Re'eh discusses the LORD's warning against idol-worshiping, regulations about clean and unclean food, sabbatical year, livestock firstborn, as well as revisiting the three key feasts of the LORD: Passover, Shavuot (Feast of Weeks) and Sukkot (Feast of Booths/Ingathering).

The Hebrew root Ra'ah ראה means to see. The title of this Parasha comes from its first verse.

*"Behold (Look/Re'eh/ראה), I set before you today a blessing and a curse:* **Deuteronomy 11:26**

**The root verb See Ra'ah ראה is made of 3 letters:**

- ר Resh meaning the head,
- א Aleph meaning strength and
- ה Hey meaning to Reveal.

We can say when we are able to see something, the strength of our head is revealed. To reveal something is as if a veil is removed, something being uncovered.

Like a light bulb comes on... an "Ah-ha" moment.

Ironically, sight-impaired people can often "see" better than those with perfect eyesight, without hindrance and distractions. Their other senses are heightened and therefore able to "see" and discern people and situations with deeper insight.

The word See ראה Ra'ah is seen in this Parashat Ra'ah 5 times! The number 5 is known to be a number for Grace. The Hebrew alphabet ה Hey is the 5th one out of the 22 Hebrew letters. Its ancient form is shaped as "a man with his hands lifted up," then later evolved to be "an open window." It is no accident that the letter ה Hey is in the word See ראה Ra'ah. I think the picture of someone lifting up his hands and then something being revealed (open window) shows the interesting connection between the gesture of lifting of the hands in humility and surrender and seeing!

The first time the word See ראה Ra'ah appears in the Torah is in Genesis 1 —

*And God said, "Let there be light," and there was light.*
*God <u>saw</u> that the light was good, and he separated the light from the darkness.*
**Genesis 1:3-4**

This is right after GOD had fashioned the first creation, light. GOD is the first "seer," the first one seeing something, in the Torah. He saw the

Light as good! He modeled for us what seeing is intended for, seeing the light, seeing the good, the truly good things, and seeing His perspective.

However, between the time having been instructed not to eat or touch the Tree of the knowledge of good and evil and the time having heard the serpent challenging GOD's Word, Eve "saw the fruit of the tree was good for food and pleasing to the eye."

> *15 The Lord God took the man and put him in the Garden of Eden to work it and take care of it. 16 And the Lord God commanded the man, "You are free to eat from any tree in the garden; 17 but you must not eat from the tree of the knowledge of good and evil, for when you eat from it you will certainly die."*
> **Genesis 2:15-16**

> *4 "You will not certainly die," the serpent said to the woman. 5 "For God knows that when you eat from it your eyes will be opened, and you will be like God, knowing good and evil."*
> *6 When the woman saw that the fruit of the tree was good for food and pleasing to the eye, and also desirable for gaining wisdom, she took some and ate it. She also gave some to her husband, who was with her, and he ate it.*
> **Genesis 3:4-6**

What Eve saw was clouded by what she wanted to see and her own self-centered desire. What Eve chose to see for temporary and instant gratification forfeited GOD's perfect vision for her and her husband! What a huge tradeoff, foregoing the precious eternal gift for a counterfeit.

In the beginning of this Torah Portion, the LORD laid out a blessing and a curse for His people to choose.

> *"Behold, I set before you today a blessing and a curse: the blessing, if you obey the commandments of the Lord your God which I command you today; and the curse, if you do not obey the commandments of the Lord your God, but turn aside from the way which I command you today, to go after other gods which you have not known. Now it shall be, when the Lord your God has brought you into the land which you go to possess,* that you shall <u>put the blessing on Mount Gerizim and the curse on Mount Ebal</u>.
> **Deuteronomy 11:26-29**

The LORD told His children to put the blessing on Mt. Gerizim.

Mt. Gerizim is a mountain in Northern Israel, Gerizim derives from the word גרז Garaz meaning "cut off". The only time this word used in the Bible is in Psalm 31.

> *In my alarm I said,*
> *"I am **cut off** (גרז Garaz) from **your sight** (your eyes)!"*
> *Yet you heard my cry for mercy*
> *when I called to you for help.*
> **Psalm 31:22**

I sense that this verse gives us a clue as to what the LORD meant about putting a blessing on Mt. Gerizim. The blessing had to do with GOD's warning of His people cutting off themselves from the idol-worshippers around them as they entered the Promise Land. Psalm 31:22 also alludes to GOD's mercy, His hearing of our cry, as a direct result of our humility, which goes back to the letter ה Hey discussed before. Remember, the letter ה Hey comes from the picture of a man lifting up his hands, a sign of humility.

The LORD told His children to put the curse on Mt. Ebal. Ebal is an Edomite name, possibly meaning Bald. Mount Bald signifies no growth, lifeless. A curse leads to death and destruction, the opposite of life.

I'd like to suggest to you that perhaps when we choose to obey and follow GOD's Word, we choose blessing. GOD tells us where to put the blessing and where to put the curse. When the LORD says, "Behold," "Look," He has blessings in mind for us, blessings that lead to life, not death.

Truth is right before our eyes if we only choose to see.

> *From the rest he makes a god, his idol;*
> *he bows down to it and worships.*
> *He prays to it and says,*
> *"Save me! You are my god!"*
> *They know nothing, they understand nothing;*
> *their eyes are plastered over so they cannot see,*
> *and their minds closed so they cannot understand.*
> **Isaiah 44:17-18**

> *"Announce this to the descendants of Jacob*
> *and proclaim it in Judah:*
> *²¹ Hear this, you foolish and senseless people,*
> *who have eyes but do not see,*
> *who have ears but do not hear:*
> *²² <u>Should you not fear me</u>?" declares the Lord.*
> *"Should you not tremble in my presence?*
> *I made the sand a boundary for the sea,*
> *an everlasting barrier it cannot cross.*
> *The waves may roll, but they cannot prevail;*
> *they may roar, but they cannot cross it.*
> *²³ But these people have <u>stubborn and rebellious hearts</u>;*
> *they have turned aside and gone away.*
> **Jeremiah 5:20-23**

Why would anyone choose to be blind? Is it a choice or simply a consequence of another choice or experience?

Have you met or heard about a slim woman that sees herself as an overweight person in the mirror? Have you known a beautiful young woman who had experienced abuse and hurt in the past, seeing herself as ugly, unworthy, unwanted and kept going from one abusive partner to another? This demonstrates a huge gap between reality and perception.

In recent years, I have witnessed some people being paralyzed by "the unknown upcoming apocalypse" and the "what if's" projected by the world. They live in depression and despair; they've stopped living because of the fear of illnesses and death. My eldest uncle was diagnosed with lung cancer after years of smoking. He was put on medications, which were very costly and painful at times. After a few months of medical treatment, he decided to stop all treatments. He told his doctor he would take his chances and stop living in fear and pain while draining his finances. He thought he was going to die sooner or later. Uncle went on to live pain-free for two more years and was able to leave the money to his surviving wife that would have otherwise gone to medical expenses. Uncle chose to see joy and not live in fear.

A friend of mine was diagnosed with breast cancer and her infant child with terminal leukemia; instead of living in dread each day, she and her family chose to see the good plans the LORD had for them. It was a real struggle; definitely not easy to see the joy in that season, but it was all so worth it in the end. Now she and her child both live a healthy life, defying all odds, living in the blessings the LORD had planned for her, her husband, and their children!

What could possibly keep people from seeing the truth?

Pride, Fear, Trauma, Past Hurt, Unhealed Wounds, Accepted lies and confusion, Rebellion, Stubbornness, … . The list goes on and on…

Then, what can take the scales off the blind eye?

Focus on the LORD! Away from self, Away from distractions, Away from lies, … .

## 42. RE'EH / SEE

It is Intriguing that the Hebrew letter ע Ayin, representing the Eye, is not present in this word for seeing ראה Ra'ah. I believe it is because seeing does not necessarily require the eye.

> *And he will delight in the fear of the Lord.*
> *He will not judge by what he sees with his eyes,*
> *or decide by what he hears with his ears.*
> **Isaiah 11:3**

Fear of GOD, centering our thoughts, deeds, and words around Him, leads to revealing the strength of our heads that we may see — See Ra'ah ראה. As I am writing this chapter, I am hearing in my head a famous Christmas song by Bing Crosby, "Do You Hear What I Hear?" One verse with the phrase "Do you see what I see?" is as follows:

Said the night wind to the little lamb:
"Do you see what I see?
Way up in the sky, little lamb
Do you see what I see?
A star, a star, dancing in the night
With a tail as big as a kite
With a tail as big as a kite"

I feel like the LORD is singing to us, "Do you see what I see?" referring to His vision and best plan for us. He invites us to see what He sees in us and with us the bright star ahead of us, the blessings in store for us if we only see and choose and follow the path that leads us to them.

Following are verses listing 7 offerings:

*And there you shall bring your <u>burnt offerings</u> and your <u>sacrifices</u>, your <u>tithes</u> and the <u>contribution</u> that you <u>present</u>, your <u>vow offerings</u>, your <u>freewill offerings</u>, and <u>the firstborn of your herd and of your flock</u>. And there you shall eat before the LORD your God, and you shall rejoice, you and your households, in all that you undertake, in which the LORD your God has blessed you.*
**Deuteronomy 12:6-7**

GOD delights in watching us eat. He enjoys seeing us break bread in fellowship with Him. My mother is the best cook I know, taking after her mother. Grandmother, though illiterate, could cook anything, both Western and Chinese dishes. She was so culinarily gifted that she could taste something once and duplicate that at home. Mom has inherited that gift too. She can spend hours cleaning, cutting, cooking and preparing vegetables and meat, and present to us an 8-course meal unmatched by restaurants. Many times, she would sit down and watch us enjoy food, which is the result of her labor of love. I remember we had a party at our home celebrating our firstborn son's One-Month-Old birthday. It is a huge celebratory event in Chinese customs. The joyous event likens a wedding banquet. Friends and family bring gifts in the form of gold jewelry for the newborn baby. At our humble home, Mom offered to cook for this party. She spent hours preparing for all the delicious Cantonese Chinese dishes that are not often seen in restaurants in the U.S.. One of the dishes was chicken wings. She deboned every single small drumstick with the bone barely attached, then flipped the meat inside out, and tied a small string at the end so that the wing drumstick looks like a meatball on a stick. She breaded and deep-fried them. I was amazed at the effort she put into making every delicate dish. Over 80 people were packed into our home for that party. Though we knew our friends came because they loved us, Mom's cooking definitely convinced some to rearrange their schedule in order not to miss this occasion. At the end of the evening, when we sat down to reminisce the celebration, at one point, Mom looked at her grandson and remembered the sight of her food being enjoyed by all our guests… that was her reward, and her effort was worthwhile. I too like to cook, but I often make easy dishes due to time restraints. The other day, I spent hours spontaneously making a meal consisting of some lamb/beef meatballs and Zucchini fries for the first time. My family came home and devoured them. I was completely mesmerized by how they enjoyed my food. At that moment, I understand how Mom feels when she takes satisfaction in watching us enjoy her delicious cooking every time.

Deuteronomy 12 says we are to eat before the LORD our GOD and rejoice/be happy before the LORD. The sacrifices the LORD asked of us are not for Him, but instead, we are to enjoy eating what He has provided in His Presence. That reminds me of my mother taking delight in seeing us enjoying her food. Making offerings and sacrifices to GOD is often a solemn concept; it usually is not associated with joy. However, we clearly see that is not the case here.

Do you see what the LORD wills for you to see? His best vision for you? It makes Him happy to see you feasting in joy with His provision.

**Let's pray:**

**Our Father in Heaven** אבינו שבשמימ,

Help us see what You desire for us to see, not our flesh wants us to see, so we can hear and obey Your Word. Seeing everything in humility will allow windows to be open (like the picture word in ראה Ra'ah see), revealing things above and below outside of our environment that leads to seeing Your grace and blessings for us. You delight in cheerful givers. LORD, when we offer our sacrifice, help us to rejoice in giving of ourselves and our resources in Your Presence, for it pleases You so.

B'Shem Yeshua HaMashiach בשם ישוע המשיח.

In Jesus' Name we pray. Amen.

# 42. TORAH TASTING

## *REFLECTION*

1. What is the word, picture or theme the LORD is highlighting to you in this chapter and Torah Portion?

2. What we see through our physical eyes and our spiritual eyes do not always match? Can you think of an incident or a moment when that happened? What are the possible contributing factors that cause people to see things differently through their physical sight and their spiritual sight?

3. GOD is the One that provided the sacrifices brought to Him? Why do you think the LORD rejoices in seeing His children and bringing sacrifices and eating them in His presence?

# 43 מג
# shoftim
## (Judges)
שופטים

Deuteronomy 16:18-21:9

Isaiah 51:12-52:12

John 14:9-20

Parashat Shoftim begins with instructions regarding the appointment of judges and officers that they would rule GOD's people with justice. The LORD set up provisions for priests and Levites. He set parameters in regard to worship and worship practices that would be prohibited. There are also laws concerning cities of refuge, property boundaries, warfare, and murders.

*You shall appoint judges שפט and officers in all your gates, which the Lord your God gives you, according to your tribes, and they shall judge שפט the people with just/righteous צדק judgment שפט. You shall not pervert justice שפט; you shall not show partiality, nor take a bribe, for a bribe blinds the eyes of the wise and twists the words of the righteous צדק. You shall follow what is altogether just צדק, that you may live and inherit the land which the Lord your God is giving you.*
### Deuteronomy 16:18-20

I don't seem to be able to get past the first 3 verses of this Torah Portion when I first read it. I kept reading them over and over because the words of justice and righteousness are being echoed throughout this part.

- שפט Shafat — Justice
- צדק Tzadak- Righteousness

Justice and Righteousness in these 3 verses have been translated interchangeably in many Bible translations. However, I do think it is important to display the original (Hebrew) words used in order to understand this Portion's beginning verses deeper that sets the backdrop of the text focused in this week's Portion.

The first time the word Tzadak צדק righteousness used in the Torah is in Genesis 15.

*And he (Abram) believed (אמן Aman, confirm, support) in the Lord, and He accounted it to him for righteousness (צדק Tzadak).*
### Genesis 15:6

Abram believed in the LORD; the LORD considered Abram righteous! Is "our belief in GOD" what makes us righteous? I think that is what the LORD is saying here for the first time Tzadak צדק Righteousness being mentioned. We, on our own, cannot be righteous, but when we align our faith with GOD and אמן Aman (as in Amen) agree/trust/establish and believe in Him, we are considered righteous, like Abraham.

Righteousness is a concept applied to individuals. What we each do individually accounts for us to be righteous. My righteousness does not automatically make those around me righteous, though it may help influence them to emulate.

- צדק Tzadak Righteousness is made up of the three Hebrew letters:
- צ Tzade — Fishhook, catch, desire
- ד Dalet — Door, enter, path to life
- ק Qoof — Follow, behind, back of the head

I believe the picture of the word צדק Tzadak reveal to us that Righteousness is when we are hooked and desire to enter and follow the path of life.

*The fruit of the <u>righteous</u> is a tree of <u>life</u>, and he who wins souls is wise.*
**Proverbs 11:30**

*Blessed are those who <u>hunger and thirst</u> (desire, hooked) for <u>righteousness</u>, For they shall be <u>filled</u> (fed, satisfied and live).*
**Matthew 5:6**

When we have the inner desire to follow after the LORD on the path of life and believe in Him like Abram did, we too are accounted as Righteous.

As for the word Justice, the first time שפט Shafat Justice (noun) /Judge (verb) used is in Genesis 16 in Sarai's words to Abram, her husband, in the context that she had given her maid Hagar to Abram to have a child with.

*Then Sarai said to Abram, "My wrong be upon you! I gave my maid into your embrace; and when she saw that she had conceived, I became despised (belittled) in her eyes. The Lord judge (שפט Shafat) between you and me."*
**Genesis 16:5**

This verse indicates to us that the LORD is the One that judges.

**שפט Shafat Justice is made up of the three Hebrew letters:**

- ש Shin — Consume, destroy, devour
- פ Pey — Speak, word, open
- ט Tet — Surround, snake

I believe the pictures formed from these Hebrew letters reveal to us that Justice has to do with something around us. Justice is to destroy and devour the words spoken by the Snake in our surroundings. How often do we see evil deeds and words spread to create injustice in the world? GOD is our Judge, but He instructs us to open our mouths and speak justice and judge righteously to straighten and destroy injustice for the poor and needy.

> *Open your mouth, judge (שפט Shafat) righteously (צדק Tzadak),*
> *And plead the cause of the poor and needy.*
> **Proverbs 31:9-11**

> *Then the men rose from there and looked toward Sodom, and Abraham went with them to send them on the way. And the Lord said, "Shall I hide from Abraham what I am doing, since Abraham shall surely become a great and mighty nation, and all the nations of the earth shall be blessed in him? For I have known him, in order that he may command his children and his household after him, that they keep the way of the Lord, to do <u>righteousness</u> (צדק Tzadak) and <u>justice</u> (שפט Shafat), that the Lord may bring to Abraham what He has spoken to him."*
> **Genesis 18:16-19**

Doing righteousness and justice is the way/path of the LORD! Apart from HIM, there is no righteousness and no justice.

It seems nowadays, we cannot go about our day without seeing "justice" being thrown around like some kind of injustice we need to undo. I have not heard justice being discussed in pop culture as much as the recent few years. DC Comics has the Justice League made up of a team of superheroes like Superman, Wonder Woman and Batman saving the world. There is a sense of justice and righteousness built inside every child. Just look at how little boys are fascinated by Superman or Spiderman. Yes, there is a "cool factor" to be a superhero, but more than anything, righting the wrong, defeating the villains and eradicating evil is what motivates the admiration inside of us. Little did we know, the King of the Universe had the same thing in mind in His Master Plan, saving the world as the Ultimate Superhero. His plan to straighten out injustice is written in His Word.

As much as we marvel at these iconic superheroes, none compares to the Utmost, Unsurpassable and Incomparable Superhero in the LORD, who is the Most Righteous Judge. When we see injustice, we know He brings Justice at the proper time, beyond our knowledge and understanding.

Justice is at times controversial and subjective with the world that gives us "relative truth" instead of the Absolute Truth. Laws are at times bent in the name of "justice." Empathy overrules well-established statutes and ordinances, regardless of tragic circumstances. As a result, all in the name of fairness for all. Even to the point of taking another's innocent life can be justified by "preserving someone else's human right."

The world has a very distorted view of what justice is, unlike what we know from the Author of Justice, the One and Master of All Things, who instituted Justice and Righteousness. Those, who know the LORD, believe that justice lies … only with… and in the LORD.

The Lady of Justice statue in front of a courthouse that has a blindfold over her is a pertinent visual for Deuteronomy 16:19, "You shall not pervert justice שפט Shafat; you shall not show partiality, nor take a bribe, for a bribe blinds the eyes of the wise and twists the words of the righteous צדק Tzadik." GOD has gifted us the Ten Commandments as the basis of Justice and Righteousness. We are to pursue justice because our GOD is a GOD of justice. We are to pursue righteousness because our GOD is a

GOD of righteousness. I believe scriptures use Justice and Righteousness interchangeably because when we trust in the LORD and align our lives desiring Him, only then do we see what Justice is meant to be and created to be in its originated sense. Justice and righteousness are different, yet they go together like salt and pepper.

> *How blessed are those who keep <u>justice</u>,*
> *Who practice <u>righteousness</u> at all times!*
> **Psalm 106:3**

> *For <u>I, the Lord, love justice</u>,*
> *I hate robbery in the burnt offering;*
> *And I will faithfully give them their recompense*
> *And make an everlasting covenant with them.*
> **Isaiah 61:8**

> *Therefore the Lord longs to be gracious to you,*
> *And therefore He waits on high to have compassion on you.*
> *For <u>the Lord is a God of justice</u>;*
> *<u>How blessed are all those who long (wait, following) for Him</u>.*
> **Isaiah 30:18**

Without GOD, there can be NO JUSTICE. Apart from GOD, there is NO RIGHTEOUSNESS. The rules are set for all, the same for all, with no partiality. The LORD judges the wicked for their evildoings. Justice in history has been distorted in order to further certain ideologies and satisfy an agenda. My Grandfather was born in the City of Guilin in GuangXi Province (Southwestern part of China). Guilin is known for the breath-taking views of its picturesque mountains and the Li River. He grew up in a wealthy family. His father had built a 4-story house, the tallest in the city overlooking the magnificent Guilin. When the Communists won the Civil War and took over China, one of their beliefs was that all landlords were heinous and had to be punished for exploiting the poor. They confiscated my Great-grandfather's properties and persecuted his large family. Those who survived the persecution were thrown into farmlands to live as peasants. The Chinese Communists propagandized that it was "unjust" that the uneducated and poor were unfairly treated and oppressed. Therefore, confiscated lands from wealthy families were distributed and appropriated to them. They felt that the educated and intellects were polluting minds of the masses, and they were to be despised, hated, and "dealt with". Class struggle was their weapon to divide the Chinese people at the start of their reign in the 1950s. They constantly provoked and fueled the discontent between classes during the years of the Cultural Revolution to break down society and weaken individuality to promote corporate identity and loyalty to the Party. Fast forward half a century later, I visited our relatives in China. Their lives were forever changed the day they had everything stripped away from them and thrown into the countryside with a little piece of land to raise pigs and grow fruit trees, with absolutely no previous knowledge or training. As if that was not cruel enough, my Great-grandfather was executed in public, and his wife knelt on broken glass parading around town to be humiliated unto death. No crime had been committed. No law had been broken. The charge for the punishment and execution was simply due to their social and intellect status. ...

But according to the regime in power, "Justice is served."

Reality is, Justice was "hijacked" to fulfill a certain group's plan and desire to achieve power. The horrific stories told to me by my grandparents and their family are unrighteousness and injustice being flipped and justified.

However, True Righteous Justice is with GOD! We need to be able to distinguish what Justice really is from the LORD's Word.

Deuteronomy 20 starts with instructions from the LORD to Moses regarding going into battle. They offer extraordinary insights about victory in battles against the enemy —

> "When you go out to battle against your enemies, and *see horses and chariots and people more numerous than you, do not be afraid of them; for the Lord your God is with you, who brought you up from the land of Egypt.* ² So it shall be, when you are on the verge of battle, *that the priest shall approach and speak to the people.* ³ And he shall say to them, 'Hear, O Israel: Today you are on the verge of battle with your enemies. <u>Do not let your heart faint, do not be afraid, and do not tremble or be terrified because of them;</u> ⁴ <u>for the Lord your God is He who goes with you, to fight for you against your enemies, to save you.</u>'
> "Then the officers shall speak to the people, saying: 'What man is there <u>who has built a new house and has not dedicated it</u>? Let him go and return to his house, lest he die in the battle and another man dedicate it. ⁶ Also what man is there <u>who has planted a vineyard and has not eaten of it</u>? Let him go and return to his house, lest he die in the battle and another man eat of it. ⁷ And what man is there <u>who is betrothed to a woman and has not married her</u>? Let him go and return to his house, lest he die in the battle and another man marry her.'
> "The officers shall speak further to the people, and say, 'What man is there <u>who is fearful and fainthearted</u>? Let him go and return to his house, lest the heart of his brethren faint like his heart.' ⁹ And so it shall be, when the officers have finished speaking to the people, that they shall make captains of the armies to lead the people.
> **Deuteronomy 20:1-9**

In the matter of warfare, when facing enemies who are MORE NUMEROUS / SEEM BIGGER, the LORD instructed to NOT BE AFRAID of them!

Following are the 4 points demonstrated in Deuteronomy 20:1-9.

| The Priest is to tell the children of Israel | Because | Send these away: |
|---|---|---|
| 1. Do not let your heart faint* | The LORD is your GOD | Built a house, Not yet vindicated |
| 2. Do not be afraid** | The LORD goes with you | Planted a vineyard Not yet eaten of it |
| 3. Do not tremble | The LORD fights for you | Betrothed a woman Not yet married |
| 4. Do not be terrified | The LORD saves you | Fearful & Fainthearted (*,**) |

The 1st point is echoed in the 4th point.

First of all, in Kingdom principles, numbers do not always equate strength and sure triumph. Just like how the LORD defeated Goliath through David (a giant was destroyed by a skinny, "inexperienced" young man), against human logic and reasoning, GOD defeats our enemy, who seem to be more powerful than we are. He demonstrates to us the blueprint of winning a battle. The LORD reminds the Israelites repeatedly of Him bringing them out of Egypt. The memory of that Epic Deliverance should be enough to shake off any fear and strengthen our faith in the Might of our GOD. Once we settle in our mind to not lose heart nor be afraid, our bodies are to follow and not to tremble and be terrified any longer. The Priest is to explain why we should have NO FEAR — The LORD is our GOD — because GOD goes with us, GOD fights for us, and GOD saves us. These 4 points are timeless and absolute eternal truths.

In this text, the Israelites were outnumbered but were not outnumbered enough, according to GOD.

4 groups of soldiers would need to be sent home and eliminated from the victory troop — Those who built a house but not yet dedicated

it, those who planted a vineyard but not yet eaten of it, those who betrothed a woman but not yet married, and lastly those who are fearful & fainthearted.

I feel that justice is reclaiming and securing what the LORD willed for us to be and to have, reversing things to be what they ought to be.

1. The LORD is our GOD, that the enemy should be fainthearted and NOT dedicate the house we have built. — NO USURPATION — JUSTICE!
2. The LORD goes with us, that the enemy should be afraid and not eat of the vineyard we have planted. — NO USURPATION — JUSTICE!
3. The LORD fights for us, that the enemy should tremble and not marry the one we are betrothed to. — NO USURPATION — JUSTICE!
4. The LORD saves us, that the Enemy should be terrified, and his minions be fearful and fainthearted. Ultimate JUSTICE!

There is another time that GOD sent away soldiers so that He would receive all the credit for battle victory. One of my favorite stories is Gideon. We have all been doubtful at one time or another, looking to the LORD for reassurance (Judges 6-7). After Gideon got the confirmation that it was indeed the LORD speaking to him to go to battle against the Midianites, following is their exchange —

*And the Lord said to Gideon, "The people who are with you are <u>too many for Me to give the Midianites into their hands</u>, lest Israel claim glory for itself against Me, saying, 'My own hand has saved me.' ³ Now therefore, proclaim in the hearing of the people, saying, <u>'Whoever is fearful and afraid, let him turn and depart at once from Mount Gilead.'</u> " And twenty-two thousand of the people returned, and ten thousand remained.*
*⁴ But the Lord said to Gideon, "<u>The people are still too many</u>; bring them down to the water, and I will test them for you there. Then it will be, that of whom I say to you, 'This one shall go with you,' the same shall go with you; and of whomever I say to you, 'This one shall not go with you,' the same shall not go." ⁵ So he brought the people down to the water. And the Lord said to Gideon, "<u>Everyone who laps from the water with his tongue, as a dog laps, you shall set apart by himself</u>; likewise everyone who gets down on his knees to drink." ⁶ And the number of those who lapped, putting their hand to their mouth, was three hundred men; but all the rest of the people got down on their knees to drink water. ⁷ Then the Lord said to Gideon, "By the three hundred men who lapped I will save you, and deliver the Midianites into your hand. Let all the other people go, every man to his place." ⁸ So the people took provisions and their trumpets in their hands. And he sent away all the rest of Israel, every man to his tent, and retained those three hundred men. Now the camp of Midian was below him in the valley.*

## Judges 7:2-8

The 2 groups of soldiers The LORD told Gideon to send away are <u>those who are fearful and afraid</u> and <u>those who drink water like a dog with their tongues</u>. Notice that in both scenarios in Deuteronomy and Judges, the fearful ones were sent home., The fearful group is the last group in Deuteronomy, and they are the first group in Judges. I believe the elimination test is to filter out the weaker ones in faith. Fear not only debilitates a person's physical strength, but it also weakens those around him mentally and physically. In order to win a battle with GOD, walk in righteousness and justice in faith, we need to be strong and eliminate the fearful ones around us.

> *A little leaven leavens the whole lump.*
> **Galatians 5:9**

> *He who walks with wise men will be wise,*
> *But the companion of fools will be destroyed.*
> **Proverbs 13:20**

GOD had to eliminate the fainthearted ones before leading His people to victory. The harsh reality is that we need to do the same in order to win battles in life. I am not saying to cut off every weak-faithed person. Who you allow to go to battle with you, shoulder to shoulder, bringing victory and standing in faith matters. Fools are ones who lack wisdom and understanding. At times, they are even prideful, other times fearful. Basically, they do not have their whole heart trusting in the LORD. Walking righteously and justly requires faith, courage, and FEAR OF GOD. I believe this Torah Portion shows us what the LORD wants to highlight about Justice, not what the world or anyone tries to define it apart from GOD. If we trust in our Father in Heaven, we know He is the One that brings about justice. Through Yeshua Jesus, our Mashiach, we are able to walk righteously, pursue justice, and have the right standing with GOD.

Let's pray:

**Our Father in Heaven** אבינו שבשמימ,

Thank You that You are the Only One that can bring Justice and Righteousness in the world. Apart from you, there cannot be justice. Righting the wrong and restoring Justice is taking our rightful place in You as Your children through Yeshua Jesus and His atonement. When we acknowledge all that You have done and who You are in our lives, the enemy is the one that is terrified in fear and panic while we know that You are our GOD, You are with us, You go everywhere with us and You save us. Please help us be aware to not be affected by the fearful ones around us, but instead, their faith is strengthened seeing our trust in You in all circumstances.

B'Shem Yeshua HaMashiach בשם ישוע המשיח.

In Jesus' Name we pray. Amen.

# 43. TORAH TASTING
## *REFLECTION*

1. What is the word, picture or theme the LORD is highlighting to you in this chapter and Torah Portion?

2. What are some of the ways justice is twisted in the world? If the world distorts what justice truly is, why do you think so many believe its distorted version? Have you, at one point or another, believed the twisted version of justice in the name of empathy or compassion or any other reasons?

3. The LORD laid out his instructions for victory in life. "Do not fear" is on top of the list. Fear is not only toxic, but it is also contagious. Have you had to distance yourself from fear or fearful individuals in order to survive a situation? What are some of the challenges in doing that?

# 44 מד
# Ki Tetze
## (When You Go Out)
### כי תצא

Deuteronomy 21:10-25:19

Isaiah 54:1-10

Matthew 24:29-42

*When you go out (תצא Tatza) to war against your enemies, and the Lord your God delivers them into your hand, and you take them captive, and you see among the captives a beautiful woman, and desire her and would take her for your wife, then you shall bring her home to your house, and she shall shave her head and trim her nails. She shall put off the clothes of her captivity, remain in your house, and mourn her father and her mother **a full month** (Yerach Yamim ירח ימים); after that you may go in to her and be her husband, and she shall be your wife.*
**Deuteronomy 21:10-13**

The above verses open up this week's Torah Portion. It is jam-packed with GOD's instructions after battle victory on female prisoners of war, firstborns' inheritance rights, punishment of a rebellious son, laws about sexual immorality, who would be excluded from the Assembly of GOD, and those that would be included after a certain period of time, interest on loans, divorce, leprosy, compassion on hired workers and the less-fortunate, and so much more. Some of the laws we may scratch our heads and are puzzled at their reasoning. I do think cultural and historical context is necessary for making sense of them.

I sense GOD's compassion for women throughout this Parasha. In world history, the stereotypical perception about women is that their status is less than their male counterparts, starting with ancient times; especially during wartimes, women were targeted and captured for evil intentions. One remarkable example in modern history is when the Japanese military invaded China in the 1930's. Instant death would be mercy compared to the unimaginably evil atrocity done to countless women in China and many other countries in the Southeast Asian region. Japanese soldiers were unleashed on foreign soil as blood-thirsty possessed demons to hunt for their prey. Many survivors lived to tell the horrors that they endured and miraculously survived. My grandmother lived through the Japanese invasion. She retold stories of avoiding those brutal soldiers, putting dirt and mud on her face to disguise as a boy, so the Japanese soldiers would leave her alone. The terror of war that generation lived through, and their wounds are deeply seared in their souls, for which only the LORD is able to bring full healing and redemption. Unfortunately, war brutality was common throughout history in every corner of the globe with evil demonic force behind it to destroy GOD's people.

This parasha mentions the female captives that the Israelites have captured. They are not to treat them as property but instead with respect. If the man finds her attractive, he is not to use her for his own fleshly desire but instead to marry her. The woman is to shave her head and trim her nails, change out her clothing and mourn for her parents for an entire month. This type of female captives' treatment is utterly unheard of, at least for me. And the entire month the woman captured looks nothing like when he first met her, with no hair and no pretty long nails. She is to be kept away. This is like curbing instant physical gratification for the man, who would have a month to seriously consider this woman as his wife, not any casual relationship. This tells me the compassion the LORD wanted His people to have, unlike the nations known to them. The month's waiting period allows the man and the woman to process the things they had experienced at war times, good and bad, before entering into the sacred covenant of marriage. Despite unthinkable tragedy and loss at wars, the LORD can somehow produce beauty and restoration.

The phrase "a full month" caught my attention. Perhaps this specific time period indicates something else. This exact phrase, Yerach Yamim ירח ימים — A Full Month, is only used one other time in the Torah.

*Shallum the son of Jabesh became king in the thirty-ninth year of Uzziah king of Judah; and he reigned <u>a full month</u> (Yerach Yamim ירח ימים) in Samaria.*
**2 Kings 15:13**

To give you some context about Shallum, his name means Perfect/Agreeable, The Requited One, Retaliation, Repayment. In 2 Kings 15, we are told that Shallum conspired against and killed King Zachariah of Israel. He reigned for exactly one month as King of Judah before being dethroned by Menahem. According to Smith's Bible Dictionary (Bible Hub), Shallum was a keeper of the gate during David's reign (1 Chronicles 9:17), a **high priest, son of Tikvah** meaning **Hope/Glory** (2 Kings 22:14), and **married to Huldah, the Prophetess** (2 Kings 22:14).

Shallum lived in a time of political turmoil in Israel. The ruling class was constantly conspiring against other groups to gain more power. War was a common scene, just as in the time of Moses before and after entering into the Promise Land. The instability and uncertainty of life was the shared background for both this Torah Portion's prisoners of war and Shallum's reign.

I feel that the One Full Month period through the mention of Shallum's brief reign in 2 Kings 15, being the common factor with the female captive's One Full Month waiting time, alludes to the fact in the time of unrest, the only way out of the chaos is waiting for the LORD and trusting in His Hope and Glory. Being a child of the High Priest, Gatekeeper of the King, married to a Prophetess did not guarantee Shallum's success. Yerach Yamim literally means Month of Days.

Without much information on the reasons behind Shallum's loss of grace, one thing we can learn is we need to make every day count. Each day that we devote our life to GOD, each day that Shallum may have stayed true to the LORD and ruled for His glory, each day during the month of mourning the female captive and the male captor may decide for their potential marriage matters. The LORD has given us life each day, and we are never hopeless, only if we put our Hope in Him.

This Parasha's title "Ki Tetze" comes from the Hebrew root Yatza יצא To go out.

*And the earth brought forth (יצא Yatza) grass, the herb that yields seed according to its kind, and the tree that yields fruit, whose seed is in itself according to its kind. And God saw that it was good. [13] So the evening and the morning were the third.*
**Genesis 1:12**

The Hebrew root יצא Yatza Go Out is seen for the first time in the context of fruits and plants being produced. On the 3rd day of Creation, the LORD brought forth vegetation. It is harvest time! There is something hopeful and anticipative about fruit being brought forth, as in a woman bringing forth a child from a seed being planted and developed into a newborn delivered into the world. I do believe it is no accident that GOD brought forth fruits onto the earth on the 3rd day.

The number 3 represents completeness. A complete set comes in 3's.

Israel's 3 patriarchs are Abraham, Isaac and Jacob. A person is made up of mind, body and soul. For those of us who believe Yeshua Jesus the

Mashiach sent by the LORD as the long-awaited Messiah, know the 3 parts of ONE GOD as the Father, the Son and the Holy Spirit.

The 3rd Hebrew Alphabet ג Gimmel is a camel in its pictograph form. ג Gimmel signifies to lift up, benefit, yield … yielding fruits? Perhaps like vegetation being brought forth?

Near the conclusion of the worldwide flood and GOD's redemption of the world through Noah, the word יצא Yatza once again pops up.

*And with every living creature that is with you: the birds, the cattle, and every beast of the earth with you, of all that go out (יצא Yatza) of the ark, every beast of the earth. Thus I establish My covenant with you: Never again shall all flesh be cut off by the waters of the flood; never again shall there be a flood to destroy the earth."*
**Genesis 9:10,11**

One cannot help but see the theme of new life and hope through the appearance of יצא Yatza Go Out reading these verses. The end of this epic flood story displays the picture of a new beginning when Noah's family and all the animals step off the ark.

The connection of the word יצא Yatza of a Female Captive's fresh start in Parashat Ki Tetze (Deuteronomy 21:10), the 3rd Day of Creation and the Deliverance of Noah's family after the flood show us the bringing forth of New Life. A woman's role of bringing forth children and new life from the womb underlines her being a large part of His Master Plan.

This portion is the first time we see Levirate Marriage Law being discussed (a law commanding a widow to marry the dead husband's brother in order to further the lineage of the family). Building upon women's influence in GOD's Master Plan, two women in the line of King David are hinted at in this Torah Portion, and subsequently, the Mashiach is implied as well. Their connection to this Parasha's Levirate Law cannot be overlooked.

## TAMAR – MEANS PALM TREE

After Judah's two sons and wife died and had no intention to give his youngest son to Tamar to produce children, Tamar disguised herself as a prostitute (קדשה Kedeshah) in order that she would carry on the lineage of the House of Judah through her father-in-law.

> *So he returned to Judah and said, "I cannot find her. Also, the men of the place said there was no harlot/prostitute (קדשה Kedeshah) in this place."… ²⁶ So Judah acknowledged them and said, <u>"She has been more righteous than I</u>, because I did not give her to Shelah my son." And he never knew her again.*
> **Genesis 38:21, 26**

Ki Tetze's mention of the law prohibiting prostitution in Israel reminds us of the story of Tamar's disguise.

> *There shall be no ritual harlot (קדשה Kedeshah) of the daughters of Israel, or a perverted one of the sons of Israel.*
> **Deuteronomy 23:17**

Tamar's righteous act of furthering Judah's bloodline, eventually acknowledged by Judah, preceded Ki Tetze's mention of the Levirate Marriage Law (a law commanding a widow to marry the dead husband's brother in order to further the lineage of the family).

> *If brothers dwell together, and one of them dies and has no son, <u>the widow of the dead man shall not be married to a stranger outside the family; her husband's brother shall go in to her, take her as his wife, and perform the duty of a husband's brother to her.</u> ⁶ And it shall be that the firstborn son which she bears will succeed to the name of his dead brother, that his name may not be blotted out of Israel.*
> **Deuteronomy 25:5-6**

# 44. KI TETZE / WHEN YOU GO OUT

**RUTH – MEANS FRIENDSHIP**

Parashat Ki Tetze sets up the law for GOD's people to leave some of their harvest for strangers, orphans and widows.

> *When you reap your harvest in your field, and forget a sheaf in the field, you shall not go back to get it; it shall be for the stranger, the fatherless, and the widow, that the Lord your God may bless you in all the work of your hands.*
> **Deuteronomy 24:19**

In Ruth 2, Ruth was provided for when she returned to Bethlehem with her mother-in-law, Naomi, because of this Israelite practice.

> *There was a relative of Naomi's husband, a man of great wealth, of the family of Elimelech. His name was Boaz. So Ruth the Moabitess said to Naomi, "Please let me go to the field, <u>and glean heads of grain</u> after him in whose sight I may find favor."*
> **Ruth 2:1**

The following verses in Parashat Ki Tetze set up the Law of Levirate Marriage to provide for preserving the lineage of the House of Judah. Through the obedience and faithfulness of a Moabite woman, Ruth was able to produce an heir with Boaz and became the Great-Grandmother of the Greatest King of Israel, David!

*"If brothers dwell together, and one of them dies and has no son, the widow of the dead man shall not be married to a stranger outside the family; her husband's brother shall go in to her, take her as his wife, and perform the duty of a husband's brother to her. ⁶ And it shall be that the firstborn son which she bears will succeed to the name of his dead brother, that his name may not be blotted out of Israel. ⁷ But if the man does not want to take his brother's wife, then let his brother's wife go up to the gate to the elders, and say, 'My husband's brother refuses to raise up a name to his brother in Israel; he will not perform the duty of my husband's brother.' ⁸ Then the elders of his city shall call him and speak to him. But if he stands firm and says, 'I do not want to take her,' ⁹ <u>then his brother's wife shall come to him in the presence of the elders, remove his sandal from his foot</u>, spit in his face, and answer and say, 'So shall it be done to the man who will not build up his brother's house.' ¹⁰ And his name shall be called in Israel, 'The house of him who had his sandal removed.'*
**Deuteronomy 25:5-10**

*Then Boaz said, "On the day you buy the field from the hand of Naomi, <u>you must also buy it from Ruth the Moabitess, the wife of the dead, to perpetuate the name of the dead through his inheritance."</u>… Now this was the custom in former times in Israel concerning redeeming and exchanging, to confirm anything: <u>one man took off his sandal and gave it to the other, and this was a confirmation in Israel</u>. Therefore the close relative said to Boaz, "Buy it for yourself." So he took off his sandal.*
**Ruth 4:5,7,8**

Tamar braced herself against ridicule and taboos, and courageously risked everything she had to do what is right. The Name of Tamar means Palm Tree. Psalm 92:12 describes as "flourishing." It is tall and Jeremiah 10:5 says the palm is "upright." In Revelation 7:9, palm branches are a symbol of victory.

Jericho was later named "the City of Palm Trees" in Deuteronomy 34:3. Tamar was rewarded by giving birth to twins, Perez and Zerah. From

Perez to Boaz (Ruth's husband) was 6 generations. Tamar's brave acts were righteous and upright. Through her, the Messiah would be brought forth bringing victory for GOD.

Meanwhile, Ruth may not have understood the full scope of what her mother-in-law had in mind in returning to Bethlehem, nor would Naomi have known what the LORD had planned for their return. Nonetheless, Ruth followed faithfully like a loyal Friend (as in her name). Every step of the way, despite of being a foreign woman, perhaps despised at times for being a Moabite woman, she was ultimately respected as an honorable daughter-in-law. Her devotion went above and beyond duty.

Male or female, we can all acknowledge that our eternal destiny is being One in Yeshua Jesus our Mashiach, with the LORD!

> *There is neither Jew nor Greek, there is neither slave nor free, there is neither male nor female; for you are all one in Christ Jesus.*
> **Galatians 3:28**

The enemy has come to steal, kill and destroy, as well as dividing GOD's people to believe His wicked lies and deception, one being "the battle of the sexes" in malicious ways. The truth is we can all appreciate the person GOD has made in each of us, man or woman, with unique gifts and backgrounds that made us who we are, individually. In this Torah Portion, what is highlighted are the incredible lessons the LORD teaches through women, the sacred covenant of marriage, and the beautiful responsibility of producing progeny for the LORD and His righteousness.

Jewish people have been anticipating for thousands of years that the Mashiach, the Anointed One, the Christ, would be brought forth through a woman. She is the one that will bring light into the darkness, birth forth the HOPE into the World. Every Shabbat, a woman is the one, not a man, lighting the Shabbat candles as a weekly reminder of that Truth. No matter her previous background, Jew or gentile, The LORD, through

His Word, has every intention to honor the significance of a woman's role in His Eternal Story.

Let's pray:

**Our Father in Heaven** אבינו שבשמימ,

Thank You for every good thing that You bring forth that provides hope and new beginnings. Even through adversity, help us know your compassion and mercy in our midst. LORD, we ask You to open our eyes to see and process lessons You are teaching in the "waiting." Like in this Torah Portion's "full month," we do not make hasty decisions based on fleshly desires, but we decree and declare daily, "You will be done, Your Kingdom come on earth as it is in heaven." No matter man, woman, Jew or gentile, show us how to embrace the individuals that you've made us to be, for the greater purposes of Your Master Plan that Father, You will be glorified in all we do.

B'Shem Yeshua HaMashiach בשם ישוע המשיח.

In Jesus' Name we pray. Amen.

# 44. TORAH TASTING

## *REFLECTION*

1. What is the word, picture or theme the LORD is highlighting to you in this chapter and Torah Portion?

2. Have you ever had to wait for a period of time for something you so desired to have? After the waiting time, did it change your desire for it?

3. The Torah Portion shows how GOD can bring forth hope and good things through difficult times, even amazing things, through 2 ordinary women like Tamar and Ruth. What are other examples you have seen, heard, or experienced that good things were brought forth from painful and challenging times?

# 45 מה
## ki tavo
## (When You Come In)
כי תבוא

Deuteronomy 26:1-29:8

Isaiah 60:1-22

Matthew 4:13-24

*This week's parasha is titled "When you come in", named after its first verse. And it shall be, <u>when you come into</u> the land which the Lord your God is giving you as an inheritance, and you possess it and dwell in it…*
**Deuteronomy 26:1**

This Torah Portion opens with the LORD's instructions to His Children, spoken through Moses, what they are to do when they enter the Promise Land. The instructions include the First Fruits offering, inscribing GOD's laws on stones and building an altar. Also, the twelve curses mentioned, as well as blessings and curses, are consequences of obedience and disobedience, respectively. Lastly, in Moab, the covenant between the LORD and His people was renewed.

The Hebrew root for תבוא Tavo in this Portion's Ki Tavo is בוא Bo Come. בוא Bo Come is made up of 3 Hebrew alphabets:

- ב Bet — House
- ו Vav — Secure, Add
- א Aleph — A silent alphabet representing GOD and His strength.

The word בוא Bo Come gives us a word picture that "In the House of the LORD, we are secure and safe". The LORD's words "When you come in…" sounds to me as He is already there and has prepared everything for His people. He didn't say when you go there, He said, "When you come in". When someone opens the door and says, "Come in…", that usually means that person was already inside there, inviting you to come in. "Come in" sounds so inviting and warm. You need not to fear. GOD opens this Parasha inviting the Children of Israel to come into the Promise Land without fear. Their "coming in" to the Promise Land will find REST and SAFETY in the LORD when they obey His instructions.

> *This day the Lord your God commands you to observe these statutes and judgments; therefore you shall be careful to observe them <u>with all your heart and with all your soul.</u>*
> **Deuteronomy 26:16**

This verse reminds us of the V'Ahavta ("And you shall love"), as part of the SHEMA, the central creed of the Torah, the Jewish faith.

> *"Hear, O Israel: The Lord our God, the Lord is one! <u>You shall love the Lord your God</u> with all your heart, with all your soul, and with all your strength.*
> **Deuteronomy 6:4-5**

V'Ahavta commands, "You shall love the LORD with <u>all your heart</u>, <u>all our soul</u> and <u>all your strength</u>", and in this Parasha, we see "all your heart" and "all your soul" in Deuteronomy 26, however, "all your strength" is missing.

## 45. KI TAVO / WHEN YOU COME IN

But wait...

Coincidentally, the word בוא Bo Come appears 15 times in this Parasha. 15 is the number for יה Yah (the number for י Yod is 10 and ה Hey is 5) — יה Yah is one of the names of GOD.

The first time יה Yah appears in the Torah is in the beginning of the Song of Moses.

> "*The Lord (יה Yah) is my strength and my defense;*
> *he has become my salvation.*
> *He is my God, and I will praise him,*
> *my father's God, and I will exalt him.*
> **Exodus 15:2**

This verse echoes the theme יה Yah the LORD's provision and His salvation in this Torah Portion, and we are to praise and rejoice in Him. The LORD is my STRENGTH! He commanded us to observe the law with all our heart and all our soul, AND <u>He is our Strength</u>, the strength that we need to do the statutes. Not all by our own strength, but GOD and His strength is with us, and it is here to help us!

Isn't that amazing?!

**Read the following verses to see what they remind you of —**

> *That you shall <u>take some of the first of all the produce</u> of the ground, which you shall bring from your land that the Lord your God is giving you, <u>and put it in a basket</u> and go to the place where the Lord your God chooses to make His name abide.* ³ *And you shall go to the one who is priest in those days, and say to him, 'I declare today to the Lord your God that I have come to the country which the Lord swore to our fathers to give us.'.…* ⁸ *So the Lord brought us out of Egypt with a mighty hand and with an outstretched arm, with great terror and with signs and wonders.* ⁹ *He has brought us to this place and has given us this land, "a land flowing with milk and honey";* ¹⁰ *and now, behold, I have <u>brought the first fruits of the land which you, O Lord, have given me.</u>' "Then <u>you shall set it before the Lord your God,</u> and <u>worship (bow down)</u> before the Lord your God.* ¹¹ *So <u>you shall rejoice in every good thing which the Lord your God has given to you and your house,</u> you and the Levite and the stranger who is among you.*
> **Deuteronomy 26:2-3, 8-11**

This looks like a scene from America, our Nation's first Thanksgiving meal of the Pilgrims after the tumultuous trans-Atlantic travels, harsh winter, farming in the new land, in the fulfillment of the "Promise Land" and religious freedom the LORD had promised to them. Much like the Pilgrims, the Children of Israel had their own version of a Thanksgiving meal.

Israel's first fruits offering of thanksgiving and joy is mentioned before the guarantee of blessings as a consequence of obeying GOD's law. With thankful hearts, we acknowledge that all that we have comes from the LORD. We are grateful and want to do His will for we trust Him with our lives. Anything and everything we have is because of GOD's love, faithfulness, and mercy. We don't feel any sense of entitlement or pride from what is given to us, earthly possessions, health, relationships, safety from harm, …. Do you give thanks before seeing GOD's fulfillment of promise?

Another evident common denominator of both Thanksgivings, the Pilgrims' and the Israelites', is enjoying a meal in the Presence of the LORD. Food is created for our nourishment and enjoyment. Many offerings and sacrifices to the LORD are to be eaten by His beloved children. Our Father in Heaven wants us to enjoy food with Him and taste His goodness.

My husband, Paul, loves a good peach. He says when he takes a bite into a perfectly ripened peach at that perfect time, he closes his eyes and takes in the sweetness of the fruit with gratitude for GOD's goodness. That's what a perfect peach does to his soul. I believe GOD delights in family and friends "breaking bread" and sharing a meal together while grateful hearts unite together and honor The LORD The Provider. Many cultures have their own unique cuisines highlighting their heritage and geographic advantages with the types of meat and plants.

> *Go, eat your bread with joy,*
> *And drink your wine with a merry heart;*
> *For God has already accepted your works.*
> **Ecclesiastes 9:7**

As a Chinese, I know a thing or two about gathering around a table filled with mouth-watering food with family for special occasions like Grandma's birthdays and Chinese New Year's. From delicately steamed fish from right out of a fish tank, a freshly cooked whole chicken bought from the chicken farmer on the same day, to green vegetables plucked moments before stir-fried with garlic and ginger in the wok, just to name a few simple and yet scrumptious dishes I am familiar with.

Fond memories and conversations are remembered for those family times. The Biblical Feasts of the LORD calls for sharing meals together with loved ones. Jewish people around the world celebrate Holy Days like Passover and Sukkot annually with food like Matzah Ball soup and Gefilte fish for Ashkenazi families. There is a popular saying among Jews regarding these Feasts, "The enemy tried to kill us. We won. Let's eat!" This pretty much sums up every Holy Day, except for Yom Kippur, Day of Atonement (a 24-hour fast is called). We give thanks for the gift of GOD's provision in our physical and spiritual needs, as well as relationships and health. The peace and joy associated with being together and tasting the goodness of a meal is not ever to be underestimated!

Humility is a close friend to Gratitude, knowing "Apart from GOD, I can do nothing" (John 15:5).

Here is a story of the 10 lepers that Yeshua Jesus healed in the Book of Luke —

> *[11]* Now it happened as He went to Jerusalem that He passed through the midst of Samaria and Galilee. *[12]* Then as He entered a certain village, there met Him ten men who were lepers, who stood afar off. *[13]* And they lifted up their voices and said, "Jesus, Master, have mercy on us!" *[14]* So when He saw them, He said to them, "Go, show yourselves to the priests." And so it was that as they went, they were cleansed. *[15]* <u>And one of them, when he saw that **he was healed**, returned, and with a loud voice glorified God, *[16]* and fell down on his face at His feet, giving Him thanks. And he was a Samaritan. *[17]* So Jesus answered and said, "Were there not ten cleansed? But where are the nine? *[18]*</u> Were there not any found who returned to give glory to God except this foreigner?"
> *[19]* And He said to him, <u>"Arise, go your way. Your faith has made you well (saved you/rescued you)."</u>
> Luke 17:11-19

Ten lepers were healed, but only one returned to glorify and give thanks to the LORD. I could see how humble and thankful this healed leper must have been, falling down on his face at the feet of His Healer that he came all the way back to Yeshua Jesus and glorified the LORD. I am going to speculate here that Yeshua Jesus's words to the former leper, "Arise, go your way. Your faith has made well," not only was he telling him to get up off the ground physically, but he sent him off with a blessing. "Arise" as that he was no longer oppressed by the life-debilitating disease. He can go his way, on the path of living his life to the full that the Anointed One had set him free to live. His faith in the LORD has made him well.

Life is good because GOD's goodness is displayed in and through his life from this day forward.

You see how his return of Thanksgiving and Joy had him leaving with a tremendous and unexpected gift of the blessing of the Healer! I believe the LORD delights in our thankful hearts, reciprocating our love to His.

One more thing...

This scripture of the Thankful Leper had Yeshua Jesus telling him, "Arise.." Coincidentally, the Haftorah for this Torah Portion is Isaiah 60 which begins with —

> *<u>Arise</u>, shine;*
> *For your light has come!*
> *And the glory of the Lord is risen upon you.*
> *For behold, the darkness shall cover the earth,*
> *And deep darkness the people;*
> *But <u>the Lord will arise over you,</u>*
> *And His glory will be seen upon you.*
> *³ <u>The Gentiles shall come to your light,</u>*
> *<u>And kings to the brightness of your rising.</u>*
> **Isaiah 60:1-3**

Indeed, the Glory of the LORD was rising over the Thankful Leper. Those 9 lepers, who had not returned to see Yeshua Jesus, had no idea the tremendous blessing they were missing. The Glory of GOD over the Thankful Leper would no doubt draw many to see his testimony of GOD's goodness and be transformed by His Light!

My sister and I grew up thanking our mother for everything. We told her thanks for taking us for a nice meal, for clothing us, for providing us shelter.... Although it is a mother's duty to provide food for her children, but our mother treated us with many nice things, not out of obligation but with love. As a single mom, she juggled different jobs and businesses, often away from home to provide for us. She never complained about how hard she worked. She did not have to treat us to high-end restaurant dinners and or take us on trips to experience the good things in life. Nonetheless, she did it because she wanted us to enjoy the fruits of her hard work. It brings her joy to bless us to know the good things available to us. She did not ask us to get a job to help out the family during school as she did as a child so that we could focus on our education. Never once she shared her struggles with us until we became adults and later found out about some of the hardships she went through to get us through school. We were always thankful to her and never took things for granted. We became the persons we are today because of our mother's love. My husband and I teach our kids to be grateful for everything. They are respectful and grateful when someone does anything for them, small or big. One time we stopped to get a quick bite to eat at a fast-food restaurant. Our children went inside ahead of us to place their orders. When Paul and I walked in, the manager could not stop raving about how polite and respectful our children were. After getting our food, we got into our car and asked Matthew and Mollie what they had done that the manager was so impressed. They said they talked to him respectfully and said "Thank You" when he gave them the food. Even though the manager gets paid for doing his job, but a little respect and appreciation from customers can really bring the blessing of joy.

You never know how big the impact is of the small things we do and say in our daily life.

Many years ago, I had a friend repeating a quote, "Thankful people are never depressed". Indeed, I believe we have seen even in this Parasha that joy and thanksgiving go hand-in-hand.

This Torah Portion lists 10 specific blessings if we obey the voice of the LORD and do His Commandments. Interesting GOD gave the <u>Ten Commandments</u> on Mt. Sinai, and here He stated <u>10 blessings</u>:

# 45. KI TAVO / WHEN YOU COME IN

"Now it shall come to pass, if you diligently obey the voice of the Lord your God, to observe carefully all His commandments which I command you today, that the Lord your God will set you high above all nations of the earth.
² And all these blessings shall <u>come upon you and overtake (catch up, suddenly, unexpectantly) you, because you obey the voice of the Lord your God</u>:

1. ³ "Blessed (ברך Barach) shall you be in the city, and blessed shall you be in the country (field, land).
2. ⁴ "Blessed (ברך Barach) shall be the fruit of your body, the produce of your ground and the increase of your herds, the increase of your cattle and the offspring of your flocks.
3. ⁵ "Blessed (ברך Barach) shall be your basket and your kneading bowl.
4. ⁶ "Blessed (ברך Barach) shall you be <u>when you come in</u>, and blessed (ברך Barach) shall you be <u>when you go out</u>.
5. ⁷ "The Lord will cause your enemies who rise against you to be defeated before your face; they shall come out against you one way and flee before you seven ways.
6. ⁸ "The Lord will command the blessing (ברך Barach) on you in your storehouses and in all to which you set your hand, and He will bless (ברך Barach) you in the land which the Lord your God is giving you.
7. ⁹ "The Lord will establish you as a holy people to Himself, just as He has sworn to you if you keep the commandments of the Lord your God and walk in His ways. ¹⁰ Then all peoples of the earth shall see that you are called by the name of the Lord, and they shall be afraid of you.
8. ¹¹ And the Lord will grant you plenty of goods, in the fruit of your body, in the increase of your livestock, and in the produce of your ground, in the land of which the Lord swore to your fathers to give you.
9. ¹² The Lord will open to you His good treasure, the heavens, to give the rain to your land in its season, and to bless (ברך Barach) all the work of your hand. You shall lend to many nations, but you shall not borrow.

10. *¹³ And the Lord will make you the head and not the tail; you shall be above only, and not be beneath,*

*If you heed the commandments of the Lord your God, which I command you today, and are careful to observe them. ¹⁴ So you shall not turn aside from any of the words which I command you this day, to the right or the left, to go after other gods to serve them.*
**Deuteronomy 28:1-14**

A few things to note in the "10 Blessings" verses:

The Hebrew root ברך Barach was used 8 times. 8 signifies new beginnings. There were 8 people on Noah's Ark. There are 7 days in a week, the 8th one starts a new week.

As the Israelites were about to enter this land the LORD had promised them. GOD gave them the key to His 10 blessings in their new season. These 10 blessings cover every provision anyone would ever need, physical needs, safety, peace, victory, protection from harm, fertility for posterity, .... . All they needed to do is to follow GOD's commandments.

These blessings will "overtake" you when you obey the LORD is a strong sense that they will chase after you suddenly and unexpectedly. We do not do what is right to gain something with GOD, but out of our devotion toward Him, so we expect nothing back because He has first loved us.

I like the visual of blessings chasing after us and overtaking us. How incredible are the promises of GOD when we believe and follow His Word!

Giving thanks for GOD's goodness and rejoicing in Him is seen throughout GOD's Word.

*<u>Give thanks</u> to the Lord, for **he is good**.*
*His love endures forever.*
**Psalm 136:1**

> *Enter into His gates with <u>thanksgiving</u>,*
> *And into His courts with praise.*
> *<u>Be thankful</u> to Him, and bless His name.*
> *⁵ For the Lord is good;*
> *His mercy is everlasting,*
> *And His truth endures to all generations.*
> **Psalm 100:5**

The LORD is good, and He gives good things to those who seek Him.

> *The young lions lack and suffer hunger; But those who seek the Lord*
> *<u>shall not lack any good thing</u>.*
> **Psalm 34:10**

> *<u>Every good gift and every perfect gift is from above</u>, and comes down*
> *from the Father of lights, with whom there is no variation or shadow*
> *of turning.*
> **James 1:17**

There is a Hebrew song (taken from Psalm 136:1-3) that every time I sing it, I feel an overwhelming sense of peace and gratitude. It soothes my soul to meditate on the goodness of GOD.

| Hodu L'Adonai ki tov | Give thanks to the LORD for He is good | הודו ליהוה כי טוב |
|---|---|---|
| Ki l'olam Chasdo | For His mercy is forever | כי לעולם כסדו |
| Hodu l'Adonai ki tov | Give thanks to the LORD for He is good | הודו ליהוה כי טוב |
| Ki l'olam Chasdo | For His mercy is forever | כי לעולם כסדו |
| Hodu Hodu Hodu Hodu | Give thanks, Give thanks, Give thanks, Give thanks | |
| Hodu l'Adonai ki tov | Give thanks to the LORD for He is good | |

There is a sentiment of contentment and peace that comes with thanksgiving. That joy and thanksgiving celebrating GOD's goodness in His Presence is powerful!

Blessing #4 of Deuteronomy 28:6 touches me the most because I have a plaque of this particular verse hung on the wall by our front door, "**Blessed** (ברך Barach) shall you be <u>when you come in</u> and blessed (ברך Barach) shall you be <u>when you go out</u>." It echoes the Parasha title of last week Ki Tetze, "When you go out," and this week Ki Tavo, "When you come in", sort of like this week is a sequel. As we discussed last week, how Ki Tetze alludes to hope and new life, this week, Ki Tavo mirrors new beginnings and joy.

Parashat Ki Tetze shows "When you go out," victory is delivered from the LORD, you will find peace from the aftermath of the chaos of war; and Parashat Ki Tavo gives the visual "When You Come In" to the place GOD has already prepared with abundant provision, you are to give thanks and rejoice in the blessings promised by GOD for our obedience to His instructions. He is with us when we go out. He is with us when we come in. The LORD is with us and will never leave nor forsake us in every situation and at all times. The LORD is good, and His goodness is forever.

## 45. KI TAVO / WHEN YOU COME IN

Let's pray:

**Our Father in Heaven** אבינו שבשמימ,

We thank You for the fulfillment of your promises beyond our eyes can see. Thank You for showing the power of a thankful heart. We humble ourselves and acknowledge that You are LORD and King of the universe in everything that we do. We have every good blessing, physical and spiritual because You are good. We can do nothing apart from you, but we thank You that we can do all things through Yeshua HaMashiach, who gives us strength. Help us rejoice in Your goodness and declare Your greatness in every situation.

B'Shem Yeshua HaMashiach בשם ישוע המשיח.

In Jesus' Name we pray. Amen.

# 45. TORAH TASTING

## *REFLECTION*

1. What is the word, picture or theme the LORD is highlighting to you in this chapter and Torah Portion?

2. Does the Thanksgiving theme in the Torah Portion remind you of any childhood or past pleasant memories of family and friends gathering together? What are some of your favorite dishes that remind you of those times?

3. Thanksgiving and joy go hand-in-hand. You want more joy? Then, find things you are grateful for and give thanks. What are you thankful for today? Who would you like to call, write to, or tell that you are thankful for them and why?

# 46 מו
# nitzavim
## (Stand)
נצבימ

Deuteronomy 29:9-30:20

Isaiah 61:10-63:9

John 12:41-50

This week's Torah Portion is titled Nitzavim Stand, drawn from one of the words in the beginning of the portion.

*All of you <u>stand (יצב Yatzav)</u> today before the Lord your God: your leaders and your tribes and your elders and your officers, all the men of Israel, ... that you may <u>enter into (עבר Cross over/Pass over)</u> covenant with the Lord your God, and into His oath, which the Lord your God makes with you today,*
**Deuteronomy 29:10,12**

Moses spoke to the Israelites, "All of you stand…" for the solemn sworn covenant.

It may sound silly, but what other posture would they be in? Were there chairs? I suppose they could have all grabbed a rock and sat or just squatted but not likely.

However, all joking aside, people usually stand when taking an oath, getting sworn into office. It is like an exchange that they accept the responsibility of becoming an elected official, and at the same time, promise to uphold the Constitution and the law. I cannot imagine someone sworn into office sitting (unless due to special circumstance), can you?

There is a very solemn sentiment reading the first few verses in this portion. Can you imagine hearing a pin drop during Moses' speech? They were all standing, participating in a historic event… together… in unity… at the end of a very, very, long journey.

> *…That He may establish you today as a people for Himself, and that He may be God to you, just as He has spoken to you, and just as He has sworn to your fathers, to Abraham, Isaac, and Jacob.*
> **Deuteronomy 29:13**

The Children of Israel are about to enter into this covenant and into an oath made with the LORD. They stand witnessing the fulfillment of GOD's promises to their forefathers. Can you fathom the overwhelming emotions?

> *…"I make this covenant and this oath, not with you (plural, you all) alone,* [15] *but <u>with him who stands here with us today</u> before the Lord our God, as well as <u>with him who is not here with us today</u>.*
> **Deuteronomy 29:14-15**

This verse is a little interesting…

Did you catch that? They are making this covenant… with him who stands here with us today… and with him who is not here with us today. The phrase "with him who stands here with us" represents a united group of people, and "with him who is not here with us" in singular form as a united body as well. Nonetheless, they are all part of this sworn covenant. So, who was not there? Those who could not come that day? Sure. Perhaps those who have passed on before them and the future generations? I think so. This covenant includes everyone.

"Your little ones and your wives — also the stranger who is in your camp, from the one who cuts your wood to the one who draws your water" in Deuteronomy 29:11, past and future generations as witnesses. You and I and our future generations reading this, as if we are participating in this historic event, are all included in this covenant too!

Deuteronomy 29:12 really caught my attention —

> "You may <u>enter into (Avar עבר Cross over/Pass over)</u> covenant with the Lord your God."

<u>Avar עבר Cross over/Pass over</u> is used in the context of entering into a covenant with GOD. Where have we seen this before?

> *Now when the sun was going down, **a deep sleep** (תרדמה **Tardem**) fell upon Abram; and behold, horror and great darkness fell upon him. <sup>13</sup> Then He said to Abram: "Know certainly that your descendants will be <u>strangers in a land that is not theirs</u>, and will serve them, and they will afflict them <u>four hundred years</u>. <sup>14</sup> And also the nation whom they serve I will judge; afterward they shall come out with great possessions. <sup>15</sup> Now as for you, you shall go to your fathers in peace; you shall be buried at a good old age. <sup>16</sup> But in the fourth generation they shall return here, for the iniquity of the Amorites is not yet complete."*
> *And it came to pass, when the sun went down and it was dark, that behold, there appeared a smoking oven and a burning torch that **passed between** (עבר **Avar**) those pieces.*
> *<sup>18</sup> On the same day **the Lord made a covenant with Abram**, saying, "To your descendants I have given this land, from the river of Egypt to the great river, the River Euphrates — <sup>19</sup> the Kenites, the Kenezzites, the Kadmonites, <sup>20</sup> the Hittites, the Perizzites, the Rephaim, <sup>21</sup> the Amorites, the Canaanites, the Girgashites, and the Jebusites."*
> **Genesis 15:12-21**

Is it a coincidence that Nitzavim Torah Portion's opening phrase the verse "You may <u>**enter into (Avar** עבר **Cross over/Pass over)**,</u> somehow reflects and fulfills the covenant the Lord made with Abraham? I think not. There is no Mere Coincidence, only Divine Providence. The Genesis verses display the LORD's prophecy to Abram while he was in a deep sleep, that his descendants would be in slavery for 400 years and they would return here into this land promised to him after 4 generations!!!

This Parasha truly is GOD's Epic Promises-Made-Promises-Kept moment right before the Israelites' eyes!

Another significant covenant the LORD established while someone was in a deep sleep was with Adam.

## 46. NITZVAIM / STAND

> *And the Lord God caused **a deep sleep** (תרדמה Tardem) to fall on Adam, and he slept; and He took one of his ribs, and closed up the flesh in its place. ²² Then the rib which the Lord God had taken from man He made into a woman, and He brought her to the man.*
> **Genesis 2:21-22**

תרדמה Tardemah Deep Sleep is only used twice in the Torah (the 5 Books of Moses), referring to Adam, with his rib the LORD made his wife Eve establishing the marriage covenant, and to Abram, the covenant was established that the LORD would be his GOD. The first 2 covenants GOD established with man happened during their deep sleep. Their part was to receive.

During deep sleep, we are in complete rest mode. Rest and receive GOD's goodness and faithfulness is our part too when it comes to GOD's covenant with us.

Furthermore, the exact phrase, "enter into a covenant לעברך בברית L'Avrecha Bivrit (Hebrew root of עבר **Avar** Cross Over/Pass Over & **Brit** ברית Covenant)" is only used ONCE in the entire Torah. That is right here in this Parashat Nitzavim. I think it calls for some serious attention. The Abrahamic Covenant is being fulfilled in this Parasha in magnificent ways. The LORD foretold to Abram that his descendants would be enslaved, but He would deliver them bringing them to the land promised to Abraham.

> *For **I will pass through** (עבר Avar) the land of Egypt on that night, and will strike all the firstborn in the land of Egypt, both man and beast; and against all the gods of Egypt I will execute judgment: I am the Lord. ¹³ Now the blood shall be a sign for you on the houses where you are. And when I see the blood, I will **pass over** (עבר Avar) you; and the plague shall not be on you to destroy you when I strike the land of Egypt.*
> **Genesis 12:12-13**

Just as the LORD "passed through" (עבר **Avar**) when establishing the covenant with Abram while he was in a deep sleep resting, GOD also brought salvation and deliverance to Abram's descendants, fulfilling the promises by He Himself passing over (עבר **Avar**) while they rested inside their own homes feasting on GOD's provision. They rested and received GOD's salvation.

The connection of GOD's Promises-Made-Promise-Kept between the Abrahamic Covenant in Genesis 15 and its fulfillment in Deuteronomy 29 just keeps on going...

The first man ever called a Hebrew (עברית Ivrit, its Hebrew root is עבר Avar) is...

> *A man who had escaped came and reported this to **Abram the Hebrew** (עברית Ivrit). Now Abram was living near the great trees of Mamre the Amorite, a brother of Eshkol and Aner, all of whom were allied with Abram.*
> **Genesis 14:13**

After Abram's nephew Lot had been captured along with his possessions, Abram was notified of the incident. He was referred to as a "Hebrew." Hebrew (עברית Ivrit, its Hebrew root is עבר Avar) means Cross over or עבר Ever/Eber also means region beyond, or he is someone from a region beyond. Nonetheless, Abraham's faith in GOD made him a Hebrew, a "Crossed-Over." He left all that was familiar to him to a land he was called to go, simply to be obedient to the One True GOD!

The second person with that same title referenced is Joseph when he was wrongly accused by Potiphar's wife for assault after being sold into slavery.

> *[14] she called her household servants. "Look," she said to them, "**this Hebrew** (עברית Ivrit) (Joseph) has been brought to us to make sport of us! He came in here to sleep with me, but I screamed...*
> **Genesis 39:14**

And then, we are told that Joseph was taken from "the land of the Hebrews."

*But when all goes well with you, remember me and show me kindness; mention me to Pharaoh and get me out of this prison.* $^{15}$ *I (Joseph) was forcibly carried off from* **the land of the Hebrews (**עברית *Ivrit*)*, and even here I have done nothing to deserve being put in a dungeon."*
**Genesis 40:15**

Looks like between Abram being the first Hebrew to his descendants, growing to be lots of "the Hebrews" is 2 generations, from Abraham, Isaac to Jacob, Joseph's being Jacob's son.

*Therefore, <u>the promise comes by faith</u>, so that it may be by grace and may be guaranteed to all Abraham's offspring — not only to those who are of the law but also to those who have the faith of Abraham. He is the father of us all.*
**Romans 4:16**

*So also <u>Abraham "believed God,</u> and it was credited to him as righteousness. Understand, then, that <u>those who have faith are children of Abraham</u>. Scripture foresaw that God would justify the Gentiles by faith, and announced the gospel in advance to Abraham: "All nations will be blessed through you." So those who rely on faith are blessed along with Abraham, the man of faith.*
**Galatians 4:6-9**

If Abraham became a Hebrew by believing in GOD, then the LORD provided a way for us to be Abraham's children and partake in the promises of Abraham too.

What is amazing is that the LORD is the One first "pass through/cross over" in Genesis 15:17, "a burning torch that **passed between (**עבר *Avar***)** those pieces," establishing the covenant with Abram.

עבר Avar Pass over/Cross over is made of 2 components —

- ע Ayin — Eye
- בר Bar — Son

You can say crossing over in faith means seeing and believing in the Son (the Son of GOD as the Messiah/Mashiach). My husband, Paul, was raised an Orthodox Jew in New York. Years later, he accepted Yeshua Jesus as His LORD and Mashiach, acknowledging Him as the Jewish long-anticipated Mashiach, the Anointed One. Whenever a Christian says to him, "Congratulations, now you've converted." Paul's reply would be, "No, I didn't convert. You did. Yeshua was a Jewish Rabbi, and I am a Jew that follows the Jewish Mashiach. You've 'converted,' You've crossed over as a Hebrew."

What an enlightening concept!

Being a Hebrew is to Enter into Covenant / Crossing over GOD's Covenant, Abraham the Hebrew is accounted to be righteous because he believed GOD.

Are you a "Crossed-Over" Hebrew? Do you too follow our forefather Abraham's righteous footstep and believe in the One True GOD?

עברית Ivrit Hebrew can mean the Hebrew people or the Hebrew language.

**The word עברית Ivrit Hebrew (people and the language) is made up of 2 components-**

- ע Ayin — Eye/see
- ברית Brit — Covenant.

As someone who believes in GOD, crossed over can "See the Covenant."

Isn't that Good News to know that when we "cross over" and believe in the LORD, trusting in Him alone, we can see The Covenant? Would it be possible that Abraham saw the promises of GOD in GOD's prophetic word for him and his descendants when he was called a Hebrew? I believe so.

We see how "the LORD's Word never returns void" demonstrated in the word עבר **Avar Pass Over/Cross**. GOD made the covenant with Abram by Himself passing through עבר **Avar,** the meat of sacrifice. Abraham answered the LORD's call by crossing over עבר **Avar,** becoming a Hebrew, he believed GOD. The LORD passed over עבר **Avar** the homes with the Blood of the lamb and brought deliverance for Abraham's descendants, fulfilling His Covenant promises. Israel then crossed over עבר **Avar** and entered into the Promise Land, witnessing the fulfillment of GOD's promise to Abraham. In order to enter into the Promise Land seeing GOD's promises in our lives, we too have to say yes in faith like our forefather Abraham did. We too, have to do our part to cross over spiritually, receiving salvation by seeing the Son of GOD as our LORD.

*The secret things belong to the Lord our God, but those things which are revealed belong to us and to our children forever, that we may do all the words of this law.*
**Deuteronomy 29:29**

This is one of my favorite verses. I love secret things, don't you? Knowledge that only a few chosen have the privilege to possess. I even have these verses in Hebrew on my phone wallpaper. This verse is tucked in between Deuteronomy 29's curses and blessings verses laid out by the LORD for us to choose. I believe choosing the LORD and following Him will unlock the mystery things and secret things to be revealed to us. They would belong to us and our children forever as inheritance enabling us to do His law.

Wow! We are all curious to know a secret, especially those that belong to GOD. We have a Mighty GOD that is ready to impart and entrust His secrets with us. There are times that the LORD gave me a glimpse of a secret thing through a dream or a sign that He later confirmed, and I would stand in awe of His goodness and in humility that He would share that with me.

Are you ready to have secret things revealed to you? Get ready because that's the LORD's desire too. That is how much He loves you.

Stand (Hebrew root: יצב Yatzav) …

> *¹³ And Moses said to the people, "Do not be afraid. Stand still, and see the salvation of the Lord, which He will accomplish for you today. For the Egyptians whom you see today, you shall see again no more forever. ¹⁴ The Lord will fight for you, and you shall hold your peace."*
> **Exodus 14:13-14**

At the edge of the Red Sea, with the Egyptian army drawing near, Moses encouraged the Children of Israel not to be afraid, **stand still (יצי Yatzav)** and see the salvation of the LORD.

Going back to the name of this Parasha, Stand. We are reminded who is Our Provider, Our Defender, Our Deliverer, … . Adam and Abram rested to receive GOD's gifts of covenants for them, and they stood to see the fulfillment.

GOD kept a 400-year promise to Abraham and fulfilled it. As witnesses to that fulfillment, we know He is faithful to keep His promises to us too.

How reassuring is that to us?

The opening scene of this Torah Portion is Moses speaking to all those who were about to enter into the promise, preparing them to enter into the solemn covenant with the LORD.

> *¹² That you may enter into covenant with the Lord your God, and into His oath, which the Lord your God makes with you today, ¹³ that <u>He may establish you today as a people for Himself</u>, and that <u>He may be God to you</u>, just as He has spoken to you, and just as He has sworn to your fathers, to Abraham, Isaac, and Jacob.*
> **Deuteronomy 29:12-13**

## 46. NITZVAIM / STAND

This is a "déjà vu" moment from another episode in the Torah earlier:

> *I will take you as My people, and I will be your God. Then you shall know that I am the Lord your God who brings you out from under the burdens of the Egyptians.*
> **Exodus 6:7**

At Mt. Sinai, there was a vow exchange between the LORD and Israel that likens a wedding ceremony.

> *Now therefore, if you will indeed obey My voice and keep My covenant, then you shall be a special treasure to Me above all people; for all the earth is Mine...*
> *So Moses came and told the people all the words of the Lord and all the judgments. And all the people answered with one voice and said, "All the words which the Lord has said we will do."...*
> *Now the glory of the Lord rested on Mount Sinai, and the cloud covered it six days. And on the seventh day He called to Moses out of the midst of the cloud. ¹⁷ The sight of the glory of the Lord was like a consuming fire on the top of the mountain in the eyes of the children of Israel.*
> **Exodus 19:5, 24:3,16**

If Exodus 19-24 was the wedding ceremony, then Deuteronomy 29 would be a vow renewal. It is a sworn covenant they are entering into with the LORD before the Promise Land entry. They are saying "I do" again. Abraham chose GOD, he crossed over. He became a Hebrew. I can choose GOD and be a Hebrew. We are children of Abraham. We are Hebrews by faith. Every morning upon awakening, we can proclaim to the LORD, "I choose you. You are still the One I love. I will follow You. I will trust You." It is like renewing a wedding vow with the One you love.

**The chorus of a pop ballad "Still The One" by Shania Twain goes like this:**

You're still the one I run to
The one that I belong to
You're still the one I want for life
You're still the one
You're still the one that I love

Imagine singing to GOD professing your love in response to His never-failing love for you... Just rest in the goodness and faithfulness provided by the LORD's covenant. Then, stand and see His salvation, deliverance, and fulfillment of His promises. Trust in Him as He reveals to us the secret things that we get to possess with our children forever.

Rest and stand!

Let's pray:

> **Our Father in Heaven אבינו שבשמימ,**
>
> We are thankful that You are a covenant-making and covenant-keeping GOD. You are faithful to Your Word. You have demonstrated to us how You kept the 400-year promise to Abraham and his children and their children. You are still keeping many promises today. Your Word never fails. We need only to rest in Your goodness and then stand and see Your faithfulness manifested. LORD, please teach us to be still and steadfast in our faith in You. We are Hebrews, sons and daughters of Abraham, seeing The Ultimate Covenant You have kept through the Son of GOD, the Mashiach sent to us. We believe in You and Your Word. We trust in You wherever You call us to go and the good things prepared for us. Thank You!
>
> B'Shem Yeshua HaMashiach בשם ישוע המשיח.
>
> In Jesus' Name we pray. Amen.

# 46. TORAH TASTING
## *REFLECTION*

1. What is the word, picture or theme the LORD is highlighting to you in this chapter and Torah Portion?

2. GOD established his covenant with Abram through passing through the sacrifice; Abram accepted the covenant as a Hebrew crossing over in faith, believing in GOD. Do you remember the moment when you received the LORD as your GOD that you too became a Hebrew in faith? If you have not done that before, would you like to receive Him as GOD over your life, acknowledging that He alone is your Provider, Protector, Deliverer and Savior in Yeshua Jesus?

3. If so, please see the Salvation Prayer at the end of this book.

4. Exodus 14:13 says, "Do not be afraid. stand still, and see the salvation of the LORD" The opposite of being afraid is standing still in faith and confidence. Standing still requires staying alert to fight off the enemies' scare tactics. What are you standing still to see GOD's salvation for in this season? Each morning, how do you remind yourself of GOD's steadfast love for you?

# 47 מז
# vayelech
## (And He Went)
## וילך

Deuteronomy 30:1-31:30

Isaiah 55:6-56:8

Matthew 21:9-17

This week's Torah Portion is Vayelech meaning, "And he went," drawn from its first verse, "And Moses went…". This Parasha is the whole chapter of Deuteronomy 31, comparably shorter than most other chapters. It covers the commissioning of Joshua as Moses' successor in leading GOD's Children into the Promise Land, the commandment of the Law to be read every 7 years, the finale of Moses' farewell speech and the Song of Moses being written and read.

The phrase "And he went and spoke these words to all Israel" connects the end of Parashat Nitzvaim from last week —

> *"I have set before you life and death, blessing and cursing; therefore choose life, that both you and your descendants may live, that you may love the Lord your God, that you may obey His voice, and that you may cling to Him, for He is your life and the length of your days; and that you may dwell in the land which the Lord swore to your fathers, to Abraham, Isaac, and Jacob, to give them."*
> **Deuteronomy 30:19-20**

and the beginning of Parashat Vayelech from this week —

> *"Joshua himself crosses over before you, just as the Lord has said. Be strong and of good courage, do not fear nor be afraid of them; for the Lord your God, He is the One who goes with you. He will not leave you nor forsake you."*
> **Deuteronomy 31:3,6**

From one promise GOD would fulfill to another that GOD will faithfully keep, that is GOD's heart for His people, regardless of what they choose to do. The LORD, our GOD, stays truthful and faithful.

Right now, we are feeling a little relief from the scorching Texas heat as the season of Fall is approaching. The anticipation of the High Holy days of Rosh Hashana (Feast of Trumpets/Jewish New Year), Yom Kippur (Day of Atonement) and Sukkot (Feast of Tabernacles/Feast of Booths) is the in the atmosphere. In a couple of weeks, we will be observing Sukkot this year (2021) in a Sabbatical year (שנת השמטה Sh'net Shemitah). It is timely that this Parasha covers GOD's commandment of reading the Law at Sukkot.

⁹ *So Moses wrote this law and delivered it to the priests, the sons of Levi, who bore the ark of the covenant of the Lord, and to all the elders of Israel. And Moses commanded them, saying: "At the end of every seven years, at the appointed time in the year of release (שנת השמטה Sh'net Shemitah), at the Feast of Tabernacles,* ¹¹ *when all Israel comes to appear before the Lord your God in the place which He chooses, you shall read this law before all Israel in their hearing.* ¹² *Gather the people together, <u>men and women and little ones, and the stranger who is within your gates</u>, <u>that they may hear and that they may learn to fear</u> <u>the Lord your God and carefully observe all the words of this law</u>,* ¹³ *and that their children, who have not known it, may hear and learn to fear the Lord your God as long as you live in the land which you cross the Jordan to possess."*
**Deuteronomy 31:9-13**

Sukkot (Feast of Tabernacles) in the Sabbatical year is a time of Thanksgiving reflecting on the LORD's goodness and faithfulness to His people providing for them all that they needed in the Wilderness as well as His very presence with them. There is no better time than this to hear and be reminded of the Law of GOD. Moses gave the law to the priests and the elders of Israel and the responsibility to remind Israel of it every 7 years. All men, women, little ones, and strangers in the land are included in this. This tells us that the blessing of the law and the responsibility of observing and following GOD's commandments are not exclusively for the Israelites, but they also apply to all "within their gates," all who were with GOD's people.

³³ Then the Lord spoke to Moses, saying, ³⁴ "Speak to the children of Israel, saying: '_The fifteenth day of **this seventh month** shall be the Feast of Tabernacles (Sukkot) for **seven days** to the Lord._ ³⁵ On the first day there shall be a holy convocation. You shall do no customary work on it. ³⁶ For **seven days** you shall offer an offering made by fire to the Lord. On the eighth day you shall have a holy convocation, and you shall offer an offering made by fire to the Lord. It is a sacred assembly, and you shall do no customary work on it. ³⁹ 'Also on the fifteenth day of the **seventh month**, when you have gathered in the fruit of the land, you shall keep the feast of the Lord for **seven days**; **on the first day there shall be a sabbath-rest, and on the eighth day a sabbath-rest**. ⁴⁰ And you shall take for yourselves on the first day the fruit of beautiful trees, branches of palm trees, the boughs of leafy trees, and willows of the brook; and _you shall rejoice before the Lord your God for **seven days**_. ⁴¹ You shall keep it as a feast to the Lord for **seven days** in the year. It shall be a statute forever in your generations. You shall celebrate it in the **seventh month**. ⁴² _You shall dwell in booths for **seven days**_. All who are native Israelites shall dwell in booths, ⁴³ that your generations may know that I made the children of Israel dwell in booths when I brought them out of the land of Egypt: I am the Lord your God.'

Among all the feasts and different appointed years, the LORD chose Sukkot (Feast of Tabernacles) in a Sabbatical Year for the law to be read to His people (every 7 years).

Sukkot is a joyous occasion to be celebrated for 7 days.

Notice all the 7's? 7 days, 7 months, Sabbath (7<sup>th</sup> day), seven years... .

In the Shemitah (7<sup>th</sup> year), Year of Release or Sabbatical Year, no sowing nor reaping is allowed. It is during the Sukkot in Every Shemitah (every 7 years), while the Israelites were enjoying food that they did not work for that year, resting (no work allowed during Sukkot nor Shemitah) and enjoying time with family and friends during the Feast of Tabernacles, that they were reminded that GOD provided for all their needs, even their shoes and clothing would not wear out. It is so like GOD to have us remember His lovingkindness while enjoying His substantial and tangible goodness and provision.

7 is a number for completion and perfection. The LORD created the world in 6 days and rested on the 7<sup>th</sup>. All the 7s in Sukkot that we observe is as if we are to follow the LORD and rest in His Perfection for us. Isn't it fascinating that the LORD made the 7<sup>th</sup> Commandment in the Ten Commandments to be "Do not commit adultery"? 7 is to represent a perfect union between us and the LORD, staying faithful and devoted to each other. His intention is that when we stay close to Him, following His instructions, living in His perfect will, we will be in perfect union with Him, reflecting His perfect love for us for the world to see. Violating the 7<sup>th</sup> commandment and committing adultery would completely go against the perfect union.

I believe this is the only time that the Sabbatical Year/the Year of Release (שנת השמטה Sh'net Shemitah) and Sukkot (סכות Feast of Tabernacles) are mentioned together in the Torah. The significance of the law being read and heard every seventh year at Sukkot, a time of joy and Thanksgiving, is not to be underestimated.

"<u>At the end of every seven years</u>, at the appointed time in the year of release, at the Feast of Tabernacles," you may ask, "I thought Sukkot comes right after the Jewish New Year and Day of Atonement. Why is this then the end of the seven years? Should it not be the beginning of a new year?"

According to the Torah, the LORD appointed Passover to be the New Year when they were delivered out of slavery and bondage, therefore, and Sukkot comes later, near the end of the year, as the last of the Fall Feasts. It was not until much later that the Feast of Trumpets (תרועה ים Yom Teruah in Hebrew) was recognized to be the civil or agricultural new year, which we know today as Rosh HaShanah (רש השנה Head of the

Year). It marks the beginning of another year of sowing new crops after the harvest. Sukkot, the Feast of Tabernacles or Feast of Booths, is a time remembering the LORD dwelling among us.

> *"So the cloud of the Lord was over the tabernacle by day, and fire was in the cloud by night, in the sight of all the Israelites during all their travels."*
> **Exodus 40:38**

GOD's presence is everything that we need. GOD through fire or cloud or anything else makes His presence known to us and offers us comfort. We need nothing else. Yeshua Jesus is GOD's Word manifested.

> *In the beginning was the Word, and the Word was with God, and the Word was God.*
> *² He was with God in the beginning.*
> **John 1:1-2**

Whenever GOD's Word is read, heard or spoken, it testifies of the LORD being with us.

Do you want to feel GOD's presence?

Read His Word, the Torah, the Bible. Ask the LORD in faith to show His love through His Word. I promise you… He never disappoints.

In last week's Parashat Nitzvaim (Stand) and this week's Parashat Vayelech (And He Went), GOD called heaven and earth, His law and a song as witnesses against Israel.

> *I (The LORD) call heaven and earth as witnesses today against you, that I have set before you life and death, blessing and cursing; therefore choose life, that both you and your descendants may live.*
> **Deuteronomy 30:19**

## 47. VAYELECH / AND HE WENT

> *Now therefore, write down this song for yourselves, and teach it to the children of Israel; <u>put it in their mouths</u>, that **this song may be a witness** (עֵד Ed) **for Me against the children of Israel**...* ²¹ *Then it shall be, when many evils and troubles have come upon them, that **this song will testify against them as a witness** (עֵד Ed);...*
> *Take this **Book of the Law, and put it beside the ark of the covenant of the Lord your God, that it may be there as a witness** (Ed עֵד) **against you**...* ²⁸ *Gather to me all the elders of your tribes, and your officers, that I may speak these words <u>in their hearing</u> and **call heaven and earth to witness** (Ed עֵד) **against them**.*
> **Deuteronomy 31:19, 21, 26, 28**

When we think of a witness, a person on a stand in a courtroom comes to mind. However, it is interesting that GOD calls many things to be witnesses for Him and His people. The very first time we see a witness in the Torah is when Israel's Patriarch Jacob had a dispute with his uncle/father-in-law, Laban.

> ⁴⁵ *So Jacob took a stone and set it up as a pillar.* ⁴⁶ *Then Jacob said to his brethren, "Gather stones." And they took stones and made a heap, and they ate there on the heap.* ⁴⁷ *Laban called it Jegar Sahadutha, but Jacob called it Galeed.* ⁴⁸ *And Laban said, "**This heap is a witness** (Ed עֵד) **between you and me this day.**"*
> *Then Laban said to Jacob, "Here is this heap and here is this pillar, which I have placed between you and me.* ⁵² ***This heap is a witness** (Ed עֵד), **and this pillar is a witness** (Ed עֵד), **that I will not pass beyond this heap to you, and you will not pass beyond this heap and this pillar to me, for harm**.*
> **Genesis 31:45-48, 51-52**

Did they have any actual person that could be witnesses? They had to use a stone and a heap of stones to be witnesses? A witness is to remain neutral to the Truth. The stone is neutral and non-partial to either party. Also, notice that the words of the song (Deuteronomy 31) were put in the Israelites' mouths to testify for GOD's love for His people and against His people's eventual rebellion. The Song the LORD given to Moses to write and to be sung will be passed on from generation to generation by mouth standing for GOD's love for His people, despite of the foreknowledge GOD had about their rebellion.

Someday the words of truth sung will bring the ultimate restoration and redemption as GOD's mercy intended:

*And I saw what looked like a sea of glass glowing with fire and, standing beside the sea, those who had been victorious over the beast and its image and over the number of its name. They held harps given them by God ³ and sang the song of God's servant Moses and of the Lamb*
**Revelation 15:2-3**

The Song of Moses is a finale of the Torah, as well as for the New Testament in the Book of Revelation. It is a victory song sung by GOD's people.

**The two Hebrew alphabets of ע Ayin and דDalet together make the word עד Ed/Witness or עד Ad/Until, with different vowels:**

- The letter ע Ayin — the Eye
- the letter ד Dalet — the Door
- Ed עד (Witness) together looks like — the Eye guarding the Door (to the Truth). A witness is someone who has seen an event firsthand and can testify of it.
- Ad עד (Until) — a witness is necessary when called for a purpose to testify for the Truth. A witness stands by, going about life as usual, <u>until</u> a time that a witness is needed.

From the referenced scriptures above, the Law, the heaven and earth and the Song were called by GOD as witnesses for Him against His people. It is to stand witness against their rebellion. These witnesses stand the test of time. From the time Moses taught the Israelites the Song of Moses to GOD's people singing the song, there is a sense of eternity and GOD's story coming to completion and fulfillment someday. The words we speak of GOD, His law, and ordinances that we proclaim and live out in obedience testify of our Eternal LORD. Yes, He knew His people would stray away from His law. Yes, He knew they would break His heart after He had poured out His love on them. No matter, He charged Joshua to lead them into the Promise Land. No matter, He would continue to keep His end of the bargain, His end of the Covenant, because He is true to His Word. From the beginning, He had a plan to bring His people back to Himself. His Word was spoken through Moses, written on tablets, repeated through priests and the elders, heard לדר ודר L'Dor V'Dor from generation to generation… then ultimately manifested in Israel's long-awaited Mashiach Yeshua Jesus, personified in a physical form. The Mashiach would teach everything Father GOD had intended for His people to learn about Him and the Kingdom, reconciling them to His heart. The LORD's Law, Moses' Song, heaven & earth, and Yeshua continue to be witnesses to GOD and His Truth to us throughout the ages, until the age to come, for eternity, עד עלם Ad Olam forever.

*Heaven and earth will pass away, but my words will never pass away.*
**Matthew 24:35**

**Let's pray:**

**Our Father in Heaven** אבינו שבשמימ,

Thank You for Your faithfulness, which is not dependent on what we do. You remind us of Your Goodness in the Year of Rest and Release, a time of joy celebrating Your provision in our lives. Instead of the Song of Moses being a witness against our rebellion, teach us to be witnesses standing for Your lovingkindness declaring Your Eternal Word to the World. We choose life over death, good over evil, blessing over curse. I choose YOU!

B'Shem Yeshua HaMashiach בשם ישוע המשיח.

In Jesus' Name we pray. Amen.

# 47. TORAH TASTING

## *REFLECTION*

1. What is the word, picture or theme the LORD is highlighting to you in this chapter and Torah Portion?

2. In the Sabbatical year, every 7 years, no work is to be done, yet GOD's people had no lack. GOD provided for them then, He still does. What area are you striving to fulfill a need that you need to trust the LORD as Your Provider?

3. What do you think a witness is? Throughout the Bible, GOD highlights the importance of a witness. Have you ever seen how a witness helped resolve a conflict or situation or how the lack of one led to a tragic ending?

# 48 מח
# ha azinu
## (Give Ear)
### האזינו

Deuteronomy 32:1-32:52

2 Samuel 22:1-511

John 6:26-35

This week's Parasha is only one chapter long, Deuteronomy 32. It mostly comprises of the Song of Moses that Moses taught Israel to sing, and it concludes with the death of Israel's first and greatest prophet. The song is full of poetic imagery. It begins with telling the heavens to האזינו Ha Azinu "Give ear," to take heed and pay attention, and the earth to hear his words. Of course, we know the heavens and the earth are being personified. I cannot help but wonder about the "personhood" given to GOD's non-human creations. We have read scriptures that talk about the rocks crying out, trees clapping, and all created things singing praises to the LORD. While the pagans worship creation, as believers of the One True GOD, we believe all creation, made up of atoms and molecules, acknowledge and worship our Creator in one form or another; they are not to be worshipped. Their very existence displays the magnificent, intelligent design of our Creator.

This Song of Moses in Deuteronomy 34 is the Second Version. The First one was sung right after Israel had crossed the Red Sea, having been delivered by the LORD from bondage. It is a victory song proclaiming the LORD and His glory. Moses begins this second Song of Moses by calling out one of the names of the LORD Our GOD, the Rock.

> *He is **the Rock**, His work is perfect;*
> *For all His ways are justice,*
> *A God of truth and without injustice;*
> *Righteous and upright is He.*
> **Deuteronomy 32:4**

**As a matter of fact, 7 times of "The Rock" הצור HaTzur mentioned in this Song of Moses state the characteristics of The Rock:**

- Verse 4- The Rock is just and righteous.
- Verse 13- Not only the Rock provides water, but he also supplies honey and oil.
- Verse 15- The Rock is our Salvation.
- Verse 18- The Rock "begot us" gave birth to us. He gave us life.
- Verse 30- The Rock is more powerful than the enemies in battle.
- Verse 31- Our Rock is mightier and unlike any other rocks; even our enemies recognize that.
- Verse 37- The Rock is our refuge.

The number 7 in the 7 times of הצור HaTzur The Rock mentioned is amazing. The Rock definitely is a major theme highlighted in the Song of Moses in this Torah Portion. 7 alludes to perfection and completion. The Rock is perfect and complete. We now begin to see The Rock as a metaphor for a particular someone. This is not just any rock; this is הצור HaTzur The Rock that has been referenced throughout the Torah. The Rock gives us life. The Rock is powerful. The Rock is nurturing, providing honey that has health-beneficial properties to heal physical bodies. The Rock provides oil, yet another element suggests provision of physical healing as well as mental and spiritual healing, as in the oil of gladness (Psalm 45:7). The Rock is the ultimate Provider and Protector. The Hebrew word for Rock is צור Tzur. צור Tzur is a rock, a cliff or a stone. הצור HaTzur The Rock can be fairly large in size.

The first time the Rock appears in the Torah is in Exodus 17.

*And the Lord said to Moses, "Go on before the people, and take with you some of the elders of Israel. Also take in your hand your rod with which you struck the river, and go.*
*⁶ Behold, I will stand before you there on the rock in Horeb; and you shall strike the rock, and water will come out of it, that the people may drink."*
**Exodus 17:6**

The very first time the Rock of Israel came on the scene of world history and His first Salvation act was providing water during the first water shortage among the Children of Israel. Water is one of the most essential necessities of living. How could anyone survive wandering in the desert without water? They could not!

My husband grew up in New York City and me in Hong Kong. We recall whenever our respective Big Cities shut off water supplies for water conservation or our apartment buildings were working on repairs, we had to live without water for a period of time. Forget about showers, cooking, washing; of course, drinking water would not be possible. We usually were forewarned about the water shut-off. Buckets of water were filled up in preparation. Sometimes we even had to bring empty buckets and walk 2 blocks to get water to bring home. Can you imagine living and traveling around the desert without water? We often think of the Israelites being whiny. However, thirst and fatigue can make anyone grumpy.

During the 40 years in the Wilderness, it is this "traveling Rock" that supplied water for millions of the wandering Israelites until the death of Israel's prophetess Miriam, sister of Moses. That interesting timing led to Jewish traditions connecting the death of Miriam and the second water crisis. It is believed the miraculous water provision was attributed to Miriam. Exodus 15:21-27 tells us that right after Miriam's song praising GOD, water was provided by The Rock. At her passing, The Rock stopped supplying water.

An interesting note is when הצור **HaTzur The Rock** is mentioned in Exodus 17 for the first time, the LORD said He would stand on The Rock before them and that Moses would strike the Rock and water would come out for the people to drink. It is as if the LORD would stand on His Provision, our part is to obey and follow His instruction, even striking The Rock in faith that water would come out as He had said that it would. Have you heard of "Standing on the promises of GOD"? Can you see GOD Himself standing there on the Rock? Or is this another metaphor? Nonetheless, He stands on The Rock, unmovable, unshakable until His Word and promises come to pass. Do you believe in the supernatural? Well, the Torah is full of supernatural and miraculous things. Many Bible scholars believe there were at least 2 million Israelites with Moses in the Wilderness. The Rock, like a water fountain, with an unlimited supply of water for Israel was going to wherever those millions were traveling. What a sight that must have been! I believe GOD demonstrated to us the miraculous things He did thousands of years ago; He has never stopped doing. He did not say He would stop doing. I believe there are yet many more miraculous supernatural things the LORD is doing in our midst if you dare to believe. I have heard modern miracles of GOD supplying food for the needy when there was no logical reason to explain the "Yeshua-feeding-thousands-with 5 loaves-of-bread-and-2-fish" type of miracles.

Many believers of Yeshua Jesus HaMashiach The Messiah believe The Rock is none other than a type or foreshadow of the Mashiach Himself —

*All were baptized into Moses in the cloud and in the sea, ³ all ate the same spiritual food, ⁴ and all drank the same spiritual drink. For they drank of that spiritual Rock that followed them, and that Rock was Christ.*
1 Corinthians 10:4

At every Hanukkah, we sing the song מעוז צור Maoz Tzur, The Rock of Ages after lighting the Hanukkiah candles on the 8 nights. This is a traditional Hanukkah song proclaiming the LORD being "The Rock of My Salvation," particularly referring to the Maccabees story of Hanukkah. The story tells of the Maccabees miraculously defeated the strongest military force of their time, the Assyrian army. They drove out the enemies, cleaned out the altar and rededicated the Temple to the LORD, who had delivered victory.

## MAOZ TZUR — YESHUATI
### My Refuge My Rock of Salvation

*מָעוֹז צוּר יְשׁוּעָתִי, לְךָ נָאֶה לְשַׁבֵּחַ*
*תִּכּוֹן בֵּית תְּפִלָּתִי, וְשָׁם תּוֹדָה נְזַבֵּחַ.*
*לְעֵת תָּכִין מַטְבֵּחַ מִצָּר הַמְנַבֵּחַ.*
*אָז אֶגְמוֹר בְּשִׁיר מִזְמוֹר חֲנֻכַּת הַמִּזְבֵּחַ.*

*My Refuge, my Rock of Salvation! 'Tis pleasant to sing Your praises. Let our house of prayer be restored. And there we will offer You our thanks. When You will have slaughtered the barking foe. Then we will celebrate with song and psalm the altar's dedication.*

Whenever we sing מעוז צור Maoz Tzur (The Rock of Ages), we can sense GOD's mighty hand over us. Nothing and no one can be against us. This song is perfect for Hanukkah / The Feast of Dedication as we remember the Hanukkah story of the Maccabees. GOD is our Rock, He defended and protected His people against all odds. Imagine the tough battles the Maccabees facing their powerful enemies, being chased after and having to hide from danger. The LORD offered constant strength and safety as The Rock. He is fiercely faithful to His Word, keeping His Covenant with

His people. He provides safety and unmovable stability He is trustworthy throughout the ages. He is the Rock that we can lean on in times of weariness. The Rock is our Refuge in times of trouble. Even Hannah, the mother Israel's great prophet Samuel, offered these words of praise to the LORD after He had granted her request for a son:

> *There is no one holy like the Lord;*
> *there is no one besides you;*
> *there is no **Rock** like our God.*
> **2 Samuel 2:2**

Hannah referenced the LORD as the Mightiest; no Rock can compare to Him. Her Thanksgiving Prayer tells us that The Rock was a commonly used metaphor for GOD. In addition, מעוז צור **Maoz Tzur The Rock** represents strength and has been used numerous times in the Book of Job, many Psalms and the Book of Isaiah to symbolize GOD's strength and His faithfulness to His people. Following are a few examples.

> *My flesh and my heart fail;*
> *But God is the strength (מעוז צור Maoz Tzur) of my heart and my portion forever.*
> **Psalm 73:26**

> *May these words of my mouth and this meditation of my heart be pleasing in your sight, Lord, my Rock (מעוז צור Maoz Tzur) and my Redeemer.*
> **Psalm 19:14**

> *Truly he is my rock (מעוז צור Maoz Tzur) and my salvation;*
> *he is my fortress, I will never be shaken.*
> **Psalm 62:2**

Not only GOD is The Rock, but He is also my Rock and my strength. He is unshakable, and so am I when I call on Him.

The 3 Hebrew letters making up the word צור Tzur are:

- צ Tsade — hook.
- ו Vav — to secure.
- ר Resh — the highest.

It seems to me that strength and securing comes from hooking and securing ourselves to the "Highest," which is the LORD. This gives me a visual of rock-climbing. You have to look up and focus on the goal and not look down when you climb up on the rock. Looking down triggers fear. Focus on the highest point of the climber's destination gives hope. The Rock, indeed is our salvation when we gravitate toward GOD The Most High.

Here is a song by David praising GOD for delivering him from his enemies recorded in 2 Samuel 22 and Psalm 18, mirroring the Deuteronomy 32 Song of Moses. The theme of the LORD being The Rock, our strength, cannot be more crystal-clear.

> *The Lord is my rock, my fortress and my deliverer;*
> *³ my God is my rock, in whom I take refuge,*
> *my shield and the horn of my salvation.*
> *He is my stronghold, my refuge and my savior —*
> *from violent people you save me.*
> **2 Samuel 22:2**

> *The Lord is my rock, my fortress and my deliverer;*
> *my God is my rock, in whom I take refuge,*
> *my shield and the horn of my salvation, my stronghold.*
> **Psalm 18**

David wrote Psalm 18 praising GOD for delivering him from his enemies. I wonder if, by any chance, he penned this psalm reminiscing the time the LORD miraculously saved him when he was hiding in a cave/a rock. A fascinating rabbinical story in the Talmud (meaning learning), Jewish

Traditions, tells of a time when David was running for his life, being chased by his father-in-law, Saul, who was trying to kill him. David found a cave (or a rock) and quickly ran in there to hide. Fear paralyzed him as Saul's soldiers drew near. This is when David noticed a big spider spinning a web at the opening of the rock. Right before David's eyes, the spider covered the entire opening of the rock with his web that he had so magnificently crafted. When Saul's soldiers arrived at the cave, they found the spider web and said to one another, "Look, the spider web covers the opening and is untorn. David could not have gone inside the rock without breaking it. Let's go look for him elsewhere." David's life was spared because of the spider web.

I wonder if David's words of praise, "The LORD is my rock... my GOD is my rock..." in Psalm 18 have anything to do with this "legend."

Could he be reliving the moments in the Rock, his refuge and shield; his life was spared, time after time, including the spider-web rescue? I believe so.

The majestic stature of the Rock and His power gives us a sense of security. A large rock may resemble a small mountain. Yet, a rock, no matter how large, seems to be more approachable than a mountain. The rock is the symbol reminding us to put our trust in the LORD, not the rock, not any human, not succumbing to fear. Just as the Rock provides protection and defense, the LORD is Our Defense and Our Deliverer. No matter how dire or desperate the situation we may be in, we have the Rock of Ages. His deliverance can come in any form, a rock, a cave, or even a spider web. We need only to trust Him.

Upon Moses' death, these are his last words in the Song of Moses.

*Rejoice, O Gentiles, with His people;*
*For He will avenge the blood of His servants,*
*And render vengeance to His adversaries;*
*He will provide atonement for His land and His people.*
**Deuteronomy 32:43**

Although Moses spoke much of Israel's disobedience and the consequence they faced because of their turning-away from the LORD, he concluded the Song and his speech with hope and GOD's promise to His people.

GOD's judgment is often followed by GOD's mercy. No matter how messed up the Israelites were, their eventual repentance was always the LORD's desire. His redemption has always been the plan of reconciliation. How appropriate this being one of the last Torah Portions, is read on Shabbat highlighting The LORD our ROCK! He is our source of strength when we are strong; He is still our strength when we have no energy left. When we are at the end of the road, He is there for us.

Do you see the Father's heart? Do you see the Father's lovingkindness waiting at the door, looking out for his prodigal son's return every day (Luke 15:11-31)?

> *"Great and marvelous are Your works,*
> *Lord God Almighty!*
> *Just and true are Your ways,*
> *O King of the saints!*
> **Revelation 15:3**

One day we will all sing with the Lamb who was slain for the world, the Mashiach, the Song of Moses, the Original Version.

**Let's pray:**

> **Our Father in Heaven** אבינו שבשמים,
>
> Thank You for being The Rock — our Rock and our strength. Your promise of provision and protection never fails. There is no god like You. No other rock compares to You. How majestic are You as The Rock! Your righteousness and justice bring us salvation and life. LORD, teach us to trust in You in all circumstances and to lean on You as The Rock, The Rock of All Ages. May these words of our mouths and the meditation of our hearts be pleasing in Your sight, LORD, our Rock (צור **Maoz Tzur**) and our Redeemer.
>
> B'Shem Yeshua HaMashiach בשם ישוע המשיח.
>
> In Jesus' Name we pray. Amen.

# 48. TORAH TASTING

## *REFLECTION*

1. What is the word, picture or theme the LORD is highlighting to you in this chapter and Torah Portion?

2. Out of the seven characteristics of the Rock listed in the beginning of this chapter (Deuteronomy 32:4-37), which one stands out to you, and why?

3. Some describe rocks and mountains in places like Colorado as "Majestic." Have you ever been among rocks in nature that you sensed anything that reminds you of the characteristics of GOD as the Rock?

# 49 מט
# V'zot haBrachah
## (This Is the Blessing)

וזאת הברכה

Deuteronomy 33:1-34:12

Joshua 1:1-18

Acts 1:1-14

This is the official "last Torah Portion" to be read traditionally on the day of Simchat Torah (Rejoicing of the Torah) immediately following Sukkot (Feast of Tabernacles/Feast of Booths), rather than on a Shabbat. Simchat Torah is a celebration of completion of the reading of the entire Torah scroll and then rolling back to the very beginning of the first book to begin all over again. Orthodox synagogues would have multiple scrolls carried by rabbis and congregants, dancing with the Torah all around the synagogues with joy. This reminds me of a scene in 2 Samuel 6:16-22. Upon the return of the Ark to Jerusalem —

"King David and all Israel were celebrating with all their might before the Lord, with castanets, harps, lyres, timbrels, sistrums and cymbals."

Their joy and love of GOD and His presence caused them to sing in joy, with no care of who may be watching.

The first chapter in the Book of John tells us GOD's word becoming flesh; the Torah scroll is the best picture of the LORD manifested in physical form today. If the Messiah manifested in human form, would you embrace Him in excitement with such blissful joy?

The LORD's Word indeed gives us endless joy that we ought to celebrate the Hope He brings through His written Word each day.

Parashat V'zot HaBracha is read to conclude the Torah reading for the year, along with the first Torah Portion, Bereshit, in Genesis, displaying the end and the beginning of the annual reading cycle of the Torah. This Parasha tells of Moses' final blessings for Israel's 12 tribes and him overlooking the Promise Land on Mt. Nebo one last time before his death and burial.

Following is a chart laying out the words spoken over the 12 tribes of Israel recorded in Genesis 49 and Deuteronomy 33.

| Twelve Tribes | Deuteronomy 33 — *words spoken by Moses* | Genesis 49 — *words spoken by Jacob* |
| --- | --- | --- |
| Reuben | "Let Reuben live, and not die, Nor let his men be few." | You are my firstborn, My might and the beginning of my strength, The excellency of dignity and the excellency of power.[4] Unstable as water, you shall not excel, Because you went up to your father's bed; Then you defiled it — He went up to my couch. |

## 49. V'ZOT HABRACHACH / THIS IS THE BLESSING

| | | |
|---|---|---|
| Judah | "Hear, Lord, the voice of Judah, And bring him to his people; Let his hands be sufficient for him, And may You be a help against his enemies." | "Judah, you are he whom your brothers shall praise; Your hand shall be on the neck of your enemies; Your father's children shall bow down before you. ⁹ Judah is a lion's whelp; From the prey, my son, you have gone up. He bows down, he lies down as a lion; And as a lion, who shall rouse him? ¹⁰ The scepter shall not depart from Judah, Nor a lawgiver from between his feet, Until Shiloh comes; And to Him shall be the obedience of the people. ¹¹ Binding his donkey to the vine, And his donkey's colt to the choice vine, He washed his garments in wine, And his clothes in the blood of grapes. ¹² His eyes are darker than wine, And his teeth whiter than milk. |
| Levi | "Let Your Thummim and Your Urim be with Your holy one, Whom You tested at Massah, And with whom You contended at the waters of Meribah, ⁹ Who says of his father and mother, 'I have not seen them'; Nor did he acknowledge his brothers, Or know his own children; For they have observed Your word And kept Your covenant. ¹⁰ They shall teach Jacob Your judgments, And Israel Your law. They shall put incense before You, And a whole burnt sacrifice on Your altar. ¹¹ Bless his substance, Lord, And accept the work of his hands; Strike the loins of those who rise against him, And of those who hate him, that they rise not again." | |

| | | |
|---|---|---|
| Joseph | "Blessed of the Lord is his land, With the precious things of heaven, with the dew, And the deep lying beneath, [14] With the precious fruits of the sun, With the precious produce of the months, [15] With the best things of the ancient mountains, With the precious things of the everlasting hills, [16] With the precious things of the earth and its fullness, And the favor of Him who dwelt in the bush. Let the blessing come 'on the head of Joseph, And on the crown of the head of him who was separate from his brothers.' [17] His glory is like a firstborn bull, And his horns like the horns of the wild ox; Together with them He shall push the peoples To the ends of the earth; They are the ten thousands of Ephraim, And they are the thousands of Manasseh." | "Joseph is a fruitful bough, A fruitful bough by a well; His branches run over the wall. [23] The archers have bitterly grieved him, Shot at him and hated him. [24] But his bow remained in strength, And the arms of his hands were [g]made strong By the hands of the Mighty God of Jacob (From there is the Shepherd, the Stone of Israel), [25] By the God of your father who will help you, And by the Almighty who will bless you With blessings of heaven above, Blessings of the deep that lies beneath, Blessings of the breasts and of the womb. [26] The blessings of your father Have excelled the blessings of my ancestors, Up to the utmost bound of the everlasting hills. They shall be on the head of Joseph, And on the crown of the head of him who was separate from his brothers. |
| Zebulun | "Rejoice, Zebulun, in your going out, And Issachar in your tents! [19] They shall call the peoples to the mountain; There they shall offer sacrifices of righteousness; For they shall partake of the abundance of the seas And of treasures hidden in the sand." | Zebulun shall dwell by the haven of the sea; He shall become a haven for ships, And his border shall adjoin Sidon. |
| Gad | "Blessed is he who enlarges Gad; He dwells as a lion, And tears the arm and the crown of his head. [21] He provided the first part for himself, Because a lawgiver's portion was reserved there. He came with the heads of the people; He administered the justice of the Lord, And His judgments with Israel." | Gad, a troop shall tramp upon him, But he shall triumph at last. |

| | | |
|---|---|---|
| Dan | "Dan is a lion's whelp; He shall leap from Bashan." | "Dan shall judge his people As one of the tribes of Israel. [17] Dan shall be a serpent by the way, A viper by the path, That bites the horse's heels So that its rider shall fall backward. [18] I have waited for your salvation, O Lord! |
| Naphatali | "O Naphtali, satisfied with favor, And full of the blessing of the Lord, Possess the west and the south." | "Naphtali is a deer let loose; He uses beautiful words. |
| Asher | Asher is most blessed of sons; Let him be favored by his brothers, And let him dip his foot in oil. [25] Your sandals shall be iron and bronze; As your days, so shall your strength be.<br><br>[26] "There is no one like the God of Jeshurun, Who rides the heavens to help you, And in His excellency on the clouds. [27] The eternal God is your refuge, And underneath are the everlasting arms; He will thrust out the enemy from before you, And will say, 'Destroy!' | "Bread from Asher shall be rich, And he shall yield royal dainties. |
| Simeon and Levi | | Simeon and Levi are brothers; Instruments of cruelty are in their dwelling place. [6] Let not my soul enter their council; Let not my honor be united to their assembly; For in their anger they slew a man, And in their self-will they hamstrung an ox. [7] Cursed be their anger, for it is fierce; And their wrath, for it is cruel! I will divide them in Jacob And scatter them in Israel. |

| | | |
|---|---|---|
| Issachar | "Rejoice, Zebulun, in your going out, And Issachar in your tents! [19] They shall call the peoples to the mountain; There they shall offer sacrifices of righteousness; For they shall partake of the abundance of the seas And of treasures hidden in the sand." | "Issachar is a strong donkey, Lying down between two burdens; [15] He saw that rest was good, And that the land was pleasant; He bowed his shoulder to bear a burden, And became a band of slaves. |
| Benjamin | "The beloved of the Lord shall dwell in safety by Him, Who shelters him all the day long; And he shall dwell between His shoulders." | "Benjamin is a ravenous wolf; In the morning he shall devour the prey, And at night he shall divide the spoil." |
| Israel | [28] Then Israel shall dwell in safety, The fountain of Jacob alone, In a land of grain and new wine; His heavens shall also drop dew. [29] Happy are you, O Israel! Who is like you, a people saved by the Lord, The shield of your help And the sword of your majesty! Your enemies shall submit to you, And you shall tread down their [c] high places." | [28] All these are the twelve tribes of Israel, and this is what their father spoke to them. And he blessed them; he blessed each one according to his own blessing. |

Here I see parallels between Deuteronomy 33 and Genesis 49, the blessings of Israel right before the death and burial of Moses in Deuteronomy and the blessings of Israel right before the death and burial of Jacob and in Genesis 49. There are so many things to explore in these 2 passages, so many riddles to unpack.

Jacob died around 1885 B.C. at the age of 147, whereas Moses died approximately in 1404 B.C. at the age of 120. There were approximately 480 years between those 2 blessers.

The words of the blessings for Israel by Jacob were to prepare them for their upcoming years of hardship being enslaved in Egypt, as well as their wandering time in the Wilderness.

The words of the blessing for Israel by Moses were to prepare them for the entering of Canaan, with Joshua leading the charge. We see in both incidents that the LORD did not leave His people on their own. He equipped insightful words of wisdom, both corporately as well as for individual tribes, as powerful weapons to grasp victory and fulfilling their eternal destiny.

Similarly, we have been given the WORD of GOD, with countless promises and mind-boggling ammunition and shield, protection, and provision beyond comprehension to live life abundantly.

*But we all, with unveiled face, beholding as in a mirror the glory of the Lord, are being transformed into the same image from glory to glory, just as by the Spirit of the Lord.*
**2 Corinthians 3:18**

Every time when looking at all that the LORD has done for Israel in hindsight (this last Torah Portion in Deuteronomy), then looking ahead to the Very Beginning of Creation (the First Torah Portion in Genesis), I believe the LORD always takes us higher to see things clearer, from a different angle, through a new perspective, Kingdom perspective, the Almighty's perspective, the Father's perspective.

*Moses was one hundred and twenty years old when he died. His eyes were not dim, nor his natural vigor diminished. ⁸ And the children of Israel wept for Moses in the plains of Moab thirty days. So the days of weeping and mourning for Moses ended.*
*⁹ Now Joshua the son of Nun was full of the spirit of wisdom, for Moses had laid his hands on him; so the children of Israel heeded him, and did as the Lord had commanded Moses. ¹⁰ But since then there has not arisen in Israel a prophet like Moses, whom the Lord knew face to face, ¹¹ in all the signs and wonders which the Lord sent him to do in the land of Egypt, before Pharaoh, before all his servants, and in all his land, ² and by all that mighty power and all the great terror which Moses performed in the sight of all Israel.*
**Deuteronomy 33:7-12**

The last verses of this Parasha play like a movie's final scene, alluding to a sequel, Joshua being Moses' successor. The Children of Israel mourned for Moses' death. They wept for Moses' death for thirty days as if he was their father; and that he was, he loved and led Israel as his own children. Moses was Israel's National Father, as George Washington was America's. As Israel's National Father, Moses cared for, interceded, cried, rejoiced for his people with the LORD. He devoted his life to serving the LORD and His people to the end.

Growing up, Mom taught me about the National Father of Modern China, Dr. Sun Yat-Sen (孫中山先生 Sun Zhong Shan XianSheng). In late, 1880s, Dr. Sun studied the U.S. Constitution and the American democracy principles, as well as Christianity, during his schooling years in the U.S. He brought those ideas back when he returned to China. There is a story of Dr. Sun breaking a temple god statue out of disgust when he saw the polytheists worshipping.

Sounds familiar?

A rabbinic midrash has a legend of Israel's Patriarch Abraham, a monotheist. As a child smashing idols in his father's shop, he later blamed it on the god to prove the point how powerless those gods were.

Interesting coincidence!

Dr. Sun led the revolution overthrowing the Qing Dynasty, the last Chinese dynasty, ending the Imperial Era. He was well-respected by all Chinese people of different political ideologies for his contributions in Modern Chinese history. Dr. Sun's legacy lives on, and he remains revered until this day. His heart desiring and leading his nation to freedom mirrors Moses'.

As for Moses in this last Torah Portion… no, he did not grow weak and fade into the afterlife. He was strong as ever, almost like showing us a glimpse of his past glory of confidently speaking to the most powerful ruler of the day, Pharaoh, "Let my people go," and splitting the Red Sea with such faith in the GOD Almighty like no other, leading GOD's children many times like an eagle soaring so majestically, solo. That's the Moses Israel is to remember, the servant of GOD so inspires us all.

We are to honor the one and only, the "most humble" leader Israel (Numbers 12:3) ever saw before Yeshua Jesus. He is the Greatest prophet of Israel, the only one "the LORD knew face to face, as a man speaks to his friend" (Exodus 33:11).

Moving beyond this Parasha is the "prequel" of Genesis, where it all began. The prequel often explains much of the main feature film. Going back to the beginning helps us see the future. New and already possessed revelation of the character of GOD, the forefathers and their children's failings, yet the LORD's steadfast love and the unimaginable depths of his mercy and kindness are all and more we can look forward to revisiting and receiving in the New Year's cycle of Torah reading. Let the new journey begin...again...

**Let's pray:**

**Our Father in Heaven** אבינו שבשמימ,

Thank You for the amazing blessings and promises You have spoken through the Great prophet of Moses and Israel's Patriarch Jacob over Your children for those who have ears to hear and receive in faith. The end of the Torah cycle brings us back to begin another annual cycle of reading and partaking Your Word, the Living Bread, that sustains us for another year. We declare and decree that Your Word is our Defense. Your Word that provides everything we need, Everything! Your Word that brings joy and hope like no other. Just as Jewish people around the world on Simchat Torah dancing around with the Torah scroll in bliss and love for You and Your Word, with the Messiah inside us, may we be filled with the same if not more passion, to delve into Your Word, which gives us life, mind, body, soul, and spirit, abundantly.

B'Shem Yeshua HaMashiach בשם ישוע המשיח.

In Jesus' Name we pray. Amen.

## 49. TORAH TASTING

### *REFLECTION*

1. What is the word, picture or theme the LORD is highlighting to you in this chapter and Torah Portion?

2. Nothing compares to spiritual blessings spoken over us by our elders. Have you ever had words of blessings spoken over you before? Who spoke the words and what were the words? If not, who would you like to ask to speak blessings over you? Also, who would you like to speak blessings over? Would it be wonderful to make a point to speak blessings over those around us often?

3. Whenever we are near the end of a time or a season, entering into a new one is often bittersweet. What was the last time you were there? What are the things you look back on that make you feel proud? Any regrets? And what were you looking forward to about the next season?

# Glossary

| Bar Mitzvah | Son of the Law. It is a rite of passage for 13-year-old boys and girls in the Jewish faith |
|---|---|
| Bat Mitzvah | Daughter of the Law. It is a rite of passage for 13-year-old girls, and 12-year-old girls in the Jewish faith |
| Bat Mitzvah | Children of the Law |
| Brit Hadashah | New Testament |
| Gentiles | The nations, usually refers to anyone who is not a Hebrew or a Jew |
| ה Ha | Prefix in Hebrew for an article of "the" |
| Haftorah | A selection of readings from the Books of Prophets to be read on Shabbats |
| Ketubah | a Jewish marriage contract between the bridegroom and the bride, establishing a covenant |
| Mashiach | Messiah, Christ, The Anointed One |
| Parasha | Torah Portion |
| Parashiot | Torah Portions |
| Parashat | Torah Portion of (ex. Parashat Bo — The Torah Portion of Bo "Come") |
| Tanakh | Old Testament |
| Torah | The first 5 books in the Old Testament of the Bible, sometimes is referred to as The Five Books of Moses |
| ו V' | Prefix in Hebrew as a conjunction of "and" in most cases. |
| Yeshua | Jesus in Hebrew meaning Salvation |

If you would like to take a moment and surrender your life to the LORD right now, please say this prayer —

## Repentance Prayer

Our Father in Heaven אבינו שבשמים,

Thank You for Your lovingkindness and unfailing love for me. I acknowledge that I am nothing and can do nothing apart from You. I am sorry for everything that I have done against Your will and commandments. I am repenting for my sins, changing my ways, and surrendering my life to You today. Thank You for sending the Messiah, Yeshua Jesus Christ, to atone for my sins! Only through Yeshua Jesus, I am whole, healed, righteous and perfect. I need You, and I declare that You alone are my Deliverer, Provider, Protector, Defender, and all that I need. I am humbled that the Creator of the Universe, the One True GOD has claimed me as Your own. I invite Your Holy Spirit into my life to guide and direct me in all that I do.

LORD, please help me fulfill the purposes You have created me for, that I can be all that You have made me to be, ultimately all for Your Glory.

B'Shem Yeshua HaMashiach בשם ישוע המשיח

In Jesus' Name I pray. Amen.

# torah portions
## Calendar 2021-2023

**GENESIS**

|  |  | 2021-2022<br>5782 | 2022-2023<br>5783 |
|---|---|---|---|
| Bereshit | Gen 1:1-6:8 | Oct 2, '21 | Oct 22, '22 |
| Noah | Gen 6:9 — 11:32 | Oct 9, '21 | Oct 29, '22 |
| Lekh-Lekha | Gen 12:1 — 17:27 | Oct 16, '21 | Nov 5, '22 |
| Vayera | Gen 18:1 — 22:24 | Oct 23, '21 | Nov 12, '22 |
| Chayei Sarah | Gen 23:1 — 25:18 | Oct 30, '21 | Nov 19, '22 |
| Toldot | Gen 25:19 — 28:9 | Nov 6, '21 | Nov 26, '22 |
| Vayetze | Gen 28:10 — 32:3 | Nov 13, '21 | Dec 2, '22 |
| Vayishlach | Gen 32:4 — 36:43 | Nov 20, '21 | Dec 10, '22 |
| Vayeshev | Gen 37:1 — 40:23 | Nov 27, '21 | Dec 17, '22 |

| Miketz | Gen 41:1 — 44:17 | Dec 4, '21 | Dec 24, '22 |
| --- | --- | --- | --- |
| Vayigash | Gen 44:18 — 47:27 | Dec 11, '21 | Dec 31, '22 |
| Vayechi | Gen 47:28 — 50:26 | Dec 18, '21 | Jan 7, '23 |

## EXODUS

| | | 2021-2022 5782 | 2022-2023 5783 |
| --- | --- | --- | --- |
| Shemot | Ex 1:1 — 6:1 | Dec 25, '21 | Jan 14, '23 |
| Va-eyra | Ex 6:2 — 9:35 | Jan 1, '22 | Jan 21, '23 |
| Bo | Ex 10:1 — 13:16 | Jan 8, '22 | Jan 28, '23 |
| Beshallach | Ex 13:17 — 17:16 | Jan 15, '22 | Feb 4, '23 |
| Yitro | Ex 18:1 — 20:23 | Jan 22, '22 | Feb 11, '23 |
| Mishpatim | Ex 21:1 — 24:18 | Jan 29, '22 | Feb 18, '23 |
| Terumah | Ex 25:1 — 27:19 | Feb 5, '22 | Feb 25, '23 |
| Tetzaveh | Ex 27:20 — 30:10 | Feb 12, '22 | Mar 4, '23 |
| Ki Tisa | Ex 30:11 — 34:35 | Feb 19, '22 | Mar 11, '23 |
| Vayakhel | Ex 35:1 — 38:20 | Feb 26, '22 | Mar 18, '23* |
| Pekuday | Ex 38:21 — 40:38 | Mar 5, '22 | Mar 18, '23* |

## LEVITICUS

|  |  | 2021-2022<br>5782 | 2022-2023<br>5783 |
|---|---|---|---|
| Vayikra | Lev 1:1 — 5:26 | Mar 12, '22 | Mar 25, '23 |
| Tzav | Lev 6:1 — 8:36 | Mar 19, '22 | Apr 1, '23 |
| Shemini | Lev 9:1 — 11:47 | Mar 26, '22 | Apr 15, '23 |
| Tazria | Lev 12:1 — 13:59 | Apr 2, '22 | Apr 22, '23* |
| Metzora | Lev 14:1 — 15:33 | Apr 9, '22 | Apr 22, '23* |
| Acharey Mot | Lev 16:1 — 18:30 | Apr 30, '22 | Apr 29, '23* |
| Kedoshim | Lev 19:1 — 20:27 | May 7, '22 | Apr 29, '23* |
| Emor | Lev 21:1 — 24:23 | May 14, '22 | May 6, '23 |
| Behar | Lev 25:1 — 26:2 | May 21, '22 | May 13, '23* |
| Bechukotai | Lev 26:3 — 27:34 | May 28, '22 | May 13, '23* |

## NUMBERS

|  |  | 2021-2022 5782 | 2022-2023 5783 |
|---|---|---|---|
| Bamidbar | Num 1:1 — 4:20 | June 4, '22 | May 20, '23 |
| Naso | Num 4:21 — 7:89 | June 11, '22 | June 3, '23 |
| Beha'alotekha | Num 8:1 — 12:16 | June 18, '22 | June 10, '23 |
| Shelach Lekha | Num 13:1 — 15:41 | June 25, '22 | June 17, '23 |
| Korach | Num 16:1 — 18:32 | July 2, '22 | June 24, '23 |
| Chukat | Num 19:1 — 22:1 | July 9, '22 | July 1, '23* |
| Balak | Num 22:2 — 25:9 | July 16, '22 | July 1, '23* |
| Pinchas | Num 25:10 — 30:1 | July 23, '22 | July 8, '23 |
| Mattot | Num 30:2 — 32:42 | July 30, '22* | July 15, '23* |
| Massei | Num 33:1 — 36:13 | July 30, '22* | July 15, '23* |

## DEUTERONOMY

|  |  | 2021-2022<br>5782 | 2022-2023<br>5783 |
|---|---|---|---|
| D'varim | Deu 1:1 — 3:22 | Aug 6, '22 | July 22, '23 |
| V'Etchanan | Deu 3:23 — 7:11 | Aug 13, '22 | July 29, '23 |
| Ekev | Deu 7:12 — 11:25 | Aug 20, '22 | Aug 5, '23 |
| Re'eh | Deu 11:26 — 16:17 | Aug 27, '22 | Aug 12, '23 |
| Shoftim | Deu 16:18 — 21:9 | Sep 3, '22 | Aug 19, '23 |
| Ki Tetze | Deu 21:10 — 25:19 | Sep 10, '22 | Aug 26, '23 |
| Ki Tavo | Deu 26:1 — 29:8 | Sep 17, '22 | Sep 2, '23 |
| Nitzavim | Deu 29:9 — 30:20 | Sep 24, '22 | Sep 9, '23* |
| Vayelekh | Deu 31:1 — 31:30 | Oct 1, '22 | Sep 9, '23* |
| Ha'azinu | Deu 32:1 — 32:52 | Oct 8, '22 | Sep 23, '23 |
| Vezot HaBrakha | Deu 33:1 — 34:12<br>(Simchat Torah) | Oct 18, '22 | Oct 8, '23 |

For more information:

www.ElenaGlassman.Media
www.TorahTasting.com

www.ingramcontent.com/pod-product-compliance
Lightning Source LLC
Chambersburg PA
CBHW051856160426
43209CB00006B/1325